The Robert Hall Diaries 1954–61

The Robert Hall Diaries 1954–61

Edited by
ALEC CAIRNCROSS

London
UNWIN HYMAN
Boston Sydney Wellington

Published by the Academic Division of
Unwin Hyman Ltd
15/17 Broadwick Street, London W1V 1FP, UK

Unwin Hyman Inc.
955 Massachusetts Avenue, Cambridge, MA 02139, USA

Allen & Unwin (Australia) Ltd
8 Napier Street, North Sydney, NSW 2060, Australia

Allen & Unwin (New Zealand) Ltd
in association with the Port Nicholson Press Ltd
Compusales Building, 75 Ghuznee Street, Wellington 1, New Zealand

First published in 1991

Cover from a painting by Perilla Hall

British Library Cataloguing in Publication Data

Hall, Robert, Sir *1901–1988*
The Robert Hall diaries 1954–1961.
1. Great Britain. Civil Service. Hall, Robert, 1901–1988
I. Title II. Cairncross, Sir, Alec *1911–*
354.41006092

ISBN 0–04–445274-8

Library of Congress Cataloging in Publication Data

Available from the Library of Congress

Typeset in 10 on 11 point Times
and printed in Great Britain by Cambridge University Press

Contents

Preface		*page* ix
Robert Hall remembered:		
1	Lord Plowden	xiii
2	Sir Kit McMahon	xv
3	David Worswick	xvii
Introduction		xxi
I	Butler's last years as Chancellor, 1 January 1954 to 20 December 1955	1
II	Macmillan's Chancellorship, 20 December 1955 to 9 January 1957	53
III	Thorneycroft's Chancellorship, 9 January 1957 to 6 January 1958	89
IV	Heathcoat Amory's first year, 6 January 1958 to 31 December 1958	141
V	Reflation under Heathcoat Amory, 1 January 1959 to 27 July 1960	183
VI	Selwyn Lloyd's first year, 27 July 1960 to 21 April 1961	239
Notes		269
Appendices		
1	Summary of monetary measures, 1954–60	280
2	Main characters referred to	281
3	Members of the Economic Section, 1954–61	286
4	Initials and abbreviations	288
Bibliography		292
Index		294

Preface

In his first six years as Director of the Economic Section, Robert Hall lived through a succession of economic crises in each of which he took a leading part. When, in the autumn of 1953, he moved from the Cabinet Office to the Treasury, taking with him the Economic Section and the additional title of 'Economic Adviser to HMG', the years that followed were by no means free of anxiety but were rather less hectic. They were also years in which the problems facing the government had a closer family resemblance to those of the recent past.

First came a succession of crises in 1955: a monetary crisis in the form of a severe credit squeeze that seemed to have little effect; an exchange crisis when talk of a wider spread in exchange rates was thought to herald a fall in sterling towards its lower limit; and a fiscal crisis when an autumn Budget was required in order to put back (in a different form) some of the taxation removed in the spring by a cut in the rate of income tax near the top of a boom. A few months later Butler ceased to be Chancellor and was succeeded by Macmillan. In 1956 came Suez and shortly afterwards the resignation of Eden. Macmillan took his place as Prime Minister and Thorneycroft took over as Chancellor. In September 1957 the latter made a fresh effort to halt inflation by striking at what he took to be its root – the growth either in the stock of money or in money expenditure (he seemed to think that it was all one). Thorneycroft, however, lasted only for a year like his predecessor, resigning in January 1958 along with the two junior Treasury Ministers, Enoch Powell and Nigel Birch, when he failed to secure agreement to the last £50 million of cuts in government expenditure.

The years between 1955 and 1957 were also critical in commercial policy although this receives less attention in the Diaries. It was after those years between the Messina Conference in June 1955 and the Treaty of Rome in March 1957 that Europe came to be at Sixes and Sevens. The establishment of the EEC was accompanied by an effort to build the bridge of a free trade area, and when this failed in 1958, EFTA was created in 1959.

Meanwhile Heathcoat Amory had succeeded Thorneycroft to become the third Chancellor in three years. As he took office in 1958 a depression had already begun and brought economic growth in Britain to a halt. The deflationary zeal of ministers in 1957 gave way to something like panic as unemployment rose to over half a million in 1958. Just as the depression was bottoming out, the government piled one expansionary measure on another. The upswing was still in progress under yet another Chancellor, Selwyn Lloyd, when Robert Hall retired in April 1961, but the next crisis was only a few months away.

What occupied Hall throughout those years was the struggle to contain inflation at a high level of output and employment. For this purpose demand management had to be combined with moderate wage settlements; and such moderation could not be guaranteed merely by reducing the pressure of demand, whether by fiscal or monetary measures. There was, as the Economic Section had long maintained, an indeterminacy in wage-bargaining which afforded scope for the play of public opinion if suitably mobilized (as in West Germany), but also carried the threat of escalation if left to the trade unions. Since prices were set as a mark-up on costs, and profit margins were relatively inelastic, cost-push could become a more immediate threat than demand-pull. Of the two main elements in cost, materials and labour, the first varied with import prices over which the government had little or no control and the second with wage settlements which the government made no attempt to influence, but on which it might at least offer some guidance. In Hall's mind wage policy lay at the heart of anti-inflationary strategy.

A second danger was that of excess demand. Hall was conscious of powerful forces making for inflation from the side of demand and the limitations of the instruments available for demand management. The banks seemed able to expand credit without any effective check, and the Budget, although by far the most valuable of controls, was subject to political pressures and technical limitations that removed much of its potential. Looking back in 1957 on ten years as the government's chief economic adviser, Hall cited as 'the greatest difficulty in the economic field'

> the contradiction between the almost universal desire to have the government spending more money in all directions and the almost universal conviction that taxation was too high. The political forces which pull us in an inflationary direction are always extremely strong, and great courage and resolution is needed for even moderate deflationary measures . . . I now think [he added] that a turnover tax on the Russian model would be extremely desirable.[1]

The diary for 1954–61 is more leisurely and meditative than that for 1947–53. The entries are longer, the names more familiar and the references to official documents fewer. As a result the diary makes easier reading. On the other hand, it adds less to what we already know. It is also, in the first few years, punctuated by long breaks. These begin in 1953, where there are only six entries after 22 April, and continue in 1954: apart from comments on the Commonwealth Conference in Sydney in the first half of January, there is only a single

[1] 'Mr Downie on economic policy', 21 January 1957, in PRO T 230/305.

entry before mid-August and again only one entry between the end of October and early March 1955, four months later. Fortunately 1953 and 1954 were among the least eventful of the postwar years and as the pace quickens in 1955–7 the diary entries become more continuous and fuller.

Throughout the diary Hall makes frequent comments on the personalities – official and political – who shaped the policies adopted and on the defects in Treasury organization that limited its effectiveness. He takes a hard look from time to time at his colleagues and returns again and again to an analysis of the character of Butler and his successors. There is nothing so dramatic as the row in 1952 over Robot. But there is a similar interest in the battles with the Bank of England over monetary policy and with the Inland Revenue over the investment allowance.

Nor is the picture presented confined to the Treasury and the problems of the United Kingdom. As Hall makes repeated journeys to the United States and Canada – usually at least twice a year – and visits other parts of the world – Australia, India and Paris – the entries lengthen and the perspective widens. Quite a high proportion of the text is the fruit of those journeys when he was free of office duties and able to reflect at more leisure. Britain and her problems are seen from a different angle and brought into relation with those of the rest of the world, especially the United States.

Apart from the light it throws on personalities and events the diary has an additional interest in the picture it affords of Hall himself. We are able to enter into the mind of a highly successful adviser endowed with good judgement and an abundance of common sense as he observes the ways of Whitehall from a position of great influence, and conveys with clarity and verve what life in the Treasury was like in the 1950s.

As in the first volume of the Diaries, I have inserted a few background passages for the convenience of readers unfamiliar with the period or in order to provide a more continuous account of developments. I have also divided the narrative into six sections to accord with the term of office of successive Chancellors (except that Heathcoat Amory is allowed separate sections for deflation in 1958 and recovery in 1959–60). Square brackets in the text indicate editorial insertions to offer guidance as to either the post held by someone referred to or the department to which they were attached. Where I have been able to trace documents mentioned in the text I have provided the reference (or sometimes the PRO call number) in an insertion (also in square brackets) or in an explanatory note. These notes and others clarifying points in the text appear at the end of the diary (pages 269 ff). Details of the main characters in the story are given in an appendix and the various initials and abbreviations are spelt out in another appendix. In view of the frequency with which Bank Rate changes are discussed I have thought it worthwhile to add a note of all changes between January 1954 and April 1961 (Appendix 1).

I had thought of including a memoir of Lord Roberthall but decided against it, partly because it would have delayed publication. I am glad, however, to be able to include, as giving a picture of the author as he appeared to some of his colleagues, the text of three tributes paid to him at the crowded memorial service in the crypt of the House of Lords on 28 November 1988. This I do with the permission of the authors, Lord Plowden, Sir Kit McMahon and David Worswick.

Lastly, I gladly acknowledge my indebtedness to the Leverhulme Trust for its continuing assistance in meeting typing costs. I am grateful also to Mrs K. Jones who has greatly eased my task by preparing Appendices 2 and 4 and, once again, to Mrs Anne Robinson for skilfully deciphering and typing the text of the Diaries and my editorial additions.

A.K.C

Robert Hall remembered

1 Lord Plowden

Robert Hall came to this country from Australia: one of the sons of a family living in a countryside very different from the cities in which he was to spend his active working life. He once said to me that he was one of the few people whose life covered the horse age and that of the internal combustion engine.

He and his younger brother used to return to school after the holidays by driving for two days in a horse-drawn sulky. Robert, I believe, always did the driving. At home they rode everywhere, as did all their neighbours.

He read engineering at the University of Queensland and then came as a Rhodes Scholar to Oxford, and it was at Oxford he became an economist. I always felt that his approach to economic problems was influenced by that earlier civil engineering training – a meticulous attention to detail and accuracy.

I first met Robert in 1947 when he became Head of the Economic Section in the Cabinet Office. Over the next six years we were to work closely together. Certainly for me more closely than I ever did with anyone else. We were complementary in our working. Robert was a master of lucidity on paper but less so when speaking. Rab Butler described our relationship as follows: 'Robert Hall was our strong silent man who came to have more and more influence. I depended on Edwin Plowden to interpret and to act as publicist for the ideas of the less voluble and extrovert Hall.'

Indeed when Perilla asked me to say something today, my first instinct was to reach for the telephone and ask Robert what I should say and would he please write something for me.

Robert took over responsibility for the Economic Section at a time when nearly all the senior economists who had been there in the war had returned to academic life. Consequently there was a shortage of experienced people. He set out to overcome this by recruitment and training. He succeeded.

He was an extremely hard worker who at first literally lived on the job. He had a bed installed in his office and during the week lived there.

When he became Head of the Economic Section the Labour Government of the day did not seem to know how to use his economists. To overcome this Robert set out to integrate the Section into the official civil service machine – particularly the Treasury after Cripps became Chancellor.

He was the senior economic adviser to governments from 1947 to 1961. He was admired and trusted by both Labour and Conservative Chancellors – by men with as differing views as Cripps and Thorneycroft. His influence was very great.

I will illustrate this by two incidents. The first Devaluation with Cripps, and the second Robot with Butler.

Early in 1949 devaluation of sterling became a favourite topic of debate among informed outside opinion. At about this time, as our dollar balance of payments moved increasingly into deficit, he said to me that he believed all the advantages were in favour of devaluation.

He went on to say that he believed that the onus was certainly on those who said that devaluation would not be a remedy for our problems to prove their case. It was to be a long and difficult task to persuade those opponents.

Cripps thought it immoral when other countries held their reserves in sterling. Edward Bridges, like Cripps, saw devaluation as a dishonest and almost sordid action. He gave the policy of devaluation the code name of Caliban, which he told Robert stood for all that was unsavoury and underhand. He also feared that one devaluation might be followed by others.

The Bank of England was strongly opposed because they did not believe it would remedy for any length of time the root causes of Britain's external problems.

Throughout this period Robert played a key role, setting out the case for devaluation in a series of those lucid papers of which he was such a master.

The Cabinet decided in principle on July 29th that the pound might be devalued. The rate was not decided until Bevin and Cripps arrived in Washington early in September accompanied by a group of advisers including Robert and myself. After discussion, officials favoured a rate of 2.80 dollars to the pound. Later at a meeting with Cripps and Bevin, both of whom favoured a higher rate, Bevin turned to me and asked what effect a rate of 2.80 would have on the price of the standard loaf of bread.

We had anticipated he would ask this and had cabled London for the information. Our answer satisfied him.

In this way was the rate of $2.80 to the pound settled, a rate that was to stand for eighteen years. We had no computers but we had Robert.

The second incident in which Robert played a key role was Robot – a proposal made early in 1952 by the Bank of England and part of the Treasury for dealing with the seriously deteriorating balance of payments. It proposed to make sterling fully convertible at a floating rate and to block compulsorily most of the sterling balances.

It was accepted by the proposers that Robot would have serious and unpleasant consequences for the United Kingdom and indeed for the world economy. None the less it was put forward as the only solution to our economic problems and that it had to be instituted at once.

On February 22nd the Chancellor at a meeting of a small group of senior ministers pressed for its adoption. Only Lord Cherwell opposed it. Because of its wide-ranging implications for Britain's foreign relations it was decided that the Foreign Secretary must be consulted.

He was in Lisbon at a NATO meeting. I was also there. Two senior officials came out bearing various documents including two letters for me. One from Edward Bridges and one from Robert. The one from Edward Bridges seemed to imply that a decision to adopt Robot had more or less been taken and that Eden's agreement was virtually a formality.

The other from Robert by contrast said he was appalled at the suggestion. He was convinced that Ministers did not really understand what the proposals meant and what the consequences might be.

After reading the letters I went to see Eden. He had read the papers and seemed generally supportive of the Robot proposition.

I told him of the arguments in Robert's letter and said that he should not allow a decision to be taken on a matter of such importance without having heard the argument himself. After some discussion he agreed.

On my return to London I found that Robert, together with Donald MacDougall, had drafted a paper for Lord Cherwell highly critical of Robot.

The argument and the exchange of minutes went on for some time. Eventually Robot was rejected.

I have mentioned these two incidents – both extremely important – to show what a key role Robert played in the formulation of economic policy. In the case of devaluation he advocated a policy and it was accepted. In the case of Robot he opposed a policy and saw it rejected.

When he left Whitehall I was fortunate to be able to persuade him to join me at Tube Investments as Economic Consultant and once again to work closely with him.

From 1969 when he became a life peer he attended the House of Lords regularly and spoke in economic debates.

It would not be possible to speak about Robert without mentioning his love of working on his allotments in Oxford and in later years with Perilla in their windswept garden in Cornwall.

In remembering Robert today we can count ourselves privileged to have been able to call this resolute but modest man our friend.

2 Sir Kit McMahon

Edwin has just spoken of Robert as a colleague in Whitehall; and in a few minutes David will speak of him as a colleague at Oxford and the National Institute. I want to speak for a younger generation – those who worked for him, learned from him, admired him and loved him. We called ourselves proudly 'Robert Hall's young men'.

Of course, we all knew him for many years after we ceased to work for him – and after two of our number had themselves held with distinction the post he occupied for so long. We grew to become his friends, to owe him new debts, over fields much wider – and, certainly in my own case, in aspects much deeper – than the purely professional.

But it was Robert the public economist, the Head of the Economic Section, who made the initial and outstanding impression on us. It has been a great pleasure to me over the past few days to talk to a number of my ex-colleagues about Robert, to have memories rekindled and to find such a clear unanimous appreciation of his great and unusual qualities.

Perhaps the most striking thing about him, professionally and intellectually, was his grip on reality. Edwin has spoken of his original training as an engineer; and it may have been this that gave him what often seemed an instinctive or intuitive understanding of the way in which highly complex political and economic systems work. Certainly his training in mathematics must have helped form his very severe judgements on the role that subject could play in the assessment of the economy.

It is tempting to describe Robert's approach as common sense – and so in a way it was. But except to those who knew him well, it would be a misleading description. There was nothing bluff or plain about Robert's common sense: there was nothing of the evasion of thought and theory which characterizes what usually passes itself off as common sense in exalted places. Robert's common sense was subtle and hard-won. Something only seemed simple once he had said it.

And those ways he had of saying it. All of us here can see him now, in our minds' eyes: see him as he strove to make a point, stuttering, gasping a little, moving body and hands and then suddenly bringing out, with a modest and triumphant smile, some exact judgement or comment. His 'incoherent lucidity', in Dick Ross's happy phrase, constantly charmed and inspired us all.

Robert was an unusual man to work for. There was little structured objective-setting or formal bureaucratic good practice. Everything proceeded by indirection. We were put into bat in Committee with others often two or three ranks our senior; or got on with producing economic forecasts very much on our own. We were stimulated by nods and laconic comments on misguided views he was fighting elsewhere; we were warned by grunts and by his extraordinary ability to tell when our figures were wrong when there seemed no way he could have known it. It was all very exciting.

And, of course, it was very successful. It is common in some quarters today to look patronizingly at the postwar years, taking the criticism of Stop–Go made at the time at face value. But the fluctuations and changes of policy thrust were in those days tiny compared with what we have seen later – and the record in terms of growth, employment and inflation was probably better while Robert was Economic Adviser than at any other period of this century. Of course, the circumstances were favourable. Robert would certainly have acknowledged – did acknowledge – that his successors had to work under much more difficult conditions. But that should not be allowed to obscure the fact that as effectively the first peacetime Government economic adviser, bringing economic advice and economic thinking to a Whitehall that compared with today was almost unimaginably economically illiterate, success was achieved in all the areas Robert would have counted most important.

He was certainly proud of this. He was the exact opposite of a mere technician or operator, though – as Edwin has indicated – he could be a very powerful operator indeed when occasion demanded. He was a deeply emotional man, idealistic in his approach to his work (though he would perhaps have grunted if he had heard me say this); subject to the turbulences, doubts and distress of all who feel strongly: and he had great moral courage. It was good for his friends to see the happiness he found, at great cost, in his love for Perilla and the garden at Quarry.

It is impossible, as both Edwin and David have found, to speak of Robert without mentioning his gardening. Year after year at the Treasury Horticultural Society his sweetcorn used to win the prize for Any Other Vegetable – a suitable emblem perhaps of modesty and success combined. And one of my happiest memories of him is sitting with Perilla surveying the Quarry garden and the sea, in his old clothes with a gin and tonic in his hand. Life, as he himself said, stripped down to its bare luxuries.

3 *David Worswick*

I first came across the name of Robert Hall as one half of a celebrated economics double act – Hall and Hitch – authors of an article published in 1939 in which they introduced the kinked demand curve. The authors claimed that the evidence about the way in which firms actually fixed prices was at variance with the way economic theory said they ought to. This scepticism about 'current doctrine' was characteristic of the Oxford economists of the 1930s, and it was an attitude which Robert maintained all his life.

I did not meet Robert until he returned to Oxford after the war. And then it was Margaret, a colleague of the sub-faculty of economics, whom I got to know best, and later on Felicity and Anthea, who came to me for tutorials in economics. These were enjoyable encounters, which were to provide valuable material in proposing toasts at weddings.

Robert himself was working in London, and quite often abroad. When he was in Oxford, at weekends, he liked to switch off by digging on his allotment. But he found time to keep in touch with old colleagues, and to meet the younger economists.

The main work of the Economic Section, of which he was in charge, was to study the economy, and to make economic forecasts, to be used as the basis of advice on economic policy. This work was not made public, and, following the suggestion of Christopher Dow and Bryan Hopkin, Robert helped to persuade the National Institute of Economic and Social Research to set up a team which would undertake similar studies, but publish the results. He thought it wrong that there was no independent check on the apparatus on which the government depended for advice. The *Economic Review* was launched in 1959, and quickly established a position of some authority.

Soon after he left the Treasury in 1961, Robert took over the Chairmanship of the Executive Committee of the National Institute, which he was to hold for the next nine years. This is an honorary post, but he gave much time and thought to the Institute, to which he became devoted. When he wrote to me in 1964, inviting me to succeed Christopher Saunders as Director, I remember him saying that it was the *Review* which mattered most.

Both my predecessors had come from Whitehall, and, though the Institute was independent, nevertheless a knowledge of the way round that remarkable village was very useful. I had had an exclusively academic background in Oxford, and was an outsider. Robert proved to be a splendid mentor. He made himself available whenever I wished to consult him – on the research programme, on the state of the economy, on the Institute's finances, or on the recruitment of staff.

He never thrust his own views upon me. He might occasionally say: 'I don't think I would do that myself, but, if you feel strongly that you must, then go ahead.' And, on the rare occasions when I did not follow his advice, he would back my decision just as strongly as on the majority of occasions when I did.

The Institute was in deep financial trouble in 1965, and I have to admit that I used to find Robert's cheerful trust that Providence would come up with something a little unnerving. But his practical advice was sound. What Providence produced was the Social Science Research Council, to which the Institute immediately applied for a large grant. Meanwhile, I had myself been appointed to the Council, and thus was in a position of some delicacy. How should an honourable man behave when the Institute's application appeared on the table? Should I stay away from the meeting altogether? I asked Robert, who simply said: 'You stay glued to your chair, until they pull you out.'

Robert did not lose interest in the Institute when he ceased to be Chairman at the end of 1970. He used to drop in on his way to the House of Lords to talk to Kit Jones, the Secretary, or to me about the affairs of the Institute or the state of the national economy. These visits gradually became less frequent, as Robert and Perilla spent more and more time in Cornwall.

But he attended the Annual Meeting of the Governors unfailingly, the last time being only three years ago. More often than not, he would put a question on finance, or make a trenchant observation on the research programme. He clearly believed in the value of the Institute, to which, as Chairman, he had himself contributed so much.

He was an indifferent speaker, and in Committee preferred a few words to lengthy exposition. Yet, you always felt he had grasped the problem, and was guiding the Committee towards the right decision. Beneath his modest demeanour, there was strength and determination.

And there was a warmth about him. He inspired respect, but also affection. I owed much to him for his wisdom and support; and, seeing him at close quarters, I came to appreciate how fortunate we had all been to have such a man at the centre of economic affairs in the difficult years of recovery after the war.

I

Butler's last years as Chancellor,

1 January 1954 to 20 December 1955

Friday, January 1st 1954

My KCMG was announced this morning, and when I went to Bernard Gilbert's Friday Forum meeting, they were all very nice indeed.[1] I got a good many notes from Civil Servants during the day but as I am off early tomorrow, Miss Whitby will have to deal with most of them. As people always tell me, one of the nicest things about Honours is the letters one gets, in which one's friends and acquaintances are more forthcoming than usual.

The Commonwealth Conference in Sydney is very much a routine one although it has not been routine to have them in the past; there was one in January 1952 and one (of Prime Ministers) in December 1952 so that the interval is roughly a year. Great labours have been going on in Whitehall for quite a long time to get ready for this one. Although there have been mild runs on the old lines, they have been much less violent than they were, and the question of what to do if there were a recession in the US was treated far more amicably than I thought possible. We agreed that if it got at all bad, there would be a strong case for increasing credits available both in EPU [European Payments Union] and in the sterling area, and approaches to the US and Canada for the same reasons. Most of the other stuff was fairly routine but on development the influence of William Armstrong, who took Martin Flett's place, is already showing in that he has attempted both to quantify what is happening and to relate it to the [Economic] Survey Target: and the whole approach is more liberal. I tried to get the question of the £300–£350 mn [balance of payments] target re-examined before we left but did not succeed.[2] However Arnold France has promised to have it looked at when we get back.

The size of the US recession, or rather what size we should plan for, has also been interesting. My people, and Fred Atkinson in Washington, have been predicting a rather more serious down-turn than seems to me to be likely on political grounds. The recession has certainly been going on for some months now but in a very gentle and orderly way, and I find it hard to think, after all that Hauge [President's Assistant for Economic Affairs] says, that they will let it go very far. This is the line we are going to take in Sydney, i.e. that the most probable hypothesis is that it will be 'moderate and short' and that our best line is to try to see it through. If it gets worse then we will think again. I don't believe that our own position is so weak that we will not have time to think as we go along, and it wouldn't be very sensible to act now as if there were going to be a serious slump, particularly as we have dismantled so many controls in pursuit of Tory policies: but I haven't objected strongly since if we are going convertible we ought to make these first steps in good time – the policy of taking the temperature I tried unsuccessfully to get H.G. [Gaitskell] to adopt.

Actually I think that we are very much nearer to being able to go convertible, if there is no bad US slump, than we were two years ago.

Commodity prices are low and show little sign of getting much higher, and even food which until recently seemed to be perpetually scarce, is getting more plentiful. There is almost a glut of wheat, and British agricultural policy has become all a question of subsidies, since imports have become so much cheaper.

On the collective approach [to convertibility], there is very little to say, since the US have given no indication of what they will do, and European countries dislike either convertibility, or the floating rate, or both.

Monday, January 4th (Singapore)

I have been on time so far: spent a night at Beirut and dined at Karachi last night with Gilbert Laithwaite, the High Commissioner. He talked about Trinity all the time, being so glad to see someone who was closely connected with it.[3] The only local thing he mentioned was that the Paks were now building a big dam on the lower Indus which would develop a great deal of country there. We flew on to Calcutta that night and at about 2 a.m. picked up both Deshmukh, the Indian, and Mohammed Ali, the Pakistan, Finance Ministers. The latter looks a most engaging person. I do not remember having seen either of them before but both have high reputations. We got to Singapore about 1.30 and I had a sleep. Malcolm MacDonald, the High Commissioner, invited me to a dinner he was giving for the Chancellor. A lot of local bankers, Federation senior officials and so on were there.

After dinner we sat in the open and they asked questions of the Chancellor, who as usual handled them very well. Nearly all about rubber, where the planters, etc., are worried because if the price falls much lower it will not be profitable – and the Federation Government because most of their income depends on the export tax which falls off rapidly as the price falls. They think that if the price goes much lower they will have to borrow for, or stop, their development programme for schools, hospitals, etc. The Chancellor was not too well up in rubber. I tried to explain that I did not think the US could do much about synthetics and that the industry would have to struggle. On the Government side, I felt pretty clear that it would be cheaper for the UK to lend or give them enough, than for us to try to support rubber prices. However I think the US might be a *little* more helpful on their synthetic policy.

Wednesday, January 13th (Sydney)

I felt very much exhausted when I arrived - four days flying is too much, or rather the change of 10 hours so quickly. The Conference is nearly over now and it seems to me and I think to most others to have been very successful. Leslie Rowan and Roland Wilson [Secretary, Australian

Treasury] did a very good job on the official meetings and produced a good report for the Ministers, who began on the 8th. Menzies [the Australian Prime Minister] is obviously a very able man and he has held himself in and been a first-class Chairman. The Chancellor has had to do all the work and has done it well – all his speeches have to be prepared carefully as he is asked to open every topic, and he speaks at lunches and so on, so that the UK Del. has had a tough time. But I have not done very much, nor has Frank Lee who is also here. The main load fell on Leslie [Rowan] himself, William Armstrong and Matthew Stevenson. Also Louis Petch, the Chancellor's Secretary.

We are all in the Australia, for accommodation as well as Conference, which is a great help. The Australians have been extremely hospitable and done a first-class job on arrangements, including the Conference Secretariat. In the best Norman Brook style, which is not surprising as the Australians have sent several people to the Cabinet Office Secretariat as well as to the Economic Section.

There has not been anything unexpected or dramatic but I think the Conference is none the worse for that and one gets the feeling that the sterling area really has some coherence, much more so in this context than the Commonwealth, since the Canadians almost ostentatiously take very little part except to give everyone else rather sanctimonious advice.

The part of the discussion which I thought most useful was on the trade prospects and especially in relation to US business conditions. Here the UK line – (a) that as a working hypothesis we should assume that any recession would be moderate and short, (b) that it might be worse than this and that, if so, the general object should be to keep up the level of trade and not to have any more restriction than could be avoided, (c) that Commonwealth countries should keep in touch, and be prepared to concert measures if things got bad – was adopted by general consent. This gives us a very useful beginning – the Official Report spoke of credits between sterling area and OEEC countries and the possibility of collective discrimination. As this seems to me to be the principal thing to worry about on the horizon, I was very glad to have got so far, especially as in London a few months back OF had been nervous about opening the subject at all.

As might have been expected, development got most publicity. The Chancellor in his early public utterances talked about taking risks and the need for a bold policy, and the Australian press and politicians naturally took this to mean that there would be much more money. Partly to counteract this at home and partly to help Menzies, who was afraid he would lose his grip on the State Treasurers, the Chancellor then began to talk not only about the limits to UK resources but about the sacrifices this would mean. The Press then played this up and even talked about the need to return to rationing in the UK and to cut the housing programme. This was just as bad domestically for R.A.B. as the previous line – he tried to show that we could increase our loans without suffering, by diverting some of our increased production. This was the right line but I don't know if it stuck. Incidentally, all RSA [rest of the sterling area] countries realized that we could lend much more easily if they provided a fairly good market for our goods.

The only awkward subject was connected with Imperial Preference and trade restrictions. The Chancellor was most anxious to persuade Australia to relax further on the [import] restrictions she had imposed on inessentials early in 1952, and which had borne very heavily on the UK. The Australians are prepared to make some changes, probably in February, but did not want to seem to make them as a result of pressure at the Conference itself. R.A.B. wanted to take back something tangible, to console his supporters for the inability to get any further with Imperial Preference, so he pressed the Australians in a way which they thought would give him less tangible results than would have followed if he had said very little. In the end the reference in the communiqué was very guarded. On preference itself, the new Central African Federation people were very forthcoming and said they wanted as much Imperial Preference as they could get.

Sir O. Goonetilleke [Finance Minister, Ceylon], who was the bad boy of the Conference, made several impassioned speeches to the effect that the sterling area was buying things from outside the area and thus causing surpluses to accumulate within it. Menzies was rather keen on this 'buying from one another' as it was called, and seemed to think that it was an alternative to written preferences, which indeed it could be if there was state trading or at least import licensing. But there is a lot of difficulty about price, especially now when the US is so near to dumping its agricultural surpluses.

Tuesday, January 19th (Silver Spur)

The Conference ended about 12.30 on Friday, Jan. 15th. The main trouble at the end was of course the communiqué. After a great deal of trouble and rewriting, the officials produced a very good one but with no peroration, which they felt should be provided by Ministers. Menzies, who was drinking very heavily during the latter stages, produced at a late hour on Thursday a very flowery and unsuitable peroration, and an introduction as well. About 10 p.m. I found a meeting going on in the Chancellor's room, with all his senior officials telling him very firmly that these would not do. He was in an obstinate mood as he did not want to offend Menzies, and kept on saying that it was not too bad; however he did a draft that cut out the worst parts of the epilogue, but then the prologue was produced and he could not bear any more and went home.

Next day Ministers passed the main part, which had been redrafted on their instructions during the night. They then shut themselves up alone to consider the beginning and end, and soon after emerged with the great part of the Menzies draft. So it is still there, for all to read. It is however very unsuitable for a Finance Ministers meeting and is disapproved of by all the senior officials. But Ministers did not seem to mind and most of them thought it was the kind of stuff the Press would like.

On the Conference as a whole, Menzies was a very good Chairman indeed. He is a large and commanding figure, with a first-class voice and a ready command of language. As Chairman he was clearly the man in authority, he pushed on the discussions and made good summaries when needed. We were told that he had risen to the occasion and was not always so good, but I felt sure that he was outstanding and the next best Australian Minister, Sir A. Fadden, the Treasurer, was a long way behind. The main load fell on Mr Butler who was marked off to open, or occasionally to conclude, all the meetings. He was well served by his officials (we wrote him speeches for each meeting and these were continually worked over) but he was good enough to be worth working for and showed great adaptability in discussion. He has a very bad habit, however, of working on papers during discussion, and though he was able to keep an ear for any points that needed comment, it produced a bad impression.

The Australians ran the Conference very well indeed, under the direction of Allen Brown [Secretary, Prime Minister's Department] who has no doubt used his people who had experience of the UK Cabinet Office. They had also borrowed F. A. Bishop, but B. told me he had very little to do. Everyone was hospitable, and the Australia itself is in almost all respects a good hotel.

I got the evening plane to Brisbane and stayed at Lennon's Hotel, which has become a first-class international hotel. But Brisbane itself seemed little changed. Since then I stayed two nights in Toowoomba and am now at Silver Spur, where I came when I was two and which has been the home of the family ever since. There isn't much left of the old township, and our house was burned down in 1943 – mother lives in what was the combined Post Office and Company Office. The surroundings are of course unchanged, and the view one of the best in the world.

Thursday, April 8th

I came back by Washington and enjoyed my visit very much. Leslie Rowan was there also and we had long talks with [Arthur] Burns [Chairman of the Council of Economic Advisers] and [Gabriel] Hauge about the recession, and with various people about the Randall Report, convertibility and so on.[4] I found Burns very confident about the economic situation and about his ability to get the US Administration to take the necessary steps to check it if he thought this necessary. Win Riefler [Federal Reserve Board] was obviously in a much stronger position than when I was there before – he has continued to establish his position with Bill Martin [Chairman of the Board of Governors], who told me that he had made Win the Secretary of the Open Market Committee and that he was in a very strong position on policy. My general impression was that the Administration was still fairly weak and that they were not doing any work on our Memorandum.[5]

Since then the main interest has been the Budget, which was announced two days ago. The NIF [National Income Forecasts] Working Party came to the conclusion that there would be a little slack in the system towards the end of this year, and that if the US recession got any worse this might lead to a stock run-down here which would produce rather more slack.[6] I had been rather worried by last year's events as they seemed to show that we had over-estimated the slack last year – there ought to have been more unemployment, having regard to the small increase in production compared to the trend line.[7] So I rather modified the picture and said I thought there was only a little room for concession. At that time a Budget surplus of about £60 mn was forecast. The main changes since last year were that some of the tax concessions, especially Initial Allowances, came in and that the agricultural subsidies were much more expensive than was expected a year ago.

However about three weeks before the Budget, the Inland Revenue announced that their sample of profits showed that the revenue would be about £90 mn less than had been forecast before. They also reduced their estimate for 1955/56 by about £150 mn, showing an expected above the line deficit in that year of about £300 mn or more. This produced a sudden reversion to pre-war principles: the Chancellor seemed to think that we were on the verge of ruin and must never have an above the line deficit: Bridges, Gilbert, Brittain and Rowan took more or less the same view. I had quite a struggle to get them to realize that the principles of the Budgets since 1948 made the surplus or deficit accidental. For a while it seemed likely that we should actually put on new taxes to avoid a deficit this year. As for next year, the drop was largely due to Inland Revenue having taken the NIF forecast of a slump here due to the US recession – so the moral would have been an *easier* Budget this year.

In the end we managed to avoid any new taxes this year, though the accounts were shaded a bit to produce a surplus. For next year, there is to be a campaign against Government expenditure which is all to the good though I do not suppose it will produce much. I managed to get the Chancellor to play down the loss of revenue expected because of a hypothetical US slump.[8]

Thursday, August 12th

It seems hardly worth going on when I write so rarely and yet I am reluctant to give up something I have been doing since I began this job. I am on leave at present but had to be in London and I was reminded of the diary because a young man from *The Observer* came to see me to talk about Edwin Plowden, of whom they are doing a profile. He wanted to know what I thought Edwin's main contribution had been, and I felt no doubt that it was getting the planning machinery going for a full employment economy: the Investment Programmes Committee, the Programmes Committee and the Budget Committee as it has been since the end of 1947. The first is now the TIC [Treasury Investments Committee]; the second is getting less and less to do as controls are being given up; but the main structure is going well and will or at least should continue – in some form it will, just because full employment will remain a major object of policy.

He also asked me questions about *why* E.P. was so successful, a subject I have often considered. I feel pretty sure that it is because he has so much courage and tenacity, and because Cripps felt in him a similar spirit, wanting to get on with the job and not thinking about his career. Edwin worries a great deal about a decision after it is taken, and he thinks a great deal about his career when that is the principal thing he has to think about. But when he is in a struggle he concentrates on that and would be willing to throw his career and everything else away rather than concede anything substantial on a point he felt strongly about. Oliver Franks used to say that Cripps felt that E.P. would resign rather than give up a point of principle, whereas the ordinary Civil Servant is trained to do anything rather than resign. I have often wondered how this view squares with the state of mind E.P. got into after he learnt that R.A.B. had no real confidence in him. But I think they are compatible – when E.P. heard this, the main battle about convertibility was over and there was no struggle on so he was able to concentrate on his personal difficulties. If there had been another battle he would have gone into it unaffected by the doubts and fears that had been assailing him.

The Budget went off all right and the investment allowance was generally welcomed. The Finance Bill took longer than was expected because Customs, and especially Inland Revenue, shoved a lot of things that they said were routine or mechanical into the Bill, taking advantage of the fewness of the changes of substance. And some of these were much more awkward than had been expected. There has been a general look at Budget procedure as a result but I don't suppose there will be much change. The trouble is that we try to base the Budget on figures and forecasts made too near the time – the financial year should close in December and the Budget be opened in late May or early June.

I have been struggling a bit more about the evils of attaching any importance to an above the line balance. R.A.B. has been worrying a good deal about next year and would like to settle it now, which is ridiculous. The Civil Economies Committee of Ministers has done a good deal of work and made some useful minor economies, but there is nothing big without a change of policy except the food subsidies, or perhaps we should say also the agricultural subsidies, since policy is rather unclear there.[9] I think that there is also some struggle behind the scenes about the defence vote but I don't think that we can foresee the outcome of any of this because there is no clear view in Ministers' minds. It would be nice to have lower taxes but it would also be nice to spend more on social services, defence, etc. The hydrogen bomb has made a big query about all defence but it needs a very bold man to carry this line of thought to any conclusion at all.

The time has been very quiet on the economic front and Ministers including R.A.B. have spent a lot of time on Crichel Down and members' pay, neither of which are in my line, though I gave some advice casually at office meetings on the latter.[10] I thought (a) that expenses would go down better than a pay increase, (b) that once they had had a free vote they ought to have accepted it and put it through at once. They rejected (b) and consequently went back to (a). I was never consulted about Crichel Down but I think the House, the Press and the public have all drawn the wrong moral, since they all feel that the Civil Service is a tyrant that must be curbed, whereas it is entirely their own creature. And the Civil Service ought to exercise more rather than less initiative if it is to carry out well all the tasks that have been put on it.

The main thing on the economic front from the point of view of my great controversies is that R.A.B. has decided that he cannot carry through convertibility before the election – none of his colleagues wanted to and the Foreign Secretary took very much against – I don't believe that he himself wanted to move, he has spent the last two years or so getting off the hook that OF and the Bank put him on when he was a new boy. This is really a complete victory for me: and as our economic position has improved so much that I think we wouldn't come such a crash now if we moved, the two sides are a good deal nearer. However my relations with T.L.R. [Rowan] are no better and I had to complain to B. Gilbert about them a few weeks ago. He won't do much – he doesn't do much and it is a farce that he should preside over the Official Committee on External Economic Policy [PRO CAB 134/869] when he asserts, and with a good deal of truth, that he does not understand the issues [appointed in July, the committee was dissolved in November – Ed.].

However this is all becoming rather a mock battle and I do not worry about it like I used to do. The internal situation is almost too good to be true and causes a lot of thought - employment is over-full and coal is short of labour but apart from this there are no signs of inflation. My staff think that there has been some restocking in the production boom, and that things will slacken off in the late autumn. The Stock Exchange seems to me to be having a terrific boom and I don't think it will last but it is hard to pick the turns.

Thursday, September 2nd

I have been on leave most of the time since I wrote, but came back in the middle of last week. Everything is very quiet on the economic front, because it is all going so well. The NIF Working Party have just finished their mid-year review, and the results are very interesting. GNP has gone up by over £300 mn in the last 12 months, and nearly £100 mn of this has gone to exports and about the same to restocking.[11] So that the use to which we have been putting the boom is very non-vulnerable in the sense that two-thirds of the increase has improved our liquid capital position. The LCES [London and Cambridge Economic Service] has just come out with a very bullish analysis of the position, not very encouraging as they have generally been wrong in the past.

Most senior people have been taking leave. The Chancellor has been in for occasional meetings, and seems in fairly good shape though he is very worried about his wife's health. She has a growth on her jaw and they fear it is cancer, and it puts a great strain on him, not only mentally but because she expects him to do a great deal for her, and in his job there is hardly any time for a private life: it becomes disrupted if there are exactions on it.

Tuesday, September 28th (Washington, DC)

The Chancellor wanted me to come with him and the rather large party to the annual meeting of the IMF and IBRD – I don't usually come though I had a feeling that I was here once before when it was going on, one of the visits with Wilson Smith it was.[12] This is the Chancellor's first visit, and it was originally thought by OF that a great deal of progress towards convertibility would be made, in discussions with the USA, and possibly with senior members of the Fund staff about the stand-by credit which we hope to get. Anyway there was more than even the usual thorough preparation and we came away with a mountain of briefs.[13]

Originally the Chancellor had meant to cross by sea and I thought I had better do the same. Later both his decision to go that way, and my feeling that I ought to keep an eye on him, changed. But as I have not crossed by sea since I came with O.S.F. [Franks] on the 2nd Rubber Study Group meeting in early 1945, and as things were for once peaceful, I let it stand and came on the *Queen Mary* with Leslie Rowan, Maudling, Stevenson and John Owen who represents the Treasury on the EPU Managing Board in Paris. We did very little work there: I saw quite a lot of Maudling who is a pleasant man but rather self-indulgent. He is a reasonably good economist and has some political sense but I doubt if he will reach the top of the Ministerial ladder. He told me, a little to my surprise, that he hardly knows the Chancellor personally.

We got here on the night of Sept. 21st and the Chancellor came by air from New York the next day. He looked very poorly when he got here and has not seemed very well ever since. His Secretary Louis Petch says that his wife has had to go to hospital again and that it is almost a continuous strain on him now.

We have had several talks with the Americans under Humphrey [Secretary of US Treasury]. Burgess, Stassen, Sam Waugh, Hauge and Burns have been there: they seem to be more or less of a team on the economic side though I suppose that the Commerce Dept is usually included. Very little progress has been made. The Americans and everyone else know that we are not going to move at all quickly on convertibility and as far as I can see they do not mind. Unlike the previous Administration they feel strongly that it is our responsibility and don't want to press us to do anything we don't feel strong enough to do.

They have repeatedly said that the President is determined to get action on the Randall Report early in next year's Congress: that he simply could not fit so difficult an operation into this year's crowded programme: that he has persuaded Randall to stay another year and would not have done so if it had not been that R. was persuaded of full Presidential support. However, it is also clear that Humphrey and Weeks are protectionist rather than free traders, and Humphrey indeed has told us plainly that he thinks tariffs are necessary to maintain employment, in the same breath as he has told us that it is of the first importance to reduce expenditure while at the same time keeping the Budget balanced. However he does not appear to be able to carry out these tactics which are so pre-Keynesian that it is almost curious to hear them enunciated from such a quarter.

In our plans, we have always envisaged 'trade rules' under which countries would be bound not to discriminate after convertibility, nor to make use of q.r. except in balance of payments crises and then with a commitment to justify the action to IMF and GATT. It now seems very likely that we shall have a good deal of difficulty in getting GATT renewed at the review which begins in November, even with its present rather loose language. The Americans will have trouble to get Congress to renew it at all and most other countries want discretion to behave as they please though no doubt they would try to be well behaved. At any rate our idea that GATT could be used for our trade rules has become less rather than more likely if we expect rigid rules.[14]

The US therefore are coming to the idea that we and other countries which get IMF credits should accept unilateral commitments in return for such credits. It would be very difficult to get the UK to agree to this, especially as there is little enthusiasm either for convertibility or for free trade. And many officials, including myself, would be very much opposed to making any more commitments of this kind, which we would probably be unable or unwilling to carry out.

I have had talks with Hauge and Burns: and Fred Atkinson had a number of the national income forecasters to dinner to meet me. Burns is still reasonably confident that there will be some increase in activity this year, largely because he says that the latest figures for construction, etc., are still rising. The economists were a little more uncertain than they had been, and I thought Hauge was a little uncertain also. They have done very well so far, in preventing the recession from getting at all serious, but now that they want an expansion again they cannot quite see how to bring it about. The problem is to reconcile expansion with Republican philosophy – Hauge told me that quite a large section of Congress are opposed to deficit finance and really think that large Budgets are undermining the economy. I suppose they feel that the expansion of recent years is somehow a bubble, in spite of the obvious contrary evidence. He says that they refuse to increase the debt limit as a check on themselves (Congress) just as much as on the President. So the Council [of Economic Advisers] is making an inter-Departmental study of the conditions for growth, and this will be the theme of the next Economic Report.

I have seen a lot of other people, including the Alsops and Dick Bissell, but nothing very interesting has happened. Today I took

Viscount Harcourt to lunch. He is to replace both Denis Rickett as Economic Minister, and Hall-Patch as UK Director of the IBRD and the IMF. I had met him several times in London where he spent some time in the Treasury, and had also discussed with him the problem of replacing Atkinson. Grieve-Smith is to come instead – he is rather too young for the job but wants to try it and I feel sure that he is one of my ablest young men. Atkinson has done very well indeed here and is clearly quite highly regarded by the economists in the US Government and this goes quite a way up – both Burns and Burgess have spoken to me warmly about him.

I have not had a proper chance to talk to Harcourt before and was very favourably impressed by him. He did law at Oxford but then went into Morgan Grenfell's (I think his mother or his grandmother was a Morgan). He seemed not unnaturally a bit lost in London but I thought he had got quite sensible ideas here both about personalities and about the work. I advised him to play the Collective Approach very slowly and indeed to do nothing here till after the election and not much then. I don't think there is any pressure on us at all.

We discussed the IMF Credit [the amount that could be drawn unconditionally] and agreed that it would be a great mistake to use it, or to use very much of it, at all – its only virtue was to give us confidence to use our own reserves. I also told him that it was part of his job to give advice to London; I don't think either Leslie Rowan or Denis Rickett did this enough, Leslie especially was inclined to take his instructions as military orders and do a good deal of damage to the cause in the process. Our people here are or ought to be much more an intelligence and policy service than just diplomats who carry out instructions. I don't suppose diplomats would say that that was their role but most of the FO behave like that. Anyway it was quite an encouraging meal.

Wednesday, September 29th

The £ has got weaker in the past week and George Bolton says that it is because the bankers here believe that the Chancellor has decided never to move on convertibility till it can be a bipartisan policy. This is because he has let it be known that he thinks it would be unwise to move until after an election. Sterling tends to be weak seasonally at this time anyway and I do not think there is much to worry about. But George thinks that the Chancellor should make it clear that it is only the timing that has changed.[15] Harcourt told me that he thought the best thing to do would be for us to make several more moves towards convertibility, even of a minor kind, just to show that we intended to progress.

I have been urging for a long time that we ought to make as many moves as possible *before* convertibility, so that we can reduce the strain at the time and particularly so that we can find out where the strains are, economically and politically. We do not know exactly what industries will be upset by American competition, how we can operate a tariff, or what pledges we may have given about dollar-saving industries. We don't know much about the effect of removing US discrimination in the sterling area, though S. Africa has done it and there does not seem to be much change there.[16]

There is a peculiar schizophrenia about OF. They have always been urging us to hurry on to convertibility and yet they are now hanging back on practical steps. They have a catchword, that we ought not to do much 'without the protection of the rate and of the stand-by credits'. I don't myself think either of them would give us much protection. It would be a mistake to get a credit if we intended to make use of it except to counteract a simple and obvious threat of a speculative or confidence kind. And the more we study the floating rate the more uncertain we become about it. Harcourt was very sound on the first – on the second he seemed to think that the rate was much more likely to rise than to fall – on our studies this would be likely if the initial movement was upward, i.e. the rate has an explosive tendency or I should say destabilizing at first – I don't think it is really explosive unless monetary policy at home allows it to be as in an uncontrolled inflation.

Thursday, September 30th

We had a busy day yesterday. Delegation meeting at 9 in the Mayflower. At 10 saw Humphrey and a number of others at the Treasury. The conversation was very frank and I must say that I thought Humphrey's character was admirable – calm, decided, absolutely honest and straightforward – it made an unusually marked impression. The general line of the discussion was the rate at which we would move to convertibility. They said we must be the judge and they would give us any help they could. R.A.B. explained our position, with reference to the European political scene and a good deal less candour than Humphrey had used, and pointed out that our conditions had not been fulfilled and especially they hadn't done anything to let us see a dependable balance. H. said that as far as he was concerned they would not make any large or general tariff reductions – much more likely to have to move up in a few lines. We ought not to let it be thought that the *US* was holding up the move to convertibility – they did not think they were, and taking all their actions together they had been a good not a bad creditor for several years. Stassen pointed out that this was the result of deliberate policy.

R.A.B. rose to quite statesmanlike heights at this point. He said that, rightly or wrongly, people did not trust future US policy – all these noble acts which had more than balanced any gap were fully recognized but they were not accompanied by any change in allowing others to earn. And in this suspicious atmosphere, even small movements of an adverse kind (e.g. the tariff on Swiss watches) aroused resentment and encouraged the cynical. It would be wrong to conceal from the US side that this was there. He would do what he could but his hands were very much tied by not being able to say what would take the place of aid if moves were made that cast doubts on the prospects of trade. He referred in passing to Stassen's ideas for SE Asia: anything like this would do. Both Humphrey and R.A.B. stuck to their guns very well with good humour and good temper. At the end H. made an appeal that neither of us should try to blame the other for delay – we should try to seem to the outside world to be 'back to back'.

Afterwards I saw Aschinger, a Swiss journalist [*Neue Zürcher Zeitung*], whom I had met several times in London and who asked me the most pointed and direct questions possible, in the extremist manner of the reporter who expects the person interviewed to look after his own interests. On the whole I thought that he considered the slower pace to be desirable and he did not seem to feel either himself or as a reporter that there was any alarm or disappointment.

Dick Bissell [CIA, 1954–62] took me to lunch and we talked all the time about (a) whether Mendès-France [the French Prime Minister] was trying to build up a neutral Europe, and get all the US troops out of it, which is being constantly reported to the US and the UK; (b) how to deal with Fascist groups in a democracy and how far majorities ought to go (i) in tolerating, (ii) in fighting against minorities. On (a) we didn't get much beyond conjectures but agreed that if it really were his policy it wasn't likely to succeed. In this connection I said how relieved I was that the Labour Party had voted for German rearmament, even though the majority was small. On (b) it was rather a hackneyed discussion, though Dick handled it with great elegance and learning. His main thesis was that Fascist tendencies in the US were largely supported by the Irish Roman Catholics, but that this meant that at any time a surprising number of US citizens were not at least democrats.

In the afternoon we met Stassen [Director, Foreign Operations Administration] to talk about his plans for SE Asia – he has a lot of money and wants to use it to get some form of economic progress. His ideas were very sensible, mainly on the lines that they must take the leading part and that it must not seem to be a US–UK action in kindly making plans and finding money for them. London had said the same and in nearly all points we were agreed – though of course we haven't yet been asked to find any money. I thought Stassen was very impressive both then and at the Humphrey meeting earlier. Abbot Moffat (with whom I am staying) [and who served in ECA, MSA and FOA, 1948–53] says that S. has in the past been 'all things to all men' and that he had no principles. Also he began in his present job by getting rid of his top staff and not being able to replace them (some of this in bitterness, as A.L.M. was a victim): but he agreed that S. is growing up to his job. I could not help feeling that he was very good in his ideas and in his personality.

Afterwards I had an amusing interview – apparently a number of US Agencies have an officer called the Executive Secretary and I saw the FOA one, a man called Toner. He wanted to find out how we co-ordinated the work and kept the top staff informed in London as this was his job in FOA and Stassen had told him the British do these things much better than the US (including Toner) do! He explained their system which is more elaborate and formal than ours and which ought to produce better results. If it doesn't it must be because they change their staff too often. In the UK the fundamental thing is that everyone has been brought up in the Civil Service and to the knowledge that it is a serious crime *not* to keep people informed – though at the top policy level I don't think it works too well; at any rate I often have to complain to B. Gilbert that *he* does not tell *me* what is happening.

Then I saw Marcus Fleming, now working with IMF – his hair is completely white, most impressive. He says that there is tremendous jealousy and that no one consults anyone else if he can possibly avoid it. [Eddie] Bernstein and [Irving] Friedman will not speak to one another and Rooth [Managing Director] goes direct to the staff member dealing with a point, even if there are 3 or 4 grades between them. Abbot Moffat told me that the Bank, where he has gone to work, is full of prima donnas who spend a lot of time trying to stop others from getting their work away from them. I imagine that both bodies are over-staffed and that the staffs are all anxiously working for promotion.

Then I dined with Atkinson, to meet Meehan [Director, Office of Business Economics] of the Dept of Commerce (who does the National Income calculations) and Win Riefler of FRB [Federal Reserve Board]. The party began inauspiciously as Meehan had not brought his wife – he spent 45 minutes going back to get her. I was so exhausted by about 10 p.m. that I could hardly think or speak. Meehan seemed rather disgruntled about the economy and thought it would go down next year if nothing were done. Riefler was very careful but told me privately afterwards that he thought it wisest to make no predictions about 1955 – he meant that the outlook was uncertain. Meehan was very positive that there was nothing to make for expansion in the system and it is clear that this is their main worry. On this Riefler talked a certain amount of nonsense about Hire Purchase, as if the tendency to get into debt was their main hope.

It was a *very* hot day and I saw people without a break from breakfast at 7.30 to midnight. How the Chancellor does it I can't think, unless he rests deliberately. It is the strong animal spirit that a Minister needs first of all.

Friday, October 1st

Yesterday was mainly meetings with Commonwealth Finance Ministers. The Chancellor was in very good form all day and explained the issues against a background of very little willingness to say much by the others. In the morning I gave my views on the US position at some length and the Ec. Sec. about the UK but no one else said much and the Canadians especially were disappointing. Their new Finance Minister, Harris, was in the lead for the Can. Del. but he was very cautious and also he spoke in a very low voice. I met him at dinner at the British Embassy last night and he seemed a pleasant and fairly able man but very shy. He told me that the first moment at which he knew he was to be Finance Minister was when he heard the Privy Council Minute read aloud.

The Chancellor spoke at the National Press Club lunch and did it very well, managing to maintain with great tact that the US needed to take action on trade policy without accusing them of holding up convertibility. In fact he has now launched his new line publicly, convinced himself of it and as it is certainly a sensible line I would expect it to 'stick'. It is that there are still a great many things to do before the world can take so serious a step, but we are well on the way and will keep moving. All the same, it represents a *conversion of himself* to this view, and political considerations were one of the elements in his conversion though I should like to think that I was another.

In the afternoon we discussed the Collective Approach [to convertibility] with the Commonwealth and I found it most interesting to see how easily everyone but the Canadians accepted and endorsed the new UK line. I always believed, and I am sure this diary would support my recollection, that the Commonwealth were not in fact, and would not be when the time came, nearly so enthusiastic for convertibility as they seemed to be at the first meeting of officials and under the apostolic efforts of the fanatical Leslie [entry for October 14th 1952]. In fact Andrew Strachan of Rhodesia (now Central African Federation), who was the only man to counsel moderation then, and I congratulated ourselves last night at the change; we who were the outcasts of Nov. 1952, if not the heroes of Sept. 1954, are at any rate the successful prophets. Even the Canadians were much less fervent than they used to be and this isn't all the change of Harris for Abbot [as Canadian Minister of Finance].

I saw the Chancellor for about 1/2 hr after the meeting. We had a general chat and he told me that he wanted to explore the possibilities of profit-sharing as soon as we returned. (We have asked Inland Revenue to do this already.) He also talked in a very loose way about the importance of stability and I deduced from this that he was almost detached from the floating rate. I don't think he ever understood the arguments and indeed they are difficult and when put fairly inconclusive. Finally he said he wanted to talk to Gaitskell about the situation and prospects, based on the proposition that either he (Butler) or G. would have to take the responsibility and that there might as well be some discussion. I said I thought (a) that it would be a very good thing but that he could not expect G. to give any commitments at all, (b) that I was very doubtful whether the Labour Party, if in opposition, would attack convertibility very strongly if it were done when the situation warranted. I felt however that they would probably much prefer the move to be made by the Tories than by themselves. And indeed I feel that in spite of all their commitments it would be intensely painful to the Labour Party to have to move. I cannot however see them going back to rationing and I doubt if they would go back to material controls unless there were a crisis.

I have left out the most interesting event of the afternoon. There had been some talk about a piece of work which had been done by the

Commonwealth Liaison Committee [the forerunner of the Commonwealth Office] in London on instructions from Sydney, and done very poorly. Deshmukh said he thought the Committee should be used more and made to work harder. There was then a general discussion at which *everyone* agreed: the Chancellor with great skill picked this up, stressing that more information and better representation would be needed and that no policy issues should be raised. However I never thought to see the day when the Indians would take the lead on this. It just shows that the Economic Section have always been right in saying that the CRO [Commonwealth Relations Office] and to some extent OF [Overseas Finance] have been morbidly afraid of the Dominions thinking that London was trying to dominate them, long after the time when the Dominions had felt that this was a dead issue.

The dinner at night was pleasant enough. There were 34 at one table at the Embassy and the room seemed to hold them very easily, while the ballroom afterwards seemed almost empty. I sat next to Mehta, the Indian Ambassador to Washington, and we talked about great men we had known – his leader was Gandhi, mine was Cripps, though I would put the PM before him if I had ever known him. Afterwards we had a long talk with Mohammed Ali, the Pakistan Finance Minister, mainly about Japan. This is a horrible problem, entirely for political reasons.

Saturday, October 2nd

I am leaving Washington at lunch time and to the UK tonight – the Chancellor will be on the same 'plane. Yesterday we had the last session of the Commonwealth Finance Ministers – mostly about GATT and the Trade Rules. The Ministers were nearly all anxious to have escape clauses and safeguards against what they might need to do – I have never thought that the GATT Revision would make the rules stiffer and if this is a preview of the talks, they will certainly be more woolly.

The Chancellor mentioned the rate, I think to get on at once with his new-found interest in stability, and the talk was quite interesting. Mohammed Ali was the most sensible – he said that it was unnecessary and unwise to settle anything definite about this till you had to. I thought there was a great variety of view, but that on the whole the positions on this, which were never unanimous, have not changed much.

I lunched with Jo Alsop and had the usual discussion of foreign affairs and atom bombs. He said he and Stew [Alsop] might be imprisoned because of what they wrote on the fall-out from the H bomb and for once I think he is right, i.e. they *might* be imprisoned. He said that Mendès-France was exactly like Bob Taft [Republican Senator] in personality, narrow, able, practical, reasoning from fixed premises without examining them, hardly interested in the problems of other countries except as they touched on the interests of France. We had our usual discussion about the need to resist aggression whenever it came and however small it was – that if we were afraid of a big war we would gradually lose so much ground that we had to fight a war of despair. As we have agreed on this for years it didn't help much. I said that the UK had no leaders up to the problem and thought that on the whole it was time and more that the PM went (E.P. has told me this – he sees him a great deal and says he is painfully slow). Jo had very little to say about the US scene, and is hardly interested in anything but defence against Russia and the horrors of an H-bomb war. I think he is really in favour of a preventive war and in a way I suppose I am too – if one does not believe that one's way of life is worth being killed for one will soon lose that way – that is badly put, I mean that there is nothing convincing about the argument that a war will be so awful that anything is better than it. And if so, then unless one thinks it very likely that the Russians will live quietly with us, the most sensible course is to fight when you seem most likely to win. I do not know that I even feel glad that I don't have to take the decision, probably I do but that is a weakness. As I get older my thinking becomes more and more dominated by evolutionary considerations – what does it matter about one generation when a way of life is involved? That is just what Communists do and they will survive unless we can think as hard as they do – the danger of freedom is that with democracy it leads to soft thought and soft bodies too.

At night the Millers and some people called Norton (he is in Air side of Defence) came to dinner at the Moffats. John Miller has given up *The Times* to be the IBRD representative in Europe. He is particularly gloomy about the Republicans and the whole US scene, mainly I think because of McCarthy but in general he thinks it is all very reactionary. However I think that McCarthy and McCarthyism are over the peak, not only because of the Senate Report but because historically these things do have a peak and it is caused by something like the Senate Report. Everyone on the liberal side seems to be very pleased that [Senator] McCarran is dead, and I gather there are hopes for [Senator] Milliken too. I feel fairly sure that there will be a Republican House and probably Senate (no one else thinks the latter): and that our fortunes on the trade side will mend. I think the political outlook is better too, with the agreement on European defence in London and the Labour Party vote for German rearmament and H.G. doing so much better than Nye [Bevan] for the party Treasurership.

I think the whole trip has been satisfactory. I did not expect any positive results about convertibility and would have thought them ill-judged if they had been taken. The Chancellor has finally got out of the dangerous position he got into early in 1952 and has managed to get the Commonwealth out of it too – a very good result from this meeting. So that our policy is at last a realistic one. The US understand our position and I am fairly sure that Humphrey, Burns, Hauge and Stassen sympathize with it and that Dulles does not even think about it. Now we can move forward unhampered. The whole thing is a lesson in the dangers of ill-considered idealism in a field in which such a thing is quite unnecessary.

Sunday, October 3rd

This is written at 7.30 a.m. GMT on the flight to England. The Chancellor, L. Petch, Frank Lee and Edgar Cohen of the Board of Trade are all on board. The Chancellor asked me to dine with him last night, i.e. have dinner in the next seat. He seemed a bit tired but drank a good deal of champagne and gradually warmed up and told me all his thoughts and plans or at any rate much more than he has ever done before.

We began on the trip and I said that I thought it was a great success and that I felt much happier than I had done for a long time, because we had now got complete freedom of action and could move forward without having to be bound by any formula or timetable. This had been achieved quite honourably and with the full knowledge and consent of the US and the sterling area. After some discussion he fully agreed with this and even said that he had been out on a limb and had now got back. He is worried about his colleagues and the public but I said I thought that all these problems were manageable because we could now deal with the sore spots if we had to. He has the very good idea of talking to industrial leaders as well as to H.G.

We then got on to Treasury personnel and I was very indiscreet, looking back on it now, and told him more or less exactly what I thought and what I would do. I advised him to consult Norman Brook at all stages as he would be the man who would have to run it. The main problem is to get someone to take Bernard Gilbert's place as second in command with charge of the economic side. He said there was no one obvious – he had tried to get O.S.F. – I might have to do it. (I am very doubtful about either whether he means this, or whether it would be a good idea – both as regards what the Civil Service would think and of my character.) We ran over most of the people, including T.L.R. who I thought might go to the Cabinet Office. What about Tom Padmore? I said he could well stay where he was. He said T. had told him he knew nothing of economics or finance and this was very shocking. We both agreed that Strath, Trend and Armstrong were the best of the younger ones. He has clearly given all this a great deal of thought and thinks, or pretended to me to think, very much as I do. Denis Rickett is a problem – I said he could take Eddy Playfair's place and Eddy go to IR. The snag he said was that Inland Revenue wanted Evans. R. Makins had spoken in almost exaggerated terms of Denis's merits. We ran over a number of others.

He then told me about the current political situation, relations with the old man, Eden, Salisbury, etc. I had better not write this down. He showed an awareness of the situation and the personalities involved which was very much wider than I had expected. The crucial problem *au fond* is to hold the party together which he could do if he had some time. I asked him if he were really the man to take the course he had sketched. He said that he had considered the problem in general for years and specifically for 6 months and thought he was though he could see my point. Apparently he had told [Vincent] Massey [Governor-General of

Canada] about all this and M. had asked the same question. Well – if he has thought of it so carefully perhaps he is. It was all intensely interesting.

Wednesday, October 13th

The journey seems to have been considered a success here. Now we have to get on with all the things that must be done before we can be comfortable about the final step, and especially we must let in some US goods to see whether they will cause political trouble. The Board of Trade have been making a study of this for most of the year but I wish the Programmes Committee would recommend some changes. There has been a good deal of discussion between the Treasury and the Board of Trade about the future of tariff machinery – whether to revive IDAC [Import Duties Advisory Committee] as the President wants, or to have a new advisory body. I think there will have to be legislation anyway as the old [prewar] IDAC terms of reference were written for quite other times, and they are now suspended by emergency legislation.

Last week the travel allowance[17] was put up from £50 to £100 and *The Economist* made this the occasion for an attack on R.A.B., saying that he was afraid both of his officials and of the Tory Party and was moving much too slowly towards convertibility, etc. It had attacked him a little earlier for moving or appearing to move too fast. He is very much annoyed and wanted to cancel his subscription but as he had cancelled it about 6 months ago he was not able to – however he goes round saying that he has. He had already asked me to see Crowther and I am doing so on Thursday, but meanwhile Eddy Playfair has spoken to him and I think E. Plowden was going to last night, so Geoffrey will feel that a concerted attack is being made.

The Chancellor is in a difficult position and needs all the help he can get. Although he has much more freedom of manoeuvre than before, he now has to carry the country along to something like a free trade world when neither of the great parties is temperamentally in favour of it. No one quite realizes the implications of the commitment made in 1944/45 to ITO and now to GATT. However I think it can be done. The Chancellor said yesterday that he had got a vote for free trade from the Conservative Party Conference at Blackpool, although no one knew what they were doing. Now he wanted to play it quietly and that is why he dislikes *The Economist* so much, since it is trying to exacerbate the troubles.

Thursday, October 21st

I took Crowther to lunch and did not mention R.A.B., and after about 1/2 hr he brought it up himself and said that everyone was telling him how unpopular he was in that quarter. This distressed him because

(a) he liked R.A.B., (b) he had always supported him in *general*, (c) he was very conscious at present that the strain on him (because his wife is dying) is almost unbearable. *But* he had been Editor of *The Economist* under ten Chancellors, had written what he liked about them and none of them had been exactly pleased. Also it would soon ruin journalism if journalists could not write as they felt and say what was legitimate news.

I said that as far as I was concerned he could and should write as he pleased – if *The Economist* made mistakes of fact or drew wrong inferences I would feel entitled to say so and in fact did say so and had always been treated fairly. However if he wanted my views about R.A.B., I would say that he was unduly sensitive but I thought he had some grounds for complaint. *The Economist* wrote about the troubles he was going to have with the Tory party with every appearance of *Schadenfreude*. This would make a hard struggle worse. *The Economist* said that it was in favour of more freedom and of what R.A.B. was trying to do. Could he not expect therefore that it would represent him as a leader doing a job in the national interest and in a difficult position, rather than as a man whose intentions were (possibly) good but who was going to make no progress because he was surrounded by men of ill will whom he was more or less deceiving?

G. said that he had not intended to give this impression and didn't think he had but I said I thought that it was not unfair. I also said that it seemed very odd to the Treasury that when the tourist allowance was doubled, as a step in the right direction, it should be made the occasion for an unbridled attack on all concerned. G. said he had a 'thing' about tourism (an obsession or fixation) and felt that now was the time to free it. To go to £100 would invite it to be put back again soon. I said this was not what I expected to happen.

G. was determined not to admit that he had done anything unfriendly or that it wasn't his duty to write as he pleased. I agreed with the latter but not the former. He then talked at length about the forthcoming leading article about R.A.B.'s Blackpool slogan 'Invest in Success' in which he had tried to be friendly but he feared he had again said that the Tories (among others) would not like it. We left it there but I told Louis Petch to put a note on *The Economist* calling the Chancellor's attention to the article and saying that it was helpful, if it were at all possible to say so, so that he would come to it in the right frame of mind. In fact the article was friendly and Louis was able to put a commending note and when I saw R.A.B. on Monday he told me to convey to G. that he was pleased about it, which I did. He (R.A.B.) got into a great state about his Mansion House speech but it seemed all right at the end.

By the end of October, when unemployment had fallen to about 250,000 and inflationary pressure was growing, Hall was still insisting on the need to encourage industrial investment, apparently unaware of the increase already taking place. The current balance of payments was deteriorating and nowhere near the surplus of £350 million referred to in the entry for

October 27th. The November forecast of a surplus of £155 million in 1955 proved to be much too optimistic and by February second thoughts had already substituted a deficit of £70 million – a change for the worse of £280 million in comparison with the expected outturn in 1954.

Efforts to formulate a wage policy had also revived as the labour market tightened; but although a White Paper was drafted, it was not until March 1956 that one was issued (The Economic Implications of Full Employment).

Wednesday, October 27th

Things are fairly quiet. The Chancellor makes far too many speeches but I suppose that most politicians feel unhappy unless they are doing so – H.G. used to get restless if he did not have a number of engagements. However his mind seems to be working in a more forward direction than that of his officials. He said the other day that he had popularized his new slogan (Invest in Success) but that no one knew what it meant and we were to have some work done on a long-term investment policy for the UK. He also appears to have given commitments to Cabinet about a large road programme, which I have thought very necessary but which nearly all the senior Treasury advisers regard as extravagant. It is very interesting to see him coming round by himself to the more advanced views of the Economic Section. I told him that he could do roads all right if he would cut housing and Louis [Petch] told me that he has absorbed this.[18]

However I wish that things were not so inflationary at home or at any rate that there was more unemployment. The October figures show that things have been more or less steady, but at a slightly over-full rate, since about April – in fact the seasonally corrected figures are about flat. The balance of payments result* which has just come out [P(54)93] is very good, above the £350 mn target and at least as high as we can continue to finance unless we lend a good deal more. There are no very severe shop shortages though cars are difficult and there has been a squeeze on some of the Hire Purchase things. Coal stays bad and it is extraordinary that all this investment should produce such poor results. The Minister [Geoffrey Lloyd] came to see me on Monday (on his way to the Chancellor) but it was mainly to ask about the implications for coal of R.A.B. having said at Blackpool that we could double the national income in 25 years. He seemed to be moving in the right direction, at any rate he told me that he was putting more drive into fuel efficiency and also that he wanted to change most of the Board. However we kept off price. Ian Little has written another paper about this which is going to be looked at soon in the Treasury.[19]

* Feb. 1957 – This was the cause of our long complacency and why we took so long to start to deflate.

I have been spending some time on the Sidney Ball lecture which I have to give in Oxford on November 5th. It is about the place of the economist in Government service and is largely the result of my direct experience in the last 7 years – it could almost be called 'How I succeeded as a government economist'. The most interesting part of it to me is the discussion of forecasting and the stress on probability – I suppose I always knew it intuitively but it looks even plainer when one writes it out.[20]

The dock strike is becoming a serious problem and was talked about at 2nd Secs yesterday. I was surprised to hear that many Ministers were keen to use troops and to find that several of my colleagues were too. However N.B. is very sensible and I should think has a good deal of influence on Cabinet. I am sure that one should never use troops until it is quite clear that you have public opinion behind you. Also that it is a mistake to try to prevent the public suffering from a strike – the more they suffer the better.

Thursday, October 28th

Strath and I talked to Ian Little and Jack Robertson yesterday about the forward look on investment which is to interpret 'Invest in Success'. The TIC [Treasury Investment Committee] is just beginning its annual exercise, which in any case gets views from Departments for from 3 to 5 years ahead, and I do not think it is ever much use looking for more than 5 years. There will be a new steel programme exercise anyway and probably coal, railways and roads. The NIF Working Party will have to look at the extent to which it can be financed. L. Petch told me that Eccles wants to make a splash in the Ministry of Education, by building more schools. It is being realized that the easiest way to do roads and schools is to cut on housing but whether Sandys [Minister of Housing and Local Government] will take this or not is as yet unknown. Really there should be plenty of room to invest more out of the growth of the National Income but no one has grasped this yet and it is a bit awkward that the resources are so much under pressure at this moment.

Strath is almost detached from CEPS [Central Economic Planning Staff] for the next 3 months to make a fundamental examination of our defence strategy for Norman Brook. This is because of the hydrogen bomb which has altered all the assumptions. As far as I can see, it alters the basic one (that we can keep going) so completely that we ought to plan for the stages of preventing a war instead of for what happens when we are in it, which in my view means keeping as strong as possible so that there won't be any local actions or if there are that we will win them. And a good deal of this is political, to have Nigerias instead of Kenyas and Ceylons instead of Malayas.[21]

A good deal of time is being given to various questions about profits, dividends, reserves, etc. A long time ago the Minister of Labour [Sir Walter Monckton] decided to make a statement about Wages in a Full Employment Society and this has been bandied about in draft between

Treasury and Ministry of Labour for a long time. We made an early mistake in letting S. C. Leslie take charge of the Treasury drafting – he does not seem to have the feel for the economic aspects and is inclined also to make woolly statements that sound good. I have got disheartened about this subject over the years, although I still feel that it is a major one (how to keep prices fairly steady in a full employment system). Anyway after great tribulations the Minister took his statement at the NJAC [National Joint Advisory Council] yesterday but the Trade Union representatives did not like it and so the discussion was put off. I feel sure that no Ministers will ever deal adequately with this, though R.A.B. looks more like it than he used to.

There has been a great deal of sniping because of the rapid increase of dividend distribution this year, and there are a lot of PQ's at present. To add to our troubles, the Chancellor made a speech recently to the Chamber of Shipping in which he said extemporaneously that British companies did not put as much to reserve as European ones did (which apparently is untrue) and that they ought to invest more and pay less attention to 'awards to shareholders or anybody else'. This has led to very sharp attacks in papers like the *Financial Times* and the *Telegraph*. We decided to try to get Ministers to fix on what their policy was, since if they say that dividends are increasing too fast they ought to be ready to act. This resulted in quite a good statement, drafted by E.B. and me, which we showed the Chancellor but I don't think he has really thought about it much. Now I am trying to draft a speech which he might make. The dividend problem is the same as the wage problem – full employment makes profits high just as it creates demand conditions for labour. Unless the workers are restrained, and the employers act reasonably, you get both price instability and bad feeling. However I am not quite sure myself of what the theoretical answer ought to be.

Thursday, January 20th 1955

It is hardly worth keeping a diary when the entries are so far apart – I do not know why my interest has flagged so much, partly that the whole situation is quieter, partly that I am more used to it all and think less about it, partly advancing age I suppose or fear. Looking at the last entry, all the questions have moved ahead. I set up a Working Party to look explicitly at the future in the light of the Chancellor's statement that we ought to double the standard of living in 25 years. We are looking in detail at the next 5 years to see what ought to be done then to be consistent with the 25 year target.[22] The TIC Report was finished just about Christmas and some of the work done for that will be useful. The Iron and Steel Board have asked for a new forward look on steel and that comes in. We also have the new road and rail programmes although both are very sketchy.

Strath has set up a group to look specifically at fall-out problems and has got permission from No. 10 to put me on the group.[23] It is a very Top Secret affair – not I think because the material we are using is secret since the Alsops have published most of it and it seems to be almost common talk in the USA – but because the facts are not absorbed here and are so unpleasant that it is very tricky to know how best to act to get them absorbed. I have been doing some work for Strath's Group on economic effects but I think for the UK the fall-out is not nearly so important as the events that cause it. I do not know much about how the rest of Strath's activities go.

Talking of atomic energy at all, Jukes who worked so long with me has gone with my agreement to be economic adviser to the Atomic Energy Authority which means Edwin P. I see a good deal of Edwin as we lunch together about once a fortnight and he drops in occasionally. He seems to be doing quite well with his prima donna. The outline of the power station programme was finished some time ago by Burke Trend's Working Party and there was a meeting this week of the BEA and the AEA about the new programme, which B. Gilbert told me was extremely friendly. BEA wanted to go ahead even faster than AEA did. And B. Gilbert himself is far more enterprising and energetic about this than anything else. I suppose one reason for all this enterprise is the general pessimism about the coal situation. Anyway it looks as if we shall be getting the first power from the experimental plant (I believe at Dounreay) in about 2 years and if all goes well the new stations start coming in in the early 60s or before.[24]

On wages, etc., we are in the middle of a new upward movement and one rather more marked than last year. The main event has been the threat of a railway strike. The workers quite rightly felt that their wages were too low and Brian Robertson felt that if he raised them to what was wanted he would be certain to make losses and then would have broken the clause in the Transport Act which says they must pay their way 'one year with another'. We got very near to a strike and Ministers, although they did not want one, were quite prepared for it rather than a complete surrender. However, it is hard to say what the result represents except that it was not morally a surrender, i.e. Ministers *were* prepared to face a strike and if the result looks little different from a surrender this is the result of manoeuvres rather than cowardice.

We all agreed that the railwaymen were not getting enough, and that the clause in the Transport Act must be interpreted with latitude, i.e. it could not mean 'pay every year'. We also felt that there was no evidence that the railways could not pay comparable wages if they were properly run (*we* is senior Treasury officials). One problem was that the workers were uneconomically used and had persistently refused redeployment, as it is called, although they had constantly said they would co-operate. But there were also the new powers to alter charges to get the most traffic, and the big modernization scheme.

Against this background the Minister of Labour spent an enormous time with both parties trying to stop a strike. I think that what happened was that B. Robertson, when he found that Ministers took a broader view of his obligations than he did, felt that he was absolved from any obligations and looked for a formula to concede all claims. He would not just concede them as the NUR wanted, and there was nearly a strike about this. But once the strike was suspended and negotiations began, he gave them more or less what they had sought. All this was somewhat complicated by the Court of Inquiry – it was part of the Ministerial line that every effort should be made to accept the Court's recommendations but when they appeared they included some nonsense passages about willing the end and the means which no one could accept.[25] However taken altogether I think it is a good thing that there was no strike, and that the statement which will be made by the Government (probably the Chancellor) will put things in proper perspective.

The first NIF appreciation was finished in December and showed that we will have quite enough employment, if not too much, without any tax concessions. (Since then the Programmes Committee has started its next review and the balance of payments for 1955 looks like a *deficit* – I don't believe this but at any rate it looks worse.) However the boom of 1954 has raised the revenue so much that there is a big surplus in prospect for this financial year and quite a good-sized one for next.[26]

As the Chancellor must act as if it is an election year, the pressure to spend some of the surplus is very great and no doubt it will be spent. Most senior Treasury officials really think that above the line balance is the proper doctrine in spite of all that has been learnt in recent years! So much for my efforts. However I would not mind this – I can deal with them all if necessary – but one must admit that the Chancellor is in a bad spot and that human nature cannot be expected to do nothing. I feel that the economy is fundamentally a good deal stronger than it has been since 1939 or say 1945 since the war years mean nothing and that it will stand a bit more strain than it has done in the intervening period. However it is funny to find myself in the most austere position. We haven't really got down to Budget work yet but I can see how it is going.

One trouble in all this is that the date of the next election is completely uncertain. The PM is the only person who can fix it, unless Providence removes him, and it is quite certain that he has not fixed it in his own mind. Like Prince Seithenyn in [T. L. Peacock's] *The Misfortunes of Elphin*, his motto is 'A Little More'. When 1956 was a long way off he said he would resign well before then – now it is only next year he says there is no need for an election yet. And I feel sure that he will soon be considering pretexts for leading his party at that time. This is unfortunate from many points of view – the Government would be much stronger if they were not thinking of early votes all the time: and it complicates Budget calculations a great deal, since they don't want to give everything away if there is *not* going to be an election.

I haven't seen the Chancellor privately for a long time. His wife died in December, he had known this was coming since August and probably before that – she was very tough and would not go to hospital though dying of cancer of the jaw – it must have been a dreadful business waiting for and no doubt hoping for the end. So when it came it was a relief rather than a shock, but no doubt the totality of the events was a severe shock and it remains to be seen how he will feel it. I would guess that he would need some prop or other. But so far he seems to be recovering well, and people are treating him normally again which must be a help.

The Collective Approach and all that is in rather a mess. The main problems are that the dollar position is less strong than it was, and that the implications of the Trade Rules and so on on British industry are beginning to be seen. However the Chancellor is being tougher than I expected – he told a large meeting of the FBI today that he was practically a follower of Cobden! I suppose they felt he was so much a good Tory that he could only mean this in a Tory sense. The complications involved in negotiating a new GATT at Geneva are terrific. I still think that it is all very precarious in relation to the political situation here, but the Chancellor knows much more about this than I do and he has played it very carefully since his initial mistake, now almost 3 years ago. I have been going to meetings at the Board of Trade about the future of the tariff, which make it quite clear that we cannot do much about it until we give up the promises of no new tariffs against Dominion goods. And even if we did this we have bound a good many of our tariffs under the GATT procedure. The Board of Trade are well aware of this and also that we shall have great trouble when we have to give up q.r. as we ought to do in the near future even under the existing GATT and quite apart from convertibility.

On January 20th the Bank had again sought permission to support the rate for transferable sterling and hold it a little below the official rate. This was to be allowed to fluctuate between undeclared limits of $2.70 and $2.90. After a long argument and against the advice of Robert Hall, the first part of the proposal was put to the Cabinet by the Chancellor, somewhat casually, and was accepted. From February, transferable sterling was held within about 1 per cent of the official rate so that sterling was virtually convertible de facto. *The proposal for a wider spread in exchange rates, which had not been accepted, continued to be debated and re-submitted to the Chancellor. It became widely known both in the City and on the Continent. There was much talk of inflation and for this and other reasons it was generally assumed that if a wider spread were adopted the pound would fall towards the lower limit. Speculative pressure developed over the summer months; and although the Treasury had earlier wanted to combine convertibility with a floating pound the Chancellor was obliged to deny categorically, both in the House of Commons in July and at the IMF meeting in Istanbul in September, any intention of changing the exchange parity after convertibility (or, by implication, of letting the pound float).*

Meanwhile Churchill finally resigned on April 6th and was succeeded by Eden. An election had been widely expected and was held on May 26th. Between these two events came the Budget on April 19th. Despite the evidence of boom, the Chancellor took sixpence off the income tax, relying on 'the resources of a flexible monetary policy' to keep inflation in check. The ensuing credit squeeze was slow to take effect and caused much friction between the Treasury and the Bank of England.

Thursday, March 3rd

On the day I wrote the above entry (Jan. 20th) the Governor approached the Chancellor with new proposals which were in substance the same old ones he had brought nearly 3 years before, and so often since then, namely to operate in the transferable market, bring the two rates together, and hold them within the range $2.70–2.90: so it was more or less convertibility for non-resident sterling with a floating rate. I was not brought in at first but after about a week I was: the general Treasury view was against the proposals for obvious reasons. I had been urging that we needed a tighter monetary policy for some time, and at the end of January the Bank of England put the bank rate up to 3 1/2%. They were against putting it up any more as they wanted to bring the market up against the new rates slowly. On the same day Leslie Rowan showed the Chancellor the new Programmes Committee Report [P(55)18] which forecast a slight deficit for the second half of 1954 and a substantial one both for the UK and the RSA for 1955. The Chancellor was very angry as he said he would have had the rate moved by 1% if he had known.

The significance of this was of course that it was the first clear sign we had had which could be said to point definitely to a too inflationary situation at home – the previous forecast had been for a surplus which though lower than in late 1953 and the first half of 1954 was still not a bad one.[27]

The story then gets confused. The Chancellor asked what could be done and I at once wrote a minute to B. Gilbert saying that a lot could be done: (a) Bank rate and tighter credit, (b) new restrictions on hire purchase, (c) letting prices reflect costs where this wasn't done, especially on coal, (d) tighter agricultural policy, (d) implementing the Cabinet decision to reduce the number of council houses, which Sandys had been flouting.[28]

At the same time the Governor got more and more fussed about the rate for transferable sterling – he claimed that Continental opinion regarded this rate as the true valuation of the £ and they could not understand why we did not support this rate. He said that until we did this there would be no confidence in sterling and he would not take the responsibility for the position. We (Treasury officials) agreed that the weakness of sterling, both official and transferable, was related to the worsening balance of payments and required internal measures. But T.L.R. and I were very much against operating on the transferable rate as we could not follow the Bank's reasoning and thought that it would not be sensible to spend your own dollars to support a rate the lowness of which was alleged to be losing you dollars.

The argument went on for about 10 days in a most confused way as the Bank got more and more insistent but with less and less coherence – they also clouded counsel a good deal by changing their line on what should be done on monetary policy – one day they said they didn't think they needed to put bank rate up just yet, another that they needed to, a third that it would not make sense unless they could operate on transferable sterling at the same time. The Chancellor was very worried by all this – he always feels that the Bank have to do the job and are his principal advisers on exchange and monetary questions, and he doesn't seem to be worried by inconsistencies unless it suits him to point them out, i.e. unless they appear in the case of people who want to do things he dislikes having to do.

After a good deal of confusion he decided to accept the Bank views, with E.B. and B.W.G. on their side and T.L.R. and I isolated on the other – a position we have not been in since we were both in favour of devaluation against E.B., B.W.G. and the Bank in early 1949.[29]

At the same time it was decided to adopt all the internal measures I had suggested and for once Ministers were quite active. The President of the Board of Trade [Thornycroft] accepted the hire purchase restrictions and an Order in Council was made restoring the Defence Regulations under which the old HP regulations had been made. G. Lloyd agreed to put up the price of coal and would have done so if Cabinet had not stopped him on the ground that it had nothing to do with the balance of payments.[30] The Chancellor endeavoured to explain that T.L.R. and I thought that the exchange move would put the timing on convertibility out of our hands but no one was interested – in fact coal was the only thing they cared about. Discussions are going on with Sandys about council houses. Meanwhile Amory [Minister of Agriculture] and R.A.B. have decided that they cannot squeeze £9 mn or any sum out of the farmers and they are now talking about settling on the basis of *giving* the farmers £9 or £18 mn.

The main measures were announced by R.A.B. in the House on February 24th. We all went down and sat in the box. It was a most interesting occasion as Labour were so obviously delighted that the Government was having some bad luck at last – they talked about grossly misleading the country and so on but of course they were a bit vulnerable after the events of 1951.

The first effect was a shock to the Stock Exchange but that soon wore off. On the whole it was well received. I saw M. Green of *The Times* and the man who was going to write the *Financial Times* leader, and in both cases they produced leaders more or less as I had wanted. It is very early to say whether all this will work but I must say that R.A.B. acted very quickly and has certainly enhanced his reputation in the country. It is odd that he, who seems to me so weak a man, can be capable of what everyone thinks to be early and resolute action. I think it is because he cannot bear to have an uncertain situation hanging over his head. But of course it is much easier to put up Bank Rate and restore HP regulations than to do a lot of other things.

The B. is still quite unsettled but clearly R.A.B. and most of the officials want to make substantial tax cuts. Of course the NIF review now looks worse because of the balance of payments development, though I still feel very sceptical about the forecasts. I have been trying to keep the position open. R.A.B. is already getting fussed about his speech and I have written him a draft to defend concessions, just to show him how it might go, though I have made it clear that there is at present no validity in the arguments used.

One effect of all this is that the Economic Section is now in favour of early convertibility on a floating rate, on the ground that we really have no defences now and cannot restore them. So as our policy is to rely on Bank and exchange rates, let us at least let them work.

Thursday, April 7th

The past month has been dominated by the approach to and then the resignation of the PM, and consequently the date of the general election and the effect of this date on the character of the Budget. The PM planned for a long time a dinner for April 4th to which the Queen and his closest friends and those who worked with him would go, and the general idea was that he would resign then. But he changed his mind quite a lot in the interim, or at any rate gave Eden and R.A.B. the idea that he changed it: there were innumerable discussions and changes and for some time Eden and the PM were not on speaking terms and according to R.A.B. communicated largely through him.

By about the middle of March it was too late for a Budget on March 29th and April 19th was finally settled. After a lot of talk May 26th was chosen as the most probable date for the election and it was thought that Eden would announce this almost as soon as he became PM, which meant that the Budget would be *between* the announcement and the election. The economic picture hardly changed, that is, it seemed if anything to need a stiffer Budget, but almost everyone felt that it would be politically impossible to do nothing: it was a question of how to make it look as little like bribery of the electorate as possible and also not taking too many risks with the economy. The standard rate seemed by far the best bet for this and I myself thought so, since to reduce it is a real achievement even if we run a few balance of payments risks in the process.

Everything else got more and more dominated by electoral considerations and I realized for the first time how very important it is that the PM should have the power alone of deciding this and should give as short notice as possible. The farmers got £28 mn in the end and the pattern will not be much improved. Coal prices and railway fares have both been put off.

There has been a great deal of pressure from Lancashire about cotton imports and Purchase Tax. The Treasury is very much against abolishing PT which would do little good and make the problem of reforming the tax much harder. But when we have just been pressing so hard at Geneva for a stiffer GATT, it looks especially hypocritical to put a quota on imports and in the process offend against the principle of free Commonwealth entry. No decision has been reached yet after nearly as many meetings as there have been about coal prices. But I think there will be a quota announced as a holding operation until a tariff can be put on. Ministers will have to face [up to it].[31]

The PM finally resigned on April 5th – I think until almost the last moment no one was quite sure whether he would go or not. The election date is still being discussed hotly as Eden and several others want to put it off – R.A.B. and Salisbury want it soon. I think it will be decided at Chequers this weekend in favour of May 26th.

Tuesday, April 19th

This is the morning of the Budget. Things have been dominated by the election date and prospects. The new PM [Eden] was very doubtful about an early election, and so were some other Ministers. The Chancellor and the LP [Salisbury] wanted it early and made a good deal of play with the effect of uncertainty on the economic prospects, themselves somewhat uncertain. The new Foreign Secretary [Selwyn Lloyd] seems to have sat on the fence. Maudling told me that when he saw Eden on April 8th to be offered the M/Supply, the PM spoke as if May 26th was settled but they hovered all the next week and I do not believe the really final decision was taken until the afternoon of the 15th, the broadcast being that evening.

The Budget was of course fixed in time but there was a good deal of discussion of its content on different hypotheses. My own view, which I think the Chancellor would have accepted, was that if the election were to be e.g. in 12 months' time, it would be a mistake to have made more than minor concessions. With the situation somewhat inflationary, and no one at all clear about the effect of the delay on political sentiment, the chances of an adverse confidence movement were high enough without any easing on the fiscal side. But in the end this did not arise.

The other problem which is hardly settled even yet is what to do about Lancashire. When the deputation saw Churchill, he practically promised that something would be done and the Chancellor wanted to impose a temporary quota pending a tariff. This would have been very much against the line we have taken on GATT, would have breached ad hoc the sacred principle of Commonwealth free entry, and would almost certainly have been used against us in the various US discussions now going on about their policy both in general and on such specific things as the tariff recommendation on bicycles. However the Treasury reluctantly took the view that this would be the best of a bad lot.

After discussion with the Indian Government it appeared that they might reduce the duty on our cotton goods and this turned the scale against using the quota now and produced great pressure for abolishing the Purchase Tax. This would have made the Budget look silly and would have compromised the hopes of reforming the tax (I do not think we can keep it in its present shape for another year) and would have helped Lancashire very little since Indian and Hong Kong imports are cheap cloth not subject to tax and it is very doubtful whether PT really affects the home market much. However the Chancellor made a small concession and we thought that this would do. But at yesterday's Cabinet there was almost a revolt and instead of leaving for Windsor at 4.45 the Chancellor stayed another hour trying to reach some compromise. In the end he decided that there wasn't time, or a case, for any change. Then he went off and the FST, EST, Trend, France and I struggled with a bit of the speech. The President of the Board of Trade came over at 7.30 and by 8.15 we had arrived back at the first point and there I think we must stay, i.e. a small concession this afternoon but little reference to textiles otherwise, and a not very helpful statement by the President of the Board of Trade during the Budget debate, either on Wednesday or Thursday.

It has been a very awkward one because of the possibility that what is done will swing the election, and because officials felt so strongly that almost any course other than doing nothing would seriously compromise important long-term objectives. However I do not think officials come out of it too well as they didn't really do enough work on the PT prospects to let the Chancellor consider all alternatives. I don't think myself that it will swing the election but it will be very uncomfortable as a piece of history if it does.

The Chancellor has been his usual self in all these discussions, including the usual interminable drafting and redrafting of the speech. The bringing in of Trend to do it, as was done last year, has helped a great deal: it was always too much of a strain on the principal PS and Petch, the present one, is not altogether at one with the Chancellor in his feeling for words and for the balance of emphasis. But the Chancellor always tries to have it all ways. The big troubles this year are (a) that on our usual methods, we are taking a risk this year, i.e. the balance of payments doesn't really warrant the concessions with over-full employment, (b) if we stress monetary policy too much it seems to contradict the stress laid on more investment.

In addition the Bank of England haven't been as co-operative on monetary policy as they might have been. They have never been too keen on being tough with the Banks. Now the Governor tells the Chancellor that he *is* being tough with them, but Oliver Franks (now Chairman of Lloyds) tells me that this is not so, and E.P. got the same story from the Chairman of the Westminster [Lord Aldenham] and T.L.R. from the Chairman of Barclays [A. W. Tuke]. Altogether we are working up to some sort of *éclaircissement* with the Governor, but whether the Chancellor will support us I don't know – he has always felt that the Governor is in the saddle and that it is a very serious thing to disagree with him.

Monday, May 2nd

I am writing in Paris where I came last night for a meeting of the Expert Group of Economists of which I am the Chairman.[32] The Budget went off smoothly enough and was rather less criticized than I expected. Tony Crosland made the best speech technically, arguing that the Chancellor ought to have increased taxation rather than decreased it, which was certainly right if we assume that we still have a balance of payments target of £300 mn or so surplus. Most other Labour people, if they referred to it, questioned the surplus but, like H. Gaitskell, said that an outsider could not tell and went on to criticize the reduction in standard rate and to argue that it was a Budget for the rich. The reason was of course that they did not want to be against reducing taxation.

The discussions about Lancashire have gone on ever since as Cabinet generally were very anxious to do something but the whole thing had got into so awkward a position that it was hard to see what. The Chancellor really wants a quota but our whole position makes that awkward: even a tariff needs a lot of thought. To give away all P. Tax on textiles is against the Budget pattern and compromises the reform of the tax, and to reduce the Budget concession (1/2 on piece goods) to zero also raises complications. However this is the cheapest way and likely to make most impression, and the EST and I have been in favour. It is possible that the Chancellor will do nothing at all; but the election prospects are extremely uncertain though it is my present view that the Conservatives will win.

Parliament rises on Friday (May 6th) and I suppose there will be no more decisions and little work until after the election. R.A.B. has been very fortunate as a Chancellor since he came in at a trough that was bound to go up unless he acted very stupidly. I think his great merit has been that he gave his good luck a chance: he wanted to introduce more freedom into the whole economy and events allowed him to do this with success. This has been good for him and his party and the country. It was certainly a good thing to start to use Bank Rate again, and to encourage the Bank to be more active in its interventions, which I think it has done: everyone is learning in the process. I also think that the tax reductions have been generally in the right place though we could do with some more if we are to regain some free taxable capacity.

The most controversial part of his programme, as it seemed to me and to officials generally, was the move towards convertibility and non-discrimination which was forced on him (though temperamentally it was congenial to him) by the Bank and OF early in 1952 when he was quite new to the job and in a balance of payments crisis. He has certainly regretted it a great deal since then and will still have to face a troublesome time both in getting it finally accepted by his colleagues and then making it work (if he is still Chancellor). However he was saved from the immediate plunge, I think largely by Edwin Plowden and me, and he has staved off subsequent pressure, with my support, by himself.

Meanwhile, however, he has taken under Bank and OF pressure a number of steps which have made it morally very hard for him to go back, and dismantled the structure from which he has climbed and which would be very hard to rebuild – the structure of controls, bilateral and other agreements and State purchases. In fact the Labour Party if returned will hardly be able to unscramble the eggs especially as it is clear that the end of food rationing is very popular, so much so that the Labour Party manifesto says that the story that Labour will reintroduce food rationing is 'a Tory lie', the most extreme statement in the whole thing and one that compares ill with all that they said about fair shares as rationing was dismantled.

R.A.B. does not seem to me a very strong man but as he is second in the Conservative hierarchy now this must be a comparative statement and my friends say it is youthful romanticism on my part and that present Ministers are a fair average sample. He is a very good politician in the sense that he has a good idea of what will please his party and the country and I now see what I did not see at first, why he admires and wants to emulate Peel. It was Peel who faced the fact that the Tory Party would have to move with the times, give up Catholic disfranchisement and the Corn Laws and accept the logic of the Reform Bill, and it was Peel who made it possible for the Tory party to survive in full strength in the 19th and early 20th centuries. Now it is to be Butler a little more than 100 years later who is going to accept the welfare state and full employment and so on.

We do not now think of Peel as a weak man - I used to feel that R.A.B. was so much a politician that he would prefer to be in power than to follow any particular line but I now think that this isn't true but that he realizes that he cannot be in power unless he follows some lines and thus he accepts these as his framework of reference. But the great difficulty about his character is to know whether he is as straightforward as public opinion, taken over the long run, compels him to be, i.e. he would not act shabbily because it might be found out and damage his position, or whether there is any more deep principle. But perhaps this does not mean anything. He has a good deal of personal charm and I *think* he likes me which always commends a person to another; he is not particularly good at seeing the right line having regard to the economics of the position but of course that is what he pays experts to do for him; and what my staff do for me within the general limits which I set for them.

Thursday, May 5th

We have met for two days and will finish today. These meetings [of the Expert Group] are really something quite exceptional for economists and I should think are quite new in the history of the world, in the sense that economic experts, if they existed at all as Government advisers, were not generally very important people until Keynes's ideas had been commonly accepted in the West. So that there were not the people to meet as we do: now we have 7 or 8 or 9 people who are by and large the chief professional economic advisers of the main Western Governments except Canada, and who all have the same responsibility to the facts, since if their facts are wrong they will be discredited, and all have more or less the same professional training in that they understand how to maintain the level of activity and what forces operate on it. And although the US and the Germans are much more for free enterprise and not too full employment, and the French and Italians want much more regulation of international trade, than the others – still there is a much greater basic similarity than at a meeting that included either Iron Curtain or underdeveloped countries.

Wednesday, May 11th

Life is very quiet now and will be until the election. The Chancellor was in today – he is mostly in his constituency but spends part of 2 or 3 days a week here. He seemed fairly cheerful and I think he expects that his party will win the election. It is very hard to know what will happen as I cannot see any sharp issue on which a lot of people will act – so they will vote more or less according to their parties, and what will the unattached do? The Conservatives have a very good record as far as the mass of people are concerned, since they have been so lucky. But I feel that there is still an underlying trend towards Labour. We are trying to do some work on what to do if Labour gets in and there is (as seems likely) a balance of payments crisis.

Thursday, May 26th

Today is Polling Day. I am going to the US on Saturday if the Conservatives are returned, which seems likely as I write. Very little has happened, but Leslie Rowan has prepared a long paper about the next steps for convertibility, with alternative endings according to which Government is returned.[33] The general aim is for a Conservative Government to decide fairly soon to make the final move, but not actually to do it until the internal situation is a bit less inflationary. A Labour Government, it is suggested, should announce its adherence to the aims of multilateralism (to which it has always adhered) and say that it must review timetable, conditions, etc.

We have also prepared a good deal of material for a Labour Chancellor, including a review of the internal situation, a Programmes Committee Report and a WEP Report. E.B., B.W.G., T.L.R. and I have had some discussion about what to do if Labour gets in and there is a crisis. We think that it will be necessary to keep credit tight and to make some statements indicating that external policy will not be reversed.

The economic situation is not too bad, not as bad as I had feared. We seem to have had a slight overall surplus on balance of payments in the second half of 1954 and to be running a rather bigger surplus now; but the second half of 1955 is still expected to show a deficit.[34] Production has been rising fairly well and it looks as if we ought to have enough capacity to produce the programmed, or rather expected, level of exports. The main mistake we seem to have made was on wages which have risen a good deal faster than we thought they would, so that it looks as if prices will rise or else consumption will increase, more than we had expected. There are a series of small strikes going on which are a nuisance, and another railway strike is threatened for Saturday.

The most interesting feature is that credit policy is now on the verge of affecting the situation. The banks have been extremely reluctant to cut down on advances and have sold short-term securities at a loss rather than face this but we are told that the continual reduction of their liquidity is now causing them to squeeze their customers' overdrafts. It is so long since they reduced or made any bones about overdrafts on good security that they can hardly bear to do it now but they will have to learn. I must say that the Bank of England has been tougher and more resolute than I expected them to be.

The interesting thing will be to see what happens as the squeeze develops. It may cause a reduction in stock-holding but I should think it will cause the Stock Exchange to weaken, reduce private facilities and to some extent affect fixed investment. It might even cause a few bankruptcies. The Chancellor will not like it much if it reduces long-term investment but I think he will have to face it: we left him several loopholes in the Budget speech. Nobody really knows how Bank Rate will act in England when there is a real boom as at present – of course it *can* stop anything if credit is made tight enough, but we don't know how the process works for moderate changes. In 1952 it worked along with a recession caused by overproduction of textiles and the severe Australian import cuts.[35]

Ian Little has been very helpful on all this question of convertibility ever since he arrived, and under his influence I have removed much of the optimism from the Rowan draft and said (a) we must move because we are exposed, (b) it will be very risky to do so unless there is some slack in the system.

I lunched with N. Kaldor today. He is worried about our inflation, but he talked mainly about his tax Commission.[36] We also discussed Tony Crosland and what he would do if he does not get in at this election.

I am getting increasingly worried about staff for next year, as Little and Ross are both going and I have not found any replacements yet. It is also likely that Nita Watts will go for several years. It will be all right after October 1956 as Downie and perhaps Dow will come back then but I don't know what to do in the meantime. However my new assistants are all shaping fairly well and Fred Atkinson will be useful. I tried to persuade Campion to lend me Saunders for a year but as usual he said it was impossible. However I suppose I will manage. The great advantage of the Economic Section is that apart from National Income forecasts, we can reduce our work if we haven't got the staff. This does less damage to us and everyone else than if we did it badly.

I have not seen much of the Chancellor lately as he has been electioneering. I must say that I rather hope the Tories will get in this time as I think that they will be better for the country and I do not believe they will go back to the bad old times as the *Daily Mirror* has been suggesting. Also, as I advised the Chancellor and the PM, it would be just as well to have an election as the economic position was a bit shaky and would be hurt by continued uncertainty.

Saturday, May 28th

The election is safely over and being, for really the first time, thoroughly conditioned in the modern methods of prediction I felt sure of the result after the first two results had been announced on Thursday night. The final total was just about right as Ministers will not have to work nearly as much in the House of Commons, or go without pairs, as they did: and Eden can feel that the country has endorsed him. But it isn't big enough to make the Tories feel overconfident and in fact I should think it confirms both R.A.B. and the policy he has worked for of going as far as he could towards welfare state ideas. His personal standing with the PM must have gone up.

I saw him this morning as I had come in to collect some papers etc. from Washington and he had summoned Rowan and Strath to have some preliminary briefing for the OEEC Council Meeting in Paris the week after next. He is going to Rome for a holiday but it seems a bit tough to bring these people in on Whit Saturday. He was looking tired but obviously felt delighted and told me that the PM had fully recognized his responsibility for the present state of affairs. It was very useful for me to see him as he gave me his line on convertibility, which I will no doubt be asked about a good deal in Washington. It is to move as slowly as he decently can or even slower – he has by now grasped the fact that it is unpopular and its effect uncertain. Anyway he said he had *no timetable* (with great emphasis) and also that Deshmukh had told him that Sept. 1956 would be a good time which is an indirect way of saying that he thinks so but without commitment. Even I think that that is too slow, since I doubt if we can avoid moving if things go badly or that we ought to hold back if they go well.

Leslie R. came in for a short talk afterwards to give me the OF line on the same subject which is also no timetable – he said that for some time now we shall have a struggle between the Bank who want to move and the Treasury and R.A.B. who want to go slow – and that means must be found to overcome the technical difficulties which the Bank will parade.

I also had quite a long talk to Bill Strath. He has now given up all the work on the H. bomb and the Cabinet Office has brought in Richard Chilver, from Civil Aviation and the brother of Guy, whom I have known for so many years in Oxford and during the war, to be the head of the War Plans Secretariat. And Denis Rickett, in case I have not noted it already, has replaced Playfair as Deputy to T.L.R. in OF. Crombie has gone to Customs to replace Croft and Playfair to replace Crombie, in charge of Social Services, Agriculture, etc. The other change of importance is that Bamford is returning from Revenue and being succeeded by Hancock from Food. H. was second man in BRMM [British Raw Materials Mission] in Washington when I went there in 1942 and I was not much impressed then or since – also he was at pains to keep me out of the CRMB [Combined Raw Materials Board] which seemed unwarranted. However he has worked very hard to get rid of the Ministry of Food which was sensible and realistic, hence this move – unlike Bowyer who fought tooth and nail to keep the M. of Materials and brought his career to an end in the process. All these personnel changes are on the whole useful to my way of thinking as I know most of the people well.

Crombie and his man Roberts came to see me this week to explore my views about the future of purchase tax – I had said that I thought it would not last much longer in its present form. Roberts obviously agreed, as indeed Customs has always agreed, that a wide range of goods at a low rate was the best tax but he felt strongly that we could not get enough things into the band to keep anything like the present yield if we had a low rate, say 10% wholesale which would be (more or less) 5% at retail. He also said that there was very little objection to the present taxes, which I doubt. I don't think the public mind at all because they are so used to the tax that they hardly know about it except on a few big items like cars. But the manufacturers dislike it very much and whenever they get into trouble they intrigue and exclaim and it gets harder and harder to find good reasons for not making concessions simply because so many have been made already.

Crombie is not a strong man but will be easy to work with. And I certainly prefer Rickett to Playfair at OF though neither is ideal. The result of all these personnel changes in OF has altered Leslie Rowan a good deal as he has not had nearly so clear or forceful a line from below as in the days when Otto was the strongest person there. Rickett is very intelligent but rather lazy and doesn't care much. However I like him and find him very easy and stimulating to talk to, at any rate he is aware of logical consistency.

There is a lot of speculation now about personnel changes in the Top Civil Service but I think it is all quite uncertain because E.E.B. is himself very uncertain and his move is the key to any others – besides which no one knows whether he will make most of the other changes before he retires from the field of influence if not action, or leave them as he should to his successor. The most popular view is that N.B. will succeed him, T.L.R. succeed N.B.; then it is all quite uncertain because there are no obvious choices, and anyway no one knows when B.G. will go. Frank Lee would be a strong probability for the Treasury but is now so much disliked by Ministers and senior officials that it is hard to see him being brought in. In fact it is more likely that Thorneycroft will go during the next Ministerial reconstruction, which I gather will not be for several months though I would expect *some* change at the Birthday Honours.

Monday, June 6th

I am now on my way back from Washington. I saw more or less the usual lot of people but at first felt rather less at home than usual. The people at the Embassy and UKTSD [Treasury and Supply Delegation] are now much less familiar than they used to be and I gave them no notice and found them in a busy week; Grieve-Smith is very nice and did his best but he is not so completely confident with the Americans as either Jukes or Atkinson were. Anyway I began by feeling almost unwelcome though I think it was mostly imagination and it soon went.

Monday was a holiday and I only saw Jo Alsop with whom I dined. We talked as usual about the world situation and especially what was the meaning of the Russian change of attitude; we both thought that it was because they were convinced that they would be devastated by the H. bomb if there were a war. But I said that I thought they were trying to keep the Chinese back and Jo who spent the last 6 months in the Far East said that this was not so and that the Russians had been building up Chinese strength for an attack on Formosa. However he agreed broadly that it suited the Russians to go for a release of tension in Europe because it looked as if SE Asia would fall into their laps anyway.

On Tuesday I was asked to lunch at the Treasury and sat next to George Humphrey who does not seem to have changed at all in his pre-Keynesian outlook as he talked at length about the dangers of inflation and that there was too much credit about, and also of his struggles with Congress in trying to balance the Budget. Everyone was delighted about our election, in fact I did not meet anyone in Washington who wasn't; as I was also pleased about it I did not feel that I had to be as neutral as usual. Afterwards I had a talk with R. Burgess, mostly about the prospects for convertibility – they obviously expect that we will now move quite soon and I did what I could to get them into a less anticipatory state, taking the line that it wouldn't be a popular move and that we ought to be free to choose the best time so that if there *were* economic set-backs these would not come too close in time to the move.

On Wednesday HE [R. Makins] had Hauge and Sam Waugh to lunch to meet me but we talked mostly about OEEC and GATT questions. After that I saw a lot of economists including a very full morning at the Federal Reserve. Their economic picture is clearer than it has been for a long time and they all agreed that they had been too gloomy in September. The automobile sales had exceeded all expectation and building had kept up more. Now the increase in demand had spread to nearly all sectors and was leading to increases in fixed investment and it was expected soon to increases in inventories. So things looked set at least for the rest of this year: GNP is now thought to be $375 bn annual rate against the April 1953 peak of about $370 bn. They were especially pleased about the new investment figure which had just come in and their next unemployment figures will be well down. As far as I could see they only felt some mild anxieties, about building and consumer credit generally.

Burns was extremely friendly and so was Hauge. They both seem more cheerful than they had been about 1956 prospects, not only because of the present rate of activity, but also because they have not needed to do anything on roads, schools, etc., so far and have thus got a backlog of 'real' demand which would be easier to translate into action than if it had to be manufactured. While I was in W., the Democratic majority turned down a Presidential borrowing programme for roads but I was told that this was mainly political, to prevent the Republicans from taking credit for a balanced Budget at the same time as they were borrowing for roads through a concealed capital Budget.

I saw Paul Nitze and had a talk with Roger Makins and they both explained their views on a feeling that I had that the Administration was very weak and uncertain generally, although things seemed to be going well for them. Nitze said that the people were far ahead of Congress and Congress pretty well ahead of the Administration; whereas in Truman's or Roosevelt's time all the powers of the Administration had been used to bring Congress and the public along, now they were hardly used at all but the Administration got a pretty easy run for what it could bring itself to say it wanted. Roger said that (a) the Cabinet was divided on many issues, (b) the President appeared to be unduly afraid of the right-wing Republicans – 'it almost seemed as if they had something on him' – and the Democratic majority in Congress knew how to run the machine and were willing to work with Ike on most things. By the way, Jo Alsop said that the Administration had no policy at all. I suppose this is the usual exaggeration but it is part of the same story. In spite of all this it still looks as if Ike could beat any Democrat and as if any Democrat could beat any other Republican. No one is any clearer about whether Ike will run but it is completely clear that he is under very heavy pressure to do so.

On the dollar problem, everyone agrees that there will be plenty of dollars in 1956 and probably quite a lot of military and some aid dollars after that. But the international trade side will continue to make slow progress especially now that the South is so industrialized and the Democrats slowly becoming protectionist.

I met the two new members of the Council, Davis and Saulnier. They are not very impressive and I should think Burns has got them to make sure that he remains fully in charge. Davis is rather nice and more sensible after a time than I thought at first. He is a population expert but has done a lot on agriculture in the past – however I don't suppose he will make much mark on their agricultural problems and I do not know whether the UK really wants such a mark to be made. At any rate I think a big reduction in their agricultural surpluses would not suit us at all.

I asked Win Riefler, who seems to be more and more Bill Martin's trusted adviser, how he thought our credit policy would show results. He thought that it would have marginal effects everywhere, and that these would show up all right even if we couldn't see them working. He also thought that our tighter capital market would reduce our exports to RSA and especially Australia – this seemed odd at first hearing but I can see what he means; any ease got by not making 'unrequited exports' is as good as any other ease. However we will now really see what credit restriction will do, if the picture is not obscured by the strikes which seem to have got a bit worse in the week I have been away. I must really get down to the problem of my staff now, or I shall have no one but juniors next year.

Monday, July 18th

Since the election the two big issues in the Treasury have been the next move on convertibility, and the credit squeeze. The Governor seems to be quite determined to bring the rates together and swing, say, between $2.70 and $2.90, and we think he told his Central Bank friends at Basle that he would probably do this. There has been a lot of trouble in EPU because the other Europeans want to keep the EPU in being, as really a regional clearing, *after* convertibility and also they have put a lot of pressure on us to say that we will maintain a rate with quite narrow gold points. Ostensibly this is because one can't settle easily on a monthly basis if one of the currencies has varied during the period, though I think this is a technical problem. But really it is because they think we want to use the rate movement to stimulate our exports, which is true in the sense that we want to use it to maintain a balance and that a favourable one.

Anyway the consequences of all this were that there has been quite a lot of speculation against the £ and the Governor keeps on pressing and the Chancellor wants to do what are called the 'Jan. 20th proposals' since this was when they were put forward. He wants to do this (a) because he says that he must have some freedom to balance his exchanges now he has given up controls, (b) it is a 'halfway house' which his colleagues might accept – he thinks they won't take the full Collective Approach now because of the consequences on the trade side. None of us can see any difference between the Collective Approach and Jan. 20th except that under the latter we would be acting alone, doubtful if we get a stand-by, and all the fine words we have used about consultation would be shown to have been hollow. I feel strongly that we ought to move fairly soon but that it would be a great mistake to do so when we are so inflationary at home. None of us feel that it would be wise to move without getting at least some more restriction on credit and none of us feel that we ought to do something the world will recognize for what it is, and pretend that it is a good deal less than that (us = Treasury officials).

The problem of credit is closely linked. The new Programmes Committee, now called the Balance of Payments [Prospects] Committee, produced rather a gloomy forecast for 1955/56, that we would be in approximate balance instead of surplus and probably lose a fair amount of gold, as the sterling area's position is a good deal worse than it was a year ago. They pointed out that as we did not have any direct controls now, there was nothing for it but a tight internal policy. Since then T.L.R. has been very gloomy day in and day out on his usual theme. But on this occasion I have been on his side, since the Chancellor put his money on credit squeezing in the Budget and it hasn't been made to work. The Bank of England has done its share and total bank deposits are down but advances have gone on rising and I feel very unhappy about our mechanism for controlling the supply of money.

By midsummer, with unemployment down to 200,000, it had become clear that credit restriction had done little to check the boom. The

Chancellor on July 26th called on the banks to make 'a positive and significant reduction' in their advances over the next few months and it was subsequently agreed with the banks that they should aim to cut advances by 10 per cent by the end of the year. Public alarm at the danger of inflation continued and preparations were made for an autumn Budget. On October 26th new taxation was imposed, all of it indirect, and it was reinforced by other measures such as a cut in building programmes. As the year ended, inflationary pressure still showed little sign of easing and the balance of payments continued in deficit.

Just before Christmas, Butler ceased to be Chancellor, becoming Lord Privy Seal while Harold Macmillan took over the Treasury.

Thursday, November 24th

I don't know why I cannot keep up with this diary, which is now only a disconnected series of notes.

The summer and autumn have been dominated by the attempt to get the inflation under control. Just after my last note, Sir B.G., Sir H.B. and I managed to get the Bank of England to let us talk to representatives of the Clearing Banks, with Mynors and [Maurice] Allen present. It became clear almost at once that the banks thought they were doing all that was expected but that they could do more if we 'did not mind bankruptcies or unemployment'. In fact the Bank of England had not conveyed to them that the Government was serious in trying to use monetary tightness as an anti-inflationary measure. H.B., to do him justice, reacted very well – he came back and drafted a letter for the Chancellor to send to the Governor asking the banks to get their advances down by 10% before Christmas, and to maintain a liquidity ratio of at least 32%. Naturally as soon as the Governor heard of this he protested, said it was quite unnecessary, and he would speak to the banks. They wanted (as they had told us) the Government to *say* that it wanted a squeeze so that they could refer their disgruntled customers to Government policy. The result of all this was the Chancellor's statement on July 26th, just before the House rose, saying that the banks had been asked to make a substantial cut in investment [*sic*].

The situation did not get any less inflationary and pressure on the reserves continued in August. The reasons were first that we had said so much in Basle and Paris about a floating rate, second that with so much inflation at home, and wage demands in the offing, Continental operators thought we would go convertible soon and open at the *bottom* of any range we had in mind. We therefore decided that something more might be needed, and I did not go to Istanbul as I had to stay behind to consider what might be in a Budget and what speech might be made. At that time we were in favour of making any announcement about Sept. 27th instead of waiting until Parliament met. This was because we thought that the run on the £ might get worse, and also that the position of the Chancellor would be easier if he were the first to announce that new measures were needed, instead of waiting for Parliament. It was all extremely tricky because of the view taken in April. The fact is that the Chancellor took a risk then, but took it under the impression that credit restrictions would work more severely and sharply than they did. In fact he was let down by the Bank. But this did not make it any easier for him to have to eat his words.

After the July statement I wrote a formal Minute to E.B. and the Chancellor saying that ever since November last we had been relying on credit control and that we had not had proper co-operation from the Bank on this.[37] I think it had an effect on E.B. but it didn't seem to get through to the Chancellor as he wrote on it that the Governor had told him that the inflation would have been far worse but for the increase in rate in February and the restriction of the liquidity since then. As if when you have opened a channel you were controlling far too wide you counted it for virtue that you didn't open it any wider!

Meanwhile the Chancellor repeated at Istanbul what he had already said in Parliament, that (a) we would not move to convertibility until we were stronger internally, (b) that we had no intention of departing from the present parity, with some slightly uncertain words about the present swing. This was a major reversal of policy about which I protested since the whole Collective Approach had been based on the view that the floating rate would get us out of any troubles that followed from convertibility if our payments didn't balance.[38] I had always thought and said that a floating rate was a very hazardous thing to have with sterling so widely used and the balances so large. But this was a risk which we had apparently been prepared to take.

The decision to abandon the [idea of a floating] rate was taken more or less by chance when the Chancellor had to speak in the House, and Cabinet was not consulted at all. I did not get anywhere much with my protest but T.L.R. said that he did not believe that if we had to choose between fairly full employment and a fixed rate, we would choose the latter. There it stands at present. Convertibility put off *sine die*.

After a great deal of delay, Ministers took the papers about the effect of ending discrimination, both on our dollar position and on industries at home. They took at the same time the paper that showed how little scope we had to use the tariff, between bindings under GATT and the Commonwealth free entry which resulted from the Ottawa agreements in 1932. This was all referred to a Committee under Frank Lee to look at the details more closely.[39]

When the Chancellor got back from Istanbul, Ministers decided to wait until the House met for the supplementary Budget.[40] They accepted the need to do something and more or less left it to a few Ministers. The PM and the Foreign Secretary did not like anything that would put up the cost of living but in the end the PT was approved: bread subsidy was kept. I think that all the measures taken together will amount to a good deal, since over the next 12 months there ought to be a substantial reduction in housing and in other fixed investment. The increase in coal prices, in rents and in PT will all help. But we are a bit uncertain about wage increases and in the Budget debates just coming to an end there has been a great deal of assertion that the wage increases would be stimulated by the Budget and that in the end it would have paid us better to have had no PT. I do not believe this since I think that wages claims will be made and met whether taxes are changed or not: and that such taxes as this are disinflationary on the demand side as is indeed obvious. The critics always overlook the fact that taxes remove purchasing power, while wage increases are practically neutral since the extra incomes are offset by the higher prices which result. My own view is that the tide will turn fairly soon but it is rather an anxious business to be waiting for it.

The Chancellor has been very unhappy and rather demoralized; it began with his dislike of having to have a Budget at all after the April one and it was much added to by the cool reception of the Budget by his own party and by the violent speech Gaitskell made against it the next day [October 27th]. On the following day, Friday, he came into the office looking like a defeated man and told us that it had been a great mistake and that he could not say anything in reply. This was very silly as in fact H.G. had made it very easy for him by being so immoderate himself – it would have been harder to reply if G. had been more statesmanlike.

I saw the Chancellor a good deal that day and managed to persuade him that he had a good chance, and I wrote a good deal of the speech he was to make. It was rather funny to be able to bring in bits I had put into earlier Budget speeches myself against this very contingency of having to change one's views. By the end of the day the Chancellor was in quite firm shape and he worked on the speech himself at the weekend and did very well with it: so that when he spoke in the Commons Debate on Monday [October 31st] it was thought to be one of his best performances. I must say that his speeches are better when he does not take too long over them and have innumerable drafts circulated round the office. This one was nearly all done by himself based on drafts by Trend and me and a long note by E. C. Kahn of OF Stats about the 1951 crisis.

H.G., who had behaved most honourably in the 1951 Budget, had left himself open by having the 1951 election and it was silly of him to charge R.A.B. with electioneering and to say that if *he* had been in office and made a mistake he would have acted in much better time, since when he was in office he had done all the things he now complained of and worse. R.A.B. actually showed great courage on this occasion though one would hardly use the word if one listened to him at office meetings. After the speech he felt better but we had a number of scenes during the Committee stage of the Finance Bill, where the incessant criticism of almost every single PT item got on his nerves and although he kept on repeating that the object was disinflationary so that it did not matter that particular objects were or were not affected, he kept on feeling guilty because of arguments on individual items which were irrelevant to his own thesis. However in the end he made a concession on baskets which could be made to look a special case, and perhaps is if the demand is elastic, and got through with the House in a reasonable temper.

James Crombie has done very well in his first Budget at Customs and has immensely improved the structure of the tax which is moving towards our being able to use it as a sales tax. H.G. attacked this concept in the Debate presumably on party grounds as he must know the arguments for a sales tax, but I suppose he likes taxes on luxuries for their own sake. But the reasons for taxing these, i.e. that you can screw a bit more out of the rich after you get to the limits on Surtax, are equally applicable to the poor when it is total revenue you need.

The Wages White Paper on which we have worked so hard for so many years is now in print and unless there is a last minute change it will come out about Dec. 12th.[41] Trend and Dick Ross did most of the work on this version and after so long I have found it hard to keep much enthusiasm but of course think it is a very good idea. The wages situation itself is calming down and the opposition, both in Parliament and in the TUC, is feeling a bit ashamed of itself after its recent burst of irresponsibility. H.G., who practically cheered the workers on during his first speech, was much calmer in the speech on the 'stand fast' motion at the end of the PT in Committee: while the TUC have issued a very good statement quite unlike *their* immediate post-Budget reaction.

There must be lots of other things but this will have to do. I have been recruiting the Section busily, with a big turnover taking place, and have got Figgures, an ordinary Treasury man who has just been made an Under Secretary, to help me part-time as Deputy Director for the present. Figgures is very good and was in OEEC for some years, where he much impressed all the economists there, so much so that Cairncross and Marjolin both told me I ought to get him. I was more ambitious then but am now glad to have him and think he will do my raw recruits a good deal of good.

I have had several talks with E.B. about the Planning Staff. Strath went off to help Edwin at the Atomic Energy Organization and Strath was really very glad to go because B.W.G. had been gradually reducing the activities of the planners by keeping things away from them and when in doubt *not* taking up anything that offered. E.B. suggested a choice of Rickett, Compton and Otto Clarke but he felt sure I would not want Otto because of all our rows in the past. However I thought he would be much the best because he would give it the drive and energy needed if it were not to die altogether. So Otto has been at it for about two months and already is prowling about for more things to plan.

Monday, December 5th (Washington, DC)

I came here with Leslie Rowan on Dec. 3rd; we are on our way to the meeting of the Anglo-Canadian Continuing Committee in Ottawa on Dec. 8th. Frank Lee and Hitchman who are also going came here yesterday so there is a very high-level collection of economic officials here and Jo Alsop looks very sceptical when I say that we have only dropped in on our way North. I had lunch with [Professor] John Williams at the Federal Reserve in New York on the way through and also saw Sproul [Governor of the New York Federal Reserve Bank]. They are a bit worried about the tendency to inflation here and this was underlined by Bill Martin and Riefler, whom we saw on Friday. They say they are running quite full at present and so much investment is planned for next year that they will be over-full then unless something else contracts – they feel sure that automobiles will contract but they can't say when. Last year's figures surprised everybody but contain a substantial element of borrowing since Hire Purchase terms got easier all through the year. They are tightening up slowly. Martin was worried about wage increases also, especially the new minimum wage laws. I have not seen Burns yet.

Otherwise we have talked mostly about the waiver, which Leslie is most anxious to settle.[42] I was very much in favour of a *démarche* until I talked to George Bolton and Lucius Thompson [of the Bank of England] about it but they pointed out some features of the original negotiations which had apparently been forgotten in the Treasury. (a) We said we would not claim it except *in extremis*, (b) *in extremis* was apparently defined as a shortage of dollars due to a slump, especially a bad US slump. Clearly it is quite a different matter to claim it with a US boom and with too much inflation in the UK. We had a long talk with an official group called the Burgess Committee, which discusses UK/US Treasury matters: and a short talk with Burgess and Humphrey; but we did not get anywhere. After some years in discussing the meaning of the unintelligible Article 6(iii) [of the Loan Agreement] Humphrey last spring suggested getting the Agreement changed so that we substituted some 'bisques', deferments at our option, for the rights which cannot be used. But he found that Congress was not likely to agree so we came to talk again about interpretation: and they seem now to be thinking again about a change in the Agreement. Leslie feels that this is all hopeless and that they do not take it very seriously.

Otherwise we have mostly talked in a general way. Burns is more afraid of a down-turn than the Federal Reserve, I suspect partly because he is in the Administration and it is an election year. Everyone talks about the Presidential candidate and about the new Russian offensive with the underdeveloped countries. W. Lippmann, who sums up what they nearly all say, says (a) [Adlai] Stevenson is almost certain, (b) the President will not run again, simply because (even if he would) the people have too much experience of heart disease and *know* that you have to go slow, (c) the Republicans are entirely at a loss to know what to do and this is the reason for the delay in making an announcement. A good many people say that Nixon's position (as a candidate) is getting stronger and Walter says that is so, delay is on his side: he is not a man of any strong principle and is now trying to seem or indeed to be much more moderate.

Wednesday, December 7th

We have finished here and are just going to Canada for the UK/Canadian meeting. We had another session at the Treasury yesterday and received an unhelpful answer on the waiver. The upshot is that we pay this year, which has been probable for a long time; they will give a formal reply to our suggestions about the meaning of 6(iii) but told us that they did not see that they could accept our interpretation; they will try again with Congress for the amendment and the 'bisques'. We had lunch with John Coulson, the new Minister, on Monday and Southard [US Treasury] was there – he told us that an amendment would only be made to the Agreement if it could go through both Houses more or less unopposed. We gathered that no very desperate efforts had been made to press the bisque version.

Leslie spoke very warmly at this and said that it was not fair that we should be for ever prevented from getting something that the drafters of the Agreement thought we should get on some occasions, because of an unintelligible Clause. He also said that officials would have to recommend that the matter should be explained to Parliament. Whether this will ever be done I don't know – even if we could agree a statement we might be pressed not to publish it.

I have talked to most of the people concerned about the US economic position and feel that it is fairly clear. The Federal Reserve think the boom is quite strong enough and would *like* some mild reduction in automobile sales to fit in the expected new investment. The Council of Economic Advisers agree that they are running about full but are more nervous about the dangers, and probabilities, of a slackening in automobiles (and also in housing) than the Fed. are. Hauge would like a slightly higher level of activity, recognizes that the rate of growth must steady off to the normal trend line, and feels that this is going to be very difficult. Everyone agrees that it is very improbable that as many cars will be sold this year as last but no one can form any defensible view as to what the sales will be. The biggest worries are the extent of hire purchase credit, and the outlook for used car prices. If the latter prices fall, the trade-in price would have to fall and the terms for new cars get stiffer at a time when the need for sales is to make it less stiff.

HE gave a big dinner on Monday night with about 13 from each side. I talked to Williams and McLellan (?) of the Dept of Commerce, the Deputy Secretary and one of the Under Secretaries responsible for tariff policy and so on. But did not get very far: they took the line that the policy was firm and it was just a question of the facts. On Tuesday Hauge gave a lunch at the White House Mess for Leslie Rowan, Harcourt, Frank Lee and I, and he had Burns, Sam Waugh who has recently left [the Department of] State to be the head of the Exim [Export-Import] Bank, and Prochnow who took over from Waugh at State. Hauge said he thought that the OCT [Overseas Corporation Tax] would get through Congress this Session but not the Customs Simplification. He said they were under much less pressure now that employment was getting so full again and that the President was still firm to keep down applications under the Escape Clause.

We told him we were particularly worried about the recent oil import cut, (a) because the US ought to be conserving its own oil, (b) because the procedure used – to tell the importers that they must make a voluntary cut or there would be a legal one – was a sort of blackmail, would tend to tempt people to use it to bypass complaints under GATT, and would start similar procedures by any country that wanted to cut some inconvenient import. He understood this point already. Sam Waugh was in good form after a trip to South America and seemed optimistic about the new Argentine régime. They have started in a very bad way because they inherited defaults in their short-term overseas obligations.

On the Russian move in underdeveloped countries, I don't think that there is any clear policy view either in Washington or in London. Before I left we had been getting a good deal of pressure from No. 10 to find money here and there to meet the Russian competition, such as the Aswan High Dam and the Indian Steel Works. The Treasury got the Chancellor to put in a memorandum [CP(55)168] saying that we were in a precarious position already and it would only make it worse if we gave a lot more money away. I feel that we ought to make a plan for our total expenditure on defence, hot and cold, and try to keep within it. I am sure we are spending too much on weapons that will be no use either in a big war or a small one. It is very unfortunate to have no fund and no plan and be reduced to trying to meet the Russian offer, with them deciding where and when to push.

I couldn't find that the US were reappraising their own policy either. We talked a good deal about the need for them to have a large reserve fund in the Foreign Aid Appropriation but the tendency is for Congress to tie funds up more precisely rather than less so. In general the US situation is not very encouraging since the President is doing very little indeed – he has a lot of conferences which are well advertised but he is not yet being shown any real problems – the Administration can run along quite well in a routine way but what could it do if it had to change the lines or if there were a crisis? Since the President has all the responsibility there is no need to force a unity of view on the Cabinet, and there is no one who can really take over from him.

The other general reflection that occurs to me nowadays on these visits is that our anxiety about the post-war world, because we were afraid of the US deflating the world through slumps, now seems to be much less justified by events than we had expected. Since 1947 I have made it a practice to come to Washington at least twice a year, to see how their economy was going if no other reason brought me here. We went slow on convertibility because we thought there would be a dollar shortage anyway and made worse by slumps. This was right because we weren't then strong enough ourselves but I don't see how we can take it as a long-run view. The US economy has been much more stable than anyone expected it to be; and it has kept up the supply of dollars by one form of aid or another so that for years it has been losing gold and/or piling up short-term obligations. We ought to be able to earn our share if we can keep out of inflations. It is the same point as that about the waiver – it was planned for a contingency that seems unlikely for the present.

I feel fairly sure that the ending of discrimination will cost the world some dollars; and that aid will get less and less popular as time goes on. But I don't think that this ought to prevent us from moving to convertibility as soon as things get slacker at home – we have gone too far along the road and there is no good short-term argument for turning back. What we need is a careful study of what we would do if the aid runs down and the dollar supply runs short – I do not quite know myself because of the sterling balances. What we need most of all is a nice big reserve. I don't even feel as worried as I did about our upward movement in costs, though that is bad enough, because other countries will have some of it. Incidentally Win Riefler told me that his experts think the UK is on the turn and will get the best [*sic*] of our inflation.

Harcourt seems to be getting on well, as I have thought he would do ever since I talked to him at the Bank/Fund meeting in 1954. He is clearly on good terms with the US people, including the top level ones. He is able to be quite firm but has a nice way of doing it. I keep on being forced reluctantly to think better of T.L.R. than my emotions wish me to. He works very hard, has a good mind, is more worried about real problems than E.E.B. or (especially) B.W.G. And now he is even beginning to see the weaknesses in the Collective Approach, at a time when I am losing my fear of it. It is a great pity that he has this tendency to stomach ulcers and bad temper which makes him so difficult to deal with and reduces his effectiveness so much because he lets a note of anger come into his voice and departs from reason into the current theology. But I certainly think better of him than I have since just before he returned from Washington.

Frank Lee is a strange man. I have known him fairly well since 1940 and really quite well in recent years; I used to admire him very much for the great energy and address which he showed. But he is not as impressive as a Permanent Secretary as he was at all previous levels. He is not trusted by senior Treasury officials and I am almost sure that he is disliked by the Chancellor who has had him nearly out of the Budget Committee and thinks that he does not keep the President in order. There seem to me to be three principal troubles, (a) his judgement is not very good on top policy questions – for instance when the Chancellor has made up his mind on a Budget matter he is inclined to take an independent line after it has been thrashed out among officials, presumably in order to show that he is the bold official in favour of the hard way. At that stage it only produces irritation, particularly as the Board of Trade often goes for a soft way when it is in their own field; (b) he is conceited, in a very simple-minded way and with a rather charming personality. But he is inclined to take more credit than the facts warrant for any strokes that have gone well, and he is inclined to claim as 'an old personal friend of mine' almost anyone of note who is mentioned in conversation. On this trip he insisted on having his own appointments made for a very large number of people on the US side, many of whom were already busy and despite Roger's wish that we should go together if at all. And I think all the appointments were for short periods and that he was regularly late – he irritated me when he and I were going to see Burns by turning up 15 minutes late for a half-hour appointment; (c) he gives the impression, I think wrongly, of not being as tough as he talks. It is always hard to know with a Senior Civil Servant how much this may be due to the Minister but in most cases the man doesn't leave you in much doubt, because you know his character and he generally tells you just what he thinks and what he can do. But one doesn't feel sure in Frank's case. He would, I think, very much like to come to the Treasury.

The outlook there is not at all easy. E.E.B. who used to want to retire shows little present sign of doing so. B.W.G. is expected to go early but no one knows when, and he does very little work and does his best to keep out of difficult things in the hope that they will last his time. N.B. who is the agreed successor to E.B. is not at all well and for some reason is on bad terms with E.B. and is kept out of Treasury consultations. The obvious man to succeed B.W.G. is T.L.R. but for reasons that will be clear from much of this diary he is not ideal, either to me or to anyone else. I like Herbert Brittain especially since he drafted the letter in July to make the Bank cut down on the Clearing Banks. He is thorough and firm. But I do not think he ever initiates any thought about policy and he is really as far now as he ought to have got. There is no one else at the Permanent Secretary level who seems to me at all suitable and not too much at the next level.

The two best men in the Treasury seem to me to be Trend and Armstrong, successive Private Secretaries to the Chancellor. But they are still Under Secretaries and have a long while to wait. Sometimes this year I have felt very much like leaving myself but I suppose not quite seriously enough – but I feel often that I do not know exactly what is going on and it doesn't seem to me when I talk to people that anyone else knows much more than I do.

Saturday, December 10th

We finished the talks in Canada yesterday afternoon and I am now on the way to Bermuda because the flight is routed that way – I think it will be the first time I have flown NY–London this way. The meetings in Ottawa (of the Anglo-Canadian Continuing Committee) were very friendly and open though I often feel that the Canadians press their particular points both with too much stress on the rate at which a free economy will make adjustments, and on the possible reaction of the Canadian public to our continuing in ways of which they disapprove. But I don't think we could have talks like this with any other country, not even Australia. One feature of this Committee is that many of the members have known one another for a very long time; and another is that neither country really keeps anything up its sleeve. We talked about the UK situation (too inflationary), the US situation (as above) and the Canadian which has behaved in an astonishing way as they passed in less than 12 months from being uncomfortably depressed to being (now) uncomfortably stretched. There really is a sort of world-wide boom and most countries are trying to deal with it in the same way. They pressed us to let in more Canadian imports and professed to believe that this would help us both by giving people something to buy, and by making our industry more competitive. But I did not feel that their hearts were much in it.

Yesterday Leslie and Frank and I saw Le Pan and the staff of the Royal Commission which is considering Canadian long-term prospects and they fired all sorts of questions at us, including some about our own long-term Survey. One of them, in discussing UK exports prospects, said 'The UK has nothing to offer except price'.

II

Macmillan's Chancellorship

20 December 1955 to 9 January 1957

The struggle to contain inflation continued under Macmillan. The 1956 Budget lent some support to the credit squeeze. In the first half of the year attention was fastened increasingly on the danger of wage-push which was inevitably strengthened by the intense pressure of demand. In Hall's view the government had no adequate strategy for mobilizing opinion against high settlements and did things at the wrong time and in the wrong order. The apparent failure of the credit squeeze raised a second question: how did the monetary system really work and could it be made to work better as a check on inflation? A small committee of Treasury and Bank officials, including Hall, was appointed to prepare a report and reached agreement on a document which has never been published and of which Hall at first thought highly but was subsequently much more critical.

Wednesday, December 21st 1955

Since I got back there has been more discussion about the progress of the credit squeeze and the Budget Committee had a meeting on the evidence and agreed to recommend to the Chancellor that we should talk to the Bank and tell them that more must be done, and offer them a choice of selling more securities, whatever the price, having their liquidity ratio regulated by order, and having their policy on advances regulated by order or by a voluntary arrangement. The Chancellor has agreed to this and we are to have our first meeting with the Bank people this afternoon. It is still very worrying and I have had several outside talks, notably with W. King and on Friday with Oliver Franks who drove me to Oxford and showed me the first draft of his Chairman's speech which is due fairly soon.

I told Oliver that I thought the Bank of England and the Clearing Banks were on trial as well as the Government and the Treasury and that if this did not work now, there would be no arguments against the Labour Party's return to controls, and none against nationalizing the banking system. O. took all this on board – he is not worried about Lloyds but about the whole position of the country. He said that if the Chancellor or the Governor would have a meeting with the big 5 Chairmen and make it clear that the necessary steps were to be taken, they would give the best advice possible about what the steps ought to be.

Yesterday I lunched with E.P. and we were both gloomy about the outlook. He told me that the Ministerial changes would be announced at any moment and said he thought it a good thing that R.A.B. was going, since he had lost his nerve. This was the first time I heard that he was leaving but it was confirmed by all the office gossip when I got back, and at 5 p.m. I saw the Chancellor alone to allow him to say goodbye. The changes are announced this morning.

I do not know quite what I think. On the one hand I feel that it is a great mistake for the Chancellor to go at this juncture, when the £ is weak and there is more confidence abroad in him than in the country.

I also feel that he ought to have made the credit squeeze work somehow and that this would have vindicated him after all the attacks of recent months. Finally I do not know much about Macmillan, having met him only once at dinner with E.P. and seen him occasionally at Ministerial meetings. But he always seemed rather erratic to me. If he goes back from convertibility etc. it will be a great blow to our friends in the US and Canada. If he goes back to controls it will be a severe reverse for the Government and I doubt if it will do much good when the main trouble is that we are over-inflated.

On the other side though I like R.A.B. and am personally sorry he is going. I think he has lost his nerve at the Treasury lately and is almost unable to take a strong line or to give firm instructions. He was very rattled after the reception of the Budget and was depressed by the course of the debate. He felt on the whole that the April Budget was a mistake, although he himself was responsible for it and it was put clearly to him that it was a risk unless credit restrictions were made to work. I do not think he got really good advice from the Treasury all through the year but if he had been firmer the advice would have been better.

I do not suppose R.A.B. will be Chancellor of the Exchequer again. I have always liked him personally and got on well with him, and I think that he liked me and trusted my judgement. But I could not go very far in advising him privately, and more and more as time went on he had big meetings where the need to keep the office together tended to blur the issues. It was a real difficulty that Sir B.G., who was in a position to pull things together, had no interest in doing so but neither Leslie Rowan nor Brittain nor I were the men to make a row about this and ultimately the Chancellor was not better served than he allowed himself to be.

I think that on the whole he was a weak Chancellor who came on at a time when the tide was running in his favour and was clever enough to give it a chance. He allowed the country to make great strides towards a free economy and he was responsible for convincing business and the Labour Party that full employment was a bipartisan policy, that it could be made successful, and that it wasn't a real political issue. One result of this was to stimulate the investment boom which was a very good thing for the UK, although it contributed a good deal to the difficulties of this year and, if he can be said to have fallen, to bringing him down. But in the position of a modern Chancellor, one can only be successful if one is strong enough to dominate both one's colleagues and one's advisers. And too often his advisers tended to cancel out and his colleagues to sabotage the measures he proposed. No Minister in his Chancellorship was ever a strong advocate of economy. I always told him that a Chancellor ought to be unpopular and only so would be trusted. But he could not bear unpopularity, and though I do not think he had any scruples of a conscientious kind, he was very bad at finishing off an enemy. If he had provoked and accepted one or two resignations it would have been much better.

Yet he did his party a great service in getting them to accept the welfare state and the country to believe that it had been accepted. Whether he will be PM or not seems to me to be very uncertain and at the moment I would say that the longer the PM's health holds out the worse R.A.B.'s chances will be. Of course it may be that he does not really care now that his wife, who wanted to make him king, is dead. But I doubt it.

Thursday, January 19th 1956

I went to Switzerland from Dec. 22nd to 31st and was not in the office until Jan. 2nd. Since then I have been getting to know the Chancellor and I now think much better of him than I expected to. The principal event has been in a sense due to me. On my return I saw the preliminary Dec. unemployment figures and was given an advance figure for the Dec. trade returns (which was rather worse than the final figure turned out to be). On the basis of these I decided that there was *still* no sign of deflation and that time was getting shorter and I said so quite firmly at the 2nd Secs which was in the afternoon of Jan. 3rd. E.B. said that if I felt like this I should tell the Chancellor so at once and I did a minute almost straight away which was sent on and endorsed by E.B. and on the basis of which I was instructed to draft a paper for Cabinet saying that everything was too inflationary and that we needed to take further action, and promising another paper with measures in it.[1]

The Chancellor wrote down a lot of ideas of a rather unconnected kind, which he called 'Thoughts from a Treasury Window', and notes were written on all these and a series of meetings held at which he decided which ideas to put forward in the present context. By a piece of good luck, the Treasury Investment Committee (for the survival of which I had fought two years ago) had just done its report and on the basis of this Figgures was able to recommend a lot of cuts in investment in the area controlled directly or indirectly by the Government; this takes a large part in the recommendations.[2] The Governor has also been told that he must keep up the pressure – he has been anything but helpful over this whole period but is collaborating now. The Chancellor is also recommending cuts in subsidies (bread and milk), in defence and in the Civil Service.

E.B. put a paper together yesterday [C(56)17] and it was really a very impressive and encouraging document and reflected great credit on the Treasury. I suppose that all Treasury divisions have ideas for economies but they are all turned down by a Chancellor over a few years so they are discouraged and then show a new burst of energy when there is a new man. Anyhow the Chancellor more or less accepted the paper at a meeting yesterday afternoon and it is going round tomorrow to catch the PM for a Cabinet before he leaves for the US. What will happen at Cabinet remains to be seen but it is a good start.

We had a lot of trouble over the speech the PM has just made at Bradford as it got built up in the papers to be going to be the remedies for all present troubles, and had to be built down again. The PM has very woolly ideas and is particularly keen on lowering prices, taxes, etc., rather than putting them up, and I have had to write a lot of papers arguing the opposite. I think the Chancellor, who partly belonged to the PM's school when he came, is moving round to mine.

S. C. Leslie got M. Green to invite the Chancellor to meet the group of 'responsible' City journalists, at Brown's Hotel on Monday. The Chancellor was quite good and gave them the impression that he would be firm and also that he would let interest rates rise. (They *are* being allowed to rise now as the Bank have been told not to support the market though we are still arguing about whether the Issue Dept should *sell* its long-term securities even if this drove prices down.) However the meeting went on too long and the Chancellor really got a little drunk which surprised and somewhat horrified me as I thought a man of his experience would not run any risks. He was a bit indiscreet about his plans to end rent control, and also went in for a humanitarian outburst on the horrors of unemployment which was a bit against the picture of the Iron Man he had started to build up. But Clem Leslie made post-mortem inquiries and no harm seems to have been done.

Tonight the Chancellor is having a dinner party for Bridges, Boyle and me, to meet Cobbold, O. Franks, Tommy Brand of Lazard's and P. Mills who used to be the Machine Tool Controller and is now some sort of an industrialist. This is to talk about current economic problems. I don't know how it will come out.

I have been asked by Mahalanobis of the Indian Statistical Institute to go to India to discuss their next 5-year plan and the Chancellor has approved. I suppose I will not be able to go till after the Budget.

We have begun Budget Committee meetings but it is a bit academic as yet. We are all hoping for a deflation but see no signs of it. It looks as if the Investment Allowance may be withdrawn, and there will be violent arguments about a Capital Gains Tax. Hancock, the new Chairman of Inland Revenue, has almost moral objections or says he has. I used to know him in Washington as he was Secretary of BRMM when I began there in 1942. I did not think much of him then – he came back and did various odd jobs and was a very good Permanent Secretary of the M/Food as he did his best to get rid of it after the Government had decided on this, instead of fighting all the way as was done over the Ministry of Materials by Bowyer. Hancock had a short spell at Pensions and now has this job and Bowyer will presumably see his time out at Pensions. But I am not sure that I shall get on too well with Hancock, who rather fancies himself as an economist and puts forward arguments that I don't think hold water at all.

R.A.B. has taken Trend and Bancroft with him to the Lord Privy Seal's office. This shows very good powers of judgment anyway. I don't know what they will do but I will be keeping in touch with them. R.A.B. is in the South of France having made a very tactless set of comments about the PM just before he left, no doubt deliberately.

Another personnel change which will be very good is that Fred Bishop has gone to No. 10 to replace Pitblado. Bishop has worked very closely with the Economic Section during his time in the Cabinet Office and I think he has very good ideas, as well as energy and character. But I suppose it will be a hard job. T.L.R. is going to replace N.B. in the

PM's party for Washington. This is good from the point of view of my own long-term objective but as will be apparent I have been working much more closely with him than I ever expected to. N.B. has been very ill with an alleged slipped disc, the present medical catchphrase under which they do all sorts of damage. It will upset all ideas if he is permanently damaged, just as the heart attack created a new situation in US politics.

Friday, January 20th

The Chancellor's dinner was quite interesting. Mills talked about the engineering wage settlement which he hopes to get. He said that the employers are now very nervous about the business outlook because they think the reduced activity at Austin's will spread. He thinks there might be a settlement at about one-third of what is asked for. If so it will be cheaper than I had expected. Cobbold agreed that the 'smell' of business was now much less optimistic but neither Franks nor I agreed.

After dinner the Chancellor asked for a discussion of where we were and what we ought to do. The Governor said that the credit squeeze was going on but time was short and the reserves low. He felt sure that a reduction in Government expenditure and investment was essential. O.S.F. made quite an oration on the lines that urgent action was needed, this must be Government expenditure and investment, the banks would do their share and he hoped the Governor would be making this clear. He then said that it was essential that a big block of Treasury bills should be funded as otherwise monetary management was too difficult – the banks were too liquid. But if this were done they would be competing for Treasury bills and would not have so much they wanted to lend.

There was a good deal of discussion of this – the Governor said that no funding operation could be carried out until the market felt that there was a steady period ahead and that inflation was being brought under control. I think Franks gave the impression that he wanted the operation at once which I don't think he meant. At any rate when the Governor asked if Bank Rate should be increased he replied that it should follow, not lead, monetary tightness, which I have been urging and which is now I think accepted Treasury doctrine.

The general upshot of the discussion was that the Government should make a very early statement about reductions, e.g. on subsidies, defence and Government investment. This should give figures of what had been agreed or ordered. O.S.F. put the deflation needed at £500 mn but he did not mean that the Government should do all this. I think he is on the high side and has overlooked the purchase tax effects. He is also a bit unsound about wage increases which he regards as directly adding to purchasing power, overlooking their effect on prices. But of course the general trend of his remarks was very useful and fitted in very well with what I have been saying, and with what the Chancellor is intending. I also found it very helpful that he should be so forthcoming about what was needed in monetary policy – it is not often that one gets a chance for such a free discussion with the Governor.

T. Brand did not say much except that he thought the present system of depreciation caused firms to overstate their profits very much. This led to bad labour relations and had made many firms fundamentally unsound because they hadn't got the money to replace their capital equipment.

The Governor asked about hire purchase control extension – on the whole the officials wanted extension and the non-officials didn't but this wasn't too clear. E.E.B. asked if we ought to increase taxes. The business side thought they were too high already and an increase would be very depressing. The Ec. Sec. disagreed and thought the Budget was the most powerful instrument of control.

The Chancellor was quite good – he made them feel that they could talk really freely, gave them some insight into what he had in mind, and I think it was very useful to have the Treasury sense of urgency confirmed, the measures we have been suggesting endorsed, and stress laid on the need for higher interest rates and fewer Treasury Bills. O.S.F. was the dominant figure and the Governor rather on the defensive. It was nice to be working with him again for that is really the outcome of the last month or so.

The Governor is to see the Chancellor at 11.15 this morning to discuss the funding operation suggested by O.S.F. It will be quite a tricky business and I don't think it ought to be rushed.

Tuesday, January 31st

Things have moved along fairly fast. The Chancellor put the paper recommending various measures to Cabinet and on the whole it was very well received. Bread and milk have to wait till the PM is back from Washington to settle the timing, and I suspect the substance also. The great majority of the cuts in Government and Nat. Industry Investment were approved in principle and since then the Chancellor has been seeing his colleagues to settle in detail, and Petch tells me he has been fairly successful. I don't know exactly what else has been settled but today I was told to draft the opening passages for a statement or speech which would then go on to announce the changes decided on.[3] There is still some argument about bread and milk (if agreed in the end) – whether to put them in the packet or to announce them at the same time as the results of the Agricultural Price Review, where we hope there will be an imposed settlement this year. It is thought that both will be unpopular and if announced together (i.e. lower farm prices and lower food subsidies) they will cancel one another to a large extent.

We have also had a lot of argument about a Capital Gains Tax. Hancock is very much against it, it seems to me mainly for emotional reasons. The Chancellor wanted to do it and the EST wrote a strong opinion in its favour. E.E.B. and B.W.G. and FST are against. T.L.R., N.B. and I for it. However as Hancock said that a bill could hardly be drafted in time and it would be full of bugs anyway and they would have no staff to administer it, I think the Chancellor is turning it down on administrative grounds. I wrote a note to support it and to ask that a study be made now so that if later we (or another Chancellor) wants to go ahead he won't be baffled on purely official grounds.[4]

On Saturday (Jan. 28th) in Oxford. T. Balogh asked me round to meet Harold Wilson whom I had not seen for many years and of whom I had a very poor opinion, both over devaluation and over his resignation on the 1951 Budget. But he is now in good odour and is the most probable Labour Chancellor. So he obviously felt that he ought to meet me again and after a good deal of anxiety I decided that it would be better if I met him. It all passed off in quite an easy and friendly way and T.B. was, for him, a model of tact. H.W. seemed delighted that he was likely to be Chancellor, naturally enough. He told me that they were asking for a debate on the economic situation and even read me the notes he had made for his speech. I told him I thought a debate would be o.k. if they would wait till the PM got back, and suggested that he hang his remarks mainly on the balance of payments and especially the bad December figures. Then we talked a bit about what controls would be needed and I said I thought that the most urgent were ones over investment and that it was a great pity building licensing had been given up (as the present Government are finding). He said that he thought a Labour Government would certainly have building licences and he thought some kind of import control as they would want to go back to State buying for some things. He also said that they would be much less doctrinaire about monetary policy than they had been.

Wednesday, February 8th

The Chancellor is doing very well. His measures are well forward and all depends now on the line the PM takes when he gets back and on how tough the Chancellor will be.

On Tuesday Burke Trend came to see me and said that R.A.B. wanted to talk to me and would I go in to Smith Sq. at 6.30 for a drink? So I said yes – he told E.E.B. but not the Chancellor. When I got there Rab (as I shall call him since I cannot get used to writing Lord Privy Seal) said he wanted to discuss the economic situation. He was very much mixed up in his own mind between his personal position and what was sensible or necessary now. He is obviously much worried about recent events and told me it was quite useful that people should say he had been exhausted. He complained that Cabinet had given Harold the bread subsidies but had refused them to him – and nobody knew he had demanded them. Of course the difference (if H. gets them) is that he is more determined.

But I think the main thing he wanted to know was whether I thought the whole packet was needed now or whether bread and milk could not wait till the Budget. I said that the December and January trade and unemployment figures had been disappointing, a good deal of time was gone, and no one would say if we could wait or not. I thought that a statement *without* bread and milk would not seem adequate, though the other things could be mentioned in a debate asked for by the Opposition, as opposed to a statement volunteered by the Government. He rather jumped at this and I expect he will plug it.

Yesterday we were starting to write a speech in case there is a Debate, and the Chancellor showed us a first draft *he* had done. It was a very good draft too, with some of the ideas a bit wrong but full of life. It made the redrafting a pleasure. It is a long time since anyone did his own first draft. I seem to remember that Stafford did. Hugh and Rab demanded drafts and changed them faster than we could redraft them.

I had lunch with Hall-Patch yesterday, now going to S. Africa as he is on the way to be the Chairman of the Standard Bank of S. Africa. He told me that the Bank of England are claiming that the Treasury refused all last year to do the things they recommended in monetary policy. They did just the same after devaluation. It is difficult to get used to people in such circles who tell downright lies about official secrets.

Today I had lunch with Frank Lee and we talked a bit about Russia, etc. He thinks we ought to be a bit more forthcoming. I am brooding about our whole foreign trade policy as I think we have let the best be much too much the enemy of the good.

Monday, February 20th

Most of the details were settled by the end of the week before last (Feb. 10th) which was just as well from my point of view as I was away with influenza from then until Feb. 17th. When I got back I found that there had been a terrific struggle in Cabinet about the subsidies [on February 13th, 14th and 15th], ending up with what seems to me the worst of compromises, to take 1d [0.4p] off bread. They got all the row and only 40% of the money. L. Petch told me that the Chancellor had to offer his resignation to get even that. To make up weight they threw in the Investment Allowances. I am glad as they ought to be taken off and put on according to the conjuncture and when I left, the Inland Revenue were taking the view that it was a pity to chop and change. When I got back on Friday it was all settled and he made the statement on Friday [17th] morning, Bank Rate having been put up as planned the day before.[5] We did a bit on his speech on Friday and on Sat. a.m. he (H.M.) had a meeting from 10 a.m. to 12.30 to discuss it.

He is a very satisfactory person to do that sort of thing with as he comes very quickly to the point and gets in a stenographer at once to dictate bits that are changed. There was a little brush with T.L.R. who wanted him to make a very threatening speech pointing out how favourable a year 1955 had been and how we had failed to make any use of it. H.M. said 'Whose side are you on, anyway?' which produced a collapse. T.L.R. had moods in which he thinks of himself and Ministers as the conscience of the country, quite overlooking that Ministers ought to be the guardians of the conscience.

Now I am waiting to go to the House to hear the speech, the first in a two-day Debate [on February 20th and 21st]. It is very good, very little argument or figures, just assuming that everyone agrees that we are too inflationary. The only doubt I feel is that there is a longish passage appealing to the Opposition not to exacerbate wage claims, a thing that very much needs to be said but I wonder if he will get away with it. Both in October and now, the Opposition have been very irresponsible in arguing that if any attempt is made to get the workers to share in the sacrifices, the workers are quite right to try to contract out of it. It is really rather depressing that they should take this line, in effect trying to get the workers to put any troubles on inflating (which they then criticize) and moving towards devaluing the £ which must be the result of all these wage claims. It is party politics at its worst.

I do not know at all if these measures will be enough. My rational opinion is that we have now done more than enough in the last 12 months. Bank Rate is up from 3 to 5 1/2, bank deposits and advances are both well down against the trend, Hire Purchase is very stiff, Purchase Tax and the subsidies take away about £150 mn and there are the taxes on distributed profits and the end of Investment Allowances. And Government expenditure in one form or another is well down on its trend. But no one can be quite sure what is needed in order to break a boom and we must just go on trying till it breaks. However the Stock Exchange is far down on its peak – the FT index of industrials was at about 222 in June and is now about 174 and that in itself represents a big change in psychology. What we have learnt is that financial and monetary restraints on investment are very slow-acting in modern times. I feel sure that there are two big differences:

(a) high employment and high profits mean that firms are very liquid;
(b) the *belief* in high employment means that it is much harder to alter a boom psychology once it has got established.

I am only afraid that we won't be able to restart high investment again; however there is a very big public sector slice which can be started only too easily.

Friday, March 2nd

The Debate went quite well and it did not seem to me that there was nearly as much resentment about bread and milk as S. C. Leslie had argued that there would be. He is getting to be rather arrogant just as present. B. Gilbert does not like or trust him and has always done his best to keep him out of things, and during the later R.A.B. period he was in fact out a good deal, though everyone else was really too as R.A.B. was so undecided and defeated. Anyway, the new Chancellor has a lively feeling for public relations and to some extent shares Leslie's feelings about the need to keep on good terms with Labour and the

Trade Unions. And S.C.L. has got the idea that *he* is making policy much more than before and has begun to throw his weight about, a very silly thing for a Press Officer to do especially when he is a temporary. I have argued a good deal with him (though he and I are on very good terms) about the economic situation – he is much more worried about rising wages than about the underlying inflation while I feel that until we get that out of the way it is fairly hopeless to try for agreement on wages.

I have, however, just written a long paper on the subject.[6] It was decided in Cabinet that after the statement of February 17th, the PM should see the TUC to discuss the economic situation and explain the measures. The PM has always been well to the left of Leslie and has consistently been against the Government increasing prices or taxes that would affect the cost of living. He seems to me to be dominated by the idea that he ought to get economic affairs out of party politics and that he can persuade the Trade Unions to moderation and restraint. On present form the price he would be willing to pay is much more certain, and would be much more dangerous, than any return he got would be either certain or enough to offset the risks. However meetings are all right if no commitments are made. And the first meeting is on Monday (March 5th) to be followed by meetings with BEC, FBI and the public boards.

On Tuesday E.E.B. asked me to write a brief for the Chancellor and this gave me a chance to set out my ideas, which are that the first thing to do is to end the inflation. But *then* I think that for the first time since the war ended, we might be able to go for an agreement. The reason is that I think the long rise in food prices in the UK, which took place much later here than elsewhere because we were so slow to end rationing, subsidies and M/Food contracts, is practically over and world food prices look to me as if they will be fairly steady. So if food prices are going to be fairly stable, it is much more likely that wage stability will lead to price stability.

Wednesday, March 28th

Nearly all that has happened since I wrote last was either on the Budget or on prices, wages, etc.

The main development on the Budget has been a progressive hardening of the views of Treasury Ministers. *We* began (Economic Section) with the view that we couldn't tell exactly where we were on the Trade Cycle and that it was safest to take no risks, that is, to come out with an increase of the surplus with which you went in. The Chancellor at first took the view that this meant no concessions unless balanced by taxes but he gave himself the benefit of the doubt in various ways, especially that all the savings measures would bring in more voluntary savings than they cost in lower Government surplus. However it gradually dawned on him, and even more on Boyle, that the Tory Party were sick of economic measures and wanted this to be the last, and also that the country was waiting for a tough Budget. So it now looks fairly tough but it is not settled yet. The big question is whether to put the 6d. [2.5p] back on Income Tax. Rab says he will resign if this is done and no one knows whether to believe him or not. It seems rather a dirty business to me and also a retrograde step in general, though perhaps on a narrow economic analysis it is desirable.

Thursday, April 5th

It is still not settled but I feel that the 6d. party is in the ascendant. We had a special inquiry into the economic situation, consulting all Departments concerned, but it did not tell us much that we did not know already. The March gold figures and the March trade returns are both good and incline me to think that we really are slightly turning down but this makes it all the more important to be sure of it since we can be even surer that over a few years toughness now will pay. (This sounds illogical but I mean that if one could be sure this was the last time we had to tighten up, one would have one's heart more in it – the last year has been bad for our morale.)

I will write about the wage–price negotiations when I have more time. I have also been engaged in some skirmishes with the Bank of England and hope that I have launched an inquiry into our experiences of last year. The Chancellor very nearly screwed himself up to prescribing liquidity ratios but the Governor has been much against it. He had the nerve to write to the Chancellor saying that we must begin by assuming that we had the best not the worst banking system in the world. It isn't the worst but if it is the best the others must be poor, I mean really the other Central Banks not the other member banks.

It is really almost unbelievable how little co-operation in economic policy we have had from the Bank of England over recent years. They did not even express an opinion about how the credit side would be going this year, when we had this special inquiry laid on from all sources of information. All the Governor does is to explain away the actions of the Banks and say that nothing but reduced Government expenditure will help the situation. He told me in 1953 that 1952 proved decisively that Bank Rate was a dominant factor. In the first half of 1955 he kept on telling the Chancellor that in a little while the credit squeeze would work. Then at the Mansion House he said that it was a mistake to expect monetary policy to have too much effect. If he had said this earlier we would have known where we were.

Thursday, May 3rd

The Budget is old stuff now. In the end the Chancellor decided on practically no concessions, no 6d., and to announce a proposed reduction of £100 mn in Government expenditure. This caused a lot of alarm and despondency in the Treasury where it was regarded as impossible. The

Budget Debate was very flat and went off easily enough. R.A.B. is very glad that it is over as he now has a formal Budget between himself and his own April one: so it will cease to be possible to bring it up against him. My biggest surprise was the popularity of the premium bond.

The Bank of England–Treasury Working Party to review 1955 and monetary policy generally has now got going.[7] O'Brien and M. Allen came from the Bank and Compton and I (with Fred Atkinson) from here. It is in my view a historic series of meetings as it is the first time since the Macmillan Committee that there will have been an investigation like this. So far they have been quite forthcoming and we will clearly get much nearer to a meeting of minds than we have had for years.

I had to go to Paris last week for the Expert Group Meeting of which I am still the Chairman. The level of representation remains high and if anything is improving. Nearly everyone except Burns and the Dane, Schmidt, was more worried about inflation than deflation. Burns thinks the US will stay about flat this year. But he disapproved of the Fed. Reserve having made money dearer, so I assume that he would prefer a bit of a rise, both because they are well below capacity now and because it is an election year. We also talked about the next 5 years, for which we had all submitted forecasts, and it was surprising to see how expansionist everyone expected his Government and his economy to be.

The most interesting thing to me was the gloom of the Germans about incipient inflation. They say that Germans are quite naturally morbid about this, and even the present very mild movements are causing a reduction in personal savings. I wish we had only as much to deal with. I feel that we cannot stand another round of wage increases here on the scale of the last 2 years without getting near, or to, devaluation again.

Tuesday, May 15th

I have had to spend a great deal of time lately on the wage question. Ever since about 1948 I have thought that full employment could not be reconciled with price stability unless there was some sort of self-restraint by labour, in the sense that they could get a number of possible wage increases, leading to varying price increases, without any difference in anything else. In the long run of course there would be balance of payments effects and if wages rose too fast a series of devaluations. We have drafted a number of White Papers on this subject but for one reason or another Ministers (Labour or Tory) would not agree to publish them. However the last round of wage increases was so alarming that they actually did publish the current draft as a White Paper, *The Economic Implication of Full Employment*, before the Budget.

I thought that this was bad timing as I wanted the deflation to go a bit further than it has gone – restraint won't have a chance with over-full employment. There was also the fact that a number of Government measures, or Nationalized Industry ones, were going to put up prices and these are always presented as exacerbating the situation, and being so presented they probably do. My idea was to get these all out of the way, so that there were (a) no more subsidies to be removed, (b) no need to put up any more indirect taxes, (c) no early prospect of more wage increases and price increases in the Nationalized Industries. *Then* launch a campaign, in which at least your good faith would not be continually assailed because of your own actions.

However the PM beat the gun by summoning the TUC, and after them the FBI, BEC and selections from the Boards of the NIs. As Ministers had no real policy, nor were prepared to give any firm line, the first round of talks rather flopped.

Meanwhile I said that the *next* round of wage increases, if they were like the last one, would bring devaluation into sight, not to mention the growing danger that people would not believe that money would keep its value. Finally I got the Chancellor to put a paper to Cabinet (CP(56)118] saying that the risk was grave, a firm lead must be given – *then* giving the price increases due to Government action that were still to come; that HMG saw no more in progress, *asked* employers and labour to keep down prices and wage demands – then there was a reasonable prospect of price stability for a while and this time it would be used to try to agree a long-term wage policy.

Cabinet approved this general line but did not agree that the statement should be published when I had meant it to be, that is, after the second talks with the TUC which had meanwhile been fixed for last Thursday, May 10th. I was allowed to go to this meeting, the first time the PM had allowed *any* official to go, and I thought he was very sour about it even then. But H.M. and R.A.B. had both pressed for me to go. The meeting was very friendly but the statements by Ministers had very little impact and the Press statement issued afterwards had none at all.

I don't think there is any doubt, and George Woodcock, Assistant Secretary to V. Tewson in the TUC, confirmed this to me privately, that Trade Union leaders are practically helpless with over-full and probably with full employment. In fact I think they would like employment to be something less than full, whatever they may have to say in public. But at present they have nothing to offer their members and if they don't back these extravagant demands they will lose their jobs. And I am sure it is no good making appeals to them. Probably a straight request, of the kind I had in mind, wouldn't help either but it would be better. And it would make it clear to employers that the Government expected them to stand up to the next lot of wage demands.

Since then there has been a lot of to-ing and from-ing [*sic*]. Ministers are disappointed by the Press reactions but none of them want to make a new statement and they make the most feeble suggestions, mainly that officials should do something. It was even suggested [CM(56)36] that *I* should influence *The Times* to write a strong leading article. How I could do this if I wasn't allowed to say what Government policy was I do not see.

The latest idea is that R.A.B. should say something at the Lobby Conference on May 17th and I am going to have a talk to him tomorrow. The Chancellor is very good when I talk to him or at office meetings but I don't think he can be nearly as good at Cabinet and he isn't very impressive as a public performer. Curiously enough R.A.B. who is a much weaker character fundamentally is clearer and firmer when he speaks – he was quite good with the TUC. I thought the Minister of Labour, Macleod, was good too but he was treated very much as the junior boy and not allowed to say much.

I feel a bit depressed by all this as I put in a good deal of work on it. And even if my policy wasn't much good, it was the only thing at all like a policy – now it has gone off so feebly that it is mostly thrown away. The only good feature is that all these abortive attempts to get the Press going have stirred them up so they know the Government is worried and suspect that it has a policy. William Clark, the PM's publicity man, got me to talk to N. MacRae of *The Economist* today and he is going to write a leading article about it this week.

It is also probably getting through to employers that HMG doesn't want any more wage concessions. I expect there will be some strikes in the autumn and we must try to get Ministers ready to face these. I told them that they would do better to go down defending the £ than go down because they were afraid to defend it.

Thursday, June 21st

The economic situation is looking a little better and it begins to seem as if the Budget judgment was about right. I thought then that the peak would turn out to have been about December or January and the economic indicators since then have confirmed this – the movements are modest but clearly down. The Chancellor is getting most of his £100 mn cut so that will add quite a bit but the movement is very small and slow so far and we certainly cannot be sure that we are out of the wood yet. The best news is on the balance of payments front where it looks as if we shall have a surplus of about £120 mn for the first 6 months, and the Balance of Payments Committee (which replaced the old Programmes Committee) is forecasting about the same for the next 6 months though we will I hope eliminate this forecast since it depends on our keeping on with present mildly austere policies.

E. Compton and I have finished our labours with O'Brien and Maurice Allen and our joint report will be available today or tomorrow. While it is a bit too complimentary to the Bank over the events of 1955, it puts the whole thing in a much clearer and more intelligible light. I think that their greatest fault was to allow R.A.B. to introduce the 1955 Budget, which relied on monetary policy, without telling him that *they* thought it was not likely to do the trick. And no doubt Cabinet thought it was a good thing to lower income tax, on general principles, and was well aware that an election was coming. But granted that, no one will ever convince me that they could not have put more pressure on the banks. The Report itself makes it clear that the reduction in advances in the second half of 1955 was largely due to moral suasion on the banks. We could not act as we did in July, when B.W.G., H.B. and I saw their representatives, until we were clear that so far policy had failed – and right until then Cobbold was telling R.A.B. every week that the credit squeeze was just round the corner.

But the report does describe *how* the monetary system works at present and what the practical limitations are on its operations. It is an agreed document and can be used in any subsequent discussions if it should be necessary to spell out (as I am sure it should be in future) *how* the squeeze is to be made effective. We have a forecast until March 1957 of the banks' liquidity position and can see that if all goes well things will be very tight by then. If only we had had such a forecast in April 1955. So I think it is the biggest advance in monetary policy since the Macmillan Committee in 1932 or whenever it was.

I also feel quite sure that the Bank has become much more conscious of the duty it has and much more anxious to regain and to exercise control. I do not know how much to allow for the inarticulateness of Cobbold or the vicious system under which he saw R.A.B. alone and there was no record of their talks. But if he said the right things in these talks (I don't believe he did) he has only himself to blame that no one at this end thinks he did his duty or played the part he ought to have done. And the damage to R.A.B.'s reputation is a standing memorial to the conduct of the Bank of England.

The anti-cost-inflation campaign is now well launched and I feel much more cheerful about it. In spite of the fiasco of the TUC meeting, the subsequent publicity pressure and two speeches by H.M. managed to make everyone conscious that there was something in the air. Norman MacRae did quite a bit to help by a short leading article [in *The Economist*] after our talk, to the effect that the PM was trying to say something important even if no one realized this and William Clark had to call attention to the fact that he was sounding the charge on his muted trumpet.

Wednesday, June 27th

We have had several meetings about the money report and are to discuss it with the Governor and the Chancellor on Monday. I think we will press for more reduction in advances but no fixed liquidity ratio or advances ratio if they behave. The Governor wrote to E.B. about the report, approving generally but ending up with a statement that a credit squeeze 'of this severity' would soon do more harm than good! He obviously does not think of monetary policy as an important instrument at all. Bridges replied saying that one could hardly say that the squeeze was severe when we still had over-full employment and expanding investment.[8]

On the wages front, things have been moving rather slowly. The PM saw the FBI and BEC and it was a fiasco as far as Ministers were concerned since H.M. decided at the last minute that he had to go to the House of Commons when the Finance Bill was troublesome, and the PM made no effort at all to introduce the subject. However the employers knew what it was all about and were quite good. They pressed for action by the Nationalized Industries and suggested a joint meeting with them and in effect said that *they* wouldn't make any wage concessions if they could be sure that the Nationalized Industries wouldn't, and that the Government would not put any pressure on them to settle.

It was handled all through very badly by Ministers but nevertheless made some progress and in the end it was suggested that there should be a joint meeting with FBI, BEC and the NIs and then perhaps a Government statement. (This was on June 11th but I did not have time to mention it.) After that meeting I said I thought it was time somebody on the administrative side of the Treasury should be put in charge of this and it was decided that M. Stevenson should be – in spite of B.G.'s assertion that he did not think it came on his side. As he was so reluctant to handle it E.B. has taken it over.

Yesterday Ministers saw the Nationalized Industries' representatives and they were very resentful of the implication from the FBI that it was they who had sold the pass on wages. They also said they thought it would produce very bad effects on the Trade Unions if there were a joint employers–NI meeting, and more or less refused to come to such a meeting. Since the Ministers had nearly promised this to the FBI, it was a bit awkward. However the general tone was very good and nearly all the NIs had made, or promised to make, statements actually promising to keep their prices steady until some time next year, so the campaign was getting a good start. It was very bitter to me that the Coal Board, which had done what I had wanted all along and put up its prices *before* it said it would keep them stable, was given just as much credit by everyone as the railways which had not put them up and will now be running at an even worse loss.

But I feel fairly satisfied in general because in spite of the PM the whole thing is moving quite well – or perhaps I ought not to say in spite of him since it was his determination to see the various bodies that got it moving. But I wish he would handle the meetings better and show a bit more guts about the issues. I cannot think that he is very good, at any rate in this field – he really makes very little effort to understand anything and his reactions seem to me to be very close to appeasement. It is all very well to have a political feeling that we need to handle labour relations by agreement; it is essential and the TUC themselves practically say this, that there should be a firm Government policy.

There has been a good deal of work going on on improving our statistics and I think this is in a happier state than it has ever been. The Chancellor undertook to do something in his Budget speech and there have been a lot of meetings with Figgures and Neild pushing from our side. Campion has at last come to realize that everyone is on his side in wanting to get things better: he must be the last 'informed' person to have reached this conclusion. The Economic Secretary has been very helpful and it is fairly certain that the Chancellor will make a statement before the House rises.[9]

On the other side, the improvement of economic organization, I had not heard what the Chancellor had in mind but Frank Lee told me a day or two ago that R. Makins was to be brought from Washington in October to take charge of the economic side of the Treasury and N. Brook would be Head of the Civil Service *and* still Secretary of the Cabinet. Frank himself had been asked to replace Harcourt in Washington which had annoyed him very much as it would have been a demotion: and everyone would have seen this.

Louis Petch told me that the Chancellor wanted to get rid of Leslie Rowan and that E.B. had told him (T.L.R.) that it was time he had a change and would he go to the War Office. This Leslie indignantly refused, though he might have gone if it had been put in a more flattering way. But he would have gone to the Board of Trade – hence the suggestion to Frank. So there is no change and everyone is annoyed. Leslie also told the Chancellor that the appointment of Makins was the biggest blow the Civil Service had ever received.

I am very glad that *someone* is replacing B. Gilbert – now that I look back on the last four years I can see that his taking E.P.'s place was the really big mistake. I did not think it would be a good appointment but I have only slowly come to realize how bad it has turned out to be. A good many of our troubles and a good deal of the criticism now made of the Treasury has arisen simply because he would not do anything at all until he was heavily pushed and he really made no efforts whatever either to co-ordinate or to take a lead.

I suppose that if I had been smarter I would have seen this earlier and been more active myself but it did not seem easy at the time. And R.A.B. who was very conscious of it and who suffered a good deal more than anyone else, would not do anything. But the events which began when the Bank Rate was reduced in 1953, and only ended with R.A.B.'s requests to the banks in the middle of 1955, would have gone quite differently if Plowden had been there instead of Gilbert, or indeed if I had been prepared to make much more fuss than I did.

The trouble with me was that I wasn't prepared to take a chance on it and make myself unpopular enough. It was I who pressed for the reversal which led to the request to the banks but I was weak over the Income Tax – I suppose I thought that the Government had the right to take some chances to win the election and felt afraid that there would be a violent run on sterling (which there would have been) if Labour had got in.

But wherever the responsibility is placed, it is certain that the man who was supposed to hold the key job did not lift a finger. It was he and E.E.B. who pressed R.A.B. so hard on income tax, not that he needed pressing. It is a sad story and at any rate Makins will change that era. I am a bit doubtful about the constitutional effect of the whole thing, as for one thing N. Brook will have more power than any Civil Servant will have had in the modern world. He will be a sort of Horace Wilson* unless he is very careful: and the PM is both weak and wilful.

As the summer of 1956 drew on, issues of external economic policy came to take precedence over domestic problems. On the one hand was the question what to do about the Suez Canal, now under the direct control of President Nasser; on the other was the need to arrive at a policy towards the incipient European Economic Community. On the first, officials were not much consulted and latterly were kept in ignorance of the government's intentions; the Anglo-French airborne attack on the Suez Canal, under the pretence of keeping the Israelis and the Egyptians apart, came as a thunderbolt to Hall, who had gone to India with no knowledge of what was planned. On relations with 'The Six' who were preparing the Treaty of Rome (France, West Germany, Italy, Belgium, Luxembourg and the Netherlands), officials were busy with Plan G, a British proposal for a free trade area in Europe that would embrace both 'The Six' and the other countries of Western Europe (which subsequently formed the seven members of EFTA). The proposal, which was confined to manufactures and excluded all agricultural products, was designed to reconcile free entry to Britain for Commonwealth agricultural products with preservation of access to European markets for British manufactures.

Thursday, August 30th

I have been on leave for a fortnight and got back on Tuesday (28th). A good deal of work had been done in the Section on the possible economic consequences of Suez; present results so far negligible; operations, if any, begin to be important: serious interruption of oil supplies (because of unrest, *not* because of using the Cape) disastrous. Neild and Atkinson did most of the work and when the Chancellor saw the paper he sent it to the PM, who had it circulated to the Egypt (Ministerial) Committee![10] I have not been much involved in the whole question but have been very worried about it because it seemed to me that we were taking a very bellicose attitude without considering whether we would carry it through or not. I gather that the PM and the Chancellor have been the most bellicose. It might have been all right to have an immediate operation but once you have had an international conference and got it onto a negotiating plane it is another story. One might think that, now there is a 5-power Committee and so much talk, the danger was gone. But we are still carrying on as if we thought action was far more probable than not.[11]

The wage problem is now moving towards a more serious phase. We agreed at my Publicity Committee (set up when the PM was beginning his talks) that the Chancellor ought to say something in public before the TUC Congress met, and originally tried for August 17th or so. However the Chancellor didn't want this and for one reason or other

* Horace Wilson (Chamberlain's *éminence grise*.)

it got delayed until yesterday, more or less on the eve of the Congress. Then he saw all the industrial correspondents, pointed out that his price forecasts were coming out fairly well, and made all the points in favour of restraint that had been made before. He handled the subsequent questions very well, much better than he sometimes does, and got a very good Press indeed today. However the reactions from Brighton, where the Congress is assembling, are not very hopeful. No doubt in private they will be worried but it certainly looks as if we are in for a period of strikes. It won't do so much harm, I think, if we have them fairly close together as if they were long drawn out. Also they will tend to exacerbate public opinion and worry the workers if they lose a lot of consequential as well as direct pay. The trouble is that Ministers are hardly thinking about this at all and I haven't been very successful in getting officials to think about it either. Anyway the Chancellor showed great courage yesterday and it is very interesting to see that the *Chronicle* Gallup Poll says that a large majority of people want wages to be stabilized if prices in fact stay fairly steady.

The economic situation is not moving too badly though still slow. However we have now passed the seasonal peak of employment and the July figures [of unemployment?] rose instead of falling. The latest forecasts of investment show that it is expected to get steady next year and the building industry is also showing great alarm which it always does if its long order books fall at all. I think that by Christmas we should have more unemployed than vacancies and can then begin to think about stabilizing or even letting up a bit. I see that Devons in one of the Bank Reviews[12] has at last got onto the point I spotted six months ago, that once subsidies are gone they can't go [on] again and that we have had most of the distortions out of the price system now – so the big extra-wage injections into prices are gone and the thesis that if wages stay down prices will stay down is much more defensible.

The final official report on Plan G is ready and goes to the Steering Committee on Monday.[13] E.B. had a preliminary meeting about it today and I think the arguments are coming into balance very nicely. It is a pleasure to go to a meeting at present with both Gilbert and Rowan away! No emotions are introduced and one gets the central points in proper perspective very quickly. I have finally decided –

(a) that the changes are very like the ones we would have had to have anyway, only we will feel them a bit quicker and a bit bigger, simply because the economy is a bit more open.

(b) The biggest economic change is to swear off tariffs and to a large extent quotas. This means that if we want to shelter a particular industry in future we will have to think up some other way or let it go. It is a reversal of policy for the last 40 years or so, to commit oneself in advance to so rigid a formula. There will therefore be bad spots.

(c) The *political* implications are certainly towards closer relations with Europe and less with the Commonwealth. But the latter was going on anyway. The effects will depend largely on how it is handled,

> and we all thought that it ought to be presented with a minimum of fuss – no suggestion that this was a great new experiment (it isn't, the startling thing is to put on paper so bluntly the way we were moving anyway).

But it is all very funny when one thinks of the Collective Approach rows.

Friday, September 21st

I am going to Washington this evening for the Bank and Fund meeting. The Chancellor left yesterday. The main interest all this time has been on Suez where I cannot think we have handled the situation very well; we have a case but have not succeeded in getting this over to the world properly because we have so much given the impression that we were quite prepared to bypass the UN. We adopted Dulles's plan for a Canal Users' Association in order to make quite sure of the US being on our side but the plan itself is very vague and impractical. The great gain from all this has been to make Nasser much more circumspect and generally better behaved than he would have been, but I doubt if we will get full credit for this and it is very likely that it will turn into something of a diplomatic defeat. The PM's prestige is very much engaged. We have been doing a revision of the appreciation of the economic effects – the worst case, which I am told is also the likely one, is that hardly any of our or US ships will use the Canal for some time and we will have to bring some oil round the Cape and buy the rest from the US. (The case of no Middle East oil at all is worse but does not now look at all likely.)

The effects on us are very small *except* for the oil but this will be very expensive, costing us between $400 and $500 mn for a year's operation. We seem to be trying to get this as a gift from the US which I do not think we ought to expect. On the other hand it would be a very big strain on our reserves at a time when they are under pressure and we certainly ought to fortify them by an Exim Bank loan; or I would prefer an IMF credit or even something on the RFC securities.[14] It would be very weak and silly, now we have got so far, to behave as if we did not expect our policy to succeed and therefore to do anything to compromise our long-term objectives, e.g. go back to exchange control or a floating rate. There has been a lot of speculation against the £ all this month and we have nearly used up all the dollars we got from the Trinidad oil sale.[15] But since our balance of payments is quite favourable, these operations must have reduced the outstanding sterling balances quite a lot. Anyway I think the main objective ought to be to get as favourable terms as we can from the US for the loan - e.g. add it to the present loan so that we have 44 years in which to pay it off. There is no very strong case for Budgetary action but it might be that we ought to think about it a bit later, if only to convince the British public that this sort of thing is expensive.

The TUC was very recalcitrant at Brighton though they now say they didn't mean that there was to be an all-out scramble. I think public opinion is coming round much more to our point of view and that strikes will be unpopular with the country but I think it is quite likely that we will have some. So far both the BMC and the Tyne and Clyde strikes have been settled quite easily. The big one in the mill now is the Engineers but we are certainly not out of the wood on coal or the railways. However Ministers have got into a firmer frame of mind. The Chancellor made another speech on Wednesday, written largely by himself and edited by me, which I think was quite a contribution – it had a fair but not excessive press; we could hardly expect to go on with front page coverage.

Petch is going from the Private Office and Maude is taking his place. Petch is the weakest of the Private Secretaries since I have been here and has done better at the end than I thought. Meanwhile Trend is to be Deputy Secretary of the Cabinet which is a very good appointment and G. Wilson to run the Lord Privy Seal's Office. I had a long talk to Geoffrey W. about R.A.B.'s character which is a subject I enjoy. Edwin Plowden whom I saw at lunch on Tuesday says he is terribly bitter about H.M. and about the Treasury. I am not surprised but as must be clear from earlier remarks in this diary it is primarily his own fault.

The economy is still deflating itself very slowly but it is going quite well and if only we could be sure that we won't get big wage increases, I would be reasonably satisfied. I have a new AP and on October 1st a man called Scammell comes from North Wales to take Alan Day's place, then J. Downie should be here some time in October and another new man called Troup towards the end of the year. In fact the staff position is not turning out so badly as I feared. Robert Neild is now finally gone but it is quite nice that someone should go straight from here to Trinity, especially not having any published work to his credit.

Ian Little is writing an article about Government economic advice for *Encounter* – he showed it to me and I felt I should show it to E.B. who was rather touchy. The main thing I didn't like was some rather forthright criticism of the Bank, which we all felt would do more harm than good, but this was the part Ian was most anxious to keep.[16] Meanwhile October 15th and the new dispensation is approaching rapidly. I am going to India in November and am rather sorry to be off the scene so quickly after R. Makins's arrival. But I hope to see him in Washington.

Tuesday, September 25th (Washington, DC)

I travelled with E. Plowden and E. Boyle; Edgar Cohen [Second Secretary, Board of Trade] was on the 'plane also and we had a very slow crossing owing to various delays. I talked mostly to E.P. whom I see rather less than I used to; he was to deliver a lecture on Atomic Energy at the Bank meeting and for this they pay his and Biddy's air passage and $75 a day for four days' subsistence. He told me that the Treasury and the Ministry of Fuel and Power were now being sticky about the maximum expansion rate of atomic power stations at home – this was new to me as the line has always been to go ahead as fast as we can and I would have thought that Suez made it even more desirable to push on. He also said that they were going faster than ever technically and that the US were afraid that we were well ahead of them on this. I don't see why we shouldn't be as their other fuel sources are so much cheaper and more reliable than ours. Anyway he has to be very careful since it remains essential to cultivate good relations: his inspired comparison of an elephant and a whale which he says he made up himself is very useful.

It was rather funny to talk as O.S.F. had had dinner with him on Monday and had apparently given him a lot of views on the economic situation which he must have got from me at a talk Oliver and I had had a few days before – the state of the economy, the time when we would be moving to stimulating it instead of contracting it, and the British political scene (I had said that both parties were struggling to occupy the middle of the road and Oliver had produced and embroidered this). We also talked a bit about Plan G where Edwin is very keen that we should go ahead and has been trying to persuade the LP to this. Incidentally the Commonwealth has now been told about it in a preliminary and non-committal way and we hope to talk about it to them at the end of this week, which is one reason why Edgar Cohen is coming (the other is that Frank Lee is laid up and the Film Agreement, which Frank normally arranges to renegotiate at this time, has to be done).

The President is going to Canada on Wednesday to do some preliminary explaining and then coming here on Thursday to help with the rest. It is rather doubtful whether the Chancellor and the President *ought* to be the first to broach it like this since they are the leading advocates of the Plan and the last Cabinet which discussed it was anything but united. It is a bit like the Collective Approach in that we are slowly moving into a position in which we are fairly deeply committed without it being clear at any stage that the Cabinet, much less the country, wants it. However the Collective Approach was gradually reversed or at least transformed by economic events leading R.A.B. to change his mind. And now it is nothing more than the objective of convertibility which we have always had. If anything the new Plan is a radical modification of it in spirit, though we say that it means lower tariffs inside an area in which all the GATT lowering tendency still continues.

However I doubt if this will go the way of the Collective Approach as it is something that has to be progressively negotiated and stands or falls more or less as a whole. What may imperil it more is the political troubles it may encounter as it is disclosed to the Commonwealth, the Tory Party and Parliament. We shall know much more about this before the year is out. And this all assumes that the Government survives what now seems to have been quite a knock about Suez. At any rate the New York papers on Sunday seemed to be quite clear that the present form of the Dulles plan is quite different from the original one and is much more a scheme for letting Nasser go on operating the Canal than one to force him either to co-operate or to refuse by acts to do so. I haven't heard anything official about it since I left London but cannot believe that the PM's prestige is not severely damaged and I should think the Government's also though no doubt there won't be an election.

John Grieve-Smith and Harcourt met me. John has done very well here in spite of his shy and diffident manner which he has not lost. I gather that Thorold is to replace Harcourt in January, and I will send Kit McMahon to replace Grieve-Smith in April. The arrangement started when I sent John Jukes with T.L.R. in 1949 has come out very well and a man from the Section is regarded by the Economic Minister as indispensable. It also does my people a great deal of good and we have put economic reporting from the US on to a new plane and established first-class contacts with the various forecasters here. This is not so necessary as we thought it would be, since the US economy has turned out to be much more stable and for one reason or another we have never been deflated by it as we thought we would be. But the contact is a good one. Incidentally, Grieve-Smith tells me that R. Makins is *not* to become the Permanent Head of the FO even after his spell at the Treasury. I don't know if this is true, it is the contrary of what I had heard in London. He says that R.M. is very disappointed by this.

The Bank and Fund meetings do not look as if they will be more exciting or useful than usual. Rooth who has not been a great success is leaving and is to be succeeded [as Managing Director of the IMF] by Per Jacobsson from the BIS whom I know fairly well – I might perhaps call on him while I am here. There does not seem to me to be very much future for the Fund but I suppose it will stagger on like nearly all international bodies which no one dares to kill.

Sunday, September 30th

This is being written just before I get into London. Per Jacobsson is on the 'plane and I have asked him to lunch on Wednesday. So is Maurice Hutton who is now the Australian manager of the Lazard investment subsidiary but who doesn't seem at all changed.

I saw a lot of people in Washington, including Burns and Hauge. The economy is running very comfortably with the index of production steady and no violent changes in sight.

The only interesting things are first whether automobile sales will pick up this autumn, and later on whether the movement will be up or down. Burns thinks it is more likely to go down than up and is I think rather angry at the Federal Reserve and Treasury who seem to be convinced that they are on the edge of inflation and talk about the shortage of savings which is a very old-fashioned view in relation to the load on the economy and rather queer to hear when the business cycle forecasters take so much credit for the sustaining effect of the capital boom and look a bit worried at the decline in housing. Burns also told me that the idea that the US is getting short of gold, in relation to her short-term foreign liabilities, is gaining ground again. He thought he had killed it last year but it is too convenient an argument for a number of purposes for it to stay dead long.

Of course the absorbing interest is the Presidential election and I heard a good deal about it at two dinners, one given by Perry Sellon of *US News and World Report* where he had only 3 of his colleagues, and one by Jo Alsop where he had Stewart [Alsop], W. Lippmann, Paul Nitze and several Democratic Committee people – Helen Kirkpatrick and Arthur Schlesinger. Everyone agrees that [Adlai] Stevenson has gained a great deal of ground and almost everyone thinks that Eisenhower will be elected but that the Republicans will lose both Houses. But Stewart Alsop who has been in Iowa says that Stevenson will win by a minority of total votes. He says that S. will win the South and the Farm States and can pick up a few others, enough to do it. This is a combination of factors: farm discontent, a drift back of Democrats, and Kefauver telling all the small men that the Democrats are for them and everyone else against them and not mentioning issues at all. The *US News* people said that there was much more apathy than they had expected and that this might mean that the floating voter who had gone so much for Ike last time would perhaps not vote at all. Ike made a little speech at the closing Bank/Fund Session and seemed quite well but he looked an old man.

On Friday afternoon we talked to the Commonwealth Finance Ministers (but they were mostly their Deputies) on the usual lines about the prospects for sterling and the reserves. It was a very dull meeting and the Chancellor did not seem able to get it alight. The most interesting things were the firm determination of the new Finance Minister of Ceylon to show that he is as attached to the sterling area, and as anxious to keep Ceylon a good risk for investment, as his predecessor – and the first appearance of the Gold Coast [Ghana] as an independent member, rather a premature one but a very good idea. On Saturday morning they began the discussion of the Common Market and as this was the first exchange (apart from Canada) it was most interesting. My impression was that everyone was anxious *not* to commit himself, since I don't think any Cabinet had been able to give it more than a very first look; that they were all keen to find out how it would work in detail; and that they more or less believed us when we said that we were determined that it shouldn't affect the Commonwealth link. Ceylon and the Gold Coast being untouched by it – since all their exports to the UK are agricultural or primary products – were able to give it a full blessing subject to its not weakening the Commonwealth. Very nice too.

There is now intense interest in it both in London and in a good deal of the non-Communist world. I gather that it has been heavily splashed in the London papers this last week and their Washington correspondents were doing their best to get stories – the Chancellor really gave them more than he ought to have done as he made it quite clear that *he* thought it a good idea. I feel sure that it will now have to be put to the public and Parliament as soon as possible so that we will at least know their reaction which we haven't had so far. Macmillan is certainly a bold man – he has taken a very strong line both on this and on Suez and burnt any boats that he might have had – it must be make or break for him.

I had a good talk to R. Makins about the prospects after October 15th when he comes. He seemed quite sensible – roughly I advised him to do as little as possible in the early days, since there is no need to do anything – except to try to mend the Planning Board fences which B. Gilbert so completely broke.

Otherwise the main thing I did was to talk to Emminger about the Expert Group Meeting which is now probably put off from October 11th where we had fixed it to about October 22nd. The big problem is the German surplus and how to handle it – I found Emminger very sensible as always but he made it clear that they thought they had a very good case and would attack others if themselves attacked.

Thursday, October 11th

Ministers are all away at the Conservative Party Conference so the office is rather quiet, though it has been fairly busy since I got back. I have written two memoranda, one discussing what we should do if we wanted to relax our present deflationary policy, and one on a long-term policy for wages.

On the first I suggested that we would be under heavy pressure on a number of fronts and that many people would expect a drop in the Bank Rate to be the first step. But I thought that it was likely that interest rates were going to remain high for a long time, owing to the general pressure for capital from developed and underdeveloped countries – so I suggested that we should go very slow on Bank Rate, and in any case that there was much to be said for letting up a bit on the Clearing Banks policy of restraint first – don't lower prices just when you are expected to deration. For the rest I argued that we ought to ease up on investment as soon as we could. There are new signs that the investment boom is passing and if that is right we ought to start in good time to stimulate it – it took a long while to stop it and we ought to have started earlier. Incidentally I had lunch with R. Brech of Unilever today and he told me that a lot of firms have surprised him by the speed with which they reacted first to the investment allowance and then to its removal.

I think this is one of the fields where the Government ought to make a positive drive. They have had a great success with Plan G and the Chancellor will, I think, get away with bouncing his colleagues here as he did with houses when he was Minister of Housing and Local Government. At any rate the public reception to what was really an indiscretion on his part (since Cabinet had reached no decision) must have been very encouraging. Otto Clarke is also showing signs of wanting to make a forward drive on investment though he is more interested in particular items, such as steel, shipbuilding and coal.

On wages, there has been an argument going on with the Ministry of Labour who regard present methods as sacrosanct, and the Treasury, who think that something new is needed. Stevenson who has been in charge of the Treasury side has often discussed it with me – he wants to go too far towards compulsory arbitration. But I have been urging that at least the Government should make it clear that they don't think increases should exceed a stated percentage every year.[17] The trouble now is that the Government's point of view is not properly presented during negotiations. We say that there are grave risks to the country if increases keep on pushing up prices, and ask for restraint. But if we don't get restraint, then we have to give more of a lead. I would not mind going further, because I think it follows from our assertion about the national interest that we are bound to pursue it. But I would like to try persuasion a bit longer, only in future in more precise terms.

Sir E. Bridges and Sir B. Gilbert end their time as civil servants tomorrow night and there is a Treasury dinner at the Reform for them. It is a pity that they are linked in this way as they have been very different people. Bridges was Secretary of the Cabinet during the war and closely trusted by Winston, then he became head of the Treasury and he must have been one of the most distinguished of Civil Servants. The Economic Section really owes its existence to him and he has always been interested in it and stuck up for it so far as he could. He is a man of courage, determination, immense energy and a very good head. But his great weakness, and it is this which has so much lowered his prestige recently, is that he tried to do too much: I think that this was combined with being too sensitive to the claims of Eady and Gilbert, whom he may have felt that he was ousting when he came here.

The result has been that he has never had time in recent years to act as the real Head of the Treasury on the economic side. When there is a crisis he will move in, but up to that point he was always giving one the impression that his mind was on his next appointment and that he was grasping at anything that seemed like a workable solution. This was very much accentuated when Plowden went and out of loyalty or unwillingness to wound he accepted, or suggested, B. Gilbert as his Deputy. He told me at the time that he realized that it was not an ideal appointment but said that we must put up with it because it got the structure right. It shows the dangers, which of course one continually experiences in life, of acquiescing in putting in the wrong man to a key job. For the result has been to demoralize the Treasury, ruin the reputation of R.A.B., cloud that of Edward B. himself, and lead to a new organization here (so that the structure for which we paid this price has not survived) and which I fear will prove a bad organization, since I think N. Brook has now got too much power and if he is not careful will become very unpopular.

B. Gilbert has surpassed all the gloomy expectations formed when he came to his new post as he has consistently thrown all his weight in the direction of doing nothing. The only exception was when he persuaded E.B. to go for 6d. [2.5p] off the Income Tax in 1955 – no doubt we were all guilty about this and the results were much worse than we expected, but he must have most of the responsibility. It is difficult to say too much about the bad effects of his régime. He has almost killed the Planning Board and given the TUC the idea that this

Government want to break off relations with them, which is far from the truth.

And so on, and so on. Whenever anyone wanted to talk about important issues he tried to shelve it. He always found reasons for doing nothing or for delaying or for losing the papers.

Of course looking back one can see that if we had expected this, or if we had been better men ourselves, we could have acted differently. The trouble is that it takes a long time to realize just how much damage is being done and why. R.A.B. and E.E.B. were in the best positions to act and did not. They have paid for this. I suppose the rest of us ought to have tried to do something, and we didn't – we haven't paid so much. But it has been a sad experience. It is one of the difficulties of such a position that one is reluctant to make a big enough fuss to get something done. And in this case we acted very badly simply because the gold reserves were so low. Having taken the initial risk on the Budget, we ought to have been quicker on money. But there I think the Treasury is not to blame, since the Governor was always telling R.A.B. that action was just coming and as soon as we had had enough time to feel *sure* it wasn't, we made the move of telling the banks to limit advances. After that I felt reasonably certain that things would turn round and if it had not been for the low reserves we could have resisted the demand for an Autumn Budget. The measures Macmillan took when he arrived were different as he was not committed. Anyway, I suppose that if one were the person to make a real fuss in such fields one would either be discredited because one had turned out wrong, or would be a much more influential person than one is.

Monday, October 15th

This is the day of the change. There was a party in Compton's room to meet the new [Joint] Permanent Secretaries [Norman Brook and Roger Makins]. N.B. looked in good form, better than he has been lately though I doubt if his health is nearly what it was. But I imagine that although there was so much hope deferred, he cannot help feeling pleased that it has come at last. Roger Makins looked his usual self. I am to see him at 6 today, and he is making a tour of the whole office tomorrow and Wednesday which is a very good idea. The dinner on Friday went off very nicely. Leslie Rowan made a short speech and E.B. a very good reply, both largely on the theme that personal relations were always quite intimate in the Treasury and (a) how we all felt E.B. was our greatest prop, (b) he felt how much he had been supported. B.G. said very little. Then they told a lot of Winston stories – of course E.B. has a great fund of them.

The Chancellor said to me at an Embassy Dinner in W. that we ought to publish the report on monetary policy [entry for June 21st] and I have been looking at it from that point of view. It is a bit critical of our policy in 1954/55, and rightly so. But I think it could be made into an interesting document. I don't suppose it will ever see the light really

– for one thing the Governor would hate it. E. Compton tells me that he (Cob) thinks that he said all that could be said on the subject at the Mansion House dinner last week. Otherwise things are quiet. The gold reserves are still falling and I hope we will borrow $500 mn from the IMF as soon as possible, against the good balance of payments; this is clearly the right course. T.L.R. says that the French are on the point of borrowing but their position is much worse than ours.

Plan G continues to have a fairly good press. The Conservative Party Conference seems to have gone off in a well-disciplined manner and R.A.B. to be to some extent on his way back. But it seems to me that H.M. will be the man of the future; it will indeed be very unjust if he is not for he at least has ideas and courage to push them. The cost of living for September is actually down again, to just over 102, so he is well on the right side of his plateau and will hardly reach his forecast by December in spite of bread and coal and the season.

Thursday, November 29th

I went to India, on the invitation of the Indian Statistical Institute, on October 26th, and the period between October 15th and then was largely taken up by a meeting in Paris of the OEEC experts. I saw a certain amount of R. Makins and he gave me the impression that he was getting hold of things quickly and in particular that he agreed that we needed to strengthen the reserves. The Paris meeting had been expected to be awkward as we wanted to talk about the German tendency to pile up gold and yet to avoid any discussion of exchange parities. In the end Burns did not come, though the meeting had been put off largely to allow him to, and the US sent a man from ECA or whatever it is called now who was no use at all. Tinbergen and Schmidt were away too and nearly all the work fell on Emminger and me. However we didn't do too badly and got a report which stressed the UK need to hold down costs, and the difficulties in which Germany was putting everybody else. Emminger gave us the impression that the most likely thing was inflation as a result of spending on social services. The French were quite good about their own troubles.

The Indian visit had been arranged some time ago. Mahalanobis is the head of the ISI [Indian Statistical Institute] and a close adviser of Nehru's on economic affairs. The ISI is supported by Government grants but is pretty well independent. It began by training statisticians but has gradually extended its activities to the economic field and both M. himself and the staff had a good deal to do with the second 5 year plan. He asks economists to go and advise them from time to time and is somewhat notorious in the UK in that he has asked a number of Russians and Poles. Anyway I was asked to advise on long-term planning and they paid the expenses of my wife and myself on quite a lavish scale and it was a pleasant trip, except for Suez. The ISI does a large sample survey which is so late in producing its material as to be much out of date. It is also beginning to construct an input–output matrix for India, has about six economists working on long-term planning and a section which appraises the validity of its statistical methods and results. All this is in Calcutta. In Delhi there are more economists, also working on long-term planning but in closer touch with the Government people.

I spent about eight days each in Calcutta and New Delhi and three days inspecting the new industrial plants, etc., in the Damodar Valley. We also made excursions by way of holiday and seeing the country to Darjeeling, Benares and Agra. It is a bit hard to form any very firm impression in so short a time. But for what they are worth, they are

(1) the quality of the top economists in the organization is very good. They fully understand the latest methods of planning and I found it quite comforting to find how much we talked the same language. The best ISI man was called Dr Nagri and I liked him very much and thought highly of him. The other chief brain is a man called Pitambar Pant who used to be, and still nominally is, Nehru's private secretary. He is not an economist by training but is making himself one. He has been to Russia and China and has got an enormous lot of material from there. He has a great deal of drive and energy and ought to be put much more in charge. The quality of the supporting staff is not nearly so good but it is tolerable.

(2) The Government people concerned with current developments are rather mixed and I don't think they have as yet anything like the drive needed to put these elaborate plans into force. They inherited a very good Civil Service machine from the British but it is not the right kind for their jobs.

(3) The current plan is quite ambitious and the tentative plans for going further ahead (10 or 15 year plans from 1961) are even more so. The biggest job will be to raise agricultural production which is a frightful job as it is in the hands of innumerable small peasants. And even if they got production up they will have a fearful job to get hold of the proceeds. Planning of their kind is done on the basis that the Government can dispose of the increments in the National Income but in a democratic country the pressures will be, already are, the other way: to raise the standard of living and improve housing and social services, which ought to come very late in the list. The UK got its expansion by treating the workers rather harshly during the early stages of the Industrial Revolution, thus accumulating big profits to finance more development. The USSR did the same by using the power of the State to hold down living standards in order to permit industrialization. Now it is getting huge dividends, but *now* is 40 years since the Revolution. Democracy in India is very like democracy here and the pressure to do something about current poverty is very severe.

(4) There is also a lot of confusion in high places between output and employment, which reflects the same thing. This finds its sharpest expression in the programme for cloth production, where they are actually holding down mill output to encourage a very inefficient village production. It would be far better to produce cloth cheaply and to find work for the villagers at almost anything that would be additional to current production.

(5) The level of industrial management, as seen in the DVC [Damodar Valley Corporation], is quite high. It is a great thing to know that if they succeed in industrializing themselves, they will have the men to do it and to run it. But they ought to turn some of their best industrial brains on to the agricultural side.

When I left London I was under the impression that Suez was settling down after we had agreed to refer the dispute to the UN. And so far as I know all the other officials had the same idea, indeed I doubt if I would have been able to go away if it had been suspected that the blocking of the Canal was so near.

I was therefore very much surprised, as well as appalled, to hear about the invasion which I did the day after I reached Calcutta. The Indians were very nice about it to me personally throughout the whole of the trip but made no secret of their views, and particularly that we *must* be hypocrites or we would have attacked Israel the aggressor rather than Egypt which was attacked. It was very uncomfortable and as I felt much the same as they did I felt much disturbed. It seemed incredible that one's own Government should act in what seemed so reckless and wanton a way without consulting anyone, officials, the Opposition, the USA, the Commonwealth.

At first I felt fairly sure that there would be enough Conservatives against the Government to compel them to withdraw but as time went on this was not realized, and though I suppose the cease-fire was a victory for the moderates, the fact that we made conditions (and are still making them) meant that we seemed to be acting grudgingly and with a bad grace.

I saw the PM Mr Nehru for an hour in Delhi and he was very realistic I thought – he said it was a great problem to say what one felt truthfully and yet not to make things worse. He was also very good on Hungary, making what I thought was the biggest deduction, that the USSR must be very startled to find that after 9 years' pressure to Communism, they were so unpopular that a revolution broke out the moment their troops went. We lunched with Malcolm MacDonald who must be very miserable, but did not talk about Suez at all.

After the invasion I sent a telegram saying that I would return if needed but N. Brook replied that it didn't seem necessary though I was to keep in touch. However, another telegram came about November 18th saying that I was to come. I said I had to go through with the Delhi talks but would come as soon as I could after that and in the end we got a 'plane on November 24th and I was in the office by Monday 26th.

In a way the most encouraging thing is to find that *all* senior officials, as far as I can see, are violently opposed to the Government's action and feel that it was disastrous. I gather that Ministers have avoided officials as much as they could and only talked on detailed matters.

The economic situation is very dangerous because of the rapid run-down of the reserves. The US disapproves of our policy strongly and it has become difficult for us to borrow from the Fund, or against the RFC securities, because until we have left Egypt they are more against us than for us. Apart from the reserves, the oil position is poor and has been made a bit worse than we expected because there is no official US encouragement, though we can buy from private companies. However it seems to me that there is a real danger that we will be driven off the present exchange parity, purely for speculative purposes, and I doubt if sterling as we know it now could stand the shock of another move so soon after 1949.

I have been writing memoranda on the economic situation and have recommended both fortifying the reserves, and an increase in taxation in order to try to offset the loss of external income due to our not getting Middle East oil.[18] The Chancellor has to make a statement on Tuesday about the reserve loss (probably over $300 mn this month) and at present he wants to announce tax changes. But we are to talk to him about the statement tomorrow.

I have seen quite a lot of R. Makins and for once T.L.R. and I are very much in the same camp. I am told that Ministers are all agreed that we *must* leave Suez soon and that this is the only way to restore US relations and to make some headway against our economic troubles. But their own back-benchers say they will revolt if this is done. So the Ministers are playing for time; it seems to me very irresponsible with so much at stake, not only the future of sterling but what is left of our position in the world. I tried to see R.A.B. but G. Wilson said it wasn't necessary: he understood the economic jam and was trying to persuade himself to face his back-benchers, without much success.

Leslie Rowan wrote a note on what we would do if we were forced off the rate. I did not agree with it at all and think he is assuming that we will be stronger at that time, or more able to control events, than we will be. I would let the rate float and not support it, in the expectation that panic sales of sterling would soon stop because it wouldn't be worth the while of the holders to get rid of it at low rates. Our current position is still quite good though it is worsening.

The oil shortage will probably cause some dislocation here both in itself and because it will put an overload on the railways. I think there is bound to be some unemployment but this must be accepted now when the balance of payments is so weak.

Wednesday, December 5th

Things moved rather quickly after that, with an enormous amount of cabling to and from Washington. The general effect was that they would do nothing until we announced a definite withdrawal from Suez, but would be as helpful as possible after that. Harold Caccia [UK Ambassador] must have had a busy time so soon after his arrival, and I think it is clear that Bill Harcourt's personal relations with Humphrey must have been enormously helpful, as they were able to speak quite plainly but stay on good terms. Anyway the details were settled by the weekend but it was not entirely clear whether our statement on Monday [December 3rd] would be satisfactory.

In fact it turned out to be quite all right; it was really very definite as to our going and made no conditions, in fact it was a complete climb-down. Meanwhile the US were very worried about sterling and I think genuinely concerned about Anglo-US relations. At any rate Humphrey became completely helpful about our application to the IMF and practically on our side about the Waiver on the Loan.

My statement on the economic position [EA(56)92] was circulated to EPC. The Budget Committee recommended tax increases but IR said they couldn't put up income tax because of PAYE complications (or rather that it would put an almost unbearable load on their staff) and in the end we had to settle for a shilling [5p] on petrol and Derv and only vague noises otherwise about Income Tax in April and watching the position. The Junior Treasury Ministers, especially H. Brooke [Financial Secretary 1954–7], violently opposed the petrol tax as they thought their back-benchers would revolt. It seemed to me that a severe statement would do a lot of good and all Treasury officials felt the same and so did the Chancellor who managed to convince his colleagues and has, I think, improved his own position as a result.[19]

Anyway we somehow produced a statement both about the way we were going to fortify the reserves, and about internal measures: and most of us went to the House yesterday afternoon to hear it. It was taken very seriously, the House almost entirely quiet, and afterwards Harold Wilson made a very good speech, as helpful as he could have been in all the circumstances. Then there were a few more exchanges and these were nearly all on a technical rather than controversial plane. Altogether it went off well, and the Press this morning has been fairly good. But it will take a few days to know what the overseas reactions will be.

Hall-Patch lunched with me yesterday and told me that his impression (he is now Chairman of the Standard Bank of South Africa) was that there was a big bear position in sterling: and if so it will probably be closed now since there cannot be the resources to go much further on the bear side and these big supplements to the reserves will take care of them. But we do not know how much there is a tendency for holders of the sterling balances to take them away altogether. I was certainly given the impression in India that they considered this question from time to time.

Whatever be the outcome here, I cannot feel any doubt that our intervention in Suez has been a disaster from a political point of view. One hesitates to say that anything is an economic disaster for a country, short of a serious loss in productive facilities or in external income. But we have certainly lost a big slice of our external income so long as the Canal is closed, and we must wait and see whether this is all there is to it. The political situation at home is very obscure, since a majority of the country appear to be in favour of the Government. But I think that informed opinion is increasingly against them and I am practically sure they will lose the next election by a substantial majority. However I do not think they will resign and it is a bit hard to see anyone to succeed Eden since Butler is disliked by the right and

Macmillan by the left. It seems a tragedy that we have to go on with such a bad PM.

Wednesday, December 12th

We have now borrowed or got on a stand-by $1300 mn from the IMF. As soon as the Canal withdrawal was clear, the Americans became very friendly and Humphrey was most helpful. But Harcourt obviously did a very good job indeed – the whole thing was handled with great skill and determination.

Here there was a bit of an outcry about petrol and the [Economic] Planning Board was quite hysterical about it – said it was the worst possible tax and would wreck the price plateau and price and wage stability, etc.[20] I do not believe a word of it and it was clear that none of them had read the Chancellor's statement. However it was something to have their views and partly as a result of them it has been announced that it is a temporary tax.

Things look a little better now than they did.

(a) The IMF loan will stop the speculation which was the big danger.
(b) The Government has at least done something deflationary.
(c) The chances of getting through this wage round on a 3% basis are very much better.
(d) The November trade returns were very good indeed.

I like R. Makins and get on very well with him – it is a great change that B.W.G. is gone and a great change that R.M. has a bit of time. He is the personification of energy and action instead of their opposites as B.G. was.

E.P. lunched with me today but didn't say much new except that Salisbury was away ill during the crisis and that if he had been here he would have insisted that we kept more in step with the US. He confirmed my views on Eden and said that R.A.B. was now disliked from both sides.

Otherwise we talked mainly about the need to cut defence and have a bigger investment programme. And he plugged as he always does the need for less taxes on earned income.

III

Thorneycroft's Chancellorship, 9 January 1957 to 6 January 1958

Although the economic situation after Suez had been alarming, the outlook rapidly improved. The revelation of British weakness, however, had a profound effect on opinion. There was a widespread uneasiness and a disposition to pursue more stringent financial measures.

Macmillan, after one year at the Treasury, succeeded Eden as Prime Minister on January 9th and Thorneycroft became Chancellor, again for one year only. The day before he left the Treasury, Macmillan had called for a cut of £200 million in defence expenditure and £80–£100 million from the social services. Thorneycroft aimed at similar economies in public expenditure and pursued them throughout the year. At the official level, OF were willing to support further deflation in order to improve the balance of payments and rebuild the reserves. The balance of payments remained in surplus in 1957 and inflation was appreciably lower than in the previous year. Public opinion, however, was said to be increasingly restive over the continuing rise in prices and the high wage settlements underlying it. The anxieties surrounding prices and wages contributed to the crisis in September.

Early in the year the Governor of the Bank of England suggested the appointment of a committee to examine the working of the monetary system. The committee was appointed in April with Lord Radcliffe in the chair and took extensive evidence, including a great deal from the Treasury and the Bank, before reporting over two years later in June 1959. Hall refers frequently to the committee and to the evidence submitted to it.

Thursday, January 10th 1957

Last night the PM resigned and as I write (about 4 p.m.) the gossip that Macmillan is to succeed him has been confirmed and the Office has begun to speculate about the next Chancellor – the obvious names being Thorneycroft, Heathcoat Amory, Eccles and Macleod in the Cabinet and Maudling not in the Cabinet. It would be a big jump for Macleod though perhaps not greater than Gaitskell's. I very much hope it wouldn't be Eccles and can hardly believe it would. Thorneycroft probably has the best claim on his record and Amory on his party standing.

However all this is a complete surprise to me – I knew that the PM was not very well and all sorts of rumours had been going around about his health, including the one that he was given a drug to cheer him up when he was taken ill at University College Hospital when he visited his wife in October, and that his extraordinary aggressiveness and self-possession until he collapsed were due to that. I suppose if I had been more awake I would have deduced that this was on the cards. When I lunched with R.A.B. last Thursday January 3rd he told me that either he or Harold would probably be PM in a few weeks because A.'s health was so poor. But I doubt very much whether anyone knew that it was coming quite so soon. I should think that the PM's intestinal troubles are somewhat affected by his state of mind and that the obvious failure of his policy and the gradual change of public opinion gradually affected what must have been bad health anyway.

The speculation both in the morning papers and in the Office put the chances at about 6/4 in favour of R.A.B. Though on personal grounds (and I think on grounds of my own personal position) I would have preferred him, I do not think he really has the character that England needs in a Prime Minister and on the whole I think the new PM has. No doubt the Queen decided as she did mainly because Salisbury told her that the Suez group would be very unhappy – I imagine publicly oppose – if R.A.B. had been appointed. But no doubt also both he and Winston thought H.M. was more the man for it, though no doubt they had been feeling for some time that Eden was anything but.

Now of course there is considerable speculation in the Treasury about the new Chancellor. I should say that Thorneycroft is the favourite and he has certainly done well over monopolies and the Customs Union though I am not too sure about him fundamentally. Amory is in good standing with his party and did very well at the Board of Trade. Macleod is freely mentioned but he seemed to me to be treated by the three Senior Ministers as a small boy during the various talks on wages last year and I find it hard to see him getting such a step [up]. Maudling is rather junior and very much a Butler man though perhaps R.A.B. would press him. I can hardly believe that Eccles would be regarded by anyone as a good choice. Finally I have a vague feeling that Sandys is a strong candidate – he is tough, a right-wing Tory, well connected. He has made a very bad reputation in his handling of staff in the Ministry of Housing and I have twice sat next to him at a Magdalen gaudy and found he would not say a word to me. So I do not relish the idea.

It is, I think, practically certain that H.M. is a man of courage and of independent ideas and as I have not got to know him at all well it would be idle to suggest that I have any idea among all the above. Clem Leslie suggests that Selwyn Lloyd might be moved here to make room for R.A.B. at the FO but this seems to me unlike H.M. and I would think it more likely that he would dispense with Lloyd. Finally it is said that Lennox-Boyd has been a good Secretary for Colonies and has some claims. We shall no doubt know by Monday if not before. I would not risk any money on anyone.

The new Chancellor will have a wonderful opportunity if he is any good and has any imagination, as the economic outlook seems to me to be almost rosy – I mean that if one looks round the skyline it looks dark and grey but if ever the sun was near the horizon and ready to make it pink it is now. This is indeed so obvious that a number of commentators and especially Roy Harrod and Nicholas Davenport are saying so very loudly already. The three great uncertainties are

(a) when the Canal will reopen;
(b) what will happen in this wage round;
(c) what will international confidence be in sterling.

(c) is of course partly dependent on the answers to (a) and (b). The prospects for the Canal are very uncertain, not that of clearing it which now looks like March/April for most ships, but whether we can use it freely when it opens. The Egyptians are still bargaining and are aware that this hurts us much more than it hurts them. However I find it hard to believe that we won't be pretty well out of our production and foreign exchange difficulties by the middle of the year. Once this happens our balance of payments should recover rapidly and so should such production as has been dislocated by oil shortage, and especially car output.

On (b), the outlook is a little worse than when I wrote last – the 'bus men were given 7/6 [37.5p] a week instead of the 6/- [30p] that the Transport Executive were offering and this may be widely taken as showing that the Government are running away. It was done without consultation. But the size of the settlement was consistent with what we had been hoping for. The engine-drivers have accepted the 3% recommendation and this should weigh with the other railwaymen. The engineers are still negotiating about their claim but I do not think we shall have much trouble there.

The worst feature is that the coal workers have just asked for 19/6 [97.5p] extra a week for non-face workers, which is more than 10%. In general they have the best claim on economic grounds as obviously no one likes working in coal mines. But it looks the biggest slice and of course the most dangerous. It was premature for me to rejoice about the deferment of the bonus shift claim since the districts have mostly rejected it.

Anyway I do not regard these things as too difficult and meanwhile we can hold the disinflation and I would hope more or less hold it through the next Budget. As we are building up a large reserve of capacity we can clearly let up as soon as we feel it is safe to do so on balance of payments grounds and are through the wage round. The big tasks for next fiscal year are to expand investment again, and to get a permanent wage settlement and I have ideas on both of these.

The Governor wrote a letter to the Chancellor on December 20th saying that we were in the last ditch, would not be regarded by US business opinion as worth supporting again, and must have an overall balance this year – if possible by cutting Government expenditure. He asked that this be shown to the PM. At about the same time the Chancellor saw the new estimates which showed an above-the-line surplus of only £186 mn and an overall deficit of about £550 mn. This put him into a great flap and he put a paper to his colleagues asking for considerable reductions in defence and civil expenditure.[1] At the office meeting it was clear that he would be lucky to get £150 mn off the estimates but it seemed to me that if he got this he would do very well and even that was mainly desirable to improve our position for later advance. It was about all this that I had lunch with R.A.B. as he wanted to know if *I* thought an overall balance was a necessity. I told him I thought £150/£200 mn would be enough. He and the Chancellor and the PM saw the Governor the following day (or that day – I am not sure). H.M. did not tell the office that this was on foot but I gather that the meeting was very inconclusive. We have just done the first Budget Committee appraisal [BC(57)3]. However this is all very uncertain now in relation to office affairs.

PS. I went to see R. Makins at this point to ask if he needed any briefing for the new Chancellor or if I ought to stay in London over the weekend. He told me there was not likely to be any announcement before late Saturday or Sunday. Also that it would probably be Thorneycroft – 'better than Eccles or Sandys or Maudling'. He is clearly pleased at this turn of events and told me that the Governor had just been in to say the City much preferred H.M. to R.A.B. Whether they are sensible to do this is another matter. It seems to me practically certain that the Government will lose the next election and the appointment of H.M. will make it a little more certain. The fact that there can be an economic recovery may make some difference but I think that as time goes on Suez will look worse and H.M. will be a bit tarred with that brush.

Monday, January 21st

It *was* Thorneycroft, and I am glad as I think he is the best of the possibles. Eccles has gone to the Board of Trade, Sandys to Defence (I am told because Head [Minister of Defence] refused to agree in advance to the cuts H.M. wanted, while Sandys said he would try), Amory stayed at Agriculture and Food at his own request. Sir P. Mills is Minister of Power with Maudling as his Deputy. I think this is a good move in principle and I like R. Maudling. One can't tell about these super-men till they have tried but it is an imaginative move and indeed it is quite a lively Cabinet, and reflects the desire of the new PM to do imaginative things. I had lunch with E.P. last week and he told me that Salisbury tried out an enormous number of Tories as he wanted to be sure his recommendation would stick (he did not want to run any risks in his advice to the Queen), and it was quite clear that H.M. commanded much more support and that people felt they did not know where they were with R.A.B. He also said that S. was now feeling rather sad as he had not been consulted about any of the new appointments. So much for king-making. I feel on the whole that H.M. is more like a PM than R.A.B. though I think he is a bit *too* adventurous for these times.

We have two new junior Ministers: N. Birch as EST whom I hardly knew, and Enoch Powell as FST of whom I had hardly heard. We had a meeting of the BC with them and the Chancellor last week and it was most interesting. The Chancellor has obviously come on a lot in recent years and was very pleasant but also clear and firm. The main thing is that all three of them feel that they had better do what they believe in and don't try to hold votes too much, which I am sure is the right line. They want to economize a good deal on this Budget with perhaps a few minor concessions on the tax side.

I am not at all clear what the Chancellor really thinks about the economic situation – we had another meeting this morning to discuss the next Cabinet when P.T. is to go on with the economy drive H.M. began a fortnight ago. He wants a big slice off defence, £100 mn or so off Civil Estimates and say £60 mn off below the line. He might just get it off defence but I don't think he can collect £100 mn off civil and the wish to cut below the line was where my doubts were raised as he seemed a bit mixed between the need for expansion on investment and the need for economies.

Leslie Rowan feels that he is in the saddle now as having called up all these reserves he says we have nothing left to call up and that we must take extreme measures. My own feeling is that this is mainly a window-dressing operation and that before the year is out we shall do some relaxing. However it will certainly make the relaxing easier if he can get some cuts in Government spending first: but the problem is to present them when the situation is so temporary, at least if the Canal really is opened fairly soon. There is nothing at all firm on that yet as the Egyptians are really refusing to talk while Israel still occupies the Gaza strip and the forts at the head of the Gulf of Aquaba.

Meanwhile the Texas Railway Commission has again refused to extend the oil flow, for February this time – I think it is now very likely that we will have to make another cut on fuel oil. So far it has hardly affected anybody, but it is alleged by Transport and Fuel & Power that this is because people are living on their stocks.

Of the other Ministerial changes, I am glad R.A.B. has gone to the Home Office as he needs a Department, and not to the FO where I am told he wanted to go – indeed it is said that Selwyn Lloyd stayed at the FO so that R.A.B. wouldn't get it! I am glad H. Brooke is promoted [to Minister of Housing and Local Government] as he is a very virtuous and conscientious man though unfortunately no speaker. And I am glad E. Boyle has got a job [as Parliamentary Secretary at the Ministry of Education] though I hope that they did not choose education to remind people of R.A.B. in the Churchill Government – the circumstances are almost precisely opposite.

Wages are still somewhat uneasily balanced but I am still hoping for the best. Unfortunately prices are bound to go up in the next six months and this will make my great move a bit more difficult even if I persuade P.T. to make it. Altogether I have a very suspended judgment about the short run both for men and for circumstances; in the longer run I still feel quite optimistic.

Thursday, February 7th

Since I wrote last I have had a number of talks with Thorneycroft and also the junior Ministers, and taken Maudling to lunch. The Chancellor certainly wants to go on economizing and to have a Budget which is tough on balance, but he is not getting on very well in his talks with individual Ministers. I feel a bit uncomfortable because I do not think anyone at the top levels in the Treasury, and especially not the Chancellor, understands the general position on investment. The Chancellor has been trying to cut investment in the Nationalized Industries, and he takes quite a restrictive view on the atomic energy programme, for reasons connected mainly with below-the-line presentation, itself more a window-dressing than a real issue. All our work suggests that the Nationalized Industries or most of them should be encouraged to invest more and I am personally certain that as an insurance policy we ought to keep moving very fast on atomic energy.

I also feel that the Chancellor does not understand that the economy is more deflated than inflated so that he will have a margin to play with – and if he commits himself to basic investment he will reduce the margin and hence the pressure to relax in some other way.[2] The TIC is moving slowly in its long-term review [of investment] as Stevenson who is in charge is not at all familiar with the concepts he must use. He is depending a good deal on my people, Downie and Richenberg.

There is not much new on the Canal but my guess is now that it will gradually open between end-February and end-April and that we shall use it and pay all or nearly all the dues to Nasser. The UN is in a mess and the US does not know what line to take – the real trouble is that the majority of the Assembly are so against Israel, on a variety of grounds, that they are taking a line which cannot really be defended as either just or reasonable, particularly in the context of the Russian attitude to Hungary and the Indian to Kashmir.

The home situation is still surprisingly good, very little loss of production because of oil, and even the motor car industry picking up a little, though Ministers are still under heavy pressure to do something, especially on P. Tax. I think we are still moving slowly in a deflationary direction. No more evidence on the wage front but no news is not too bad news now and coal output is actually increasing. The Chancellor, whom I saw alone about wages, *seemed* quite keen on my proposals and when things settle down a little I will stir them up. He also is much more favourable to building controls than I had thought.

The Bank Rate is to be reduced this morning, in fact the news is probably out as I write. This has caused a great deal of disturbance in the office and illustrates once more, as I think, the irresponsible and cynical attitude of the Bank. As I mentioned earlier, the Governor wrote to the last Chancellor on December 20th saying that we must have an overall surplus or he would not answer for the £ and he asked that this should be shown to the PM, and there was actually a meeting at No. 10. I felt that some lowering of Bank Rate would be desirable later on but that we ought to wait as long as possible.

The whole strategy was to play up the weakness of sterling and the need for toughness and it has alarmed me recently to find that the Bank has been manipulating the money market and gilt-edged market so as to produce market falls in both long- and short-term rates. This was largely in order to assist their funding operations, which have been very successful: but we have been arguing that they could have been *more* successful and that at the least they ought to have let the long-term rate fall more slowly and have pressed more securities on the market.

Of course it is very easy to criticize them but it seemed to me that they were in danger of being too keen on technicalities and losing sight of the general objective. It is quite certain that all the arguments for keeping the market sweet in order to be able to fund apply just as strongly at *any* level of interest and that we have therefore lost some room for manoeuvre. Anyway it was clear that the technical conditions were being set for a fall in Bank Rate as they were in 1954 when we made, as I think everyone would now admit, an error which it took years of hard work to restore and which may well have had the principal part in the fall of R.A.B. But I did not dream that any decision would be taken without adequate consultation.

On Tuesday (February 5th) the Chancellor had a meeting about monetary policy and said that the Governor now wanted to lower Bank Rate [from 5½ to 5 per cent] for technical reasons, as he could only push on with his funding if this were done. He suggested February 14th as he said he could square Basle at the BIS [Bank for International Settlements] meeting and the clearing banks at lunch on February 7th.[3] The Chancellor said *his* reactions were against it and I said strongly that mine were – I was supported by N. Birch the new EST who felt that the Bank had created the conditions which now made it technically necessary. It was left as I thought that we were all against it.

At 11.30 yesterday (February 6th) Roger Makins told me that the Chancellor had been talked round by the Governor and was just going to see the PM and if he agreed the rate would be lowered at once, i.e. today. R.M. himself seemed to have been convinced and more or less said that it was too much of a fuss about a small matter. He advised me to put my views on record at once, which I did, pointing out that the move was contrary to all that we had agreed we ought to do and would not be understood. After lunch Evan Maude, the Chancellor's PS, came to see me with a message from the Chancellor that it was all settled but he took my points and would see me if it would help. I did not think it would.

The next stage was that the Chancellor had agreed to meet the City Editors at Brown's Hotel at 6.30 (long before this had come up) so I went and I was glad to find that they all thought more or less as I did. The Chancellor had thought it a good occasion to tell them not to take a reduction as a green light, and went as near as decency permitted to telling them that there would be an early reduction, leaving them to assume that today was the most likely. He inveighed against the symbolic significance of the rate but was not given much change and indeed was driven to promising that more advantage would be taken of the technical advantages alleged to be obtainable than I think he could safely promise. Anyway it was very nice for me that my fears had been confirmed so strongly and so soon. (I should say that Leslie Rowan felt even worse than I did and his first minute to the Chancellor had to be returned as the Private Office felt that it would not look very seemly on the files!)

This morning the Chancellor sent for Leslie and me at 10 a.m. and he was clearly in a very chastened mood though of course going through with it now. I had told Leslie that he must appear to be good-tempered and co-operative and he made a great effort and we had a very nice talk, in the course of which the Chancellor agreed *not* to let us be bounced like this again, and to see that any recommendations by the Government were properly processed, and also that he would make it clear to the House and to the Governor that he expected the funding would be carried out very forcibly to demonstrate that we were really still in a tough frame of mind. So it may be all right.

I have to lunch with D. Jay this morning, but am trying to see W. King at the Reform just after lunch before he goes to the Bank of England Press Conference and I to the House of Commons to hear the statement which the Chancellor has undertaken to make during questions. It may all turn out for the best if the Chancellor and R.M. remain shaken and put plenty of heat on the Governor but it is really very awkward indeed, at any rate to someone like me who feels that we must preserve some logical consistency in our speech and behaviour. It is certain that Roy Harrod, and probably the *Financial Times*, will claim that this is the endorsement of the views they have been pressing on the world for some time. And W. King tells me that *The Economist* will take the same line.

Monday, February 11th

I went to the House on Thursday to hear the Chancellor (P.T.) make his statement about Bank Rate. It went off fairly quietly and he refused to be drawn by Wilson and Gaitskell, beyond referring darkly to the sale of securities as a means of controlling the volume of money. This was a clear indication that we intended a Funding operation and in fact a big issue is to be announced tomorrow, I think of interminable stock, the first good move for a long time as it reduces these perpetual conversion operations.

Press comment on the Bank Rate was not too bad, the evening papers of course said it was a sign of a great turn for the better but the Chancellor's indoctrinees in the serious morning papers took the right line, and on the whole *The Economist* did, though they are a bit split as the front part people want to let up and the back part to go on being tough. So the leading article was called 'Amber over Green', i.e. go ahead if you do it cautiously.

I feel fairly clear that we could now relax a bit, but the longer we can put it off the better. The easing of hire purchase on cars has apparently caused a substantial increase of business; my own view is that the trend of car production will be upwards from now on.

The Chancellor has just gone to Paris for the OEEC discussions on the Common Market; these will show whether we can sell our idea of excluding agriculture. If this can be agreed most of the rest should be negotiable so long as the French don't back out.

For some time now we have talked about another Macmillan Committee, on Banking and Currency, but it seemed as if nothing would persuade the Governor, and indeed I was told that he regarded the report Compton, O'Brien, Allen and Hall did last year as the last word. However the US in the Message to Congress asked for just such a Committee there and this seems to have brought the Governor round as he has now actually suggested a Committee, so we are talking about terms of reference and membership. The present suggestions are Radcliffe (if he will do it which is unlikely), Bridges, Heyworth, Franks, Harcourt, Woodcock, Sayers, Cairncross – I have said there ought to be another Labour man and that the Chancellor should consult Gaitskell.

It is a very good thing that there should be an inquiry as all our ideas have changed very much since 1932 or whenever it was [1929–31]. Keynes was a member of the [Macmillan] Committee and it is his ideas which have caused such a radical reconsideration. But it may be a little awkward for us as I do not see how they can do it without considering the Budget. The Governor wanted Harrod but neither I nor R.M. nor P.T. wanted him – he is really too eclectic altogether. If it is finally decided it will probably be announced in the Budget.

Last year H.M. said he would review the statistics and these have been very much improved. The clear evidence from everyone that this was wanted at last removed Campion's inhibitions and he has done very well. We now publish quarterly National Income estimates.[5]

There is an Ecomonic Debate tomorrow and the EST [Nigel Birch] has to speak as the Chancellor is in Paris. I don't know how he will get on – I haven't heard him yet but he did not do his questions very well on the 7th when I was there - too offhand.

Wednesday, February 20th

I did not go to the Economic Debate but was told that the EST did not do at all well as he spoke as if he had to read out what he said but felt no interest in it. H. Wilson made rather a dull speech on very familiar lines – I don't think that he can do very much work on his speeches which are hardly constructive at all. But there was no life in the Debate.

The Chancellor and Eccles spent three days in Paris but they did not make much progress on the Common Market questions. E. Cohen told me that there was no agreement on anything except to go on having talks and that the Chancellor has taken on a very heavy load in agreeing to supervise the negotiations now to take place. Figgures and France are to be put almost whole time on this. Cohen also told me that Eccles feels his nose a bit out of joint because the Chancellor has taken too much of this work with him from the Board of Trade. I think that the whole thing is getting more sticky as the Commonwealth do not like the agricultural proposals of the Six, which amount to keeping as much of the market as possible to themselves and no doubt keeping high-cost French agriculture going.

The preparations for the Budget continue rather slowly, and we will not take a view till the end of next week when we have both the final estimates of next year's Income and Expenditure, and the latest NIF report. The picture is completely dominated by the fears the Government and the Bank have about sterling which seem to me to be a bit exaggerated unless one believes that Suez will hang on indefinitely. Since production has been stable for nearly two years during a period of very high investment, there can't be much doubt that there is a great deal of slack in the economy. And unemployment and unfilled vacancies both show this up very clearly though a bit less hoarding of labour would help.

The only big stimulus likely next year is the recovery of the motor trade when Suez is out of the way. Anyway there is quite a gap and if we were budgeting for full use of resources we could give away quite a lot. But for reasons of foreign confidence, the balance of payments, and price and wages stability at home, there is no intention of filling it and the question is essentially one of judgment about how slack to keep things. Leslie Rowan is taking a very austere line.

The Chancellor announced yesterday in the House that he was reducing the subsidies on school meals and welfare milk, and adding 10d. [4p] to the charge for the Health part of the stamp. This is estimated to save £37 mn next year and £57 mn in a regular year. There is to be a meeting of senior Ministers at Chequers this weekend to try to settle defence policy and once that is over we ought to know where we are on the estimates. Since it is nearly all psychological, I have been taking the line that we only need to get the same above the line surplus this year as last – the situation being more deflationary now than it was then. I suspect that the revised estimates will show that that gives us a little in hand.

We have discussed all sorts of tax reductions – the favourite is something off earned incomes above £2,000, but it might be possible to do something for investment either generally or selectively and I hope very much that what is done for the workers will be on indirect taxation so that we can get some result in the cost of living.

Petrol duty will come off then or near to then anyway. Incidentally we have had much less dislocation from oil, etc., shortages than we expected. The weather has been unusually mild, the miners have dug up more coal, and it seems that many people used fuel oil wastefully. The Derv and petrol rationing seems to have done hardly anyone (except the new car market) any harm and I should think that most people in the country would like petrol rationing to go on for ever.

The wage situation is still moving very slowly and no big settlements have been reached. There appears to be a strike likely at Briggs which is very silly of the men as Ford can take a strike better now than at most times.[6] However this is about a shop steward, not about wages. I still think we shall get this round with 3–4% increases. Altogether I don't feel that there is much to worry about in the economic outlook except Suez – where it is no good assuming anything – and the Continental feeling for sterling, which is I think linked with Suez.

Friday, March 1st

Ministers didn't get very far on defence at Chequers but the Chancellor is still hoping for [a cut of] about £100mn this year. We have just finished the Economic Assessment for the Budget Committee [BC(57)15] and it is to be taken on Tuesday. I have finally come to the view that we ought not to give away more than is saved on defence. This will make it the most austere Budget (in relation to available resources) of the post-war period. This is a tribute to the strength of the economy since no one is very worried by anything and apart from a few economists and journalists there is little pressure to relax. I was finally decided in my mind by (a) reports from the *Manchester Guardian* and the Banks that the general feeling of industry was still confident and bullish; (b) indications that the Bank of England wants to relax the credit squeeze, and the February banking figures which suggest that they have already relaxed it quite a bit.

I also think that it would be very silly to let up while Suez is still unsettled and that we ought to get as much good out of our deflation as we can before we start to spend it. But there is clearly a good time coming before long. Our estimates put output next year at about 1½% above this year, which will mean that in 5 years we have had very little expansion indeed.

Sir D. Eccles dropped a small brick in the House on Wednesday about the likelihood that Entertainments Tax would be reduced in the Budget. He was trying to be clever but instead of saying 'Use your brain' he said 'How else can you do it?' Yesterday there was a row and the PM made it worse by refusing any sort of explanation and also referring to 'loyalty to one's colleagues' which could be said to mean that he was sticking to Eccles although he was wrong. However it isn't much and in fact Chancellors *have* said in the past some of the things they were going to do.

I went to Cambridge last night to talk to the Marshall Society about problems especially of full employment. The general theme was that we still had to learn how to live with full employment and that this needed a change in our general habits of thought. In discussion people were more interested in wages than anything else.

The preparations to announce a new Macmillan Committee in the Budget are nearly over and we have got very simple terms of reference. R. Kahn seemed to me to have got hold of it and said he hoped there would *not* be a Committee as it would only whitewash the existing bad state of affairs whereas under a Labour Government it might do some good. I think he is being too pessimistic and that it will be impossible not to bring out the major snags when the Committee get down to them. The latest studies we have made suggest that we really have very little control over the banks indeed. All our estimates last year were badly out, and in any case they sold securities to increase their Treasury bill holdings in case they might have been squeezed on liquidity. In fact it was only the directive that did any good.

Thursday, March 7th

The BC accepted the Economic Section Assessment and recommended concessions of between £50 and £100 mn, which will be roughly equivalent to the savings on defence this year. The package of reliefs recommended are all rather small things – Earned Income Relief above £2,000, some PT reductions mainly in the pots and pans group, and a rather big concession for Overseas Trade Corporations. The main proviso was that we should not let up much, at any rate at this juncture, on the credit squeeze. We are to have this out with the Bank fairly soon. Meanwhile R.M. and I are seeing the Chancellor tomorrow morning to discuss the BC recommendations, to be followed by larger meetings. The first drafts of the Budget speech have been written and the date (April 9th) is to be announced this afternoon.

The general progress of the economy continues to be good. February unemployment is up on a seasonal basis, February balance of payments is expected to be back towards the last quarter 1956 figures, all reports suggest that this slack has been got without breaking anyone's confidence. The only danger I think is the other way, since January consumption seems to have risen quite markedly.

The reserves have not done too well but I think a great deal of this is due to the combination of the big oil payments, and the continuing uncertainty about the Middle East. Here the first bright spot since the Suez thing began took place yesterday, when Syria agreed to let the IPC start to mend the pipeline. Although the Canal has been steadily cleared it always seemed to me that we couldn't *count* on a reopening at any particular time, and with the Arabs so willing to pay almost any material price in order to keep up their prestige or just to be as bloody as possible. I think that Nasser may try to sell the opening of the Canal very dearly both in claims for damages, and in conditions about the dues. But the US is now pretty deeply committed morally to struggle against his being too intransigent. Anyway I think it is very likely that we shall begin to spend less dollars on oil in the near future. Our EPU position remains fairly good.

The US Government have now agreed to a very generous settlement on the waiver, on the bisque lines put forward two years ago by Humphrey. This, if approved, gives us $100mn straight away on last year's interest payment and a useful insurance for the future.

Taken as a whole, I think the outlook is quite good and the principal difficulty is the sterling balances, of which we are becoming increasingly conscious. The EPC have taken the Report of the Sterling Area Working Party and have asked for a number of studies.[7]

Wages are still an uncertain factor. The most striking thing about this round is the extreme slowness with which it is being taken, a good thing in itself. There may be a few strikes but on the whole I think we will settle at between 3 and 4% and that there won't be much serious industrial damage. The Farm Price Review is reaching its closing stages and it still seems likely that a fairly tough settlement will be imposed – this Chancellor has much less interest in farmers than either of the previous two.

The Free Trade Area has run into frightful difficulties because the French have persuaded the Six Messina countries to include the Colonies on a sort of preferential basis – their exports to the Common Market to have preference over competing products from other places, but the Six not to have unrestricted access for their manufactures to the Colonies market.[4] This was quite contrary to our original understanding and it is very awkward for us either to join in – since this would limit our exclusion of free entry for Commonwealth agricultural products, and also wreck what is left of GATT – or to stay out since French Colonies would then be treated much better than our own. This has clouded the first rapture among the Tory Party here and is giving the Chancellor some awkward moments.

Bryan Hopkin came to see me yesterday – he wants to give up the NIESR and to come back to the Civil Service preferably to the Economic Section. He says that the NIESR would probably like Christopher Dow to succeed him. I am getting my staff position a bit clearer in my own mind. Scammell is doing very well but Troup, the other man whom I took at last year's competition, has decided to leave after only two months. He got into financial difficulties and has been offered a better job.

Wednesday, March 20th

The Budget was settled last weekend after the Chancellor had been to Chequers to talk about it – we had previously reached agreement in the office about the amount and the measures, and were a bit nervous lest the PM who was worried about by-elections and strikes, should try to go for something easier. We are going for total concessions of about £100 mn which will mean a fairly stiff Budget when one thinks of the Government economies and also of the rather deflated economy. But I suspect that it is not as deflated as all that and would go moving up again at the slightest provocation.

Meanwhile there is a shipbuilding strike, and others threatened in engineering and railways, so the outlook is highly unsettled. I have been trying to persuade people that these strikes are not the end of everything and that we have to stand up if we are to have any hope on wages. The Chancellor seemed to take the same view but I think railways have given him cold feet and that he thinks we can't stand three at the same time.

Wednesday, March 27th

We are now well ahead on the Budget Speech. The Chancellor is less troublesome about it than any of his predecessors and Fred Atkinson is helping Maude, the PS, already so maybe it will go on quietly. If so, it will be about the first time.

The wages disputes are going very badly and have produced some alarms in the Treasury. It is really a defeat for the 'plateau', etc., and whatever may have been said privately, the pattern is again the Nationalized Industries making too big a concession. As I write the outcome of the other strikes is unclear but a good deal is lost already. At any rate the Chancellor is now well aware of the problem and we will do some work on it.

Otherwise the main doings have been on credit, seeing the banks etc. I must write in more detail on this when I have time. The Chancellor saw Franks and Robarts yesterday to ask them to go on being tough on advances.

Monday, April 1st

The background to the previous remark was that the Clearing Bank advances increased by quite a lot in the February statement and at the same time the Governor was saying to us that he felt sure that advances would increase this year and that they *ought* to.[8] This after he had been telling us that an overall surplus was essential if we were to have any hope of saving the £. So there was a sort of indignation meeting here and after a good deal of discussion Compton wrote a paper with Bank concurrence, the gist of which was that we could not do much on banks' liquidity because they could and would reduce their investments and hold more Treasury bills, and so we could rely only on persuasion.

The Governor was in South Africa but Mynors and O'Brien came. They said they would like to help if they could but couldn't; and finally the Chancellor saw Franks and Robarts and told them that they must continue with restraint. They said they would but that advances of the highest priority were bound to go up anyway – and I gather that the Treasury has been asking for help both for exports and for tanker finance.

What worries me in all this is the difficulty of persuading anybody of the enormity of the situation! When I tried under Cripps to get the Bank to agree that they were at least *responsible* for the monetary position I was at the centre of the matter, and when they refused to commit themselves I ought to have realized that this was a tactical and strategic matter but also had a trace of truth in it.

Anyway the Chancellor can say in his Budget Speech that he has been assured of co-operation. Radcliffe has agreed to be Chairman of the new Macmillan Committee and the sooner it gets to work the better for me, though I am afraid it may gloss over some of the defects of the present position. I can hardly suppose the Governor would have suggested it if he had not thought this and maybe he felt that if there were one now it would be better than waiting till after an election.

The Budget is practically ready and the speech almost written. The Chancellor, of whom my opinion becomes steadily more favourable, is a very easy man for the speech, more so than any of his predecessors I have known. He takes suggestions, makes his own, and so far has shown no signs of wanting to start all over again every week or two. I think that although about £100 mn in concessions is being made, it will remain deflationary since the OTCs will affect the balance of payments and thus the target there rather than home demand, and I doubt if the net effect of all the others will be more than £60 mn or so, against which the forecasts show a bigger surplus remaining than we had on last year and the economy is certainly flattening out except for consumption, and there must now be a lot of surplus capacity.

The Government is now in very deep water as Salisbury resigned on Saturday over the decision to release Makarios;[9] and two French journalists have just published a book about Suez in which it is made clear that in some sense or other Ministers here knew that the Israeli attack was coming; and that the inefficiency of the operation once it started was due to bad leadership, etc., from the UK side. It seems quite clear that we will have to pay Nasser full tolls at an early date, as our competitors' ships are already going through.

I think there must be some general irritation on Salisbury's part, judging by what E.P. told me especially about him not being consulted on Ministerial appointments. Altogether the PM is in a sea of troubles. His behaviour suggests that he is determined to be a strong PM and if he is that is a great gain as long as there is some sense in his strength. I am sure the decision on Makarios was right and indeed that we ought to have faced it long ago that the British are not the people to hold down a possession by ruthless methods.

The strikes are now well under way but I think there is some hope that in spite of the rail settlement – or perhaps because it is settled and economic life thus not at a halt – the engineers and shipbuilders will not get anything like what they have asked for. The most extraordinary things have been said and done from an economic point of view. Thus the *Queen Mary* was taken out of repairs before she was quite finished and the dockers have been trying to stop both *Queens* from sailing – apparently arguing that the ship repairers should have a veto on what ships should sail. The ASLEF has said that productivity has nothing to do with wages, and the shipbuilders that making concessions in the interests of greater output were so valuable that they ought to have more pay. As one of the newspapers says today, they want pay increases to persuade them to be less obstructive about productivity and more pay increases if any productivity increases materialize. I have been writing a long paper on the wage question, on very familiar lines, but arguing that the present idea that the Government should be 'impartial' and not interfere in wage disputes is all wrong.

Monday, April 8th

Tomorrow is Budget Day and we have been having last-minute reviews of the Speech and the briefing for Press Conferences and the sort of criticisms that may be made by foreigners and economists and the Opposition. There will certainly be arguments from overseas that the cuts in Defence have now been dissipated by tax concessions – I think these will be unfair both because there have been a lot of other economies, and because the concessions to ordinary consumption are very small, indeed I think the biggest Opposition criticism will be that the EIR [earned income relief] is far too generous to the rich and the purchase tax concessions too trivial for the poor. Clem Leslie has just been asking me the points that I think the Chancellor ought to make in his television appearance tomorrow night.

I do not feel much doubt that this is quite an austere Budget on any of the standards of the last 10 years. We start from a much more deflated position than in any year since 1952 and a much better balance of payments background than there was then. And on any calculations we can make, the net effect of Government operations this year will be more deflationary than last year. But on the other side, we feel fairly sure that consumption will rise both because of higher wages and because we won't get this year the temporary depressing effect of Hire Purchase and personal bank advances. There is a bit of a question mark about investment which is not booming but there is very little evidence that it is falling off either and the Nationalized Industries have got a good deal more they say they are going to do.

The mechanical preparations, if one can call them so, have been extremely easy because the Chancellor takes so little exception to what is drafted for him – his secretary Maude is also very phlegmatic and indeed has economized so much on typing and duplication that we have seen far fewer versions than usual, indeed I think he has overdone it as hardly anyone really knows what the final version will look like! Finally Roger Makins is new to the job and has not grown up in the aura of extreme agitation in which most of us were trained to regard Budget speeches so he has helped to keep the temperature down. I do not feel nearly as agitated as I used to do: partly old age, partly experience, but mainly that it is now all judgment and very little arithmetic, so that the old fear, that someone would prove that the sums were wrong and therefore *on his own premises* the Chancellor ought to have given more or less than he has done, has no grounds.

However it is still worrying as the time draws near to have so much dynamite lying round one's office and of course one cannot be absolutely sure of the reaction – though I don't think we are far wrong on this, the main uncertainty is the extent of the class feeling that is around. This may be quite strong because of the attempt to work up the view that this Government is going back on the welfare state. It suits the Trade Unions to play this up because of the wage disputes, just as it suits the Labour Party electorally. However the Labour Party is having a very bad patch and they have wasted most of their chances so that it may even be possible for the Government to live down the Suez affair.

The PM is coming well out of Salisbury's resignation, for both the reasons I thought possible. The Tory Party feel that the issue was a bad one to choose, therefore Salisbury's judgment is less sound than they thought. And *The Economist* has pointed out that it shows the

PM as stronger than was thought. However there is a violent storm among all our Allies about the Defence White Paper.

The labour situation is somewhat in the balance – the shipbuilders and engineers went back after cash offers of 5 and 3½% which was what they said they must have, and subject to courts of inquiry. There are now a lot of recriminations going on in the Unions. But I think there is a more militant attitude than I had supposed, for the first time since I have been in England I am reminded of the atmosphere in Australia in the 20s. Full employment and prosperity seem to have roused the spirit of the working man and the ingrained respect for the upper classes is probably being whittled away. It is therefore becoming crucial that the employers and workers should take productivity seriously, since we can only get on with a militant attitude if there are rapid increases in output.

The Radcliffe Committee is settled and all the members will be approached on Wednesday. I am beginning to do some work for the Treasury evidence which will have to be given. I think I ought to write a paper on the elementary theory of money for a start.

Two of my staff – Troup and Richenberg – have just resigned to go to better paid jobs in industry. It is rather a good thing as they are not fliers at all and I think I can do better – and it will help me to make a case for getting my salaries increased.

Tuesday, April 30th

I am now in a 'plane approaching New York. Leslie Rowan and I are going to spend the rest of the week in Washington before going to Ottawa for the Continuing Committee.

The Budget went off very well – the speech sounded quite clear and the Chancellor held the House for nearly the whole time. Most of the concessions were welcomed though there was some jeering about pots and pans and petrol – 'You put 'em on, you take 'em off'.[10] And the size of the Surtax concession was not fully grasped at the time. Anyway the Conservatives were clearly pleased which was very good for so austere a Budget. In fact Thorneycroft reaped a good deal of what Rab and H.M. had sown.

The Labour Party were in some difficulty in attacking the proposals and H. Wilson, who made a very entertaining and polished speech, was forced to attack the Government both for being too inflationary and for not stimulating production more. The only way we could have got what he wanted was to direct production into exports and investment. There was of course a good deal of criticism of the Surtax concessions on the lines that even if there was a case, the pensioners ought to get more money before the Surtax payers. But it did not seem to me that there was much fire in the attack. I did not hear Gaitskell, who tried to make a big statesmanlike speech but it did not appear too successful. Both the Junior Treasury Ministers made surprisingly good speeches, the result of a lot of hard work and Birch, the EST, made a very good impression because he learned his by heart and did not use notes – his eyes are so bad that he could hardly have read them.

The Defence Debate seems to have been a triumph for Sandys, mainly because he seemed to be looking more realistically at the problem. It is almost invariably the case that a bold man who has really worked at a subject makes a good impression. And yet we have so few real leaders in Parliament – I still think it is the fault of democracy but it may be that there just are not the men available who have the character and ability to lead and are at the same time good enough speakers and patient enough politicians to get on.

The Radcliffe Committee was welcomed but it is not announced yet as there has been some difficulty with the membership. Franks, Sayers, Cairncross and Harcourt all accepted and so did John Henry [Woods]. Heyworth did not, I think rightly if he could not spare the time. I suggested Verdon Smith of whom I have gradually come to have a high opinion, and I think he will accept. The main trouble is with the Trade Unionists. Heyworth refused and Radcliffe very sensibly said there ought to be two as they would comfort on another – so what I wanted, that is, another Labour man got after consulting Gaitskell, was more or less secured except that it was Tewson who was consulted. It will be Woodcock and another.

Radcliffe came to see me last week and we had a talk about what the Committee was for. I thought he was very sensible. I have written a summary of why it is needed as a background for any Treasury briefs. T.L.R. has produced a formidable document suggesting that it will need to go into the whole of external economic policy. I don't think he understands the difference between policy and the instruments of it.

The Investment inquiry is under way and will take a long time to finish but at least it has more steam behind it and is over the doldrums in which Richenberg put it by his delays.[11]

Otherwise the main news is on the wages front. The Court of Inquiry has recommended a general inquiry into wage problems and the M/Labour is backing this. So the Chancellor pushed on with his own paper which has turned out to be mainly written by me and in essence says (a) that the currency will lose its value if we go on in this way, (b) present policies have all failed, (c) Government must decide the amount of the annual permissible increase and do its best to make it effective.[12]

R. Makins has had several meetings with officials, mainly Ministry of Labour – they were horrified at first and even now find it hard to see how they can conciliate if they have to support a figure fixed in advance. So I say that we must decide whether conciliation or price stability is the more important object of policy. I doubt if Cabinet will really accept anything so drastic as I have prepared, or would have the nerve to carry it through if they did, but they are bolder than at any time since Cripps was Chancellor and it may go. If they adopt the plan, there will be a tremendous lot of hard work to do. Fortunately Stevenson, who is the U/S in the Treasury in charge on the HOPS [Home and Overseas Planning Staff] side, is a great enthusiast and feels that the scheme is at least half his, as it is, so he will put some drive into it if the Chancellor will find the time to be driven.

It is a pity that I am going away at this moment but I don't think it ever makes much difference if one changes one's plans. For instance it seemed to me that we became more urgent about withdrawing from Suez and getting the IMF and Exim bank credits, because I had come back from India. But I expect it would have happened in just the same way if I had not come, since Bill Harcourt, who was handling the Washington end, had exactly the same ideas as I.

This has been a very comfortable flight. Apparently BOAC customers prefer the Boeings to the new DC-7s because of the bar; anyhow they are still used for the Monarch which is the top service. It supports my theory that if you can fly London–New York overnight, you don't really want to go any faster until you can do it between meals or at any rate by day. And even then many people prefer a night – I certainly do because it is more of a rest. On this flight they have all the ground delays reduced to a minimum and this makes the whole thing far less tiring.

Friday, May 3rd (Washington, DC)

Leslie Rowan and I had lunch with the Federal Reserve people in New York and had a lively discussion about monetary policy. They have much more control over their banks than we do partly because there is not nearly so much paper out and partly because the Federal Reserve does not feel under any obligation to subscribe to Treasury loans – at least that is what they say. In fact the Government has to borrow what it needs at the market. It would be very interesting to get some idea of the *scale* of US operations in total compared to ours.

We flew to Washington in the afternoon and went to stay with Guy Thorold who has taken Harcourt's place as Economic Minister and also his house – it is where David Butt and I stayed when we were here with Attlee in 1951 – Empson had it then. Guy seems to me to have got himself established quickly and to be very good in his own way – he was here mainly on MEW [Ministry of Economic Warfare] business during the war but has got a good deal more force and assurance since then – I suppose all of us who have survived have done the same. We dined with the Coulsons that night and have been very busy since then, meeting mostly the same people at various parties.

The first was given by Sam Waugh now head of the Exim Bank but whom we had first met when he was Under Secretary at the State Dept. It had many of the senior economic people there and after lunch he made a very moving little speech, about how depressing Suez had been and how essential it was that we should never get into that sort of mess again but we always had been able to talk about things 'between friends with perfect confidence' and we always should. It was very consoling and indeed the whole atmosphere here is as good as ever. I know that was settled at Bermuda but it is clearly a genuine feeling. No doubt the failure of US policy to make any dirt on Nasser has helped.

I had a long talk to Saulnier, the successor to Burns at CEA. He is generally thought to be a rather weak man and it was hard to understand the appointment. Hauge told me that Burns had taken his job too hard and felt himself to be worn out – I did not like to ask him about why Saulnier was chosen. Anyway I did not get too far with him except a strong feeling that he is a Budget balancer.

The economy here is clearly not going to go into a decline – capital expenditure is holding up very well and so is consumer expenditure generally. The economic official world is worried about rising prices because of rising wages and I have had to talk about how we see it quite a lot. The Federal Reserve are determined to keep money as tight as they can, which they feel will be at least a contribution. They are under fire because of their tight policy, particularly because of the way it affects housing mortgages. But Win Riefler says that when he goes to talk to Congress, the Chairman attacks him for the record while all the other members of the Committee do their best to convey to him that they really strongly approve of the stand by the Fed.

Subject to the practical certainty that there won't be any serious decline this year – much more likely to be an up movement – there are really quite conflicting strands affecting the economy. There is a lot of pressure on the Government to cut the Budget presumably in order to cut taxes. And there is a lot of worry, let by the Fed., about the wage–price spiral. So there is quite a lot of support for tough and perhaps more-deflationary-than-now policies. On the other side there are expansionists of the Keyserling school, and all who want cheaper houses, and no doubt the Government in its anxiety to get a big Budget. But between them I should say that they will go on about as at present, with the Fed. as the dominant element against an economy which still seems to me to have inherently expansionist tendencies. Not a bad combination.

We have talked a good deal to Per Jacobsson who is now Managing Director of the IMF and he gave a dinner for us last night. I suppose one of the things we are trying to do is to rouse up some sharper feelings about Germany and we sowed some seeds with him – though he thinks they are going to pull out by themselves. We were told that a year ago and they are running a bigger surplus than ever.

Otherwise we talked to Gene Black [President of the World Bank] about the possibility of the Bank Loan for the Atomic Energy Programme which he would like to make in order to have the UK on his books and also to give his people some knowledge of the technical problems of atomic energy. We said it would be useful to us but not worth doing unless we were to get a fairly big amount. I think it might be very handy to be able to borrow between 1960 and 1965 when our investment programmes will be quite a burden on us. But it is premature to think in these terms now when we haven't decided whether to draw the Exim Bank loan or not.

I have given several accounts of the UK situation and the Budget – they are generally very pleased with us because we have been able to get the position in hand and I should think British credit in US circles is at quite a high level.

Harold Caccia has been at some of the talks and all the dinners. He seems to be doing very well and has a manner of putting things which is a great asset to a diplomatist – somehow managing to be impersonal and devoid of offence even if he is saying something awkward or unpleasant. And he has as much charm as ever. But it is early days to make more than a superficial judgment.

Sunday, May 5th

I am now on the way to Canada. The last day of the talks in Washington was very interesting. We lunched at the Treasury with Burgess and had a discussion afterwards but not much happened. It was much pleasanter than it was eighteen months ago when T.L.R. had almost made a scene about the waiver – now it was safely through. The combined effect of their guilty consciences or perhaps one should say misgivings about Suez, and their feeling that we have been sensible internally, has done us a lot of good.

After the Treasury I took Kit McMahon to see Saulnier and it was most interesting. He started slowly but began to talk very freely after a while. The two things that transpired were that he has inherited Burns's feelings of irritation at the Fed. Reserve tight money policy (see entry for Sept. 30th above) and would be much happier if they eased up a bit and allowed the economy to expand. The second one is that he is an extreme empiricist which he got from Wesley Mitchell and Burns at the National Bureau. He told us that all their indicators showed that the US was or at any rate ought to be in a severe slump.

Apparently (though I have not read the articles) they studied trade cycles in the past and collected a lot of indicators which led, or lagged, or were contemporaneous with, the peak of the trade cycle. And all the leaders turned down some time ago. The 'diffusion index', which measures the relation between (for all the members of the series) where they ought to be and where they are, also suggested the same. As there are 200 items in the series it seems to be Chartism at its worst and it is queer that they have not re-examined the whole thing.

I can remember quite well when Wesley Mitchell was a visiting professor in Oxford and told us about this. Beveridge tried to do the same in a paper he read to the British Association in (I think) 1937 or 1938 but I had thought all this was dead, attempting by tremendous study to wrest the secrets from something that is well understood. Like alchemy persisting after the rise of chemistry. But I take it that Saulnier's discomfort arises from both alchemy and chemistry as his staff are certainly chemists.

Then I went to the Fed. mainly to ask Win Riefler about whether he would welcome a delegation from the Radcliffe Committee, if they wanted to come. I hope they will. Riefler is of course preoccupied with the wage–cost–price cycle and he and Martin want to keep things tight for ages yet. He showed me a draft he had done for a resolution by Congress affirming the need to prevent wage increases in one sector from taking away from other people their opportunity to share in the general increase in production. This is one of the thoughts I had in the paper which the Chancellor put to Cabinet. This is basically the way to do it since I am sure that monetary restraint alone will not succeed.

Finally I had a talk to Sam Katz who is going to London with a sort of Rockefeller Fellowship which they give to public servants. He wants to work on monetary problems from the NIF stage which sets the deficit requirements to the final operations of the Issue Dept of the Bank. He seemed to be very pleased with the way we had been managing our affairs, and as he is on the European Dept of the Fed.'s foreign intelligence section, he has no doubt played some part in the generally favourable atmosphere we have so obviously created.

I see that I have not said anything about the Common Market or the Free Trade area, though in fact we have talked a good deal about that here. We were anxious to remove an impression which US posts in Europe have been passing through, that we were trying to sabotage the whole idea. We had been trying to stop this in London and could not find out how it started. But we also wanted the US, who are very keen on the Common Market politically, to help us to get the Free Trade Area going and to push it in a multilateral rather than a two or three world direction. And as Arnold France is doing so much of the work in London it seemed a good chance to get him to make progress reports, which he has been doing.

After I finished at the Fed. on Friday, Marget gave me a lift back and told me that it was *Marjolin* who was saying that we were the wreckers – presumably because we are trying through OEEC to get the Common Market modified so that it can be a full participant in the Free Trade Area. It is only too likely that Marjolin would be taken seriously by the US people abroad – Marget told me because he hoped we *would* block the plan. It has been running into very heavy weather in Paris – that is to say, our plan has – because the Six won't discuss any changes. They say they are exhausted but it may be that they or at any rate the French want to alter nothing, as our conditions would require. Anyway I am sure there is a lot of trouble to come yet.

Tuesday, May 7th (Ottawa)

I am just leaving Ottawa for New York and London. I got here on Sunday and stayed with Jo Garner [British High Commissioner] at Earnscliffe, where Frank Lee and Alan Hitchman also stayed. Leslie Rowan and France came up the day before and the whole party had been to see the Seaway and were much impressed by the hydroelectric works. We had a Delegation meeting after dinner but not much to talk about: then spent a good deal of Monday on the current economic situation, which was not very interesting.

Canada expects to expand again this year and on the whole they think that the US will, as I do; though how much depends to some extent on how tight the Federal Reserve can keep things screwed down. We talked a bit about whether the US would become more protectionist and they said they thought it wouldn't amount to much. I think I agree with this, that it will be more bark than bite but again it depends a bit on how much they are held down.

Leslie Rowan thinks we are on the edge of a dollar shortage, because disinflation stimulates their exports and Congress will cut foreign aid. I think that this is possible and equally that more protection is possible. But after so many years in which we were apprehensive and they managed so well, I don't feel that we would be justified in doing anything or saying anything till we were fairly sure. The Canadians complained bitterly about the surplus disposal especially of wheat.

Leslie then raised the question of Germany and said that we were very worried about the contrast between what they said they would do and the way their surplus and their reserves went on rising. Rasminsky made a very useful contribution, both saying that they ought to let the exchange rate rise, and that it ought to be discussed in the IMF. So maybe what with Washington and Ottawa we have made a little progress in winning friends and influencing people.

Then Arnold France made his prepared statement on the Free Trade Area and this was debated the next day. The Canadians spoke entirely about the Common Market and said that they were alarmed by the Treaty of Rome because it seemed to them to be a move towards regionalism and away from multilateralism. At the GATT session they had asked Snoy if it was intended that the Common Market institutions would override GATT and the IMF; and Snoy had said that there was no conflict but if there was the Six would expect automatic dispensations. This the Canadians would certainly oppose: and they would consider it necessary to recover full liberty of action and to renegotiate all their present bindings, if necessary bilaterally, if the Six went on as they well might do.

Plumptre [Ministry of Finance] said that Canada was now becoming a consumer of all her own food except wheat and that farmers had not shared in the prosperity of the rest of the country. Therefore farmers were less interested in exports and more in protection. Therefore we could not expect in future that farmers would oppose protectionist moves by manufacturers. Indeed there was a hint that it might be useful if the Six broke up GATT because this would provide cover for what they would be compelled to do politically.

All this was very interesting and instructive but it practically ignored our plea that they should help us to get the Free Trade Area set up, as the best form of guarantee against excesses by the Six. So we asked them explicitly if they would give what help they could both in opposing forces in the Customs Union which were making difficulties about negotiating the FTA, and in lending public support to the FTA in Paris and elsewhere. They asked for time and after lunch said that they could not (since Ministers were hardly accessible) go beyond what

St Laurent [Canadian Prime Minister] had already said, which was a general welcome to European integration plus reservations about the trade aspects.

Arnold France then made a remarkable statement about the advantages which would be gained by negotiating the FTA because our concept would be fully consistent with the Collective Approach and because we intended to do all the running of it through OEEC where Canada and the US were associates. It then became clear that the Canadians had been so upset by the Customs Union that they had not really taken in, up to that point, the arguments we had been pressing on them to get their support of the FTA. And indeed that we ought to have sent them a written note of our views – which I later proposed that we should now do.

The rest of the talks were on the usual things especially the slowness with which we are taking away q.r.s on Canadian products and the delay in deciding the apple quota. We had made some concessions on honey and canned salmon: and we all said we would give the travel allowance to North America as soon as the moment at home came, i.e. that it would not seem as if we were easing up. Leslie made a very good statement about how we had to pay back the IMF credit and this was so important that we ought not to lose sight of it for a moment. It is all more psychological than real to my mind, since we have slack in the system at home and since transferable sterling is so very near American account sterling.

I talked to Coyne and Rasminsky [Governor and Deputy Governor of the Bank of Canada] about their Central Bank problems and about our Committee, and I think that they would welcome any inquiries. They would really like to have an inquiry into their own system, as their relations with their banks are far from watertight.

Last night I talked to the local branch of the Canadian Political Science Association, about the relation between economists and Government. It was on the lines of the Sydney Ball Lecture but a good deal more philosophical and reaching the conclusion that the ideal would be that all top policy officials knew enough about economics for it not to be necessary to have economic advisers at all. Unfortunately I realized only after the talk that they had very nearly reached this position already in Canada, so the talk fell rather flat because they did not really see what was worrying me.

When I got back to Earnscliffe the Garners and Frank Lee were still up, and Hitch came in later, and we had a long talk about what was wrong with the UK Civil Service – mainly that the pay was too low but also that full employment had made business offer much more attractive openings to young men than it used to. They also thought that the prestige of the service was much less than it had been apart from the effects of the economic changes. I don't feel too sure about this; it seems to me that top Civil Servants still have plenty of prestige and that this continues down the line. But it is hard to maintain prestige when you can't even live in the sort of way the people you meet do. I have noticed it especially at the Assistant Secretary level, where it is impossible to keep up anything like pre-war upper-middle-class standards, although Assistant Secretaries ought at least to be regarded in that light. I think that one of the troubles is that the Civil Service is so big that it makes too much of a stir if the salaries are raised. But nowadays the different attitudes of business and the Civil Service to expenses make a great deal of difference.

We also talked a bit about the position of economists and I argued that in economic departments people ought not to be moved round so much. But Garner argued strongly that they should be moved more, to broaden their experience – I think he was thinking more of geographical than job movements.

Frank Lee, who is a very sturdy advocate of women in the Civil Service, nevertheless was very warm on the subject and said that one of the effects of the lessening attraction was that more and more women would come in. And 'they were a thorough nuisance' because either they married and left, or they married and stayed and needed special treatment, or they stayed unmarried and got neuroses. I expect that either from Estab. or for personal reasons or both he has been suffering lately as I do not think he used to feel so strongly. Of course there is something in the neurotic point, though not as much as there used to be now that it is so much more usual to have affairs even if you do not marry. And even men have neuroses. But on the whole I think it is true that women are not so forceful as men, grade for grade, and that this has a physiological basis. Women could not cope with children at all unless someone gave them some help and this tends to be a man – and it would be contrary to natural selection if this did not mean that women had better survival value if they could get a man to look after them, than if they were able to look after themselves. Thus women who would have made good top Civil Servants would not have been so likely to have had adult children as women who would not have made top Civil Servants.

The more I think about it the more I come to the conclusion that the *only* principle of any philosophical validity in the field of moral philosophy or the ends of life rather than the explanation of the world – is that of survival. One cannot deny that qualities that do not survive have in some sense less validity than qualities that do. Thus truth in the logical sense will prevail because by and large those who recognize facts are likely to do better than those who don't. But right will only prevail to the extent that those who believe in it can survive. 'Treason doth never prosper, what's the reason? Why if it prosper none dare call it treason' – God is on the side of the big battalions.

I don't mean that moral principles in the ordinary sense are completely bogus if they give people the idea that they have any strength in themselves. But those who hold them must make them valid. That's why I think that it is of very doubtful validity to argue that we should extend the principles of free society to Communist citizens. It is said that if we are fighting for freedom we must not contradict it. But there is already a contradiction in tolerating what you are fighting against.

These are unhappy thoughts when one is faced by someone like McCarthy (who has just died very unlamented all over the world) and yet I think it was his methods not his ideas that were wrong, i.e. he did more harm than good in trying to establish that it was better that 20 innocent men should suffer than that one guilty one should escape.

Thursday, June 27th

The main activity since I got back from North America has been in getting ready for the Radcliffe Committee, the membership of which was announced while we were away. E. Compton and I went to see the Committee at its second meeting, to tell them why the Treasury thought the inquiry was needed – I made the two points, that we needed advice on the extent to which we should rely on monetary measures, and on the mechanism by which they should be used if it were decided to use them. R. Makins has a Committee to co-ordinate Treasury thinking, on which O'Brien of the Bank sits.[13] The Banks are turning out rather undistinguished papers at a rapid rate, and we are trying to write some.

I have the main responsibility for the paper giving a critical account of recent years. This is bringing out very clearly the imperfect nature of our thinking on the subject, and the very bad co-ordination in policy matters between ourselves and the Bank, which stems from the fact that the Governor talks privately to the Chancellor, and neither he nor the Chancellor normally tells their respective staffs what goes on. The Governor has usually spoken to Bridges or Gilbert afterwards but I don't think these conversations have helped much.

Our studies also make it clear that we have never properly faced the question of the interest rate policy we should have adopted, nor whether we needed directives as a permanent element. A year ago it seemed possible to argue that an active funding policy would give us control over liquidity ratios, but I am coming more and more to the view that it is a labour of Sisyphus, since so much old debt comes up for reconversion every year and there is no real incentive to the banks to hold long-term securities when they can earn *so* much on shorts.

I have had several talks to O. Franks and one to Sayers – I gather that they are at opposite extremes about the range of the Committee's studies, Sayers wanting to stick to the technical end and Franks to cover the whole field of economic policy. It is very interesting and beneficial to have to concentrate on this subject for a while as it makes one realize the intricacies of it.

The wages/prices battle is making very slow progress but it is hoped that the names of the new Committee of Wise Men [Council on Prices, Productivity and Incomes] and the job they have to do, will be announced before the House rises. I want the Chancellor to have another go at his colleagues to rub it into them that this Committee will only be a piece of machinery and not a substitute for resolute action. The last wage round is now over and looks as if it will be about 5½%

which is at any rate better than the nearly 8½% of the previous year. As prices won't rise by more than 2 or 3% this year, we have a good chance of getting a smaller increase next year if we are prepared to be tough about it. But at present all the Nationalized Industry prices are going up because of the last lot of wage increases.

The economic system remains well in hand and we have got over the Suez crisis with very little trouble. The balance of payments forecasts make the next 12 months look like a period of a very substantial surplus.[14] Production is rising now and I don't feel at all worried about the rate of progress. Indeed, the big study on investment which is now going on suggests that the load is going to be too big for us: though at present things are well in hand. The main troubles now are certainly connected with the belief that we shall go on inflating – partly that wages and prices will continue to rise and partly that the growth of investment will create a demand inflation again. I am not so much afraid of the latter, as I think we can control it, as I am of the former, where the outlook must remain bad and the only hope a strong Government and an informed public opinion. However we are doing something to create this and I think people are now really tired of constantly rising prices.

Herbert Brittain is retiring tomorrow and (I am told) is to be replaced by Tom Padmore. I am sorry Herbert is going and think that he has been on the whole a force for good though not a very strong one. He really understands the Treasury, he carries out policy loyally and resolutely, and when he can understand an issue he is in favour of strong action – for instance he has consistently supported the use of stronger methods to get the Bank and the banking system to conform. His main weakness in my time has been that he has never initiated anything or even been conscious of the changes of problem until these were pointed out to him. In fact a good dependable subordinate rather than a leader, in thought or action. But how much better in all respects than Eady or Gilbert.

I do not know how Tom Padmore will turn out as I have never seen him in a tight spot, or indeed doing any work of a non-Establishment kind – the Establishment work at a high level was done first by Bridges and then by G. Bush and at a low level it is very different from ordinary Treasury work, though probably needing the same qualities. At any rate the question mark is whether he will have enough force and drive.

After months of doubt and anxiety, Jack Downie is at last to be promoted. I do not know what I would have done if this had not happened as he is really my main prop.

I had lunch with Edwin yesterday – he told me they had tried to get Hitch to succeed Brittain but he wouldn't think of it. Indeed Hitch told me in Canada that he wanted to leave the Service. I told Edwin that it was time I left – I had had a talk with Padmore some time ago and he said that it was policy to get senior Civil Servants out pretty near 60, though he did not think it would apply to me, where the main question was whether the Chancellor wanted me or not. Anyway I have been thinking for some time that I ought to be thinking of a move, (a) I will have to work after 60 as my pension is very little adjusted to the price rises that have taken place, (b) it is time they got someone else to start learning this job, (c) I am getting tired, and tired of the job – in the sense that it does not fascinate me as it did, and I am often only too ready to think that it does not matter one way or the other whether I take a line or not.

Edwin said he was determined to leave the Atomic Energy job at the end of next year and had had several inquiries already, from AEI and Vickers, both of which were embarrassing as they were dealing with the Authority, so he could only tell them he had noted what they said. But I was pleased to find that he still would like very much to work with me. I think I will now have a talk to O. Franks and find out how to get a business job – I suppose I can get one, in fact I am quite sure I can get one as I have a unique experience of the Government field generally. But I do not know at all how one goes about it – I can't very well put an advertisement in a paper.

Friday, July 19th

Nothing very new in the past three weeks. The paper for the Radcliffe Committee has now been circulated to the Makins Committee and is, I think, a good document.[15] I removed the critical parts and myself wrote a note pointing out that orthodox control had broken down and that we really ought to face the fact that we need to keep the 'request' technique and probably should formalize it. I also discussed the future of gilt-edged and interest rates on the assumption that inflation will continue. E. Compton was so impressed that he asked to be associated with it so it went round as a joint paper.

The Committee has begun to talk to the Bank of England on technical matters and wants to talk to the Treasury on the same. I was told that the Governor was rather cross at the technical examination as only Sayers and Cairncross would ask him questions. They are hoping to educate themselves first and get on to the policy matters in October. Meanwhile gilt-edged fell to a $5^1/_8$% yield basis this week though they have recovered a little since.

A fair amount of publicity has been given to the inflation problem and last week the Chancellor made four speeches all mentioning it, and next week there is to be a Debate. This is all to the good as it has begun to make people take it seriously and even to think about the difference between demand inflation and cost inflation, which the Government has been talking about for years and which is even beginning to be discussed in the USA. It is extraordinary to me to realize what a gap there is between what the Economic Section knows to be happening and is telling Ministers about, and what economists and the public are discussing. The first Government pronouncement on this was in the 1944 White Paper, there were Government statements published in 1947 and 1948 and it has been mentioned in every Budget speech since. But you would think now that it has only just been discovered.

The Chancellor is still in good form and put in a paper to Cabinet this week on the economic situation, reiterating what he had said about the wage problem and saying plainly that if there was a strike we would have to face it.[16] As he has now stirred public opinion up so much, his colleagues have been forced to take it all much more seriously. At present we are working on the Debate on this subject. T. Padmore has made a good start *vice* Brittain and is doing all the co-ordination.

Wednesday, July 31st

The Debate was not particularly good and Downie who went to it thought that the Chancellor did not make the most of his case. Parliament will rise on Friday for about three months and there is already an air of release in the office and the leave season is in full blast. Certainly the whole wage–cost–inflation situation has had a thorough airing and the Government has at least begun to give the impression that resistance to wage increases must be the solution. Frank Cousins [General Secretary of the Transport and General Workers Union] has announced that at the TUC Congress he will move a motion completely rejecting wage stabilization and in the House of Lords yesterday he was attacked for this by Lord Hailsham. S. C. Leslie thinks it would be disastrous to give the impression that the Government is looking for a show-down with the Trade Unions but I do not see how this can be avoided.

Meanwhile we have run into trouble with the Council on Prices Productivity and Incomes as it is to be called, since Lord Justice Morris who was to be Chairman has turned it down. We think this was with the connivance of the Lord Chancellor who thinks it is too hot a potato and that the judges should not be too much drawn into what will be regarded as a political issue. The search for members has revealed an extraordinary emptiness of the cupboard – it is always a mistake to think that there are no great men in one's own time but we are all led to that conclusion. Certainly there is no economist with the professional standing of Keynes or the public position of Beveridge which they had ten years ago. The Chancellor pressed us very hard to put Lionel Robbins as Chairman but I felt strongly that the whole left wing of the country would regard this as the choice of a notorious reactionary to do the work of a Tory Government. It is not true as Lionel would be a very good Chairman – and the job is one for the whole country not for the Tories – but it would be said. I don't know where it stands now.

The Tory back-benchers are a poor lot who do not know what they want; they hate planners and yet they are always asking for planning measures, e.g. there has been a great outcry against the increases in prices announced by the Nationalized Industries but the only way to stop them would be subsidies. The back-benchers would also like to see hard bitten Tories in all Government appointments with not a thought of the public relations aspects. In fact they are very much the sort of people one would expect them to be, and Suez was not a fit of mania except among Ministers. As I feel extremely doubtful about the outlook if we have a Labour Government, it seems a poor prospect either way. The Chancellor is very good and sensible and on the whole I think that the PM and many other Ministers are – it is their party I dislike.

No doubt Gaitskell and many of his Ministers would be good and sensible, and maybe they could do a bit more with their party who are just as woolly-minded as the Tories are bloody-minded. The fact seems to be that democracy is an almost impossible institution, only saved by having very good leaders. As soon as the leaders deteriorate public affairs begin to deteriorate too. Then when there is a crisis a good leader is thrown up and the country will follow him. That is, if things are not so bad that the country is ruined altogether. 1930–45 is a good example.

Last night the Chancellor saw the 'inner group' of City Editors at the Reform – it was an unusually bad meeting as Oscar Hobson, George Schwartz and a man called Forge from the *Glasgow Herald* talked all the time about how the only trouble was that the Government was not willing to use monetary policy severely enough. As they refused even to admit that the Government was trying to combine full employment and price stability and was therefore rejecting large-scale unemployment as a solution, it was a most barren evening. They did, however, make it quite clear to the Chancellor that they thought the Government had sold out over the railway–engineering–shipbuilding claims earlier this year, which is quite true: and in his turn the Chancellor made it clear that the Government did not intend to do this again, though he would not admit that they had last time. He also said, very wisely, that it would only do harm to talk as if a slow-down was wanted – I am afraid Hailsham will have sold that one.

The Government's case ending with last week's debate has been made to look rather poor by two events. The 'bus strike was referred to Arbitration and the Tribunal awarded 11/- [55p] a week increase which was more than would have been needed for a settlement and about halfway between the 3/- [15p] offered and the £1 asked. The general effect is to make everyone think that a strike pays, that the refusal of employers to offer enough is only a move in a game, and that wage inflation is going on. On top of this the Agricultural Wages Tribunal has awarded 9/- [45p] a week to the agricultural workers, a larger than usual increase but, however justified, one that will tend to set a bad pattern for next round.

Lord Cherwell died last week – I had seen a great deal of him since 1951 and had come to like him in a curious way, although his temperament and outlook were so very unlike my own and when I met him before the war in Christ Church Common Room I thought him a most objectionable man. But in all the time he was Paymaster General he seemed to me to be trying hard for the right things – maybe this was because of D. MacDougall. And he was always very nice when I went to see him at Ch. Ch. after he gave up being Paymaster General. He was becoming a lonely man with Winston more and more out of things and he retired from his Chair and much less consulted. So if one has any case at all for saying that he died at a good time for himself it can be said now.

Radcliffe is having a quiet time. There is a meeting tomorrow to consider the Treasury papers of a more policy kind, including mine. But they have been talking to the Bank of England about the mechanics of that institution and now want to talk to the Treasury, and not get on to theory or policy till the autumn. I have seen O. Franks several times. He says that the inability of the Governor to talk coherently is going to be a great barrier. He also got T. Padmore to lunch to tell him that long-term interest rates should rise, a thought he had got from me.

George Meehan, the National Income expert from the Dept of Commerce, came to see me today. He is rather pessimistic about the US Business Outlook in the sense that he does not expect much increase in industrial production this year, but as he belongs to the Federal Reserve school of thought, that rising prices however caused show that deflation is needed, he is not worried.

Leslie Rowan and I have been doing (or rather getting done) a note on the world gold and dollar outlook as we think the Chancellor ought probably to speak about it at the IMF meeting in September. The Germans are the main villains but there is some doubt about the United States – according to Meehan this is not necessary as their exports are now likely to fall again. It will be very interesting if the world deflation that we were so much afraid of in the early post-war years should now be upon us, but as thought has developed so much in the period, I don't believe it would come to much harm.

At present the world seems to be very much in disequilibrium. France has been running a large deficit for some time and in spite of the present Government measures this is likely to go on. Germany has been accumulating dollars at about $1,000 mn a year and in spite of all her assertions goes on doing it. India is running down her sterling balances at at least £200 mn a year and this takes about all our surplus. Canada is now taking in dollars and the US about the turn of the year began to take them in, though it seems to be stopping now. Anyway there does seem to be a real danger of a shortage of international liquidity and if we think of the past this suggests a downward move, particularly as the US and Germany are much more worried about internal price dangers than about other countries' balances of payments.

The autumn of 1957 was unexpectedly a time of crisis. Sterling was under pressure in spite of a substantial current account surplus and simultaneously the government was contemplating deflationary measures after a series of high wage settlements. These measures, which were quite unconnected with the speculative pressure on the pound, were linked in the Chancellor's mind with a monetarist view of inflation although they were directed towards cutting government expenditure, rather than the money supply.

The sequence of events from the end of August until the statement on September 19th and after is summarized in the entry for October 29th.

Relations between the Chancellor and his officials and between the Chancellor and the Bank of England were at breaking point by the time the measures were announced. The Chancellor sought, unsuccessfully, to dismiss the Governor when the latter refused to direct the banks to cut their advances by 5 per cent. Robert Hall, although he does not say so, was twice driven to offer his resignation. His objections, however, were not primarily to the measures, of which he came to take quite a hopeful view, as to the theoretical dressing in which they were presented. Public attention, meanwhile, was deflected to the proceedings of the tribunal investigating the rumours of a leak before the increase of Bank Rate to 7 per cent on September 19th.

In the middle of these events the Treasury continued to prepare and submit evidence to the Radcliffe Committee and Hall took a particular interest in the evidence on funding.

Monday, August 19th

Since I last wrote the franc has been more or less devalued and the £ is now under very heavy pressure; to a large extent it is speculation *into* Deutschmarks but as there is a feeling that we may not be able to hold the position, it is largely sterling that is being used. We lost about $100 mn last week and pressure continued on Saturday.

T.L.R. and Denis Rickett are both on leave and I saw Arnold France, who is in charge of OF at present, on Friday and then Roger Makins. A good deal of thought is being given to drawing the Exim Bank loan, or part of it. I am rather against drawing it, and if we do I think we should either draw or arrange to draw the lot. But I think we should also consider letting the £ float which I have previously been against. I think it is quite different when one does this because another currency is undervalued, and when one's own is weak because of one's own policies. It would be much easier to defend our action and would cast much less doubt on the position of sterling in the long run.

Roger told me that the Governor was thinking about holding the £ against the dollar but letting it float against European currencies, which would be a very good thing if it were technically possible. At the moment I cannot see how this could be done because of the cross-rates – unless we go back to a much more strict use of exchange control vis-à-vis the dollar than we have now. It suggests to me the end of EPU and perhaps of transferable sterling; but I may not have worked it out (certainly in my first attempt I got it the wrong way round!). Anyway it is all to be discussed next Thursday.

Just before he went on leave the Chancellor started a new exercise on further deflation. He and the PM had been impressed by all the criticism that the Government ought to deal with wage pressures by 'orthodox' monetary measures whatever these are, and they did not like the idea of a strike. So they suggested a combination of further credit restriction, and of reducing Government investment in the Nationalized Industries aimed at producing, say 2½ or 3% unemployment. I think it is partly wishful thinking because they don't like a strike, and partly a good idea of which they have not considered the political consequences. We have had one or two technical meetings and I have written a longish Minute pointing out the difficulties.[17]

It is difficult to believe that anything will come of it. In the first place it would not come in time to affect wages this winter; second, it would need a change in the whole emphasis of policy from full employment to keeping in balance; and third, it would be putting consumption before investment. However I am in favour of running the economy less flat out than we have been doing, and it is a good policy to aim at over a period. The real trouble is the constant pressure to spend more and to reduce taxation, and until recently to keep down the prices of Nationalized Industries.

Radcliffe. The Treasury paper on Recent Experience is now in its 6th Draft and I hope practically finalized. It is, as always, a good deal better as a result and I think we have managed to keep the essentials in. Leslie Rowan objected to anything that implied either criticism of past policies or a view by the Treasury but I found quotations from speeches by Chancellors that made all the points that were needed – nearly all written by me or for me at the time. It is a comfort to find bits one put in in case they would be needed later on, coming in handy. I have been reading the evidence by O'Brien and Hollom to the Radcliffe Committee [July 11th, 16th and 26th] and O'Brien made the central point – that the whole system is too liquid for control to be got by orthodox ways – very clearly. This will make it a good deal easier for us though we will still have to deal with interest rates and what form of monetary control is appropriate to a continually rising price level.

The Council on Productivity, Prices and Incomes – COPPI – has come out better than seemed likely at one time. When L. Justice Morris refused to act, we thought it would be impossible to get a Judge as we gathered that the Lord Chancellor was against it, but somehow L. J. Cohen was persuaded to take it on and *he* suggested Howitt and Dennis Robertson as his colleagues. Dennis is not nearly so publicly objectionable to the left as Lionel, except perhaps that Joan Robinson and Richard Kahn have had so many quarrels with him. But he is certainly a highly respected figure in the economic world. I was somewhat doubtful about whether he would accept as he is not too strong and in any case thinks that we ought to deflate more and have more unemployment. But according to the Governor, he spent three hours persuading him and was finally successful. At any rate it is a very distinguished body and I should think highly competent as these things go.

The Chancellor was most anxious that they should have a top-level staff and suggested that a Treasury 3rd Secretary should go which seemed to all of us rather too much. Unfortunately Norman Brook suggested Bryan Hopkin who is so obviously suitable that I could not speak against it although it is a great blow to me. Just as it seemed as if the Section were improving in strength we get the most important accession taken away. However I have got P. D. Henderson of Oxford coming next month and before he goes R. G. Opie of the LSE will be arriving. The first attempts we made this year to get some new Assistants were unsuccessful but the second shot seems to have been a bit better and we may have one or two people by the end of September.

COPPI got on the whole a fairly good press, in fact of the papers I saw *The Spectator* was the worst – worse than the *New Statesman* or *Tribune*. I suppose *The Spectator* has to take the very subversive line it has done since it changed editors in order to keep up its circulation, but it seems to me to have very little of either sense or conscience on the political and economic side, though Nicholas Davenport who writes the end article on economics tries to be helpful. But the main part of the paper is quite against Davenport and the Government.

Tuesday, August 27th

I was supposed to start my leave last Friday, August 23rd, but as the Chancellor was to have a meeting about further deflationary measures I had to come up for it.[18] His holiday seems to have increased his conviction that it is too much money which is at the root of all our troubles, and he set out very eloquently an extended version of the ideas we had been working on. The meeting began with a discussion of the position of sterling which is under a good deal of strain because of speculation into D-Marks: but we decided quite rightly that there was nothing to do but to ride it out, meanwhile considering what more pressure could be put on the Germans to revalue. I was in favour of trying to organize discrimination against them but did not get much support.

We then went on to the need to restrict the supply of money. Dennis Robertson when the Chancellor had asked him to join COPPI had made it plain that he thought more deflation was needed, and the Economic Secretary repeated the piece he had previously said to me several times, namely that the Government was bound to lose the next election and that their own supporters were furious with them because of the continued rise in prices, the power and arrogance of Trade Unions, and the inability of the Government to *do* anything. So the Chancellor wanted to fix bank advances by direction and cut down spending by Nationalized Industries, Government Departments and Local Authorities.

I said that it was easy enough to do all this technically if the Cabinet would make up its mind to it but that they could hardly expect officials to believe that they would, when they hardly ever stood up to economy measures even in quite minor things. The Chancellor said that it would be much easier to stand up for a broad general slash with everyone hurt and we could not get him to see that broad action nevertheless requires working out in detail. He was quite eloquent about how he expected officials to tell him that there was only so much money available and that this was all that he could let his colleagues have.

I don't think he quite distinguishes in his own mind between money in the sense of the total supply of currency and credit, and money in the sense of the amount an individual has in his pocket or his bank. Anyway we went away with instructions to prepare a draft Cabinet paper and I did an outline in the afternoon before going back to Oxford and leaving Otto Clarke to fill it out, which he has done very nobly. I had to come to London anyway this afternoon and came in for a meeting at 4 p.m. but it is now 5.15 and the Chancellor is still at Cabinet so I do not know when ours will be taken.

I have had a chat with R. Makins who has so far come in almost every day of his leave, and is a bit bewildered by this turn of events. He repeated what he had said to me several times before, and I to him before that, that this Government is led by gamblers (he calls them plungers) and he thinks that they are now meditating what he calls 'an economic Suez'. I don't think there is much danger of that, as the measures the Chancellor has in mind will all need Cabinet approval and then have to be communicated to lots of other people before anything happens. One doesn't just declare a slump as one does war – or launch deflation as one does an army. And I shall be very much surprised indeed if he can get anything like his present proposals through Cabinet, if he is bold enough to make them. Nor do I believe that the Conservative Party is so keen on all this, or perhaps I should say will be so keen when they know what is involved.

I found Bryan Hopkin waiting for me when I came in at 9.45 – he had seen N. Brook yesterday about his appointment as Secretary to COPPI and wanted to make sure that I agreed. It is certainly a blow to me and I only hope that they will not keep him too long. After their first big report, I don't think that there will be anything like a full-time job there.

Wednesday, August 28th

The meeting yesterday which was to have been held at 4 did not start till 5.45 as Cabinet went on. I had to leave at 6.30 but they went on until 7.45. The Chancellor could not be shaken and a definitive draft is now to be made. Tom Padmore is back and will be the editor. I re-did the early part this morning and am going off to get the 6.5 to Oxford in the renewed hope of getting some leave. R. Makins has been back almost every day since he started *his* leave but he also hopes to go off today.

Meanwhile Roy Harrod has written to the PM saying that the economy needs a substantial stimulus and suggesting giving up *all* the Purchase Tax – about £460 mn. The PM rather approved so the Chancellor will have a tough time.

Grieve-Smith just told me he is going off to the Atomic Energy Authority.

Tuesday, October 22nd

I have missed all the important events of the last six weeks. The Chancellor took against all his officials and I think especially me and he got Lionel Robbins back from a holiday in Austria and this confirmed him in the view that it must all be done by money. The statement of Sept. 19th about the new measures was done by Ministers and they would not listen to any suggestion that what they were saying did not make much sense as economics. The biggest effect was caused by the Bank Rate change which we had not thought of in the early stages. But of course the whole situation developed against both an increasing strain on sterling and the impending meeting of the IMF.

Tuesday, October 29th

The history of the past two months really ought to be set out in some detail and it is most unfortunate that it will be 'emotion recollected in tranquillity' for me.

It started with the PM and the Chancellor having a talk which as far as I could make out was based on the completely wrong assumption that deflation would cure the wage/price spiral without forcing the Government to face a row with the Unions or a strike. This led to the instructions the Chancellor gave before he went on holiday and to the work done in the Treasury while he was away: and the meetings here after he got back, to all of which there is some reference above.

Meanwhile the reserves came under increasing pressure and the Chancellor and the Government got into a state: and the Chancellor consulted Robbins a good deal and got it firmly into his head that the supply of money was the cause of all the trouble. A working group of Ministers was set up and officials were told that it was no good their protesting because Ministers had settled the policy, and the Chancellor told me plainly at an office meeting that it was nonsense to say it was not the supply of money because everyone knew that it was.

I did not object to the policy as such, but I felt that the words chosen to announce it were dangerous as far as economists were concerned; that it would be better to produce some deflation without committing yourself publicly to produce the amount necessary to stop prices from rising; and that nothing that was done now, particularly the kind of measures announced, would produce enough unemployment this winter to ease the wage pressure, and that therefore the *immediate* object of policy must remain to stand up to wage claims especially on the railways this winter. In fact the policy I had already put forward and which the Chancellor himself had put to Cabinet in a long paper in the summer.

As the time for the Chancellor to go to Washington got nearer the atmosphere got worse and things were much complicated by our relations with the Bank. The Chancellor wanted to call for a 5% reduction in advances, which would certainly have been logical, but the banks would not accept it and the Governor refused to give them a direction. The Chancellor was advised that the 1946 Act did not give him powers either to direct the Bank to direct the clearing banks, or to dismiss the Governor, both of which courses he was contemplating! and as I thought rightly on the basis of his own policy.

R. Makins was horrified as *he* thought it would complete the débâcle over the £ if the Chancellor now began to direct or dismiss in the banking world – all the rest of us could not see how the £ could be weakened by measures aimed at strengthening the control over money. But in the end the Chancellor would not push it through.

Meanwhile the Bank decided that we ought to put the Bank Rate up to 7% and the Chancellor and the Treasury wanted it to go only to 6% so there was a row about that, but we advised the Chancellor that he would be on weak ground to sack the Governor when the Governor wanted to be tougher than he. So it was left at 7% and as it turned out this was a very good thing as it produced a crisis atmosphere which we had not wanted but in fact it turned out to be very useful.

The Chancellor was so annoyed by all this that he gave immediate instructions for a Working Party to study (a) how to control bank credit, (b) how to amend the law to give the Treasury power it thought it had already. Lionel R. was put on this Working Party and was made to stay behind from Washington to sit on it. The Bank tried hard to sabotage it and had to be more or less instructed to collaborate. J. Downie was the Secretary.[19]

We did not deal with the legal aspect at all but concentrated on means of control. I was delighted as I have always felt that it was ridiculous that we had so little power, so Lionel and I collaborated – he is of course very good in these practical problems and he came out very strong in favour of a prescribed liquidity ratio plus something like TDRs to keep down the banks' supply of Treasury bills. The Bank (Mynors) agreed that this was practicable but were very strong that it was not necessary and that if it were done it would create a very bad effect on overseas opinion – because it would be said that it was potentially very inflationary to make the banks hold Government securities.

When he came back the Chancellor accepted our recommendation that the next stage should be the study of how to do it as a practical job and O'Brien and Compton are now doing this. Meanwhile the amendment of the 1946 Act is in abeyance and the Governor made a speech at Ipswich reminding everyone that *he* had the powers to direct the banks – no doubt he is getting cold feet at the thought of the Government amending the 1946 Act.

Since the statement, the £ has recovered a good deal and the idea that we or the Germans might change our parities has been dropped for the time. The internal situation shows no signs of shock so far, except on the Stock Exchange. There has been a good deal of criticism of the Government but on the whole it has gone very well and the Chancellor may get away with it, especially as he has now come back to the idea that we must fight on the wage front after all – perhaps his statement will be a useful psychological weapon here. Today the statement, situation, etc., are to be debated and I am just going over to the House. The Chancellor and I have patched it up for the moment; he has consulted me on several occasions alone which he never did before and I have tried to get him to put his economic arguments on a plane where they cannot be attacked even if the policy is.

We have appeared before the Radcliffe Committee now for about ten periods and so far have not done too badly. The Committee are still educating themselves and range over a very wide field and go very slowly. The main trouble we have had was on funding, where I had been warning HF and R. Makins that we could not defend our policy unless we had some reason for not letting the rate of interest fall. Sure enough, they got on to it and Compton did not do at all well; on October 24th when we came away I told Roger that we were in an impossible position and suggested a statement, which he made at our first meeting the next day, putting the thing on a defensible basis and saying that we had good policy reasons for *not* funding at all costs.[20] It would indeed have required a major decision, that interest rates should be allowed to reflect the expectation of rising prices, i.e. that the Government had decided that it could not stop prices rising, if we had done this.

Otherwise the main paper has gone fairly well and I have the feeling that my own performance was a good one. We have not got on to 1955/56 yet. I have been trying hard to make the point that the period since monetary policy was reactivated in 1951 has been a period of experiment and that we could not be expected to know all about a new world the first time that we entered it. Actually I think that the Treasury and the Bank are both to blame for the slowness with which we grasped the position. It is obvious now that funding was a very uncertain operation and that our control was therefore uncertain too. But at the root of it all is the unwillingness of the Bank to admit that they were responsible for the amount of money, coupled in recent years with the Governor's view that an overall surplus would do the trick – although it was at his instance that the Nationalized Industries were taken in below the line.[21]

I cannot see exactly how the Committee is going to move at present, as between higher interest rates and some form of compulsion. But judging by what Robbins reported of Sayers's reaction to the proposal for compulsory liquidity ratio plus TDRs, I should think he will go for that. O. Franks wants to make very much wider recommendations and he has kept on asking questions both on a wide front and designed to show that they will need to go widely. One thing that seems a bit queer to me is that it looks at present as if I will go through without being asked what *I* think ought to be done, either about credit control or the use of money. Our answers have tended to indicate that we did not attach a great deal of importance to the rate of interest itself.

We still have to put in a paper on Debt Management on which we shall no doubt be taken to task again about funding. And all the OF papers have to go in.

R.M., T. Padmore, Stevenson and I have been to see COPPI and talked to them for a morning. It was a surprise to me to find how little

Cohen and Howitt knew about the background of economic affairs recently. D. H. Robertson and Bryan Hopkin have got a good deal of education to do. D.H.R. suggested that it would be wrong for them to put a figure on non-inflationary wage increases – if they don't, most of their usefulness in my eyes will have gone. But anyway I think that now the Government is going to stand up and fight this winter, they are less useful than they might have been otherwise. In fact their existence is a monument to the muddle and weakness earlier this year.

Saturday, November 9th

The Debate went fairly well for the Government in the sense that no attacks were damaging. The Chancellor made a fairly good speech at the beginning and got a serious hearing. The main thing I have noticed is that no one is anxious to be regarded as the pro-inflationist – both Labour members and Trade Unionists are making what look like fighting speeches but when you read them carefully they are very cautious. I think also that all the Unions are trying to be late in the queue for the final settlement of claims and disputes.

I have to go to America on Sunday, a trip decided on only a week ago. The main purpose is to try to get some informal Committee where we can exchange ideas about world economic conditions, against the content of the widely expressed views that the US is going to have a slump and that the fall in primary product prices will cause all sorts of economic and political troubles with underdeveloped countries. I don't think anyone has been hurt yet except perhaps by the German accumulation of reserves but it is just as well to look out. The blackest spot just now seems to be France which must be very near some kind of collapse and no doubt is expecting to be bailed out at the last moment.

Thursday, November 14th (Washington, DC)

I left London on Sunday and had the quickest flight I have ever had, being in New York at 6.15 a.m. and in Washington by 10 a.m. I am staying with Guy Thorold the Economic Minister who seems to have taken over very well from Harcourt. We are involved in a round of visits and discussions partly on general topics and partly on my assignment.

We started on Monday with a visit to the Council of Economic Advisers and Saulnier the Chairman did us very well; it was a holiday but nevertheless he had the other two members of the Council there and we talked for over 1½ hours. The two main points he made were (a) that the Council were worried about the extent to which the US recession had gone and wanted a change in policy, especially on the monetary side, (b) that he thought the US ought to take a more comprehensive view of world problems than it had done – it was thinking so far mainly in terms of the level of activity in the US as their main responsibility, plus aid in certain places as needed. (He mentioned France and India, almost as if the US had already decided on giving them fairly substantial amounts.) All this was as good an opening as we could have hoped for but I thought it better not to open up the question of regular meetings with him. In the end he said that if we had any ideas about what the US might do either itself or by lending its influence elsewhere, he hoped we would let him know.

He told me at dinner the next evening that all his series showed that the US peak was reached earlier this year and that they were well down now. He also complained almost bitterly of the amount of work in which he personally was involved because of having to write the Report of the Council. I know Arthur Burns did most of the writing with his own hand and apparently S. is following him. He said also that it had to be kept open till the last minute in order to get the emphasis up-to-date, a familiar problem to us with the [Economic] Surveys.

On Tuesday we went to see Hauge who gave us a lecture on the deficiencies of US scientific education and on the difficulties of finding Government money for important things when so much of it was tied up in 'deal' activities such as agricultural subsidies, veterans and so on. We lunched with him and Clarence Randall who always seems to me a very vague man and who cannot have got much satisfaction out of his long assignment to handle the US commercial relations, GATT tariff simplification and so on.

After lunch we broached our ideas to Hauge who was a bit jumpy at the idea of any formal co-operation between US and UK – we said we did not want anything very formal or with any powers but it seemed sensible to arrange to meet a bit regularly and not just leave it to hazard, and to put in papers occasionally. He seemed to grasp this and said he would mention it to Anderson, Saulnier and Dillon, which wasn't too bad.

Then we went on to see Anderson the new Secretary of the Treasury who replaced Humphrey in the summer. This was really a courtesy call but was most interesting – he is entirely unlike Humphrey who was a man of great force of character and always seemed to me to be absolutely honest and straightforward, but who had his mind very firmly set in what seemed to me to be quite antiquated grooves and as far as his thoughts went, Keynes might never have written anything.

Anderson is a much younger man, rather slim and nervous and with a mind which ranged very rapidly over the whole scene, especially international. In less than half an hour he had got my appreciation of the UK scene, my views on Russian economic problems, on France and on Germany and given me his on many of them. On France he thought as I do that the best thing would be to let them be until they realized that they couldn't go on living on aid but that politically it might not be possible to stick to this. On Germany he was very strong that they should now begin to be a 'good neighbour' and carry some of the load of underdeveloped countries.

His final words I thought were very good and encouraging – he said that we must be prepared to maintain a strong posture of defence in the free world for an indefinite time and we must find the economic stability and expansion that were needed as a base for this. In fact we needed an international economic policy – again the note Saulnier had struck.

Yesterday we saw Bill Martin who was extremely difficult to understand apart from the fact that he said it was now clear that the US was in a phase of recession and did not add that that was just where he wanted it to be which was his line in May. But otherwise he talked half the time about the need to kill the inflationary mentality and half the time in somewhat nursery metaphors to the effect that when people were really burned it was the time to bind up the wounds and do all you could to ease their pains.

I suppose he meant to tell us that the Fed. would not for ever persist in deflation but we could not make out where he stood now: I think it is the fundamental weakness of not recognizing that cost inflation and demand inflation are different things, that you can't talk about judging the situation by prices and about judging it by the level of activity at the same time, since there is an area in which they can move in opposite directions. However the general attitude was fairly encouraging, not that I had ever expected it to be any different, that is, I have never supposed that the US would not take counter-inflation measures if it looked as if these were needed.

Afterwards I had a very long and interesting talk with Per Jacobsson, who is doing very well as the Managing Director of the IMF. We talked about the situation in the UK, in the US where he said that the Fed. could not make up their minds what to do, and especially France where I thought he had a very good idea – namely that Gaillard should get emergency powers and that someone (e.g. the Fund) should lend them say $50 mn to tide them over up to two months, that period to be used for a package deal to be worked out with the emergency powers on the one hand and a big loan on the other.

I expect this idea has occurred to others but it was new to me – it seemed to offer the best way out of the impasse which is that no French Government seems to be in a position to promise, much less to implement, the sort of reforms that would justify a further loan. On the UK I told him the same story I have been telling everyone in Washington, that our troubles were the wage ones this winter but that I thought there was a fair chance that there would be no disastrous struggle, because it seemed to me that both the Labour Party and the Unions were being anxious not to be put in the wrong by either supporting inflation or by being too greedy.

Tuesday, November 19th

This is written just before we are due at London Airport.

On Thursday morning we saw Dillon who is now Assistant Under Secretary of State for Economic Affairs and seemed an enormous improvement on his recent predecessors – as intelligent as Willard Thorp but with what seemed like much more drive and energy. Thorold talked about the proposed new Committee for Economic Measures which had been more or less agreed following the PM/President talks, to deal with specific problems, e.g. Syria or Lebanon, that needed some concerting of views or measures. This had been discussed in London before I left and the terms of reference practically agreed.

Then I expounded our longer-range ideas. Dillon said that Hauge had mentioned them but in spite of our efforts it seemed as if Hauge had got the idea that we wanted to go a good deal further towards formality than we did. I explained that we only wanted to meet a bit more regularly, and have a bit more on an agenda, than was now the case and that it need have no title or terms of reference at all. Dillon gave us the impression that he thought it was a good idea and promised to give us a considered view before long. So we departed and sent off a telegram.

In the afternoon I saw David Lusher at the Council to get some check on the economic outlook and then Win Riefler. He at once told me that the rediscount rate had been reduced that afternoon from 3½ to 3% at four Reserve Banks – this explained Martin's peculiar performance the day before as he did not like to take too clear a view when they were on the point of so clear an action – indeed Bill himself came in to apologize for the previous day.

It seemed quite clear, putting both interviews together, that the Fed. has now become worried about the signs of recession and has begun not only to lean the other way but to hope for developments to hold things up – e.g. Win said he hoped house-building would recover, which he certainly would not have hoped in May. This was all a great relief to me as it means that all the Government authorities take the same view and of course if they want to they can change the economic outlook: in fact they do not intend (nor I think need) to pull things down any more because of the price level and can therefore turn their eyes back to the GNP. When I got back to the Embassy and told my man Kit McMahon, about this his face lit up and he said he felt much better as if he had been under a great personal strain.

On Friday I saw Baird at the Treasury who has replaced Randolph Burgess – an elderly man very conscious that he was new to the job. George Willis was there too, muttering at a table and asking a lot of questions he had prepared and taking notes. It is difficult to think he can have much effect there. Hillary King the Information Officer took me to lunch with four newspaper men from *New York Times*, *Herald Tribune*, *Business Week* and *US News and World Report*. I found it rather strange that they did not see the full significance of the rediscount change, and they argued strongly that the Administration did not know what it wanted to do in the defence field so how could one say that Federal spending would pull things up? I said that of course they did not know because they were working it out and anyhow needed to see Congress, but that the change in atmosphere was very significant.

In the afternoon I saw Dick Bissell who is now in the CIA and who characteristically had forgotten all about the visit so that it took twenty minutes for me to get into the building and for him to get out of his other engagements. However this did not affect his equanimity and we had a good talk. He wanted mainly to know about how the prospects were for the next Election in the UK and how feeling was about the US. I said I thought no one could say how the next Election would go – the Government were at present unpopular, largely from Suez but if they did as well as seemed possible on wages and prices, all this might change. I felt that the underlying feeling in the UK was not anti-US. He commented on the changes in the US Administration I had noted – especially the replacement of Humphrey, Hollister and Hoover, and getting Dillon into State instead of Prochnow. He thought that all this showed that *any* administration would improve with time and experience but a pity it took so long.

On Saturday I went to Boston but the only economist I saw there was A. Smithies, whose summary of the US position was much the same as mine. On Sunday I went back to Washington and reported to H. Caccia on what I had been doing. On Monday I had lunch with the Vice Consul General in New York (Rooke) and met Stacy May who used to be Chief Statistician to WPB [War Production Board] in the war and is now with the Rockefeller Foundation: also several British and US business men including Commander Whitehead, the Schweppes man. Stacy was very optimistic about the outlook and said he thought Defence spending might rise by as much as an annual rate of $5 bn in the next twelve months. As he is a close friend of Riefler's his opinions are worth having.

Otherwise most of the lunch was taken up by an ex-Swiss economist (I think called Runce) who now runs an advisory service on foreign economic affairs and who was arguing that UK publicity on overseas finance matters was lousy. But he seemed to be thinking altogether of short-term or market operator considerations, e.g. he wanted to soften by advance publicity bad monthly dollar figures – we have tried all sorts of dodges here but found that it is always swings and roundabouts. There was a Morgan partner there who hardly said a word but was obviously appalled at the suggestion that HMG should try for short market effects.

Wednesday, November 27th

Since I got back we have finished the main examination on the big paper for Radcliffe, which ended in a rush: and started on the OF papers. The Debt Management paper[22] is done and we are in for a nasty time on it since no economist will be able to stomach our views on the role of interest rates in affecting the propensity to hold various types of securities. I have warned everyone but it can't help what we have in fact done.

The Chancellor seems in fairly good form and certainly is better disposed towards me. But I expect he is worried about the Bank Rate

Leak Inquiry:[23] I have made a statement and so has everyone else and the Chancellor has made a very detailed one. If nothing comes out, it will have been a most unfortunate affair, since all sorts of details will be brought to light not discreditable in themselves but of a kind which one could have expected would have been kept private, e.g. that the Chancellor saw Robbins and Sayers.

The inquiry must have caused great anxiety in the City – I saw George Bolton at the Tuesday Club last night and he said that his lawyer had told him he mustn't mention Bank Rate (not the leak – but at all!) till after the inquiry. And that the City had been advised to hold *no* communication with any member of the Labour Party except by letter approved by legal advisers, till after. E. Compton said this morning that no firms were buying gilt-edged till then as their books might be inspected and why should they put down any more transactions. It all seems perfectly silly but I suppose the lawyers are having a lovely time.

The poor Treasury officials have seen one of the Treasury Solicitor lawyers about their statements but no more advice. It appears that no one suspects us. In fact none of us can remember *when* we first knew of the decision – it was taken by the PM and the Chancellor about 10.30 a.m. on Wednesday, Sept. 18th and was quite an open question till then but what time Wednesday I heard, I cannot remember. It is rather sad that the Chancellor has to disclose his talks with a few senior newspaper men and with O. Poole. The main trouble seems to be that Lazard's did some selling and Kindersley and Poole are both Lazard partners.

Wednesday, December 18th

The Bank Rate Tribunal must be near the end of its inquiries: the Chancellor has not been yet but I am told that they intend to take him last, and probably no Treasury officials (except the two PSs who went early).

The most striking thing to most people is that the members of the Court with outside interests should be placed in this difficult position. I doubt if there can be said to have been any leak in any real sense but everyone will say that no one who is constantly having to buy and sell gilt-edged ought to know. E. Compton says that he is most surprised that the members of the Court were consulted so early, as he had always supposed that they were summoned at the last moment. I did not really know though I had always thought of the Court as stooges of the Governor.

The Governor was in the witness box for over three hours on Tuesday and I did not think he did too well. He seems to have told the PM a little less than the full story about the deals by firms with members on the Court – and as Ministers do not like him much anyway, this won't help. (The Chancellor and the Ec. Sec. both want to push on with measures to control bank deposits and/or advances formally, but the Bank are obstructing the work as much as they can.) The Governor also made a very rash statement, to the effect that if the character of the Court were changed by having no City men on it, it would cease to be useful to the country and the Commonwealth. Anyway it is all very interesting and taken in conjunction with Radcliffe it may make some assault on them.

We have finished with Radcliffe except possibly for something on 'alternative techniques', i.e. methods of controlling the banks other than by liquidity conditions. We had a bad time on debt management and it ought to be clear that our policy on funding has been based on a very poor analysis of how things work – although I think it has been defensible on other grounds. So far as the Committee is concerned at present, I should say they are coming to the conclusion that monetary policy has not been used firmly enough, which is certainly true. But I am less sure that it would have been best to use it this way as I think that investment ought to be controlled more directly in a full employment economy.

The Bank put in a paper on alternative techniques which was sensible enough in substance but which said that no change in the present system was desirable 'at present' and also that the Central Bank ought (except in the last resort) to have a good deal of independence of the Government in monetary control.[24] This is a view widely held in the past but on theoretical grounds I don't think modern societies would agree to let their Central Banks control the level of activity (as the Fed. has been doing) and on practical grounds it would be more convincing if the Bank had been more of a help in the control of inflation in recent years.

The thing that I find most irritating about all our proceedings with Radcliffe is that the central fact is not being brought out and I do not suppose it can be brought out, which is that the Bank hardly collaborate with the Treasury at all in internal policy matters – the Chancellor talks to the Governor in private and the Bank neither give us their assessment of the situation, nor of the part they expect monetary policy to play in it. Now I feel that the Governor has hypnotized Roger Makins – at any rate he sits on all the papers he gets which raise questions about interest rates or funding policy. I have written a note saying that we ought to say to the Radcliffe Committee

(a) that the Government must control the supply of money;
(b) that we have lost control now and ought to regain it;
(c) that we don't feel sure that we can do it by conventional liquidity ratios;
(d) that therefore we are in principle in favour of some other technique;
(e) that we don't think it would be wise to make the Central Bank independent of Parliament.

Edmund Compton wants to hedge on (d) and to say that we would be in favour of other methods of control if the present ones fail but dodge the issue as to whether they have failed or not. I have a nasty feeling that Roger will try very hard not to contradict the Bank – I feel that this would be wrong in this case since we know that Ministers would like another technique and we ourselves have shown that the present one has failed.

The Chancellor is engaged on one of the struggles so usual at this time of the year, namely to reduce the Estimates which are coming out at about £300 mn more than last year's and £200 mn more than the probable out-turn. This is partly prices and partly that this is the year in which a big block of old age pensioners come in under the National Insurance Scheme. However the Chancellor feels quite rightly that this will make the statement of September 19th look very silly, since among other things it implied and almost said that the Government would not go on pouring out more money to meet inflated prices. I don't see how he is going to get much economy except if he cuts the family allowances which the FST wants him to do. The Chancellor to do him justice is aware that wage negotiations will be a good deal more difficult if the Government put anything more onto prices or attack the welfare state any more, but maybe he could get away with family allowances.

The economic situation is about what we expected. Production has been rising gently but employment is about stable and the further outlook is for some very gentle decline, probably not until later next year. One of the interesting things is that private investment plans do not seem to have been much affected by the statement of September 19th. The Board of Trade Survey showed some reduction in plans over those previously reported, but we had a special regional report made in November and the feeling there was almost entirely optimistic. The only place in which an early down-turn seems probable is in building.

Bryan Hopkin has been to see me about COPPI of which he is the Secretary. He feels very gloomy about it. This is partly because Howitt seems to be past the age at which he can think – he asks all sorts of questions on various topics but does not appear to remember either the questions or the answers. Cohen is more intelligent but not very forcible. However the main trouble is that Dennis Robertson seems to have hardened very much in his attitude – according to Bryan he gets a dogged look whenever the words 'full employment' are mentioned and is determined to take no account of their existence in his terms of reference. So he wants to write a report saying that it is all the fault of the Government for not taking a tough enough line on money, the Budget, etc., and in effect saying that the price stability must be aimed at and no thought given to employment levels.

The report is not likely to come out before the end of January but if this is all that it is going to say it won't have much effect, indeed it is likely to exacerbate feelings. This is just what I feared but I told the Chancellor to find out from Dennis, before he appointed him, if this was the line he would take, since if it was it would be better not to appoint him at all. Bryan may have been exaggerating the position but he seemed pretty positive about it and said that the other two members of the Council would not exercise any effective check on Dennis.

Friday, December 20th

I went to the Bank Rate Tribunal this morning to hear the Chancellor give his evidence as I thought they might ask him whether it was not self-evident from the rest of his statement (about which he spoke to Editors, the Conservative Central Office, etc.) that Bank Rate though not mentioned must be an integral part. However they did not really get on to this. The whole thing is about over now. Harold Wilson has been very lucky since the things he *thought* were wrong have turned out to be all right, while the City end of the transactions about which he knew nothing have at least seemed to be questionable.

Monday, December 30th

The last week has, of course, been very quiet and there is extremely little in my tray this (Monday) morning.

This year is ending very much better than it began, but considering that we were only just beginning to move out of Suez and that Eden was still PM, that is not saying much. The peculiar thing about 1957 from the economic point of view is that it was this Government, which sold out over the wage issue at a time when it seemed to be going the right way, which has now the best chance of getting wage stability, and which is doing it under the threat of the end of full employment.

It has been a good year apart from the troubles with wages, which led (at least in my view) to the troubles with sterling in the autumn. Basically we are certainly much stronger than we were – we got through Suez with a much better balance of payments than we expected and are ending the year with a forecast for next year of the biggest of all the post-war surpluses. Investment was at an all-time record and with a bigger concentration on industrial investment. The Rent Act came into force and looks as if it will be more or less the last of the wartime survivals to go, which have been exerting such an evil effect on the retail price index. The British people have never had so high a standard of living nor the British economy been so productive – nor (though I doubt if we will get it) has the balance of payments forecast ever been so good. Finally the over-full employment is moderating and may well get more comfortable.

Nevertheless I doubt if all these grounds for cheerfulness are appreciated or would make most people very cheerful if they were. This is primarily because the year has been one of considerable political set-backs both for the UK and for the West generally. It is also beginning to be realized how fast the Russians have caught up in the economic way: it was always inherent in the system that once they got over the early hump they would be able to go very fast and now people are becoming aware of it. In addition, the concept of full employment is going sour because of its effect on the price level and this means that the US is going down rather sharply at a time when we are still committed to deflationary action in spite of the expansionary potential in the system.

The Germans have also stopped expanding and the French must be nearer than they have ever been to a real balance of payments crisis.

Thus there is quite a lot of gloom about the prospect of some sort of world recession, with compensating action rather inhibited by the internal policies of the US, the UK and Germany. I do not think things will go down very far because the prospects here and in Germany are for a fairly steady look rather than a decline: and it is hard to think that the US will let themselves slide too far. But we are waiting for the Presidential messages with great interest.

The disturbing thing seems to me to be the absence of strong leaders in the West. The French are hopelessly stuck in Algeria and cannot get anything like a strong Government. Eisenhower is becoming more and more of a weakness at a time when it is very necessary that he should be strong. Here it is impossible to believe that we have any very strong men; I am now inclined to think that the Chancellor is the strongest but he is certainly not outstanding. The Governor of the Bank is no good at all and Roger Makins, who *is* good, is too new to this job and does not seem to me really to have got hold of it.

The best thing that could happen here would be a very moderate wage round, which would enable the Government to let up a bit on their monetary policy and if they wanted on fiscal policy too. But the Chancellor is now conducting a ferocious anti-expenditure drive and probably going to take away the child allowance for the second (i.e. first ranking) child which will add something to the view that this Government really is the enemy of the welfare state. I do not find myself too comfortable, quite apart from the episode in August and September – I think that in spite of the violence of my feelings against Trade Unions exploiting full employment, my heart is still more or less on the left and it is not very easy for me to see what I would once have called, and still perhaps call, an illiberal attitude on almost everything. But since October I have not made any further soundings for another job.

D. MacDougall, who came (with a rather economics group) to drinks last night in Oxford, took me aside to consult me about an article he is writing for the *Financial Times* on the effects of the US position for overseas trade, etc. I told him that it seemed silly to forecast what they would do when we would know the official view in a few weeks but that I agreed with him that if the US went much further down it would have a bad effect on everyone. I advised him to make the crux of the article the importance of the President's messages on the Budget, economic outlook and so on. He wants to send me the article today and get my views by 'phone tomorrow. But as he did not take much notice of what I said when he was organizing *The Times* letter earlier this year, I don't suppose he will now.[25]

Wednesday, January 1st 1958

I dined on Monday with Denis Rickett who had Rosenstein-Rodan staying with him. Rosey is working at MIT and among other things he joined with W. Rostow and Millikan in writing a report on US external economic policy, originally for the President but it was also shown to Stevenson and is now likely to be published. I read it in type as they sent O. Franks a copy for comment and he asked me to (more or less) comment for him. Anyway Rosey is very keen on this and after dinner we talked a good deal especially in the context of India.

He and I both agreed that it was essential that the Indian 5-Year Plan should not break down and I said that the UK ought to reconsider a loan to them now that the sterling balances were so low – the case was quite different when these were high as they might have spent the loan and the balances at once. But if the balances are too low for safety anyway, we get control back. And if they are not drawing on them, clearly we can afford to lend them something since the strain will be less. To my surprise, I found Denis quite sympathetic to this point of view and he said we ought to put it forward. Previously I had supposed that it would be hopeless in the present atmosphere of economy and deflation at all costs.

Meanwhile Arnold France has done a first draft of a paper to form the basis of something we might put to the USA for out joint talks, which will probably be in February. It seems to me to be too conventional and whimpering and that we ought to put it in the context of the cold war and the competition for the underdeveloped countries: this would give us a chance to work in the above ideas about India, if we can get some sort of Ministerial agreement at least to our discussing what the UK might possibly do.

R. Makins who is supposed to be on leave came in today and will be here tomorrow. He took the opportunity to discuss a number of questions about interest rates, funding and so on which have been hanging about. The Bank are selling long-term securities as fast as they can and are keeping other borrowers, especially local authorities, off the market to help them. E. Compton and I think that for once the Bank is being too active and that it would be better to keep the long-term rate high by letting the local authorities borrow, staying rather short ourselves. This is because if we are successful in steadying the price level, the long rate will probably fall and it is a pity to saddle the Exchequer with high charges in perpetuity. I feel fairly sure that the Bank are doing this partly because they have been criticized by Radcliffe and partly because they hope to do a lot of funding and thus reduce the pressure for some other way of controlling bank credit.

E. Compton tells me that the Bank have at last done some work on the 'emergency' plan for compelling reductions in Bank deposits if the September requests don't do the trick. But in the meantime I don't think it will be necessary to have any emergency action, as bank advances are falling anyway and I begin to think that there is a bit of deflation in the system. The latest National Income figures, for the third quarter of 1957, suggest strongly that stock-building *must* come to an end fairly soon and the bank advances suggest that a run-down began in October/November. Meanwhile more complaints are coming in from the building industry.

The Fin. Sec. wants to take the local authorities out of the Public Works Loan Board altogether and to wind the PWLB up.[26] This is to reduce the below-the-line deficit which he seems to think is crucial to the control of inflation. The confusion about the meaning of inflation is now at its height. Paish has an article in the *Financial Times* today in which he assumes that it means price increases. For many years the Government has been assuming that it meant pressure on resources. Now the FST and I should think a number of other Ministers think it means Government borrowing – apparently not even Government short borrowing.

R. Makins tells me that the City is in a rage against Ministers over the Bank Rate Inquiry, because they think the Attorney-General (doubtless stimulated by his colleagues) attacked the Governor and the Court and let off the politicians, especially Birch, Thorneycroft and H. Wilson, much too lightly. I think partly this is due to a feeling of guilt as they (the City end) did come out of the inquiry rather badly. Lionel Robbins came in to see me yesterday and even he felt that the position of the Bank would never be the same again. Rosenstein-Rodan said he was sure the Governor would be resigning or dismissed before long!

Incidentally the EST asked me on Monday who should take the Governor's place if he resigned (as he is said to have said he would if criticized adversely) over this inquiry. So it seems to be fairly general gossip. I said I thought O. Franks was the only really suitable person – he said he did not trust him, which I can understand but which shows a misunderstanding of his character. He would never put a foot wrong because he is so intelligent, and it is beside the point that he might be acting from expediency rather than principle. He told me that after he had been consulted, in very general terms, by the Chancellor in September he decided that Lloyds should neither buy nor sell securities until the Chancellor had left for America – this on the broadest grounds, that he now knew that there was *something* in the wind and better not to run any risks.

The Chancellor is still trying to get next year's estimates down and wants his colleagues to agree to various cuts, including the first of the child allowances – I think I have put this down once already. He had a meeting about it at No. 10 this afternoon but I don't think they will get anywhere. The PM is going to Australia early this month and will leave R.A.B. in charge – I should think he will be able to outmanoeuvre P.T. if they can avoid any dramatic occasions. I expect R.A.B. will send for me as soon as he is in charge – he has been making some approaches with that in view already. If I were Ministers I would not take my final decisions at all yet, as they will want to be able to move either way according to where they go on wages. This is all going very slowly: no show-downs at all yet and the London 'buses which are in the forefront of the battle still some way from action. Except that delays are a good thing, I would like some movement soon so that we could get an indication of the probable outcome.

IV

Heathcoat Amory's first year,

6 January 1958 to 31 December 1958

For the third time running, Robert Hall found himself under a new Chancellor at the beginning of the year. Thorneycroft had insisted, as a matter of principle, on keeping public expenditure in 1958–9 within the limits of probable expenditure in the current year. When the Cabinet was unwilling to agree to the last £50 million or so of the cuts which he proposed (about 1 per cent of total expenditure), he resigned along with the two junior Treasury Ministers, Nigel Birch and Enoch Powell. The new Chancellor, Heathcoat Amory, felt bound, in these circumstances, to refrain from taking immediate expansionary measures as production began to decline in 1958.

Wednesday, January 8th 1958

Having had so little leave, and feeling I needed a rest, I decided to take this week off and go to Brighton to get some sea air. On Friday (Jan. 3rd) I had a general talk with R. Makins and he said that it would be very odd if we found ourselves on Monday without a Chancellor or either of the two Secs. I said I thought it would be very odd indeed and he said that tempers were rising over the Chancellor's determination to get the estimates down at any cost and that he was being egged on by Birch and Powell, who in their different ways are both rather mad. And though he could hardly believe the Chancellor would be so rash it was at any rate on the cards.

I did not take it very seriously and was astonished when he telephoned me on Monday morning and said that 'when I saw the papers on Tuesday I would probably want to come back'! – which could only mean that at least the Chancellor was going though in the circumstances it seemed certain that the junior Ministers would have to go too. Sure enough it was announced on the BBC at 10.30 that they had all resigned and D. Heathcoat Amory became the new Chancellor. During the afternoon I had speculated about this and thought that, of the three probables, R.A.B. would not be wanted by the PM and would look too soft in such circumstances and Maudling would be thought too junior, so Heathcoat Amory the most likely. I am glad he was chosen as he is a sensible man whom I have liked when I met him before and whom Hitchman (his Perm. Sec.) thinks well of. For the time being Maudling is going to double the European FTA and Ec. Sec. and this is a good move and I am glad.

Altogether I was very much relieved as long as it was not going to mean any weakening on the wage front. The Chancellor was getting more and more into a rigid position which I felt sure would be impossible to hold politically and undesirable from the point of view of the whole economic position of the West, where it is essential to maintain both a fair level of activity and reasonable growth and help to the underdevelopeds. Although I admired him in many ways, and feel sure that but for him we would not have got the wage battle going so clearly and inevitably, I had been very troubled personally by the way he handled the September announcement and said such silly things about the money supply, and I was getting uncomfortable about his rigidity on things like social services and aid to underdeveloped countries where he seemed to be making principles of tactical points and thus in fact making bad errors of judgment and presumably based in the end on a sort of laissez-faire morality.

Powell, the FST, is a very queer man indeed, fanatically holding principles of economy and austerity which he does not understand in the least: and Birch the EST whom I like and find personally congenial, although I was on his side over the control of credit and against the Bank, was doctrinally in many ways an extreme right-wing Tory who felt that it was much better to go down fighting for this (very right-wing) position than to temporize. All this was obviously getting less and less congenial to the feelings of the PM, R.A.B. and Macleod and to the political judgment of all the rest. However the great thing is that the new Chancellor, if he can avoid making any speeches that put him in an exposed position, will regain the freedom of manoeuvre for later in the year which P.T. was deliberately throwing away and locking the house against. Personally of course it is much easier for me, *as long as they stand on wages* which they have asserted vigorously they mean to do.

I came to London on Tuesday and decided to stay till Friday though taking as much holiday as I could. When I arrived R.M. had been having an office meeting and I had a longish private talk with him, which made it clear that it was P.T.'s extreme rigidity which succeeded in the end in turning a Cabinet which had begun on his side unanimously against him. Roger was very glad to see the last of Birch and Powell and on the whole relieved about P.T. though he thought it was great folly to have let things get to this pass and deplored the pass itself.

We were shortly summoned to meet the new Chancellor and he gave us a little talk saying that the old policy was to be continued in all respects and that the first task was to persuade the public of this – he wanted to see the Press and especially, if possible, Tyerman the editor of *The Economist*, to try to get him not to be too violent on Friday. He (H.A.) said that it was almost impossible to understand how they had got to this stage since there was (in the minds of the rest of the Cabinet) very little between them and P.T. They saw it entirely as a matter of practical judgment. It was agreed that the wage front was the crucial one, and that in the time available £50 mn deflation through next year's estimates could have no effect at all. (This is obviously true.)

The question therefore was whether the psychological effect of sticking to a precise figure in the estimates, on opinion at home and abroad, was worth jeopardizing the hope of a reasonable wage settlement (the object of the exercise) which all the rest of Cabinet thought would be the result of cutting another £50 mn off the social services, either on family allowances or on the rest of the welfare subsidies. I must say that all my sympathies were with the Cabinet – although I can see P.T.'s point of view, it was all his fault that he had erected a symbol based on faulty economics and sworn allegiance to it so regularly and publicly that he felt he could not now disown it in public.

Thursday, January 30th

This is one of these periods when a lot of things have happened that one wishes one had written down at the time. Anyway I like the new Chancellor very much and find him most sensible and sympathetic. Both R.A.B. and Hailsham have told me personally that they not only disagreed with Thorneycroft but also with the policy of September 19th and that they are very worried that we are holding back production instead of expanding. Maudling also seems more or less on this line and to be doubtful about sterling. In fact my original instincts about the P.T. line seem to have been more than justified.

I have seen a fair bit of the Chancellor both because of the Economic Debate and because we have had a number of talks about wages. I put it to him very early that there were two separate problems – the load on resources and the pressure of wages on prices – and he emphatically agreed, and separated the two in his speech. So this was a big gain. He is also moving towards saying that we *ought* to resume expansion as soon as we are clear that we can hold prices, although he is very worried about the reserves and wants to speed up our talks with the US. These are provisionally down for February 24th but may be advanced to February 17th.

The Economic Debate [on January 23rd] went off moderately well although I think a lot of Conservatives feel instinctively that P.T. was right. They would not do so if they could see it in active terms. P.T. made a very impressive speech, the Chancellor a dull honest one in which he began to get our economic doctrine back to a manageable form, and R.A.B. an amusing one but very weak on argument. There are two more Debates next week, one on the Bank Rate Tribunal and one on Wages Policy and Industrial Relations. The Tribunal came out with more whitewash than anyone really expected – it is very useful for the Government and I think quite justified. A lot may be said about part-time directors and the way the Bank of England conducts its affairs but the Government has a ready-made answer on all this since it set up the Radcliffe Committee to look into all this about nine months ago, so it is well ahead of any public demand.

Incidentally we have at last finished with Radcliffe as we had our session on Alternative Techniques on January 16th. Unfortunately I had to leave in the middle to see the Chancellor and R.A.B. – which turned out to be a complete waste of time as R.A.B. would not get down to the economic situation which I had gone to discuss – I think he was enjoying working at the Cabinet Room table in No. 10 where (as far as my limited experience goes) all Prime Ministers sit to work. Anyway I feel on reading the Minutes that the quality of the discussion fell away a bit after I left! Probably this is simple vanity. But we made our main points, that the Government *must* be able to control the supply of money and that we did not think Parliament would pass a self-denying ordinance in favour of the Bank of England. Sayers was a bit hard to follow as he had pressed us strongly on funding in previous sessions but in this one he pressed us hard to say that funding would not do the trick – because too many Treasury bills were likely to be held outside the Clearing Banks and therefore monetizable.

On wages we are getting on quite well as Cabinet overrode the M/Labour about the 'bus dispute and accepted the Treasury line that we should only have an inquiry if it covered country as well as town 'buses. At any rate the Government strong line has got across.

Monday, February 10th

The Debate on the Parker [Tribunal] Report lasted for two days [February 3rd and 4th] and was not very edifying. H. Wilson stuck to his guns and in general seems to have confirmed the City view of him which means that they will not co-operate much when he is Chancellor – but I don't suppose this means much; after a long experience of public life I feel a good deal of doubt about whether there are such things as sinister or other forces which make much difference, in fact the Establishment which is so much talked about now is only a name for the collection of people who hold power at any time and in my view they don't hold all that much because the real power is with the electorate. A man not yet established in his career can be a bit damaged by any concerted idea that he is not sound but even then if he makes a row in his own way they soon come round. In fact nobody is all that much tougher than anybody else. Perhaps it was different when rich people were really rich and Dukes were really Dukes but I doubt it. If one reads Trollope, e.g. *The Way We Live Now*, it appears that only those who combined an upright character and a lack of aggressiveness were very susceptible to the Establishment of the day and it is the same now.

The Chancellor made an intentionally anodyne speech in the Debate but it did not prevent the temperature from rising later especially when Maudling would not say whether the PM told the Lord Chancellor that members of the Bank Court's firms had done some of the selling of gilt-edged. The Government story is that the Governor misled the PM.

On Thursday [February 6th] there was a Debate on Industrial Relations and Macleod did very well. The whole question which seems to me the dominant one of the day has moved forward a good deal since September 19th. R. Makins has had a Group working on a paper for Cabinet and it was finished last week. The M/Labour moved a good deal during the discussion and we will recommend what we now call the 'guiding light' principle, i.e. that the Government should state the figure beyond which wage increases would be inflationary (it is put at rather less than 2% in the paper – a bit low I think) and would use such influence as it had to get this accepted. This is really my doctrine which Thorneycroft put to Cabinet in his long paper in the early summer last year [C(57)168] – it has taken a lot of work to get it back there. The general atmosphere is still fairly calm and responsible. When one remembers that M/Labour were expecting the railways and/or 'buses to come to a head about Christmas and realizes that the arbitration is not for several weeks yet, one can see how slowly it is all being taken.

A good deal of pressure has been put on Cohen to get his report out – he came to see the Chancellor last Thursday and said the *printing* would hold them up so the Chancellor has been goading the Stationery Office. According to Bryan Hopkin who came to consult me last week, it won't state a figure but *will* say that this year's ought not to be as much as the cost-of-living increase, hence ought not to be as much as 4%, which is not too bad. However it is all to play for still.

Meanwhile we have had several of the usual bombshells from the Bank. On Thursday they said they wanted to lower Bank Rate in two steps to 5% because they could not hold it at 7% any longer. Also to issue a large long-term Government loan so that they could have something to stop gilt-edged rising. We all felt that it would be regarded as a clear sign that the Government was already easing up – it is *most* extraordinary that if this were done HMG would be blamed and the Bank would go on giving the impression that it was tough and austere and sold out by Civil Servants and politicians. Anyhow the Chancellor took our line and when the Governor came and heard it, he said he *could* hold the rate after all. E. Compton is now charged with trying to find out the exact meaning of not being able to hold a rate, since the Bank told Radcliffe that they *could*. As far as I can see it means that it is awkward for the Discount Market.

Today I got a paper from T.L.R. in which the Bank propose to unify the rates for sterling on the ground that we have gone so far already that we can't stop. No doubt this is true – they have moved steadily towards making sterling convertible without ever asking themselves whether it could be held there. In this paper they say that it all depends on our internal policies and that these will do just as well, or as ill, whether the two rates are unified or not. Actually the balance of payments forecast for 1958 shows a current account surplus of nearly £500 mn so our internal policies are not too bad. But that is not the point, since the strain is going to come on us as bankers and the current account surplus is only one factor in this. Anyway T.L.R. seems to have taken the right view – OF has been gradually transformed in recent years and is as thick as anything with the Economic Section.

Leslie Rowan and I are leaving for Washington on Friday (February 14th) for the first round of talks with the US, largely on this very problem, for our studies of international illiquidity seem to show that sterling will have to stand the strain.[1] It is clear that if we unified the rates now, and as a consequence had to give up dollar discrimination, *and* got driven off the fixed rate later on, this would be regarded as reckless irresponsibility and we would never be able to convince anyone that it wasn't. Especially as the Labour Party would be found to denounce it, since in all the Debates they say we must have more controls and not less.

T. Balogh talked to me over the weekend. He has been asked to submit a paper to the Radcliffe Committee and was very pleased – I am glad as he has some very good ideas which I only hope they take seriously. He also talked very wildly about the need to change key officials when and if the Labour Government came in – he seems to be in touch with H. Wilson and actually asked me if I would prefer to be Governor of the Bank or Joint Perm. Sec. of the Treasury. He hasn't got much idea of how these things are or can be done if he thinks it is going to be as easy as all that.

Tuesday, February 11th

This is the season for all the big exercises and they are now finishing. The Balance of Payments Committee shows a surplus of nearly £500 mn for 1958, a combination of better terms of trade, restricted consumption here and a reversal of stocks. The TIC shows investment very slightly up – the public sector being stabilized at somewhere about end-1957 figure and private investment still rising a little. NIF has not been done yet but J. Downie says that the prospects are for GDP about 1% up on the year, the biggest change being a large forecast reversal from stock-building to stock running down. The reserves are expected to fall in the second half of the year because the RSA will be running such big current account deficits – in spite of a big UK surplus with them, and they (especially India) getting fairly big loans abroad. I think it is certain that we ought to have a no change Budget but to keep a very open mind about what to do later in the year.

The reports about the US imply that they are going down rather faster than they expected and it certainly looks as if the change in expectations is beginning to operate. They expect about 5 million unemployed in February, a high figure. The tone of public pronouncements now seems to be for more Government action although the Administration have not yet said that any more was needed than they have announced already.

I will know a good deal more about this next week but I still do not feel at all alarmed simply because I can't believe that they won't do something about it before it goes on too long. All they have said about balanced Budgets and debt ceiling and holding inflation is round their necks so that they need a bit of time before they can reverse themselves. But surely they will do it. Commodity prices are on the low side but have been fairly steady for some time now and again I can't see them falling much further. This would sound very complacent to many ears but I am fairly confident myself and believe that modern systems are more stable, and modern Governments much more masters of their own fate, and that this reduces the amplitude of downward fluctuations. Also there is so much for the US to lose politically if they get anywhere near out of hand.

The Commonwealth official talks preparatory to the [Montreal] Conference (probably in September) begin in London today. I am not going as I do not think anything much will come up. The main flood of papers is still on the Free Trade Area, where I feel that the UK is in a much more difficult position than most people realize. Meanwhile the French bombing in Tunisia has put a large cloud on the political horizon generally.

Monday, February 17th

After a delay because of a loader's strike, we left London Airport about midnight on Friday (14th) and had a good flight and got to Washington about 3, where Guy Thorold and Pitblado met us. It was just beginning to snow and there was a very heavy fall from then on: it took an hour to drive half a mile to the Embassy for dinner and it is still thick. Leslie Rowan and I had arranged to spend today in New York to see the Federal Reserve people and lunch with Elliott Bell [editor and publisher of *Business Week*], but we decided that we would not be able to get about there. We have come to try to start the 'conversations' with the Americans which I proposed when I was there last November. We put in a paper on World Economic Problems which is to be a sort of agenda for the talks. But I think that the future of them is quite uncertain. Harold Caccia gave us that impression when we dined with him on Saturday. It is partly that it takes them so long to form anything like a 'US' view on anything and partly that they are so much stronger than we and are in doubt to say the least about any partnership idea, and partly the feeling that if anything is decided to be desirable it will somehow involve them in paying for it!

The three things in our paper are the need to continue economic growth in the West and hence to avoid recessions (i.e. the present US one), the idea that international liquidity will be insufficient when expansion does start again, and the general problems raised by under-developed countries. We have done quite a lot of work on liquidity and one result of this trip is that I have had to do some work on it myself and am beginning to feel that I understand it.

Ever since I came to the Economic Section I have had to do more on internal problems, mainly because that was the field in which it has seemed to be recognized that I was supposed to be almost the responsible authority whereas OF have almost always tried to argue that external affairs were essentially theirs and any interests I might have very peripheral. Though of course we have had a lot of struggles with OF. But I never felt that I was able to devote very much attention to it and when Marcus Fleming was Deputy I did not see eye to eye or mind to mind with him. And generally I felt a good deal less than expert in it. However it looks as if I will have to think about it much more from now on and I am glad that this is pressing me to it.

Meanwhile all our relations with OF are very much better. David Butt is in charge of OF Statistical Section which is the key place for ideas (he came on this trip with us) and Denis Rickett is far more conscious of the technical economic requirements; meanwhile Jack Downie, who is much clearer and far more diplomatic than Marcus, is putting in a great deal of time on it, and I hope I will be able to promote Atkinson and put him on the NIF work and thus let Jack do nearly all external. If by any chance we are now starting on an exercise to reconsider Bretton Woods we shall need all our strength for the job.

Wednesday, February 19th

We have now had two lots of talks with the US and are finished from a formal point of view. They put up a very good team – Dillon (State), Coughran (Treasury), Hauge, Saulnier and Marget from the Federal Reserve the first day, and the same plus Anderson, the Secretary of the Treasury, today. There were a rather large number of minor characters which slightly disturbed us as we had hoped the talks would be very informal but in fact it did not make much difference as we talked quite informally all the same.

On the first day we talked about the world (mainly US, UK and W. European) economic position and the tendencies to recession. Saulnier gave a long exposé of the US situation on lines with which we were already familiar – the gist of it was that they expected an upturn in the third quarter and that if this was going to take place they would see the signs of it in the next month or two. (Incidentally the President said this publicly last week but it was taken by the Press to be that there would be an upturn in the next month or two – I gather however that it was phased to produce this result, if so I think it was a mistake.) I got the impression that Saulnier thought it would be very much of a toss-up whether the signs came out right or not. Both he and Hauge said very firmly that whether they did or not, the policy was to prevent any sharp recession and if more were needed more would be done. We had already heard from Guy Thorold that they are working on the sort of tax cut that might be needed.

Hal Lary, about whom I had heard so much from Downie and Nita Watts because both had worked under him at ECE in Geneva, is now the expert on international economics at the Council and he was there and gave a little talk about their international balance, which on a number of fairly favourable hypotheses would show an outflow of $½bn this year though they were all nervous of this figure and I think have all got their doubts. At the end, both Hauge and Saulnier said very emphatically that whether the economy went as they hoped or not, the *policy* was to see that there was no severe recession and an early recovery, and that if more were needed to bring this about, more would be done. We talked a bit about the rest of the world and the general conclusion was that there wasn't much recession except arising from the effects of the US recession plus stationary Europe, on commodity prices.

Today at the Treasury we got on to the rest of our paper (we had put one in on our broad ideas) and especially on to the liquidity problem. Anderson, who had to go early to talk to Congress, led off with a very broad opening statement. That although we wanted a 'sustainable' rate of growth we mustn't risk inflation. The US did not think there was any overall problem of liquidity, only that the distribution of existing reserves was uneven. This was mainly due to reckless policies by the ones whose low reserves were the result of this. The UK had had a great deal of help to *its* reserves lately but they hadn't gone up – this was disquieting. The US thought that the IMF should only be used sparingly and on special occasions. In fact if we wanted higher reserves we ought to earn them. This sounded very blunt but as we had been warned both by Lary and Southard that this was the line they were going to take, it did not surprise me and I felt very grateful to Anderson for being so forthright. Then Leslie Rowan set out our case very well and in particular stressed the point that an enormous amount of thought had gone into the post-war institutions and we were hardly giving any to our own, although the cold war might well be moving into a phase where economic considerations were the dominant ones.

I said a little more on what we thought the problem might be – everyone competing for inadequate liquidity, leading to deflationary forces, and the danger that speculative movements might destroy sterling in the process. Then Marget made a longish speech giving in more detail the reasons for which they thought the problem was not one of inadequacy but of bad internal policies. Then I spoke at rather more length. We agreed that it was wrong to treat as a monetary problem the difficulties of countries which were determined to spend all they could get. But we thought there was a case for the view that total liquidity was inadequate. However even if it were not, there might well be systematic reasons which would lead to deflationary effects if the countries with inadequate reserves tried to get them from those with larger ones – we had no reason to think that e.g. Germany intended to let her reserves fall.

I also dealt with Anderson's thesis that all we needed to do to get reserves was to earn them – we were going to earn a very big surplus this year but did not expect our reserves to rise. Did they really expect us to pursue policies which would give us a substantial increase in reserves? This led to a certain amount of discussion of whether it was or was not easy to earn reserves and of our policy on overseas investment and finally to our moving towards saying that it was a sterling problem – which any liquidity problem *at present* must be since sterling is the weakest of the three forms of reserve now in use.

Thursday, March 20th

The Bank Rate was lowered today from 7 to 6%. The Bank wanted to do this about six weeks ago but we thought it would look as if we were letting up. However the economy is gradually getting easier and it looks as if there will be some slack as time goes on; and it seemed a good thing to have a move on the record, apart from what it would save on London balances and the help to the appearance of the Budget. The difficulty was to find a good story. When the Bank first came they said they wanted to move on technical grounds, as they did a year ago, but we pointed out that both Treasury and Bank had said to the Radcliffe Committee that we could keep the market in the Bank if we wanted to. They were so stung by this that they went off and have in fact kept it in the Bank ever since. We also got them to put out £300 mn of fairly long 5½% stock which has successfully prevented the gilt-edged market from rising much. Once these two were out of the way, the real pretext came from the reserves which have gone up quite fast in January and February and look like an enormous rise in March. So we could say that it was to keep London rates at least in some sort of relation with those overseas. However the Bank then began to feel doubtful, largely because they said there was an adverse reaction in the exchange markets to the bad reception the Cohen Report got.

So we went on arguing – I wanted it as far away from the Budget as possible – and finally the Governor went off on a trip and said it *could* be moved while he was away if anything happened, and for some unknown reason the Deputy, Mynors, suddenly said yesterday that they would move it. E. Compton brought me a statement yesterday which O'Brien had drafted on the right lines but too long – I cut it down and we agreed it with the Chancellor and Maudling but then Mynors wanted it changed. However we stuck to our point about relation of interest rates at home and abroad, and at least this was given in guidance to the Press (the Deputy saw some of them) and Clem Leslie passed it on all too clearly to Reuters and *The Economist*. It seems to have got clearly enough into the papers and sterling, if anything, was stronger at today's close.

This is of course the busy time on Budget, Survey and so on, and quite a lot has been happening.

Tuesday, March 25th

Quite a long time ago, it seemed to me that the Government could not very well relax its deflationary policy until it knew where it was going to be on wages. For a number of months now the economy has been moving very slowly downwards and in relation to our capacity we must be well below where we could be, but that could not be taken advantage of. I recommended this in both the preliminary and the final Budget Committee appreciations.[2] However the slackness is getting a little more marked every month and most Ministers are now in an early stage of unemployment nerves; so that I do not think a little easing now would do any harm. Faced with the need to make the Budget appear to have a little interest, the Chancellor decided to concentrate on reform and rationalization and that is now the keynote. But it started with the idea that any gifts should be offset by extra imposts.

I have been arguing that now was *not* the time to annoy anyone; quite enough annoyance has been caused by the various measures of the past two years, and I thought better to do nothing than purchase a change by an annoyance. This was warmly supported by R. Maudling and has now been accepted, and as a result we shall probably give about £50 mn away. This is of course nothing in the present context with fixed investment steady, stocks and exports probably falling and also

Government expenditure. However I hope it won't look like weakening as we are still far from any clear idea on wages. The 'bus arbitration gave 8/6 [42.5p] or about 4% to two-thirds of the London 'bus men and we are now waiting for the railway arbitration. I don't think we will get through on 3% as I had hoped but it is clear that the Government will not stick to the Thorneycroft line which would have committed them to more deflation.

Monday, March 31st

The Chancellor has a habit of collecting people, quite often Makins, me and Maudling, quite late in the day and sitting on indefinitely, long after others want to get back to their work or to go to dinner. He seems to be quite unaware of any engagements others may have though he is the soul of politeness when his attention is called to it. Anyway I am getting to know him fairly well and he is certainly a likeable person. Very slow in his conduct of business, and not liking to make up his mind until he has been over the ground a good deal. But not like R.A.B. who wanted to be proved right and would really have liked to announce a decision and then have another chance after he had seen the reactions to it. This man is just careful and modest and wants to be sure, but he has a mind and he has principles. His mind must work rather like mine I think: and he sets store on the opinion of Plowden and O. Franks, unfortunately for him as they ask me what *I* think before they go to see him.

Apart from the Budget, which is more or less settled, there are a lot of other things to keep us busy, and many of these stem from the PM who is far more interested in economics than any of his predecessors in my time. For one thing, he is clearly very nervous lest we should get into a severe slump and keeps on asking if we know what we will do and ought we not to be giving more stimulus to the economy and so on. This while the wage round is still all to play for.

He has also been very keen on a floating rate lately. According to O.S.F. this was much stimulated by Robarts of Barclays though I should not think he needed much stimulus. Anyway I have written a long and eloquent essay on the subject which he is to get this week – it was based on papers by Denis Rickett and the Bank but I was asked to do the final draft on the ground that I was particularly able to write clearly. When one thinks of 1952 it is very funny that T.L.R. should ask me to write a paper for the PM *against* floating rates. The Bank is also against them so for once we are all on the same side. But the Bank want to unify the rates for dollars and for transferable sterling which both OF and I think would be tantamount to full non-resident convertibility and would be very hard to defend publicly at a time when we are all afraid of what a US recession might do. So at any rate it is put off till after the Budget. R. Makins tends to take the Bank line if they are opposed by the Treasury and an unorthodox line if the Bank and Treasury are agreed but he is very fair and sensible about it and on the whole a very good head of Treasury, at least after the long period when E.B. had no time to spare. N. Brook is being almost too correct and keeps out of everything.[3]

Broadly speaking, we are spending a lot of time on anti-recession measures, partly to keep the Ministers from going too far. Apart from an inquiry which I have suggested to the Budget Committee about these measures in general, we are trying to dress up a 'soft spots' policy for areas of undue unemployment, so that Ministers will be able at least to appear to be sorry for them: and to explore the possibilities of short-term credits to sterling area countries whose London balances are getting too low because of the fall in commodity prices. The latter is a good example of the new co-operation in the Treasury. The CRO wrote suggesting something of the sort and it was passed around OF and came to Denis Rickett with a recommendation that it should be turned down flat. Denis sent me the papers to look at and I wrote a long Minute saying that in a recession it was logical that we should help them, and give them something to pay off in a boom when our balance of payments would be bad. This caused them all to reconsider it and now it is official doctrine and a paper was approved by the Steering Committee this morning recommending it to Ministers, whose minds are working that way already anyhow.[4]

Monday, April 14th

All is clear for the Budget tomorrow and I am sure that there has never been in my time any set of proceedings so calm and straightforward as this year. The proposed tax changes are all in the downward direction but the total to be given away (£50 mn in the first year) makes it a somewhat deflationary Budget by all previous standards or rather it leaves the total prospect for the economy deflationary because we expect stocks and exports both to fall.

The Chancellor has no doubt consulted nearly all his colleagues and as a result his proposals seem to be quite intelligently forecast in the newspapers. But he has not made any concessions to the colleagues and generally speaking it is all on the lines I have suggested. The only thing that might cause some trouble is the unification of the two profits tax rates, which will certainly be said to be provocative on wages. However I hope that the other concessions will create a fairly mild atmosphere.

He has made very easy work of the speech which only went into four drafts before going to press which it has now done. I stayed around the last few days in case I should be wanted but when I saw the Chancellor on Friday he told me that he was ready to settle for it as it stood and I agreed. It is shorter than usual and I hope makes his position clear: I expect it will sound dull because he is no orator and so much of it is dreary anyhow.

The BC agreed that we ought to make a study of anti-recession measures. This became a bit more pressing because the PM made a speech in which he said all our plans were prepared which implied rather a different state of affairs than actually obtains – so much so that Hugh Beaver, the President of the FBI, said that plans were no good unless the land had been bought already – the PM ought to have said 'there were a number of measures which could be taken at once'. Anyway I am going to edit a sort of war book and have it ready for the Chancellor about the end of this month.

The most striking developments have been the movement on the wages front. The 'bus men rejected the award and are talking about a strike on May 5th. Then last week the railways result was announced, recommending by 2–1 a no change award. I would have preferred say a 2% increase with the hope that this would become general as I cannot think that all later settlements will be nil, and the railwaymen will feel much aggrieved if they are the only people to get nothing. However the papers generally have said we must stick to this and I think the Chancellor is going to stick to it, although some of his colleagues would like to make some concessions. At first it looked as if we were sure to have a transport strike but over the weekend it has become more doubtful, largely because people believe the Government really will stand firm and partly because the Labour Party are afraid that if there is a bad strike – against the objective of steady prices – it will be bad for them politically.

Personally I do not feel at all certain that the Government are going to lose, as no doubt I have written before. Anyway nothing could more dramatize the wage issue than this nil recommendation and so far it has gone very much better than we might have expected. And the Budget won't make things worse and if anything should ease tension slightly. I have told the Chancellor that he will have to make up his mind about his wage policy before the end of this round, because I don't think the PM will wait till then before he demands a bit of reflation somewhere.

The economy is still moving gently down but it is very gentle and no one is seriously worried. So far exports have stayed up well and the balance of payments is very good, and so curiously perhaps are the gold figures. At any rate none of us thought they would be as good as they are. The US picture is a bit more alarming than I thought it was going to be – at least that is what my US friends tell me – Kit McMahon wrote quite a gloomy letter today to say that I ought to revise my views that the US Government would do all that was needed, because it was not at all likely that they would and the downward momentum would soon get a force that would need some stopping. As far as I can see, the Administration is less active than they implied that they would be when we were there in February, and more afraid of starting a boom again. But it may just be the weakness of the President plus extreme Conservatism in the Senate. Anyhow I feel that I may have been too optimistic and am now considering whether we ought to change our policies at all, though I think that the central idea, of keeping up the sterling balances by lending to those who are approaching a deficit, is the main one.

I had a talk to Norman Brook last week about my own position, on the lines of my talk to Tom Padmore last year. Norman was very nice and said that although his policy was to look very severely at Permanent Secretaries after they were 60, he did not think that my job had worn me out as much as some of them and that I certainly need not assume that I must go at 60 – on the contrary, his present view was more like 65. But he quite understood that I might want to get another job and one would get a better one and do it better if one did not leave it till too late. He did not think anyone wanted me to go, in fact they would be very sorry if I did. But he himself had determined to go at 60 and was telling everyone so as this would make it harder for him to change his mind.

I have recommended that Fred Atkinson should be promoted. (This came through end of April.) Mrs Abbot, who is now Establishments Officer, told me a little while ago that when D. Butt went to Nuffield on a year's leave in October, they would be asking me for Downie or Atkinson to take his place in OF Stats. I said I could not spare anyone but might be more reasonable if I could get Hopkin. It would be a help if Fred were promoted before then. And I would like to keep Watts for another year to help Jack Downie on the international problems. My staff difficulties remain more or less the same, that is, it is very hard to get people in fast enough to take the place of those who are leaving. But I have got a very nice man called Opie from LSE to take Scammell's place, and at the end of the year hope to get a man called Mackintosh from Birmingham. If I can get Hopkin in September to take over the NIF work from Downie and reorganize the whole thing, it will be a considerable help.

Tuesday, April 22nd

The Budget Debate ended very quietly yesterday and in doing so kept the tone which it had had all through, and which was set both by the matter, and by the Chancellor's manner. He spoke quite well and was listened to carefully but it was not at all oratorical or exciting. Labour divided on the profits tax resolution and then took the line that it was an 'irrelevant' Budget and that they would ask for a Debate soon on the economic situation, which is ridiculous since the Budget Debate has been on that since 1948 when it was put a day longer, and the Survey brought out to suit, on purpose.

Nothing very interesting happened in the Debate. Labour made a little of profits tax but couldn't get much out of it, and they talked a great deal, but mostly fairly loosely, about stagnation. Several good speeches were made on wages and I would judge that the whole problem is getting far better understood. None of the Opposition faced the problem of how to fit in the sort of expansion they wanted with our balance of payments problems, except the usual references to controls which are on the whole misleading.

The main headache for the Chancellor turned out to be with his own party because of the retrospective provisions on dividend stripping. This is much disliked on principle. Unfortunately, the Chancellor either did not mention it to Cabinet or (more probably) did it so vaguely that no one took the point. So he feels, as I would in his place, that he can't insist. It is rather a breakdown of the whole system. Officials ought to have flogged it more. And the three Treasury Ministers between them ought to have realized that there would be this trouble. And either the Chancellor or R. Maudling should have put it squarely to Cabinet. Now the Chancellor will have to give it up, and this will cause much more damage than if he had never put it in. He said last night that he would reconsider 'before the Finance Bill' but he means to drop it from the Bill and it was quite a struggle to get him not to drop it last night. The other changes were all welcome and I think my advice to put in nothing to offend anyone has paid off well. Incidentally the Chancellor did very well on TV and seems to have quite a personality for it.

The railway dispute is taking up a lot of time and is being mainly handled by the PM. They are trying to do a deal on the lines of hurrying on the modernization programme (which is useful anyway in the present down-turn) and promising to look at wages again in the autumn. I don't know if the leaders can hold the men, and the 'bus strike is still due for May 5th. The railways would be mad, if they are going to strike at all, not to choose the same day.

Until after the Budget, Hall had been content to see a slackening of activity so long as the trend in wage settlements was still uncertain. By May the increasing slack in the system was beginning to worry him. He foresaw a level of unemployment rising, first to 600,000 in January 1959 (entry for May 12th), then to 750,000 (entry for July 29th). By August, however, he was reassured by evidence that unemployment had climbed less steeply in May and June. The total number on the register (to which all his figures refer) reached a peak of 621,000 (2.8 per cent) in January 1959 but the seasonally adjusted figure had reached a peak in November 1958.

Hall was also right in judging that stockbuilding would be less than in 1957 and that there would be some falling-off in exports. The biggest drop in 1958, however, was in public expenditure on goods and services.

Monday, May 12th

The 'bus strike has now gone on for a week and no one seems to mind much. There was a Debate about it on Thursday when Macleod made a bitter attack on Gaitskell. I was not there but heard Gaitskell and the PM wind up. It seemed fairly clear that the Opposition was very much worried about the situation, as they tended to shout down all the points of any substance made from the Government benches. Gaitskell attacked Macleod on the ground that he had turned the Ministry of Labour from an impartial body to a Government stooge, but this begged the whole question of whether the Government were right to have a wages policy or not. The PM made quite a good speech but in the temper of the House it was not particularly listened to and often interrupted.

Meanwhile all the energy has been put into the railway settlement with both sides showing an astonishing amount of forbearance and caution. The PM is most anxious to settle it but some of his back-benchers led by Thorneycroft are making it clear that they will attack him if he recedes. It is being tackled mainly in terms of more capital now plus various reorganizations with a promise to reconsider the wages position later. I have not been brought in much as R. Makins and Stevenson are doing it all but I gather that the main stumbling block is that the Unions want something at once and it is hard to reconcile this with policy as announced so far.

I am beginning to get worried about the whole position. Unemployment is now quite clearly on an up trend, and as the index of production is practically steady, this must mean that labour is being squeezed out of the system. Exports have kept up well but are bound to fall away soon. Stocks have shown no signs but I cannot think that they will be built up at last year's rate. All this suggests that we shall have 600,000 or more unemployed by next January and hence that we ought to be moving already. But the philosophy of the present policy is that we should not let up until we know where we are on wages, and the wage settlements have taken such a long time that we will be moving downwards faster than I like while still committed to holding the line.

The cowardice and folly of the Government in all these wage questions is very irritating to me. In 1956 they got things moving, only to sell out over the railways in 1957 because they had been such fools over Suez. So we got a big wage settlement instead of a small one and that left it all to do again. Thorneycroft put a paper to Cabinet on the lines of my note, recommending that the Government should indicate the amount it thought reasonable, but they fluffed this and appointed the Cohen Committee which has been nothing but an embarrassment. Then an official Committee recommended the guiding light which was really what I had recommended already. No action was taken on this but meanwhile there was the September statement committing the Government to a tough line. Now they are in a position which really cannot be defended, since they can't answer those who say that *they* are holding down production, or those who say that whatever their policy means it cannot justify *no* increase which is what caused the trouble on the railways.

I have put in two more papers, one has gone to the Chancellor and the other is a draft Cabinet paper which I would like the Chancellor to put in.[5] Both say that we will have to start expanding soon and that a necessary part of this is to say something about wages. Even if there is some sort of railway settlement, the Government will have to say if it is good or not, and if they say it is good it will mean that similar settlements in the other disputes will be all right.

Lots of other rather minor things have happened including a most awkward case about dumping of butter.[6] In 1956 Ministers were stupid enough to take powers to impose anti-dumping duties against countries because *third* countries were being injured. Now New Zealand has put in a case against Swedish, Finnish and Irish butter. Once we start to police the trade of other countries we shall never stop, especially in the agricultural field. But Ministers are in a state of nerves about Commonwealth relations.

The Free Trade Area is also causing trouble as we have to change our ground and are moving towards putting duties on Commonwealth products. The Steering Committee had no less than three meetings on this last week. Leslie Rowan and I are going to the US tomorrow to resume our talks started in February. I am much more worried about the US situation than I was, as developments have been as bad as we expected and action by the US Government much less.

Saturday, May 17th (Washington, DC)

We have now finished our talks and I am going to Boston for the weekend, to see my daughter and to talk to some of the economists there.

T.L.R. and I left London on Tuesday 13th and flew by day which I have not done since the 'plane services became fast and regular. But there is a great deal to say for it as one doesn't have to rush off at the end of the day's work, but starts more or less rested – then a long lazy day to read all the papers, and arrive just in time to go to bed. We had four meetings with the US, a short one with Anderson then two with the whole team and at the end another shortish one with Anderson to take stock. I also had a long talk to Hauge and a brief one with Saulnier. Otherwise I lunched with J. Alsop and had a long talk at a dinner party with Walter Lippmann.

The general impressions are:

The US economic situation. They seem more confident that they know where they are and expect the recession, which is continuing but at a slower pace, to reach bottom in the next few months. Government expenditure and building houses are rising, consumption holding up fairly well, fixed investment well down and inventory liquidation going on fast. As soon as the pace of the latter slackens, they think the balance of the remaining forces will cause the economy to flatten out. But they seem cautious and I expect they feel uncertain about when it will rise again, though on the most general grounds they think the longer-term outlook is for a rapid expansion. I do not see myself how they can expand or at any rate how they can get back to full output if investment stays at or near its present figure since I am sure that they would save much more than this if incomes corresponded to full output.

The recession is markedly localized, being much worse in places like Detroit, Pittsburg, Chicago and to some extent in the N. England textile areas. The result of this in political terms is that although there are bitter complaints from the bad spots, they get a good many representations from those who are still worried about wages and prices but who don't feel personally much affected by the slump. The above picture was more or less confirmed by other sources but both Leslie Rowan and I heard independently that the railways are in very bad shape financially and that a number of them are on the edge of receiverships. If this is right it must be a considerable weakening factor hanging over them, since I should think business confidence would be affected. At present the stock market is holding up in a way which implies that they can see recovery not far off.

The big change since February is that the official attitude has become much less interventionist. Saulnier and Hauge both said they were more concerned at the economic and political effects on overseas countries of present tendencies, than about the internal affects. In February they both said quite plainly that the Government would intervene if necessary, but with the implication that 'necessary' meant if there was not a recovery fairly soon. Now they seem complacent. Hauge said he thought the US must get used to booms and slumps of moderate dimensions because to stop them meant too much interference. They all seem to be worried about the dangers of getting into an inflation fairly soon if they did anything much, and Hauge especially said that if they made a tax cut they would never get it back – I can well believe this but don't see why they couldn't do it in the form of a temporary discount, e.g. if you let everyone off 10% or 20% of what they owe *this* year, no rates are cut and no one ought to regard it as other than a bonus.

I feel fairly sure that the present attitude is due to a combination of the President being so ill and of the Republican dislike of deficit finance and fear of inflation and Keynes and the New Deal. W. Lippmann said that the President is very closely guarded and that he has known personally a number of people who wanted to see him and when they explained that it was about some bad news or menacing development, they were told that they just couldn't see him. I doubt if he can really be kept as much in ignorance as this implies, since he has regular Press Conferences and presumably it is out of the question to fix these in any way. But I think that there is a strong tendency in old and ailing men to pay as little attention as possible to any information that would require an output of energy, to favour the easy-going interpretation and to trust those who advise that nothing needs to be done (e.g. B. Gilbert).

Otherwise Anderson is, I suppose, less strong than I had hoped and quite close to the ultra-conservative-finance members of Congress: I am told that George Humphrey is very influential again: and I imagine that Bill Martin still thinks it is best to go through the wringer, especially as he must be very disappointed that prices still go up in spite of all this deflation. And I suppose that Saulnier and Hauge have gradually become infected by the combination of an inactive President and strong men also in favour of inaction.

Anyhow they have not done anything much – all their measures are either still being discussed, or do not amount to much. They have not even got the legislation through to extend the period of unemployment benefit, although a lot of men drop out of benefit every week. This would not matter if there were a real recovery in sight but I do not now think that there is. And if they go dragging along their present rather high floor, the movement away from it might be down as well as up.

They are I think genuinely worried about the overseas implications and conscious of the handle they are giving to anti-American feeling:

indeed the fall in commodity prices must have had at least some contributory effect in the attitude towards Nixon, who returned to a triumphal welcome while we were there, after his alarming experiences in South America, which he bore with so much fortitude. Hauge says that they are even thinking more seriously about commodity agreements which is a big change though whether it will get anything done is another matter.

On the international liquidity problem, it all went very much better this time than last. Anderson told us at our first small meeting that the US position was that nothing needed to be done and certainly that no immediate action was possible for them. In fact he warned us plainly that if it looked as if the US were under pressure to take any action (i.e. as it would seem, for Congress to vote more dollars) this would harden their hearts. NB nothing that could be dressed up as a rescue for sterling. All this is only too familiar a line particularly with this inactive Administration. H. Caccia is constantly warning us not to take it too much for gospel, as in fact they *do* react to pressure and their desire not to be criticized publicly is fundamentally the desire to pretend that all is well rather than a genuine belief that saying nothing is the best way to get Congress to act.

At the bigger meeting, however, once this caveat was repeated, we had a genuine discussion of the problem and possible techniques. Everyone was as helpful and constructive as possible, and no one seriously argued either that there was no problem, or that my account of possible strains in world trade was an alarmist one. We both agreed that an increase in IMF quotas was the most sensible and practicable way to proceed though they said that an increase by 100% was much more than they considered necessary. Anyway at this stage there was no disposition to argue and we were rather struck by the fact that Arthur Marget, who had been the most questioning of our thesis in February, made a little speech in which he said how pleased they were that the UK and the USA saw more or less eye to eye about the IMF, since this was an essential for its good working. Leslie Rowan had said earlier that we were very conscious that there was a danger of making international money available to those who wanted to live beyond their income and we fully recognized this and thought the Fund was the best place to exercise discipline and Frank Southard (who for many years had been very worried because the Fund might be misused in this way) felt obliged to caution us that we were still living in a world where politics might require us to shade our principles.

In the afternoon, after lunch with Anderson, we had our second talk with him and Coughran and I had thought he might have mentioned the tactics for the next Fund meeting, but he didn't and mostly asked us about the prospects for the Free Trade Area, which are anything but rosy. In addition to the general difficulties, the immediate French outlook is now quite uncertain because of the *crise de régime* – which broke out in the papers the morning we arrived in Washington. Of course one has been expecting the French position to fall to bits for a very long time but that does not make it any better now it is here. The news has been up and down all the week – a surprisingly large majority for Pfimlin (= anti-de Gaulle anti-authoritarian) but it does not seem to have produced much of an access of authority to the Government.

We made it clear to Anderson, as I did privately to Hauge, that the Chancellor would have to speak about the liquidity problem in September or rather October in New Delhi where the Bank/Fund meeting is to be.

The other interesting thing in Washington was that we had a long talk with Gene Black, President of IBRD, and he told us that he will be short of funds soon after 1960. The reason, of which I was not till then aware, is that the US Government has guaranteed the bulk of their borrowing in New York, and this has given them what in the UK would be trustee status. Now they are not far from the limit of the guarantee and think that their credit rating would drop if it were reached. I had thought they were building up an independent position in the investment field but apparently this was largely (though it cannot have been all) illusion. Anyway Gene wants to increase *his* resources and suggested that there should be a new look at both IBRD and IMF, and of course this would suit us very well. He also said that Congress was so disillusioned by its own loans, etc., to overseas countries that it was now much more keen on using selected international bodies.

Leslie Rowan tried on him our idea of a Commonwealth Development Fund but his reaction was just what I expected, i.e. he didn't want anyone else to cream the projects, or weaken his security, or compete for funds he might have got. In fact he said the most useful thing we could do was to provide 'equity funds' which would be loans repayable only in local currencies (not to be converted) and used for ancillary purposes to his own projects. We thought he rather overstated it but of course we can't do much without his good will. This was just the objection I had voiced in London.

Tuesday, July 29th

The last two months have been very busy and a lot of interesting things have happened. On the international scene, the US has done rather better with its economy that I expected though I still think it won't go up very fast. We had a meeting of the Economic Experts in Paris on June 16th and Saulnier told me that he hoped people would not think everything was set for a boom. They have continued to move on international liquidity and we understand that Anderson will get a letter from the President soon referring to this, which will enable a proposal to be made for a review of the resources both of the Fund and the Bank, at New Delhi in October. This is really quite fast going since we only put it to them in February and the case has not got any stronger since then.

The experts' meeting in Paris was quite significant as I got permission to raise the question of whether there was not a real downward tendency now and we all agreed (a) that there was, (b) that there ought to be expansion, (c) that the countries in the strongest position should move first, (d) that underdeveloped and primary producers needed special attention. These conclusions were endorsed by the Deputies (to Finance Ministers – Working Party 2) a week later and are now being considered and no doubt endorsed by Ministers themselves at a meeting in Paris which began yesterday. I do not suppose it will make much difference but it does show what a lot of change there is in the international economic world compared to pre-war, that there should be all this examination and a series of reflationary steps although the recessionary tendencies haven't gone very far yet.

There was a protracted meeting of officials, preparatory to the Commonwealth Economic Conference in Montreal in September, in London in the first three weeks of June [PRO CAB 130/143 and 148–9]. It did not make a great deal of progress but placed a lot of stress on commodity prices and on the need for a positive policy for the underdeveloped, which means more or less that the UK will have to lend. We have made a good deal of progress in this field as (a) we are actually lending money to Pakistan and probably to New Zealand and India too, (b) we have at last (on my instigation) set up a Committee on overseas investment which will try to decide how much we could or should lend and what mechanisms we have to influence the direction of lending.[7] This is a crying need and it shows how far we have come since the days when it was considered indecent to ask questions about the £350 mn export surplus, that this Committee was set up with no real trouble. The TIC is doing much better and now makes an annual review of the investment outlook for 3 or 4 years ahead. The only bad gap now is in HF Stats and I think we can get this filled soon, because W. Armstrong is taking over from E. Compton (see below).

Anyway, the agenda for the Commonwealth Conference is not turning out any better than on previous occasions – it seems to be standard form that Ministers decide to have one and that officials are unable to find any real business to be done. Although the Commonwealth is a very real entity and of great international significance, it is too disparate in its economic problems and indeed policies for there to be any really suitable subject. When there are common interests there is fairly continuous consultation already.

I am hoping not to have to go to the Conference but I will try to go to the IMF meeting.

On the home front things have gone very well. At Budget time we decided to make very little change, principally because the wage round was still going on, but to have another look in June. The deflationary forces went on quite mildly but steadily, and in the meantime the trend to squeeze surplus labour out became plainly established. Our projections suggested that we might have 750,000 unemployed by January and I got the Chancellor to put in a paper to EPC [EA(58)32] which indicated 700,000 and discussed the outlook generally.

He had decided to bring the request on bank advances to an end and to ease up on the CIC. These had to be done as a preliminary to any other relaxations and they went through smoothly enough. He also doubled the initial allowance concession he had made in the Budget. His colleagues who showed little alarm at first have now got rather disquieted. The whole operation of going over from the Thorneycroft line to one of expansion has been fairly tricky both because they didn't want to say too plainly that they were changing it, and also because we didn't want either to alarm foreigners or to make the Trade Unions think our views on wages were any easier.

As far as the foreigner is concerned, the pound has remained very strong. This is mainly because the terms of trade have given us such a big surplus, so that sterling has actually got scarcer. But our own policies have been on the restrictive side. The main problem here was to move gradually and not to upset anyone.

On wages, we have not done too badly. The Government showed that it was prepared to have a strike if need be by sticking for a long time to the award for the London 'buses and in fact having a strike, a very good one from their point of view as it didn't hurt anyone very badly and used up some TGWU funds. They had to do some heavy rationalization to defend the railway settlement but at 3% it was not a bad bargain. The whole round has gone much more slowly and the result been much more moderate than in any of the previous seven years and at 3½ to 4% it is almost bearable.

It was the success on these two fronts plus the growth of unemployment that made me push for the relaxations and I think the Chancellor is on the point of adding about £35 mn to the public sector investment for the rest of this year (in house repairs, etc., which can be done quickly) and also he is going to ease up on Hire Purchase. These two together should get us through to January and I hope to the next Budget if the Government holds on so long. Their popularity has suddenly increased (I think because of the 'bus strike) and there is now a lot of gossip about a possible election this autumn. However I do not expect it myself as the next Budget can be a very easy one – with the present relaxations on investment and Hire Purchase more or less worn off by then.

Hall was fond of commenting in his diary on the strengths and weaknesses of Ministers and colleagues. The entry for July 30th gives his impressions of top Treasury officials at unusual length. But just as the face of the Treasury changed over the years before 1958 as he describes, so it had changed again by the time he left in April 1961. Within eighteen months Makins had gone as Chairman to the Atomic Energy Authority and been succeeded by Frank Lee, who in turn was succeeded in 1962 by William Armstrong. By the early 1960s Padmore, Fraser and Winnifrith had all moved to other departments as Permanent Secretaries. Rickett had become Second Secretary in charge of OF, Hall had gone, and Clarke in 1964 took over the new Ministry of Technology. Hall's earlier selection (entries for October 3rd, 1954 and December 7th, 1955) of Trend and Armstrong as the two ablest members of the Treasury had been endorsed by the appointment of Trend as Cabinet Secretary and Armstrong as Permanent Secretary of the Treasury.

Wednesday, July 30th – Recent changes in the Treasury

The week before last E. Compton came to see me and told me that he was to become Comptroller and Auditor-General and W. Armstrong to take his place. The next day, Leslie Rowan told me that he was leaving in November and going to Vickers. And a Treasury notice a few days later said that he would not be replaced but that Denis Rickett would do the job, remaining as 3rd Sec. This is in accordance with what, according to office gossip, is N. Brook's policy to give up 2nd Secs altogether. I am doubtful about it as you need really good men at the head of OF and HF, and it would not be fair to keep them there when less good ones were becoming Permanent Secretaries elsewhere.

I was rather surprised about Leslie Rowan. He told me that he had developing family responsibilities and also that this job put too much strain on his health. Both of these are true (if he left at 60 he would have a child of 9) but he has been so proud of the Civil Service and so anxious to work for it that I think there must be a further element. He was very much upset when R. Makins was brought here and I think that he also feels that R.M. does not altogether trust him and that he would be glad to move him – this on top of E. Bridges trying to shift him to the War Office two years ago.

Anyway the whole face of the Treasury has now been changed since, let us say, five years ago. The top people then were Bridges, Plowden, Eady, Gilbert and Rowan: then Brittain, Playfair, Padmore and a number of lesser ones including A. Johnston and J. Crombie. Rickett was in the US, O. Clarke was an Under Sec. in OF and W. Armstrong an Under Sec. in I think HF. Now N. Brook and R. Makins are at the top, T. Padmore is the only 2nd Secretary, and the 3rd Secs will be Rickett in charge of OF, Clarke in charge of HOPS which has succeeded CEPS, Armstrong in charge of HF, and the Supply work divided between Winnifrith and Bruce Fraser. It is an astonishing change on which I will comment at some length.

Broadly speaking, all the top people in the Treasury have been ones who formed their ideas in the pre-war period, except for Plowden and me. Of course I formed mine then but being an economist at Oxford I grew up so to speak in a Keynesian atmosphere. Rowan is six years younger than I am but I do not think he is what I would call modern in his views, being temperamentally on the Thorneycroft–D. H. Robertson–Oscar Hobson side. Bridges tried hard to understand and he was in many ways a very enlightened man – his main trouble was that he tried to do far too much and couldn't really take on new ideas at all when he had so little time to use even the ones he started with. Eady was rather mad, B. Gilbert very lazy and didn't care. Brittain was a very nice man in many ways but he was essentially someone to carry out other people's ideas. E. Compton has tried very hard recently but he has never understood monetary theory as was very clear when we were dealing with Radcliffe. I ought also to mention Hancock at Inland Revenue whom I regard as an ultra-Conservative type, reasonably intelligent but using his brain to support what he thought politically desirable.

Anyway it is a most striking fact that there have been or are going to be these very widespread changes: and at the end of them there will be no one in a top position who was there five years ago, except myself: and many of the ones who are going now belong more to the pre-1939 than to the post-1939 generation of Civil Servants: either by upbringing or by temperament. E. Playfair was lively enough and on the whole understood modern ideas; if I had any quarrel with him it was that he enjoyed iconoclasm for its own sake and thought all sorts of things eikons that I did not.

Now N. Brook keeps himself strictly to establishment work and has left R. Makins free to concentrate on the economic side. R.M. spent all his life in the Foreign Office until he came here in 1956. So far as he has ideas, they were picked up in rather an All Souls atmosphere before the war. But he really came with a fairly open mind, temperamentally Conservative but not attached to any particular school of thought, and on the whole inclined to prefer my advice to anyone else's. Next to him will be T. Padmore, still something of an enigma but so far as he has views they are modern ones. He is very young (49), picked out early for promotion and had spent a great deal of the post-war period on the Establishments side. I don't really think he will be very tough. But at any rate his background will make him flexible.

The other important people will be Rickett, Clarke and Armstrong. Rickett was at All Souls and went to the Economic Advisory Council in 1931 so he was immersed in the ideas that were being developed at that time: he has comparatively little Treasury experience. I have talked a great deal to him since he went to Washington as Economic Minister in 1951 and he is rather advanced in his ideas, and indeed I think quite susceptible to people like Butt and Downie, and thinks that the Economic Section is the place with which problems should first be discussed. I do not think he is nearly so tough as Leslie Rowan and at one time I thought he did not really care very much what happened one way or another but in the last few years he has developed a good deal.

As anyone who has read this diary will be well aware (if anyone ever does) Leslie Rowan has been a great thorn in my flesh at various times. This has been much less marked in the past two years, partly because he was gradually coming under the influence of new people in OF, partly that he was coming to distrust the Bank more and more, partly that the economic situation has been improving. But with so much behind us, and with his temperament still inclined to moodiness, bad temper and prima donna-ism, I cannot really be sorry he is going, and indeed I think he was at heart a deep admirer of the later Thorneycroft and always had a tendency towards dying in the last ditch, or rather feeling that Ministers ought to do so, for very doubtful causes. He will be a loss to the Civil Service because he was a tremendous worker, had a high sense of duty, undoubted courage and ability to grasp difficult problems by the sheer force of his labours (rather than the quality of his mind). But I think the Treasury will be a better place for the sort of problems we have to face, and the sort of world we have to live in, without him.

Otto Clarke is the biggest uncertainty. He began life as a mathematician and was a financial journalist before the war. He is of course very well up in modern economic thinking and is a man of great drive, energy and ability. When he was in OF the Economic Section regarded him as Leslie Rowan's evil genius and I fully shared this view. Nevertheless, when E. Bridges asked me if I would agree to work with him if he was put in charge of HOPS [Home and Overseas Planning Staff] after Strath went, I was in favour because I was afraid that the work would wither away otherwise. I think I have been fully justified, if only because of the way he has got the investment work pulled together and put on a far better footing than it ever was in Edwin's days. He also realizes that HOPS needs to work with the Economic Section, has co-operated in lending me half one of his Under Secs [Figgures] to act as Deputy, and uses my people freely. In fact I think he would not mind at all if they were incorporated in his staff.

My main fear about him (since I don't think he can swallow me or even prevail over me at this late hour) is that he has a strong Napoleonic streak combined with a contempt for facts and a pleasure in experimental novelties. However he never seems to me to move as easily as one would expect in Ministerial or even in Permanent Secretary levels and I think he is slowing up a bit. So perhaps the monster is tamed and can be used only for good works.

Finally, E. Compton, although no one could have been nicer to me or more anxious to co-operate, has never had the brains or the personality for the HF job – he is afraid of the Bank, afraid of his own intellectual equipment, and though we have made great progress in that field, there was so much to do that I have been afraid it was the most out-of-date part of the Treasury. I like him personally, he works hard and is very thorough as a Civil Servant, with everything well documented, etc. But W. Armstrong was really trained by the Economic Section when we had to work with him (as the Chancellor's PPS) over the Budget speeches 1950/53. At that time I formed the view that he was the next man to Trend among the young Treasury men. He has a very good brain, a very strong character and quite a modern outlook.

I do not know either Winnifrith or Bruce Fraser at all well, in the sense that I have never had any arguments with them. But I do not think either of them have got any particular pre-conceived ideas and rather tend to think that the Economic Section way of looking at things is the normal one. To sum up, there will be very nearly a new team at the Treasury and they will be 'modern' in their outlook: and I at least expect to have a much easier time as long as I am here. It may be that I will be longer than I expected, since N. Brook after talking to Makins sent for me again and told me that so far from not pushing me out at 60, his view now was that I ought to stay for as long as possible – and particularly until after the next election.

The Treasury after November 1958
(Economic Side)

Sir R. Makins. 54. Winchester, Ch. Ch., All Souls. FO at 24 after All Souls. First to Treasury in 1956.
Sir T. Padmore. 49. Sheffield Sec. School, Queens, Cambridge. Inland Rev. at 22. Treasury at 25. PPS Ch. 43/45.
Sir R. Hall. 57. Queensland, Magdalen, Oxford. Don. Temp. Civil Servant 1939/45. Economic Section 1947.
Sir D. Rickett. 51. Rugby, Balliol, All Souls. Economic Advisory Council 1931/39. PPS to PM. Treasury 1947.
Mr R. W. B. Clarke. 48. Christ's Hospital, Clare, Wrangler. BEAMA 1932. *Financial News* 1932/39. Temp. Civil Servant, Treasury 1945.
Mr W. Armstrong. 43. Scotland, Exeter, Oxford. M/Education 1938. PS to Bridges, Cab. Off. 1943/46. Treasury 1946. PPS Ch./Ex. 1949/53.
Mr B. Fraser. 47. Bedford, Trinity, Cambridge. Scottish Office 1933. Treasury 1936 (PS to Hopkins).
Mr A. J. D. Winnifrith. 49. Westminster, Ch. Ch. BoT 1932. Treasury 1934.

5 Oxford. 3 Cambridge. 3 Ex-Temp. Civil Servants. No one entered Civil Service at the Treasury, but 3 transferred very early. Average age 50.

Friday, August 1st

The Chancellor has agreed to a quick £30 mn on housing repairs, etc., and to a fairly extensive easing on Hire Purchase from late August. The July unemployment figures are rather surprising as they show a small decrease after seasonal correction. In view of all this I shall be surprised if unemployment is as high as 700,000 by January but the trend then may still be upwards. The only positive stimulus so far in sight for next year is another £75 mn on the public investment programme. It certainly looks like an easy Budget. However, I think we have done enough for the present and that things will now wait until September or even October. Parliament rises today and Ministers will all be on holiday in August.

The Chancellor saw the TUC yesterday and they stayed about 30 minutes. Mostly to express their alarm about the growth of unemployment, to urge concerted international action and a number of relaxations now. They kept off prices and wages.

The Chancellor has a very good manner with them. He almost leaned over backward to make it clear that he was as much or more concerned about the pound and the price level as he was about full employment. He also said he thought it likely that unemployment would rise for the rest of this year. After the meeting Birch and Woodcock and then Leslie saw the press, and talked fairly freely.

Prices are likely to be down at least one point next month and we think more likely to fall than to rise afterwards. The index was at 108 last November, is now 110. It may well be at 108 next November. If so, it will be the first *year* of stability that I can remember and this in a year when the Rent Act added at least a point. Of course it is mainly terms of trade but it does look as if we are nearer stability than we have ever been and that a good try can be made next year.

Tuesday, August 12th

It is all very quiet and peaceful now with Parliament up and most of the Ministers away. M. Allen came to see me just after the last entry and I told him about Hire Purchase and Investment and asked him why they were doing nothing on Bank Rate. He said they hadn't been thinking about it lately but he would mention it to the Governor. It seemed to work very quickly as the Governor mentioned to the Chancellor and Makins the next day or very nearly so that *he* wanted to make a move and that we should hold up the Hire Purchase announcement until this was out of the way. So I said 'as long as he doesn't wait too long', and I think it will probably be this Thursday, 14th. If so, the Hire Purchase relaxations will probably have to wait till the first week in September. Not that it makes all that difference.

We have been doing quite a lot of work on India. The IBRD is having a meeting in Washington about Aug. 26th to discuss what might be done and Leslie Rowan is going. We have made a little progress but still are feeling rather niggardly. We have offered Pakistan £10 mn and New Zealand £20 mn but the latter turned it down. Now we are thinking about £40 mn for India this year and more to follow. At any rate we are moving in the field though I fear too little and too late. The best thing that has come out of it is the Working Party to look at the whole problem of what we can afford and how to control it.

The Chancellor came in yesterday and I had a short talk. He wanted to be reassured that we were not getting too *inflationary* again! I told him we had done all the right things and were now to wait till October and see how it went.

Thursday, August 14th

I am going to leave tomorrow for 2–3 weeks and for once do not expect to be interrupted. The Bank Rate was duly lowered today and I imagine caused as little of a ripple as any change in the post-war period. I have been doing a few odd jobs and among others considering a memo Leslie Rowan has written about moving to convertibility this year.[8] The Bank were very keen to do this – or what they call 'bringing the rates together' – in the spring but I was much against it then because I did not see how we could defend it in public with a US recession on the downward path. It is not that it is any protection but that it seems to be so and it would seem so odd to give it up in a storm.

Now however I think, and so does T.L.R., that the time is much more propitious. The £ is in fact convertible at a slight discount through EPU and we probably lose more than we gain. There is little to be said for discrimination in these circumstances and we might as well give that up too. The main troubles are the effect on EPU and what the Labour Party might say, but I think both of these can be coped with and I have just written a memo to say so.

I went to see N. Brook this morning, about a proposal to set up an economic research unit in the Treasury. This originated from my saying a year or two back that I did not think we knew nearly enough about current problems and that we ought not to be complacent. At that time I thought we should subsidize NIESR. However a Treasury Working Party was set up under O. Clarke (I was not a member – Downie was – but I talked to them) and it has recommended that the Treasury should have a special unit for this, partly to work by itself and partly to commission outside work. Norman made the point, which I had made myself to Roger, that we should not make any announcement about this until we had got a good man to take charge of it. It will probably be decided to put up the Economic Section estimate for next year and to try to get a Director of Research and if we succeed launch the whole thing subsequently.

N.B. then talked at some length about the recent Treasury changes, which I have referred to above. He said that he did not much like having a whole row of 2nd Secs with probably different ideas and all with access to the Chancellor. The idea was that Tom P. should take most of the burden of the home side (HF and Supply) and leave Roger much freer to take charge of OF direct from Denis Rickett. Roger would be expected (and be intended) to travel a good deal which would make use of his previous experience. I said that I agreed with all this subject (a) to Tom really taking the load, (b) to Roger really getting hold of the OF work. But I thought that the latter required first-class ability and that it would not be fair to keep a man there to do it and not promote him because he was too valuable where he was. I thought however that any man, however good, could fairly be expected to serve 5 or 6 years as a 3rd Sec. before being promoted, e.g. William Armstrong.

We also talked a bit about the personalities involved. I thought N.B. was very sensible about them. He said that he was very sorry Leslie was leaving the Service although he felt sure that it was a good thing that he should leave the Treasury. He implied that he had told Leslie he thought of shifting him and no doubt this was a reason for Leslie being upset. He said that Tom P. was very wise but he did not know yet how tough he could be, a view with which I concurred completely. He thought William Armstrong was very good, likely to be much better than Compton – one reason why he had moved Compton to C&AG was that he had done very good solid work but he wasn't quite up to being Roger's Deputy. Finally he thought Bruce Fraser and Winnifrith would turn out to be very sound on Supply work.

I have proposed that Bryan Hopkin should be my Deputy and R.M. hinted today that this would be o.k. D. Butt who is going to Nuffield for a year came to ask if I knew who would be taking his place in OF Stats and I said that I had agreed to release Fred Atkinson for this. David wants to show him round before he goes. It is very interesting that two successive Economic Section people should go to this key post. David said that OF were very much alarmed at Leslie not being replaced, partly because R.M. was so impetuous and partly because they did not think there would be enough bodies for international representation. This will depend on how far T.P. relieves Roger M.

The Bank Rate reduction has had a good press, and on the whole it is not thought that anything more need be done for some time now. It certainly looks as if I ought to have a quiet leave this year, but of course the international political scene is very foreboding.

Friday, August 15th

Sam Katz of the Federal Reserve has been here and in N. Europe on a year's sabbatical or study leave. He came to say goodbye this morning and we had quite a talk on Central Bank policy and especially funding, interest rates and so on. I said I thought that it had become clear last year that you could not sell gilt-edged under full employment at the rates you used to. I thought we were in an experimental period now, and must try what high long-term interest rates plus more stability of prices would get. However it would be a good deal easier if the Nationalized Industries raised more of their capital requirements through their pricing of their products. This would reduce the need for a Budget surplus and at the same time reduce the amount of borrowing the Government had to do. I thought that the US was trying to keep gilt-edged rates too low.

Tuesday, September 23rd

My leave was in fact very quiet indeed but while it was going on, the Midland Bank and then a number of others announced the personal loans scheme and this was followed by a cut in Hire Purchase charges by the main firms. When I got back, R.M. told me that they had decided to postpone the cuts in Hire Purchase deposits (which I had expected in late August) until all this blew over and when I saw the Chancellor he was rather nervous and said, only partly in joke, that he had expected me to return from leave when I had read about it. He obviously had very little idea of what might be involved and seemed a bit sceptical when I said that it would not be very much.[9] I assured him that we ought to go on with our own scheme as soon as possible but owing to the fact that the papers had played up the banks and Hire Purchase firms so much, we kept on putting it off and it was not in fact announced until Monday a week ago, Sept. 15th. Then it did not get a great deal of publicity, although as a short-term measure it will have much more effect than the other things in this field.

The general situation is quite comfortable: production is still falling slowly but we have now done rather a long list of things and the extra £30 mn on public investment, etc., is being spent. So I do not expect much further fall in activity and as the US is picking up rather faster than I had expected and there is something of a Stock Exchange boom here, we may even get an increase. The unemployment outlook, which had looked as if it might become an important political issue by Christmas, has been getting less so – it is somewhat disquieting since we certainly ought to be producing our present output with a good deal less labour than we are using. But in May it seemed that the underlying increase in unemployment was about 25,000 a month – since then the rate of increase has been much less and the mid-August figure was only 446,000. There is generally a small drop from August to September and 200,000 would be an unprecedented increase from September to January. Of course exports are falling, there may be a more marked stock change, and the easing out of surplus labour may begin again on a larger scale. But on the other side, Bank advances are rising rather quickly, business is a bit more optimistic, and we have increased the prospect of Hire Purchase sales and put in £30 mn on public investment, mainly housing and maintenance. So it would be very perverse if unemployment were as high as 650,000 in January and that does not seem nearly so alarming as 750,000.[10]

In any case there has been much less complaint than I had expected about recent trends and it may well be that Ministers and politicians have grown much more sensitive than they need have been. The object now is to get to the Budget with no more big changes (though next year's public investment increase is still to be *announced*). That will give the Chancellor the maximum freedom, and as everyone will be urging him to spend, he will only have to cope with his own fear of being accused of another 1955 Election Budget. But the reserves are still rising even in this dead season and D. Butt tells me that the current account surplus for the first half of 1958 will be no less than £334 mn which is an extraordinary figure on any view.[11]

In the first half of September the only thing moving at all was getting ready for Montreal – I had decided not to go, but to go to New Delhi for the Bank/Fund meeting for which I leave on October 1st. Our proposals on unifying the rate were discussed by a few Senior Ministers and the Chancellor was authorized to make some soundings but feeling generally was against it and still strongly in favour of a floating rate. However I expect they will come round. One of the troubles is R.A.B. who feels he has been betrayed by the Bank and OF since they made him go so hard for Robot in 1952/53 and now they have quite changed. I think I must try to see him when he gets back from S. Africa.

The big splashes at Montreal seem to be our announcement about freeing more dollar imports (which incidentally has caused still more speculation *into* sterling) and the Chancellor's announcement yesterday about ECGD loans at cost + 1/4%. Both of these have gone the way I wanted them but I hope he has made it clear that our ECGD loans will be limited. The Canadians appear to have beaten the gun on the increase of Bank/Fund resources as they are reported as having said they *will* double their Bank, and add 50% to their Fund, quotas, which is not for them to decide. However it looks as if the wind is quite favourable for New Delhi. We have decided only to go to 50% for the Fund, *if* we have to pay the basic increase in gold. I think this is rather a pity and that it would be better to go for 100% if we could get it and do as the Germans do and treat our gold subscription, which can be drawn without question, as if it were part of the reserves.

The wages front is still waiting for the engineers. The NCB seems to have made a good settlement with about 4% for the time workers and a standstill at present rates for piece workers. I have begun to draft a paper for the Wages Policy Committee on the results of this round and the attitude Ministers ought to take to the next one.[12] I still think that it is possible that the Retail Price Index in November will be at 108 (where it is now) and which will be the same as in November 1957. If we can't make a lot of propaganda about that we ought to be able to. Unfortunately the potato crop is rather badly blighted and we shall certainly get the wretched one-point or more from them in the early spring.

The Cohen Committee is trying to resign and I have got D. MacDougall lined up for the new economist member. But the Chancellor and the PM can't make up their minds about a new Chairman (we have suggested Philip Morris) so Cohen has been asked to stay on – but not to do any work – for the time being.

It has been agreed that Bryan Hopkin will be Deputy Director and he starts on October 1st and will take over all the NIF and internal reporting work, leaving Downie free for the external. Watts, who is on loan from Power, has been extended for a year and if I can get one or two new assistants I should be better off (i.e. with a better all-round team) than I have ever been. Opie from LSE has replaced Scammell – a gain – and one Macintosh is coming in January to replace David Henderson. I will give up the part-time Deputy from HOPS – it has been a help but at best is only a makeshift.

An official group has been set up to look into Initial and Investment Allowances. This was on the motion of Inland Revenue who hate Investment Allowances because they regard them as unfair. It is extraordinary that they should think there is anything objective or sacred about the current concept of 'fairness' particularly over this concession, which is generally welcome and one of the few things on which the FBI and the Labour Party are agreed. It will be very hard to find any solid evidence because so many other things are at work at the same time.

What else? I had lunch with E.P. on Friday and he talked at some length about his future. He was due to leave AEA about now but has been extended until the end of 1959 and he now seems a bit doubtful about whether he will get just what he wants. One of the jobs he had his eye on was Vickers which T.L.R. has got. We agreed that the Conservatives would probably win the next election unless there was a bad change in Foreign Affairs – at the moment this seems only too likely as the US and China are deeply embroiled over Quemoy. It is a peculiar experience to live in a world with big stocks of hydrogen bombs at a time when US/USSR relations are very tense – it hardly seems possible that the Russians would not drop one or two on London to be on the safe side even if we were not belligerents in the first stages, i.e. it is a rational possibility that one will be wiped out at any moment. However it does not produce anything beyond registering the possibility. And I still think it is very improbable that the Russians would risk such a war even if the Chinese really don't mind, as apparently they say. It is the point I made in the Strath exercise a few years ago, that if the population is reduced at least as much as the capital stock, the survivors will be better off once the radiation is gone. However it is my present impression that the radiation would take a long time to go and the early survivors therefore not necessarily be long-term survivors.

E.P. and I also agreed that the PM had turned out much better than we had expected and he told me Haley (Editor of *The Times*) agreed with this.

The Radcliffe Committee is now discussing its report. I have a drawer full of evidence submitted by various economists including a typical piece by T. Balogh attacking the incompetence of the Treasury and (especially) the Bank and saying that the Economic Section must be strengthened and given more power. O. Franks showed me a piece Sayers had written as a draft for the part on the supply of money and interest rates – it was a bit too doctrinaire, and with his usual skill he had spotted the weaknesses but wanted me to spell them out. Unfortunately Sayers has had a sort of stroke or paralysis and now has a speech impediment – it will be a great blow to the Committee if it goes on. I do not think their Report will be out now until about next June.

I expect to go to Poland for the last part of October, a return trip for a visit of Government planners which came here earlier this year. They had produced a fascinating itinerary and programme.

Wednesday, October 8th (New Delhi)

I came here last Friday, Oct. 3rd and am leaving again today, with the Chancellor. He has to go back to speak at the Conservative Party Conference at Blackpool. I had not intended to go but as soon as we had left London there was a Cabinet discussion on two papers, one from Minister of Transport on the decline in coal and steel freights (adding to the already swollen railway deficit) and one from P. Mills (Power) calling attention to the decline in coal and oil consumption and to the alarm felt by the steel industry at the falling demand.[13] So they all got into a state and asked for a paper on the economic prospects and said that momentous decisions would have to be taken on this. So R. Makins thought that the sooner I got back the better and in any case he was very much averse to the Chancellor travelling alone. It is clear that I spoke too early when I thought that Ministers were less worried about unemployment than they used to be, which is what the Chancellor had told me when I asked him explicitly earlier on if there would be a row if unemployment rose too much. He is slightly worried because the September figure shows an increase of about 30,000, but as the months May–August moved so little, it is still a good deal better than we had forecast.

The Fund/Bank meeting began on Monday but it was already fairly clear that the proposal for increases in Fund quotas and Bank capital would go through. The US were anxious that it should and all the Commonwealth countries had agreed. We came rather anxious that the actual resolution would be in favour of an increase, but the US did not like this as they thought many countries would feel that they were being rushed. So there was a compromise resolution which asked the Managing Board to report on the desirability of action, 'taking account of the views expressed at the meeting'. Since everyone who has spoken is in favour of the increase, the Board will have a clear lead. But there are some points which may be sticky. A number of countries were doubtful whether they could afford a 25% payment in gold: and there were extreme views on lending – on the one side the Philippines and India who seemed to want to be able to borrow even though there was little prospect of paying it back, and on the other the Germans (with support from the Belgians and Dutch) who took a very extreme line the other way.

Blessing [President of the Bundesbank] for Germany made what I thought a very reactionary speech, saying that it would be a disaster if the increase in Fund quotas set off fresh inflation and that any country in balance of payments difficulties could get out of them by deflating. There was not much consciousness of the poor state in which primary producers now are, or of the problem of swings for which the Fund was established. However I think that in practice the Germans are both trying to increase home use of resources and to lend abroad; though so far they have been tending to lend short, they may pluck up courage as time goes on.

The Chancellor made a good speech and of course everyone is much impressed by the recovery of sterling even though most of it is due to the terms of trade and a good deal of the rest to the extremely good creditor behaviour of the US. However internal policy has helped and we do not look such an outstanding country of cost inflation as we did.

I saw Mahalanobis but he talked all the time about the marvels of Russian planning, the similarity of India's problems to those of Poland, and especially how the Russians did not believe in the good faith of the West and hence under Chinese pressure were contemplating an H-bomb war on the ground that more of them would survive than of us. I said

I thought the West did not have any grounds for believing in Russia's good faith and that it was very speculative as to who would survive, or where, in an H-bomb war since the fall-out would be so dispersed and with so many bombs tending to high concentrations anywhere. Pitambar Pant who was there agreed with me. From what I heard elsewhere, M. really does not want to discuss Indian planning in any concrete terms. It is mainly that he now seems to me to be entirely preoccupied with the virtues of Communism and the vices of everyone else, and partly that he is probably keeping out of the way because he was so much responsible for the 2nd five-year plan and a great deal of the criticism of it is proving justified. However the fact is that they have got a great deal of improvement in their capital structure, however it was paid for, and if they can run it properly they are so much further forward.

I saw much more of the English community this time and heard very varied assessments of their efficiency but I still remain impressed by what I saw in the Damodar Valley in 1956. I did not have time to talk much about the current situation. The Chancellor, more than any of his Tory predecessors, is very anxious that we should do something substantial for India. So if only we can get our statistical exercise through in time, we may be able to make some headway. I have the utmost difficulty in getting anyone to see that as soon as the Indians have run their sterling balances to a minimum, we shall have a big strain taken off us unless someone else has started to run them down at the same sort of rate. We are already losing exports and with the pressure in the Cabinet to reflate, we shall shortly be taking up the slack at home which is what I have feared all along we would do.

A striking feature of the Fund/Bank meetings is the increasing tendency of bankers to go to them under the heading of 'special guests'. There were, I was told, 40 New York bankers and a good many others from the US. Of London people, I knew W. Monckton, Harcourt, Raismon, Denny Marris and no doubt there were many others. I suppose it is a combination of a free trip (presumably on their firms), seeing one another and a unique chance to meet Finance Ministers and senior officials en bloc. Bill Harcourt told me that they were now getting on quite quickly with Radcliffe and we had quite a talk about the relation between the Treasury and the Bank of England. The Committee have clearly got the point which I would have liked to make, that the biggest deficiency has been on internal policy. Bill said he had come to the conclusion that the Deputy Governor should concentrate on policy questions in relation to the general economic situation and be in constant touch with me. I very much agreed and also said I thought the Deputy should either be on the Budget Committee or very closely in touch with it. I gathered that I was likely to be called again before the end.

Bill is beginning to be mentioned as Governor and I think there is a good deal to be said for it – ever since I first met him I have been more and more impressed by him – although he is primarily a business man and spends his time cultivating the right people and on negotiations

– which after all is the primary requisite if you are an operator – he seems to me to have a great gift for arriving at the essence of the situation analytically, so that he is very rarely wrong on his economics even if he could not demonstrate them. I am afraid O.S.F. would not like it if he got the job. However I do not know at all when it will come up or how much there is in the rumour that Cobbold intends to resign shortly. There is no doubt that Cobbold was deeply shaken both by the proceedings following the leak, and by the whole aura connected with Radcliffe, during which he must have realized that the Bank was seriously criticized. And no doubt he suspected that a Labour Government would replace him. But maybe he will now wait and see how likely it is that there will be such a Government.

R. Maudling is here and his tendency to take life both lightly and easily is much in evidence. However I expect he has had a very heavy time with the Free Trade Area (which is now going very badly). The others in the UK Delegation are Makins, Rickett, Parsons, Thorold and two A/Ss – Symons and Copeman. R.M. is rather dissatisfied with the team. It has been I think a bit difficult for Denis since Roger is definitely in the lead. This is probably Thorold's last appearance and I am told he is being replaced shortly but I cannot remember by whom. He has done a good quiet job, after Harcourt had got us so brilliantly over the Suez crisis.

The readiness with which Ministers in September 1957 had approved deflationary measures that might raise unemployment to 2–3 per cent gave way a year later to something approaching panic when unemployment did in fact approach 2 per cent. The Chancellor cabled the Prime Minister after a Cabinet meeting on October 5th to inform him of the anxieties of his colleagues, who feared that unemployment might reach 750,000 by early spring. The Cabinet requested a paper on 'The economic situation and prospects' and one was drafted by Bryan Hopkin. It was ready for the Chancellor on his return from India and circulated, first to the Economic Policy Committee, and then to the Cabinet as an annex to a note by the Chancellor (C(568)211) listing eight separate expansionary moves that had already been taken. The Prime Minister, however, was much more 'in fear of the slump coming' than of another boom and issued a directive on October 27th (C(58)227) calling for prompt corrective measures to expand demand so long as they involved no future commitments. Hire purchase restrictions were completely withdrawn next day. The Chancellor continued to warn his colleagues, and repeated the warning in the House of Commons in the Debate on the Address, against expenditure commitments that might still be pre-empting capacity after the economy had already recovered. In a further memorandum to the Cabinet (C(58)258) he put an addition of £75 million to public investment in 1958–9 and an equal addition in 1959–60 as the maximum that he could approve. Meanwhile there were signs that vacancies were increasing and unemployment reaching a peak.

Thursday, November 20th

The past six weeks have been rather disturbed mainly because of the panic towards which Ministers have been tending in connection with increasing unemployment, the subject which led to my early return from India, and subsequently to my recall from Poland.

It is very irritating to me because I warned them in June that there was likely to be a good deal of unemployment (over 700,000) by January, that in my experience this was a very sensitive point politically, and that if they wanted to do anything they ought to start fairly soon. However they were all very bold then and it was all I could do to get the Chancellor to agree to the steps we actually took. Then as soon as he (and I) were out of the country in India the PM stimulated by Lord Mills, who is convinced that another 1929/32 is upon us, got alarmed,. When I got back I found that quite a sensible paper had been drafted by the Treasury, mostly Hopkin, and things calmed down quite a lot.

The upshot was that the PM and the Chancellor formed themselves into a small Committee [the Employment Committee], calling colleagues ad hoc, to deal with employment and particularly to deal with proposals to put up public sector investment straight away and in 1959/60. The PM sent round a directive which was very carefully worded but in places looked as if Departments were encouraged to spend as much as they wished both above and below the line. N. Brook had to have a meeting of Permanent Secretaries to try to correct this impression – it was rather a stormy meeting, mostly because Frank Lee was in a very bad temper and spoke as if everything (of which he disapproved) was the fault of Treasury officials and especially of N.B. himself.

Meanwhile the Chancellor began to regain his calm and to lean towards doing less rather than more. However on October 19th I left for a visit to Poland. While I was there, the Labour Party put down a motion of censure on the Government's economic policy for the debate on the Address and Ministers got into another flap. Consequently I was recalled in the middle of a tour of the country (after a week in Warsaw) and got back on the night of October 28th. In the interval Ministers had decided to remove the rest of the Hire Purchase restrictions. What the Chancellor really wanted to know was the figure for 1959/60 public sector investment which he should authorize. I said the figure was not really the important thing. What was needed was to get going quickly since we had lost a good deal of time already. As for a figure, I thought £150 mn which was the upper figure Otto Clarke had been suggesting was quite safe. This means the Public Sector figure, which on the Thorneycroft basis was about £1,425 mn in 1957/58 (and therefore should have been the ceiling for 1958/59 and 1959/60) and which had already been put up to £1,500 for 1959/60 in the summer review, will now be about £1,575. A lot of this is in railways and coal. And what the 1958/59 actual will turn out to be is very uncertain since more or less anything that can get going in that time will be approved. But it is all going very slowly. The Chancellor announced an increase of '£125–£150 mn' in the Debate. He made a speech which had been prepared in chaotic conditions here and appeared to fall very flat in the House but which read very well. And in later soundings in the Party he found that there was more alarm that we were moving too fast than too slowly. One unfortunate result of this is that he has rather dragged his feet in actually authorizing work to be started now and I think that no action minutes were sent out until yesterday (if then), so they have lost about 6 weeks since they got in a flap in early October. This is a lot of time when one thinks that all the alarm was generated by the prospect of the January–February unemployment figures.

The trouble is that there are now two sharply conflicting schools of thought in the Tory Party. At one end is the PM who is naturally expansionist and who is egged on by Roy Harrod on theoretical grounds and Lord Mills out of ignorance. The PM is supported by some of his Ministerial colleagues when they think of the next election and see that unemployment may be about the only good cry that the Labour Party could have. (But the Labour Party is rather shy about plugging this too hard now as they simply cannot believe that HM Government will allow unemployment to go on rising and therefore they are afraid that if they shout too loud it will put them in the position of crying 'wolf' and no wolf showing up.)

At the other end are the Nigel Birch school (Thorneycroft appears to have left it), who think inflation is the cause of all our troubles and that the country needs a bit of unemployment and that nothing will lose the Tory Party votes among its own supporters so much as appearing to get soft as soon as any results of a tough policy appear.

The Chancellor is very much afraid that he might appear to be the man who claimed that he was going to continue the Thorneycroft policy but ran away from it. So that although he is far from a deflationist, he is a very cautious expansionist. This coincides with my own view of what is needed tactically – we are not out of the wood on wages, we have an inherent tendency to overdo expansion, and in any case I like Government policy to *look* continuous and coherent even if nobody else cares about this. However I think we are going to get a big impulse from the removal of Hire Purchase and that *if* we put some energy into getting public sector expenditure up, we will be able to get through to the Budget. Exports are keeping up better than I expected because the PSA [Property Services Agency] has managed to borrow more from other countries than I thought they would. The US is picking up, so far, faster than I thought though there is now a bit of tremolo in it. Next month I am having another go with the experts in Paris to try to get a clear picture of what Europe is going to do. Business confidence is astonishingly good in the UK (since production is still falling) and bank loans are going up.

Incidentally Bank Rate came down another 1/2% today. The Bank have been finding it hard to make up their minds. Last week the Chancellor decided against a move but a week's reflection has removed the nerves – I think in a general way he likes to get used to ideas before he pushes them.

The Budget prospects at present look for as much reduction as can appear to be politically decent. In this the fact that the Chancellor cannot bear the idea of an above-the-line deficit may be important as at present the surplus doesn't look to be more than say £200 mn but I feel sure it will turn out larger. However general experience leads me to think that if we go on taking relaxing measures we will gradually build up quite strong forces the other way. NIF is doing an exercise now and we will be on slightly safer ground when that is done.

There have been a number of other interesting matters.

Personalities. Leslie Rowan finally departed on November 7th. When the time came I felt very sorry to see him leave in spite of the acute thorn he has sometimes been in my flesh and my distrust of his emotional tendencies. The Treasury is certainly much weaker with him gone – it is clear now that he was a considerable international figure and I doubt if we will easily develop anyone who will make foreigners shake in their shoes, which from time to time may be desirable. This completes the Treasury reorganization. R.M. has abandoned the 2nd Secs meetings as there is now only one 2nd Sec. (T.P.) Instead he will have a Treasury meeting to include all 3rd Secs once a fortnight, and a meeting of Permanent Secretaries of Economic Departments plus T.P., me and the Heads of Customs and Inland Revenue, on the alternate weeks.

Thorold is leaving Washington and Lord Cromer (a Baring – he is Managing Director of Barings) is to take his place. He is having lunch with me next week so I will know more about him then. These experiments have been very successful so far though I fear Denny Marris will feel that he ought to have had a turn.

Cohen Committee. The Chancellor and the PM have been so occupied with other things that they have refused to do anything about this. However we had a meeting with the Chancellor this morning and he is now going to try to persuade the PM to accept Philip Morris. There seems to be no rival to Donald MacDougall as the economist so I hope that this will go through.

Wages. There have been several meetings of the WP Committee. The Chancellor seems to have made up his mind to go for the 'guiding light' at 2½% p.a. Nearly all his colleagues, while more or less in favour of HMG deciding to have this figure in their own mind, are quite against any public pronouncement. But this does not appear to deter the Chancellor who has nearly committed himself already in public in the Mansion House and Address speeches to this and told a private meeting of City Editors at No. 11 on November 6th that 2½% was the figure he had in mind. Incidentally he did extremely well at that meeting and made a very good impression on them.

Other matters are the Free Trade Area and reunifying the Rates but I had better go at them in another entry.

Convertibility, which had been the subject of so much argument ever since 1945, arrived suddenly at the end of 1958. The initiative, curiously enough, came not from the United Kingdom but from West Germany and France.

With convertibility there was no longer any reason to discriminate against imports costing dollars but it was in fact some time before discrimination was completely abandoned.

Tuesday, December 30th

'Unifying the Rates' got itself done before I could get round to writing about it, and just as well as I would have been a very bad prophet if I had written earlier than Dec. 18th. After a good deal of thought and discussion we all (Bank and Treasury) agreed that it ought to be done before 1958 was out and I felt strongly before Parliament rose for Christmas. It was also desirable to get it done while we were discussing the IMF stand-by. However Ministers did not seem at all keen and R. Makins told me it was put off *sine die*. Then, with no notice at all, I was called to a meeting in Makins's room in the week before Christmas week and told that it had been decided to make an announcement on December 27th. The reason was that the Germans wanted to move and the French wanted to devalue and move at the same time. As far as I am concerned, it could not have been better and takes most of the sting out of any Debate. I was always against jumping out of a high window and now we have walked out of a French window.[14]

V

Reflation under Heathcoat Amory,

1 January 1959 to 27 July 1960

Tuesday, January 6th 1959

The New Year opens with the economic position very much better than it was a year ago except that production is low and the outlook for private investment a bit off. On the other hand we have got all the Thorneycroft policies reversed quite smoothly, the reserves and the pound have had good years, and the latest (November) production figures and (December) unemployment confirm my feeling that we are on the turn. The Fund and Bank resources seem to be well on the way to being increased, the whole thing having gone much more smoothly than might have been expected. The Chancellor has not done badly though of course he has been lucky, the terms of trade and the downward tendency in the economy have been just what any new Chancellor would need, very like Rab's situation in 1952. Some people are talking as if it is more like 1955, i.e. that it will be tempting to have an election Budget which we can't really afford, but this is nonsense. In 1955 we were at the top of a high boom and now we are at the bottom of the nearest thing to a post-war recession.

The convertibility operation has gone quite smoothly and the £ is fairly strong for the moment, though there is a lot of silly talk about the $ being weak which can do us nothing but harm especially as Martin and Anderson seem to have their doubts about it. Gaitskell, I think imprudently, came out very much against it – the line was right, that it weakens our defences but we will have to live with it, but I think he would have done better to be more smug, put all the responsibility on the Tories if anything goes wrong but not to be so portentous about recession and unemployment. I have very little idea about when the election will be but the Chancellor has given me the impression that it is equally balanced between about May and about October which is what I would have thought on general grounds anyway. I thought however that May would seem too soon after the Budget, so that it would look like a bribe, and also that unemployment would still be too high.

However after a great deal of nervousness and worry, Ministers seem to have made up their minds that the country is not so sensitive to unemployment as they had expected and their line is that as long as it is going down a bit, it doesn't matter if it is a good deal higher than in the past – which is a more sensible view than I thought they would reach. The economic prospects, based partly on the lastest NIF Report and partly on my own hunch and later figures, are that we are about the turn and will go up rather slowly next year, with unemployment fairly steady on the assumption that employers will continue to use labour more efficiently. Stocks, private investment and exports are all rather uncertain. The main objection to the picture is that it will still give us a very low production figure, not much better than 1955. On the basis of this, I told the Budget Committee that there was plenty of room for concessions and that the decision would be made partly on a judgment about the effect on wages and so on, and partly because we might feel that we did not want to present an above-the-line deficit. They mostly felt that the latter would be the dominant consideration, especially as we may have to borrow a bit below the line: on this basis there might be £200 mn + to give away and we all thought that Income Tax, beer and a bit of Purchase Tax would be about the right mixture.[1]

The Chancellor has become increasingly nervous that he has been doing too much and in the end began to take a fairly tough line at the PM's Employment Committee[2] – and for some reason the PM has moderated his views and seems fairly content. I think the right-wing back-benchers have been fairly vocal and the boom in Hire Purchase plus the figures of borrowing for Nationalized Industries (which are irrelevant since they cover a number of years) have led to some alarm. Anyway the Chancellor sent for me specially on Saturday morning, Dec. 20th (I had stayed here to dine with D. Rickett, q.v.) to ask me if I was *sure* he had not overdone it – of course I said I *was* sure and that we had a great deal of slack in hand and in my view we could well do more but probably would prefer to wait for the Budget. He was quite sure about this and while we were at it, we had a preliminary look at the Budget and he confirmed that on *no account* would he have an above-line deficit even though he understood it was meaningless. His figure was £200 mn – but he seemed keen on Income Tax and also said he wanted to do a few things he thought needed, especially cutting the stamp duty on Stock Exchange transactions and getting rid of Purchase Tax on commercial vehicles. The latter is o.k. but it is hard to see any good reason for reducing Stamp on Stock Exchange. The Chancellor also confirmed that he was not too worried about unemployment.

He sent for me again on New Year's Day to thank me for all my help, etc., and to ask about the impact of convertibility and the relation to an election. Clearly none of them liked having to move and their hands must have been forced by the Germans who had put pressure on the French. I said it had all gone very well and as far as I was concerned it was ideal that EPU broke up of itself and we moved in a body. As for election prospects, it seemed very probable that there would be a run on sterling because no one would believe that the Labour Party would be so tough as the Conservatives or at any rate so respectable in international banking circles. But I thought it was our duty to go through with it and mobilize as much resources as were necessary.

In this connection he asked what I thought of selling the RFC Securities and I said I would think about it. D. Rickett told me later that Erroll, the new Economic Secretary, was interested in them and thought we should manage them more but I am clear that the Chancellor was not thinking in those terms – maybe the Governor has been at him again as the Bank has always wanted to sell them. I do not think it is right for the UK to be speculating in US equities – if the value of money falls, Central Banks have got to put up with it – but I have often felt that it was nice to have something tucked away as a last resort and indeed the fact that we could pledge them to the Exim Bank shows how useful it is. Theoretically one would do better with it in gold but I wonder if we would act so sharply if the reserves + sale of securities fell from say \$3,000 mn to \$2,300 mn as we would if the reserves without them fell from \$2,300 mn to \$1,600 mn – I doubt it. Yet it is rather repugnant to think that we ought to conceal things from Ministers and the public as we do now – I am sure hardly any Ministers even know we have got these securities and that they are very like gold in the last resort in which we are likely to find ourselves.

The Common Market and the Free Trade Area are still rather in a mess. I was in Paris for a meeting of the Experts on Dec. 16th and this was the day after the row between Eccles and Couve de Murville. Since then the French have announced 80% liberalization so part of our grievance (that they intended to discriminate in quotas between the Six and the OEEC non-Six, when they were in default on OEEC liberalization obligations) has gone. But I do not find it very interesting and still think that we will reach some rather quiet position. The enthusiasm for Uniscan[3] and for retaliation against the French is dying away.

Wages are also in a mess. The previous position, that Ministers were determined not to state their policy publicly, has hardened if anything and the Chancellor has made no new indiscretions towards the guiding light. But at recent meetings the whole concept of a link between wages and productivity, which appeared to have been accepted, has been questioned again and all the nonsense that I thought they had got out of their system in July came back again, e.g. that since productivity increased at different rates in different industries it could not be a guide and (Eccles) that wages ought to be linked to export performance. The PM has been showing an interest in all this and wants to see any statement. But with Ministers so confused, and with the wage front fairly quiet, I have come to the conclusion that it would be better to have no statement than the one we are likely to get.

Meanwhile Sir Philip Morris after a lot of uncertainty decided to refuse to succeed Cohen on COPPI so we have to start again. D. MacDougall had agreed to replace Dennis Robertson as the economist *if* Morris was Chairman but that too has gone into suspense. This is one of the cases where the Chancellor's slowness and refusal to think of more than one thing at a time has been a great inconvenience.

Development of backward countries. For a long time I have thought we were not doing enough or taking the problem systematically enough. But I wanted to decide what we could afford to contribute before I moved. However we have been overtaken by events as the USA is now pushing on with a scheme for an International Development Association (IDA) to supplement IBRD with loans or grants on easier terms. The US seem to be very muddled in their ideas. D. Rickett gave a dinner on December 19th for Cromer, Gore-Booth, Parsons and Thompson-McCausland of the Bank, Arnold France and me. We talked about this at length and to my surprise we all agreed that we must do more, and that we must move in and get the US idea straight before it was allowed to go to a wider international gathering. So I have written a memo about it all and I expect we will be much occupied with this during the year.

Tuesday, January 27th

The economic position is going quite well but the January unemployment count was taken at the end of a cold spell and will show an increase over December of about 85,000. This has alarmed the PM and to a less extent the M/Labour and the PM has been pressing for more measures or an early Budget or both. But the Chancellor is now rather alarmed and in any case he feels rightly that the strategy is to wait for the Budget and he is sticking out for this. The Budget discussions are going quite smoothly and easily so far and we all (including the Chancellor) seem to be agreed that the great thing is to have a small surplus above the line and give the rest away, and probably do a bit on Post-War Credits below the line. Total say £250–£300 mn, more or less divided between Income Tax and Indirect. A bit of an argument about beer which I think is well worth doing on a number of grounds.

I had to go to Paris last week to report to the Deputies about the Experts. It all went very easily and they accepted our recommendation that we should still lean towards expansion. As we were able to make modified approving noises about Germany, the Germans were very sweet and amenable.

I had lunch with E.P. today. Hugh Gaitskell wants him to be the next Governor and he is tempted and is now finding out what H.M. would think and if *both* want him he will stay on. But he is also being tempted to go to Brit. Alum. with the reversion of the Chairmanship of Tube Investments. I told him he would find the first year at the Bank very sticky but he would not expect such a job to be a bed of roses. I think he is very much tempted.

Tuesday, February 17th

I had lunch with Edwin last week and gathered that the Chancellor said that one couldn't really be sure when the present Governor would go, since he put it a little vaguely, and that one couldn't really promise a position with no reference to what might happen in the meantime. These are both sensible points and I have often wondered if C. was not just hedging against a Labour Government. Anyway E.P. is going to go to Brit. Alum. and I think that this is right as I doubt if he would find the Bank very easy. It now seems to me that O.S.F. is the favourite is Labour wins, and if the Conservatives do, then *if* C. goes, Bill Harcourt may be the favourite.

The M/Labour took the February unemployment count on February 9th and knew the result in two days and it will show a reduction of only 5,000 which is a good deal less than was hoped – it seems as if labour is now being economized on. This caused much alarm and despondency but no new measures and I should think we can certainly live till the Budget now, only seven weeks and when three are gone no one will expect anything else to be done.

Thursday, February 19th

Since I wrote in January, the economic trends have clearly confirmed that we are moving slowly upwards but the January and February unemployment figures that labour is being used better. The Chancellor himself has moved very slowly and cautiously towards being a bit more expansionist – he made a few major concessions on quick public investment and is thinking of more and more in the Budget, though still aiming at an above-the-line surplus. This means rather more on post-war credits which come below what we had first thought of. The Budget discussions have gone very smoothly though rather too slow. Yesterday I had a long talk with the Chancellor at which he said he was now more worried that the effects of Hire Purchase would wear off too *fast* – a month ago he had felt the opposite. He was also a little disturbed because the increase in Local Authority house-building, which got quite a stimulus at the end of last year, is now reversing itself. Otto Clarke has been consistently too optimistic about this and indeed I think he has been too much afraid of another boom.

In the afternoon we had, with him, a three-hour BC and made a good deal of progress, generally on the lines we had recommended: we narrowed the range of decisions a good deal and decided against several candidates, but nothing positive reached actual finality. He is most uncertain about beer as I think his temperament is against it.

The wages front is very quiet. All his colleagues disliked the Chancellor's idea of saying that we wanted a pause, and I think that there will be no statement before the Budget speech, and even then nothing very new. If we can't have a guiding light then I would prefer this course.

We have had a great deal of worry about COPPI as we could not get anyone suitable as Chairman and in the end the Chancellor persuaded Cohen to stay on. The result of this is that Donald MacDougall, whom we wanted to replace Dennis Robertson, practically decided that *he* would not serve. He is probably seeing the Chancellor this afternoon but I am very doubtful if he will agree as he is too much worried about it being an election year and perhaps a Labour Government and be tarred with the Cohen brush.

I have had a lot of worry with a Committee on Incentive Allowances set up at Inland Revenue instigation to investigate their use. Inland Revenue have always hated the Investment Allowance and wanted a study which they hoped would come down against their re-introduction. T. Padmore was in the Chair, and the others were Evans (IR), Beales (CSO), Andrew and Stafford (BoT) and myself. As Beales came from and will no doubt go back to IR and Andrew is a violent believer in laissez-faire, the Committee turned out to be rather packed. We had a dilatory series of talks and saw a number of business men, and then without any discussion, IR drafted a most shockingly partisan report to which I was forced to object strongly. It got a bit modified in the subsequent discussion but I was forced to put in a note of dissent.

I was rather confirmed in the doubts I had previously felt about Padmore as he was not a good Chairman and as he endorsed the arguments of the Revenue and the majority on points where I felt they were plainly wrong. The whole thing was very disappointing as it is an interesting and important subject and there is a good deal to be said both for and against Investment Allowances but instead of discussing them we spent a great deal of time with the Revenue trying to establish (a) that they had had no effect in the past, (b) that they were unfair. The evidence certainly did not prove (a), and even if it had, it would not prove anything about the future; and on (b) they certainly do not offend against any fundamental principles and people do not think that they are unfair.

The funny thing is that just as we were nearing the end, a Minute from the PM to the Chancellor arrived pressing strongly the case for them. And the Chancellor himself (though he does not like them – he says they subsidize people to do what they ought to do anyway) can see that there is a strong case for them this year and indeed he suggested that we might concede them and put up profits tax at the same time, which the Economic Section have always pointed out could be made a very strong weapon of control. I was forced to say that I thought the only objection would be that it would seem too Socialist.

The external front is rather quiet except that we are having a very bad time on the Egyptian settlement. As Roger Makins says, all Tory Ministers subconsciously dislike settlements with Egypt. I think we have been very silly as we have got involved with the Smouha family who are probably rather slippery customers, and are in real danger of losing a settlement that on any wider grounds we badly need. The damned legacy of Eden and Suez.

The PM is just going to Russia, which is a popular move. He would like to make a Trade Agreement but as this would involve buying Russian oil instead of Persian Gulf oil in which we have a large financial stake, it is not a very attractive bet. However we think that as the Russians are going to export oil anyway we have less real option than we think. Meanwhile Dulles has got cancer [he died in April – Ed.] and the weakness of having two sick men at the top in the USA is even more apparent. The world political outlook seems to be extremely gloomy and one always wonders if the world won't be largely blown up and the atmosphere poisoned between any night and next morning, not to mention one's own removal from whatever scene remains!

I hardly get involved in the Economic Surveys at all these times and the whole process goes with incredibly less difficulty than it did in the days when we thought it ought to express views on current questions. Otto Clarke has had a very good effect on the Planning side as he is imaginative, a good administrator, and knows how the Treasury works. But he is still rather a dangerous factor and risks our expansion more than I like.

Friday, February 27th

Donald MacDougall finally turned down the job on COPPI last Thursday but as I was expecting it I was ready and suggested Henry Phelps Brown of LSE, whom Dennis Robertson had recommended. He came to see me on Friday and rang up on Monday to say that he would accept if LSE agreed. We finally got an announcement in the papers yesterday so did not lose much time. Henry will not be a very distinguished appointment but it is quite a safe one and has the merit of being acceptable to all concerned. On the whole I would have preferred to liquidate the Council.

Two other problems are out of the way, at least I hope so, as the agreement on Egypt is due to be signed tomorrow and the Chancellor has agreed to including beer in the Budget. Both Customs and I have been wanting this for some time but as it happens this is a good year for it – quite a lot of other things to go with it (it never looked well in near isolation) and a good chance that it will help on the wage front because of the cost of living effect.

Otherwise the Budget is moving slowly but more or less on the right lines. Before the PM left for Moscow he sent another blast on money and interest – he had not read our reply to his previous one. This time it is an inverse Thorneycroft – we contracted the money supply in 1957 and had a recession. Now let us expand it to get us out. I think all he wants is that we should get out, and he fires all these shots to keep up the pressure.

The NIF 2nd Report was done at the end of last week and I wrote my second assessment for the BC. The problem is still to do enough to affect output and employment, without *looking* as if we were being very rash. The Chancellor alternates a good deal according to the last thing that made an impact on him. In our previous session he had said that he was afraid he was doing too little. Yesterday there was a most unsatisfactory leader in *The Times* sitting on the fence on everything but saying that we must not expand consumption too much unless we could expand exports and investment at the same time. The Chancellor sent for me and although he felt as I did about the lack of merit of the article (and said the Editor was smug and tiresome) he clearly thought that if *The Times* said the Budget was too lavish it would have a bad effect on the Tory Party and foreigners. I do not believe the former as I am sure the Tory Party want unemployment to go down. (The February figures will be –12,000 instead of –5,000 which was the early figure that caused the trouble.) The Tories came in useful to me on investment allowances. When the BC discussed the paper, I was pleased to find Roger Makins on my side and as the PM and R.A.B. are there already I think there is a good chance of getting them.

I had dinner with Hugh Gaitskell and Tony Crosland this week. Hugh seemed in good form and we had a long talk about various things, especially whether there would be a run on the pound during the election. I thought that anything of this sort could and should be sat out. He also talked a bit about the Bank of England and that he would still like E.P. but as he won't be available I thought O.S.F. would be the best person. He feels he is too cold a fish but I think this is the wrong way to look at it. He and Tony want to bring N. Kaldor in to advise on tax questions – this will be all right if it is made absolutely clear to Inland Revenue that they have to co-operate.

For once, Hall seems to have misjudged the strength of the upswing in progress by the spring of 1959. On top of the various relaxations in 1958, the Budget reduced taxation by £360 million in a full year and released over £70 million in postwar credits. Public expenditure was also expanding again and the overall budget deficit for 1959–60 amounted to £730 million. This was a much higher total and a more powerful stimulus to the economy than in any previous postwar Budget. Had income tax been cut by a shilling instead of ninepence, as seemed at one time likely, the total would have been higher still. As it was, the slack in the economy was rapidly absorbed, imports expanded strongly, and by the end of 1960 the economy was nearing full employment and running a substantial balance of payments deficit.

Thursday, March 5th

The BC discussions moved a stage further yesterday. The probable above-line surplus has got larger and the scale of concessions is now approaching £400 mn which I think is quite enough, even after allowing say £100 mn for what is needed to offset the run-down of Hire Purchase. Inland Revenue have been extolling the virtues of a shilling [5p] off the Standard Rate largely because Evans is prepared to advocate anything that can be used as an argument that we don't want Investment Allowances. But I think this would be too risky from a long-run point of view, as once we got the rate down it would be very hard to get it up again: I want to do a fairly substantial block of post-war credits which we can repeat or not as we please in subsequent years.

Yesterday afternoon we had the meeting on interest rates which the PM has been wanting – on our side the Chancellor, R.M., T.P. and myself. I had to do most of the talking. The PM had a note, probably from Harrod, comparing the ratio of money supply to GNP in 1953 and now. He also said we had reversed all the 1957 measures *except* on the supply of money. And that it was 'orthodox' both to ease off on money in a recession, and to lower the price of anything if you wanted to expand its use. I said that (a) we didn't want to get back to pre-war orthodoxy which was the time of serious boom and slumps, (b) although low interest rates might have a very small stimulus, they were not likely to be quickly effective which was wanted now, (c) in any case the money supply was expanding and we had been particularly careful not to squeeze the banks on liquidity and had even bought securities to enable them to unload more of their investments. He was reduced to silence by this though I don't think he was really converted.

He kept referring to it being *his* idea which had led to the Thorneycroft packet (which he imagines was primarily a reduction in the stock of money) and seems to be extremely muddled both as to what actually happened in 1957 and as to what a Keynesian analysis requires at present. It is really too bad that Harrod should be so completely incompetent and irresponsible and put all these ideas in his head – but perhaps they are not there and all he is doing is to manoeuvre us to where on our own arguments we need a lavish Budget. But I think our present ideas are fairly lavish even though I am not sure how the PM's mind is running.

Last Thursday I had lunch at Buckingham Palace, one of the small parties the Queen is giving for people in public positions or the public eye. She was extremely nice and talked quite intelligently about my job though I imagine it is very much outside her line. I explained that it was much more hunch than figures.

On Monday R. Makins gave a dinner to say goodbye to Clem Leslie who is leaving IDT to work largely for Chandos and AEI and is to be succeeded by Raphael. I am not sorry that Clem has gone – he had too much of the idea that if possible one should get a scoop, and was always pressing that we should let him put out ideas before they were ready. I also found him a little ungenerous in the sense that I gave him a great deal of help and moral support but when he was for a short time in high favour with H.M. he rather took the line that I must accept a minor role. He was also a bit difficult during the Thorneycroft episode. No doubt these were reactions to the general treatment he got here, of being regarded as something of a nuisance and to be kept out of the picture until an actual Press release was ready. I think he did a very good job here and that Cripps was completely right to bring him in and to stress that economic policy needed public opinion behind it if it were to work at all. In the past 12 years the ideas of exports, and productivity, and price stability have all got into the public consciousness and IDT has built up a good reputation for impartiality.

On Tuesday I dined with Gore-Booth, a Group that has been dining recently to discuss current affairs.[4] The others there were Franks, Harcourt, Hoyer Millar, Rowan, Babington Smith (of Glyn Mills), Hall-Patch, Denis Rickett and Stevens of the Bank of England. We talked mostly of the Common Market and the world situation. O.S.F. very vocal.

Tuesday, April 7th (11.30 a.m.)

It is the morning of the Budget and as usual I am very glad that the time has gone. Last week there was so much Top Secret paper passing around the 2nd floor that it seemed impossible that there should not be some leak! However my nerves have now recovered and as far as I can see the Budget is likely to be well received and to be considered about right on its total concessions, but no one has predicted the composition.

In the end the Chancellor decided on ninepence [3.75p] and sixpence [2.5p] off the Income Tax and he also decided to restore Investment Allowances at 20%. It serves the Inland Revenue right that this has been done. If they had not been so unscrupulous and fanatical about it we might have reached a decision in a sensible atmosphere. But I felt bound to keep my end up and R. Makins backed me (partly because he felt that Evans was so desperate that he couldn't be right) and the PM who was stoked up by Mills and E.P. also backed it. So the Chancellor although he was rather lukewarm felt that the presentational case was very strong. He dislikes beer and keeps on saying that he is very doubtful about it but it has stayed in all the time, though there was a shock when some of the brewers put their price up by a penny a pint a week or two back. This made him say he would give up the concession but I gather that Crombie persuaded them to reverse this decision, which was not a very sensible one. Otherwise most of the last-minute dithering has been on postwar credits.

The B. Committee originally proposed repaying 4 or 5 years [postwar credits] instead of 1, but the Chancellor wanted to do something for hardship cases and very courageously (since IR did not like it much) decided to pay off the heirs of all those who had died and also the holders who were blind or totally disabled or had been on Public Assistance for a long time. This brought the total cost up to about £90 mn and the total concessions in the Budget to about £385 mn (all these figures are approximate – see tomorrow's Hansard) and this was getting towards the high side. So in the end the Chancellor cut out one year of the accelerated repayments and this brings the total nearer to £350 mn than to £400 mn (£366). Even so it will seem to most people that he has been rather bolder than they expected him to be.

My own view is that the economy can easily stand this much but I wanted to go rather gently so that we could see how we were getting on and the great bulk of the commentators have put the total at £350 mn or thereabouts, more on hunch than on calculation. The NIESR Review, which is now well launched and is far the most reliable and professional thing in this field (as it ought to be considering that the top staff were trained here), was very helpful: it gave a good analysis and the opinion that £200 mn of relief would be far too little. The speech was written in good time and has not caused much trouble. As one would expect, the Chancellor's own changes are nearly all for the better. Now we have to see what happens this afternoon – but I shall be surprised if it doesn't go off very well.

The PM has sent us a few more blasts on money and interest rates but as the level of bank advances is rising extremely quickly, and as we shall soon be borrowing on Treasury bills on a large scale (because of the big overall deficit), he is on very weak ground statistically. The Chancellor seems determined not to take any notice of him.

We had one piece of luck in this field – the March unemployment figures (they now come in very early) showed a huge drop on February and this made the PM and his colleagues feel that the Treasury wasn't doing too badly after all. The figures didn't mean all that much as they were mostly an offset to the very bad ones in January, and total employment went down, i.e. more people left the labour force than the reduction in unemployment. However no one took much notice of these refinements and Macleod had a great triumph with the figures because he was able to announce them in the middle of a debate in which the Labour Party was attacking the Government on unemployment and this took most of the sting out of the attack.

The by-elections still make the outcome look quite uncertain especially as there will be a lot of Liberal candidates this time. When the PM came back from Moscow he hinted that May wasn't off after all but the Finance Bill is far from streamlined and I am still betting on October. The PM has done a bit of good by all his travels but the international position is still deplorable. The US generals seem to be bent on a show-down, no doubt on good chess-playing calculations and maybe they are right but no one can be expected to like the idea of a nuclear war. It is extraordinarily bad luck that at this time Eisenhower and Dulles are old and sick, Adenauer is very old indeed and de Gaulle more or less mad: no wonder the PM is thought by many to be the only gleam of hope! Khrushchev has renewed some of the immediate anxieties over Berlin and no doubt he knows what the Pentagon is thinking about but it is all rather unpleasant.

Not much else. After my talk with H.G. and it being clear that E.P. was going to British Aluminium (it has been announced now) I thought it would be a good thing to talk to O.S.F. about the Bank which I did. I told him I thought he was one of the two leading candidates (Harcourt being the other) and that the betting would be on him if Labour got in and on Harcourt if the Tories did. He was obviously very much interested and had been thinking about it. I think he would be much the best man for the job now. T. Balogh keeps on hinting that I ought to be the one but I don't think I would be at all suitable.

All the White Papers are out now and had a fairly easy run this year. At the last minute, the fourth quarter investment figure came in and showed that public investment had hardly gone up at all so total fixed investment was *not* up on 1957 as we had supposed. The Survey had to be changed. It did not matter much but it is really very bad that our statistics are still so imperfect and late. P. Vinter who is now running this side for HOPS which has been re-christened National Resources (NR) is making a drive to improve them and perhaps he will do so in the course of a few years. We are now making a sort of long-term review under Otto's pressure – he is really doing a very good job there and putting things on the map much better than the Division could do under Plowden or Strath.

The wages front is fairly quiet though there are now a number of claims beginning to appear.

Thursday, May 7th

The Budget went off all right but the Speech was too long and the Chancellor nearly fainted towards the end because he had had no lunch. The Opposition have concentrated on pensions for the obvious reason they they did not want to vote against any tax reductions. There was a very good Press. However the Chancellor got extremely depressed because it has not made the Government more popular – he did not allow for the fact that when everyone *expects* tax reductions, you don't get much thanks.

However he constantly sends for me to ask me what I hear about popular reactions, and to ask if we ought not to have given more to the poor, and also if I think we will have an autumn balance of payments crisis or a lot of trouble because we have to borrow so much. All this gloom has quite depressed the office, but in the last week he seems to be cheering up. Meanwhile there is a new Minute from the PM to say that all our predictions have been too optimistic, unemployment is dropping too slowly and production rising ditto, what has gone wrong, what more can we do? As the effect of the Budget can't show up much until June, I don't know what he expects.

One trouble at present is that the preliminary index of production figures are systematically low, so we get more criticized and perhaps more alarmed than we ought to be. The April unemployment figures did not show much of a seasonal drop. But that was more or less as expected. The Minister of Labour has now leaked them early for two months and as a result is committed to putting them out early. He has now leaked the April cost of living figure, which is rather a landmark as it will be 110 or 109, and it reached 110 last April. So we have a full year of ups and downs but never rising above the point reached a year ago. And I doubt if it will go above 110 for the rest of the year, it may even drop to 108 by November, which was first reached in November 1957. I think we really will be able to claim some success then, and I don't feel that the Budget is a cheat as it is counted against us if taxes rise and anyway we have had to take in housing costs which are nothing to do with *current* policy.

I have been to a lot of meetings which take up a lot of time. Paris for the OEEC Experts on April 23rd and 24th. We all felt optimistic and decided that present policies should be continued. The Germans have gradually responded well to the pressure on them and are confident that they will more than lend their gold surplus this year and that the GNP will rise by about 4%. The US are also very confident and have done much better than I expected. We had a lot of talk about rising prices and I got them to agree to recommend that there should be a study of the actual experience of various countries –maybe it will remove some of the fallacies now prevalent.[5]

Last week I had to talk to the Fleck Committee on Fishing Subsidies, the Radcliffe Committee, and spend most of a day on the Houblon-Norman Fund, one of my few extra-curricular activities. This week we have Senior Commonwealth Officials here for a week's talks, prior to the Finance Ministers in Washington in September. Eugene Black has been here and Anderson is here now. So there is not all that time to spare.

The Fleck Committee was not very inspiring. They feel that any arguments in favour of agriculture must be equally applicable to fishing, which seems to me difficult to refute. As the Government cannot very well say that this means less for agriculture the Committee are almost sure to say more for fish. Reddaway is on it and is battling away but I expect he won't get far. Radcliffe was quite pleasant, a sort of final round-up, mostly on HF where W. Armstrong did very well and on OF where Denis Rickett and Parsons also did well. The two things that worried us in advance were whether they would go for autumn Budgets as a regular thing – but clearly they wanted and got arguments against it; and the desirable balance of payments surplus which we revised up from £300–£350 mn to £400–£450 mn. But I think we convinced them that these were necessary targets for planning, and not things that we would necessarily achieve, or that we would necessarily face disaster if we failed to achieve.

The Commonwealth talks are quite interesting. The Canadians put in a good paper on the economic outlook and took the same line as we did in Paris. There was a rather poor discussion on development. I am more and more convinced that we ought to put it all on a more systematic basis but unfortunately the US ideas seem to me to be too meagre and unimaginative. After two go's, the Chancellor managed to get agreement that we would put up some money, so we can at least talk to the Americans: but still not very constructively. A lot of the Commonwealth meetings have been on the Free Trade Area. At last the Canadians are beginning to realize that the GATT permission for Customs Unions will be contrary to the general ITO spirit, if regional unions which intend to have q.r.s or high tariffs come to be generally used.

Meanwhile we are trying to organize our own Customs Union or Free Trade Area with the Scandinavians and Swiss plus perhaps Portugal. We say that this is to persuade the Six that a European FTA is right after all. But I feel we are really moving into a new field. Jack Downie is a great help on all this and for the first time since I came to the Economic Section I feel I have a man I can trust and who has sensible ideas there. One result of this, plus Fred Atkinson in OF Stats, plus Denis R. instead of Leslie R., is that the Economic Section is beginning to become the brains department on external affairs. Jack Downie has even hypnotized L. Thompson McCausland so the Bank is also *gleichgeschaltet*.

I had lunch with Edwin P. last week and he told me that R. Makins has been offered the AEA job as his successor. I hope he won't take it. But there are difficulties about him going back to the

FO although it is likely that he was promised this. And he won't want to be at the Treasury with a Labour Government. On this, it is still anybody's guess.

Monday, June 22nd

Since I wrote last, the economic indicators have been consistently encouraging and indeed have set the Chancellor off to worrying again about whether we have done too much. Just before we were due to see the PM about his Minute that we had been consistently over-optimistic, we heard the May figures which showed a very large fall [in unemployment], about twice the seasonal one. This transformed the situation, and instead of telling us that we were making a mess of everything and needed to do more, especially on the money supply, he was quite calm, said that everything was going well and he could now turn his attention to foreign affairs, and he ended by congratulating the Chancellor (and presumably his advisers) on the way they had handled the situation. Since then the June figures show another drop of 60,000, again about twice the seasonal drop: and it is quite clear that unemployment has ceased to be a political danger to the Tories. In fact there is practically full employment in London and the SE and also in the S. Midlands where the car trade is booming. But the figures are odd because employment is not rising nearly as fast as unemployment is falling.[6] It seems as if people are leaving industry and not registering, at the same time as those out of work are being taken on again.

The index of industrial production remains very unsatisfactory and is still being revised. After being put at 107 for March, which more or less made us say that we were wrong in saying that production rose steadily from the autumn to the Budget, the figure has been revised to 109, so we were right the first time. The April figure may well be 110 which will be above the previous peak of 109 in September 1957. Productivity must be rising quite fast and as wages are fairly steady, costs are probably falling. The Chancellor has made several speeches which urge industrialists to lower prices and says they will have more and more room to do so. The May retail price index was 109 so it is lower than it was 13 months ago, and we really do have a good chance for price stability.

Our own forecasts for the rest of the year have become more bullish, and we now put the GNP at about 5% higher in the fourth quarter of 1959 than it was in in the fourth quarter of 1958, and industrial production at least 6 points up. Consumption is running quite strongly and so is house-building (where there has even been a temporary shortage of bricks). Public sector investment certainly ought to be rising but we get very bad and unreliable figures for this. Finally, and this is very encouraging, both the April and May exports have been much higher than we expected and are thus contributing more to the revival. World trade is now expanding everywhere and primary producers' incomes rising a bit, although our own terms of trade are fairly steady. The result of this plus a strong oil income is that the balance of payments forecasts have become a good deal more cheerful and the first half of 1960 looks as if it will be much the same as the first half of 1958. And all these years, 1958/60, will show a surplus of more than £300 mn.[7] The reserves will have risen a little in the six months Jan./June although we have paid back part of the IMF loan and also our subscription to the IMF increase.

The wages outlook is about as good as one can hope for though one never knows till it is over what any round will bring. The steady cost of living has removed what has been an important argument in the past. On the other hand there is the fall in unemployment and the evident signs of recovery, and it is certain that profits will rise even if people lower their prices as the Chancellor wants. At present there is a strike in the printing trades: we hope it will end in a very moderate increase, but as the employers offered 2½% it cannot be less than that. Harold Emmerson thinks that the employers are fairly firm and that the Unions will run out of funds before too long. There are now a number of claims emerging from the TU Conference going on. However there still seems a good chance that the approach of the election will keep the TUs from being too aggressive.

Ministers have consistently refused to accept the guiding light and have been reluctant even to restate the doctrine without the figure. The Chancellor thinks hardly any wage increases should be conceded which is both unrealistic, and difficult to make into a doctrine and still more to reconcile it with what has been said in the past. We had an official meeting today with the idea of putting a new paper to Ministers on what they should say if they say anything. On the one hand they must not say anything that will make an increase of up to 3% seem like a defeat or even a disaster, since it is not likely to lead to rising prices – on the other, they must not give any idea that wage increases ought to be linked to current productivity increases, since these may well turn out to be as much as 5% at the end of the year.

The Chancellor is getting worried about whether we have not done too much, and asks me whether (a) there is not a danger that home demand will check exports, (b) that we are creating conditions for fresh wage advances. I do not think there is much danger of this and certainly not over the remainder of this year. Hire Purchase ought soon to be having a braking effect, and the big slices of income from the Budget will be paid this month. Alec Johnston says they have paid out £35 mn of post-war credits already and are now slowed up because of the lack of applicants. Industrial investment is now running, so far as we can see, at about the forecast of 10% less than at this time last year.

It is evident from all this that the economic situation is extremely favourable compared to what it has been for a long time. The most uncertain factor to my mind arises from the labour situation – will some of those who are no longer registered come back into employment or will they only be drawn back by over-full conditions again?

The election still seems to be most likely for October and the results still very uncertain but so far as I can judge the Tories are a little in the lead and I think the improving economic signs are likely to support this. The people have not got used to the improvements in output and the standard of living and they feel that they are pretty well off and have something to lose. And Labour has not been able to think of a new image to replace that of the champion of the weak and underprivileged. I think many people are worried by the international situation and afraid of the H-bomb but it is hard to see how this will affect the result as no one can tell yet if there will be a Summit, or how the PM will get on if there is one, or whether Labour will be able to come forward with a policy that will appeal to people – they are having a row at present among themselves about nuclear disarmament and this cannot help. To sum up, the things in favour of Labour are the natural swing plus some strong feelings among a number of people about Suez, while the strong things for the Tories are the economic situation and the absence of any clear or compelling programme for the other side.

N. Brook saw me again last week and was rather pressing that I should not leave or if I did that he should get as much notice as possible. He also put my salary up. The Colerain Committee recommendations, which were agreed in May for the standard classes, would have meant a rise of £800 for me (he said) and he and R. Makins thought I should go to £6,000 which would have been a rise of £1,250. But apparently no intermediate Civil Servant (between Permanent Secretary and Deputy Secretary) now gets more than £5,800 so he suggested this. I was rather glad as I had been slightly nettled on the last round to go up only as much as Deputy Secretaries. At that time I was told that everyone was getting the same, i.e. they were all notionally slightly downgraded. No doubt this is due to the combined effects of R. Makins and the Chancellor both of whom, I think, think well of me. The Chancellor told me that even the PM is now disposed to think I have been right but this is no doubt fairly temporary. I have not heard any more *re* R. Makins.

I am just going to Washington for a week and then for two days to Ottawa.

Wednesday, July 1st (leaving Washington, DC, for Ottawa)

I left London on June 24th and came very quickly and comfortably to New York where we landed at 5.30 having left London at midnight. I sat in a large cool BOAC lounge and read the morning paper until 8.30 when I left for Washington and was there soon after 10. The journeys get shorter and shorter and this was a Britannia. Anything faster and one will do better by day.

I have had the usual very interesting time, at first by myself and talking mainly to economists and the last two days with Denis Rickett on more official visits. But when I think of all my past visits, this one is very different in one way, since the US is worried about its balance of payments and its loss of reserves and they are saying that we must take away our barriers to their exports and carry some of the burden of development. And meanwhile we have a large balance of payments surplus and are gaining reserves, though of course our position is very far from theirs, i.e. we are basically much weaker. Still it *is* a change and they think we have done very well and D. MacDougall and G. Crowther wrote their books at an unlucky time.[8]

I dined with Jo Alsop the first night, a very Democratic party including Dean Acheson and Paul Nitze and Bill Martin who I suppose is a Democrat but who as usual said nothing. If he is a Democrat he won't last long at the Fed. if the Democrats win as they want to grow faster and spend more and he is worried about inflation. Anyway they all talked about who the next President would be and said that the Democrats would probably have a fearful struggle over their nomination and have little time to build up their man. And meanwhile Nixon and Rockefeller are both building themselves up, though I don't think R. will be nominated unless the Republicans think he can win and Nixon can't. N. no doubt would very much like it if the President retired in good time as he would probably be nominated and have a good chance if he went in as President and would have the advantage of the chance of two terms plus 1½ years or whatever the maximum is. But I don't suppose the President will go unless his health breaks down again.

None of the party agreed on the Democratic probable except that Kennedy was a strong starter and Stevenson still very much a possibility. Kennedy's main aide was there but I stupidly did not make a chance to talk to him. The rest of the conversation was about how awful the Republicans are on foreign policy and defence and how they did not intend to do anything about Berlin for if they did so intend why were they not being more demonstrative, e.g. by putting more troops into Germany. Alsop and Acheson and Nitze also said that the Russians were probably ahead on nuclear weapons now. I did not say much but it is my impression that the US military are very far from being ready to do nothing, though of course it will be the President who will decide. And I think they thought that Europe would be comforted by a show of strength whereas I think it might have the opposite effect because it would cause at least some panic.

The other people I saw before the weekend were Win Riefler, Wallich and the two Directors of the inquiries into growth and price stability. Win Riefler said they were worried about the balance of payments and loss of reserves and asked what they ought to do. The theme of this talk and of all the others I had that touched on the subject was that they would probably get the balance of payments deficit down to $1.5 bn because exports would rise but they could not go on for long at this rate: that it was very important that they should not be pushed into action that would disorganize the joint efforts of the West: that other countries ought to get rid of dollar discrimination as soon as possible in order to remove an argument that would be increasingly used by protectionists: and that Europe must now carry more of the load of foreign aid. Of course I agree with all of this and have been saying so in London.

Henry Wallich is the most recent acquisition to the Council of Economic Advisers. He was in the Treasury for a short time and is said to be a modern Republican economist. I think he is quite good: I talked first to Hal Lary and then to him mainly on the lines already indicated.

The US has been reviving quickly and unemployment is no longer a worry to them. Saulnier whom I saw today said that they still had quite a lot of increase to come but he was worried about the steel strike mainly because of the wage effects. Bill Martin told us when we lunched at the Fed. that *he* was worried about 'the 1961 recession'. The right time to counter recessions was during a boom. If the US did not do the right things now they would have a disastrous recession. This sounded too much like George Humphrey to me and I did not pursue it, but I suppose he meant that they were getting dangerously near another 1929 which seems to me, and would to most people, to be an exaggerated view.

The Joint Committee on the Economic Report has recently commissioned a study of growth and price stability and brought a very bright young man from Harvard, called Eckstein, to be the Director. I saw him on Friday and was much impressed – I told him about our experiences and what our policy was. He said they had a subcommittee going into the institutional factors. Then I went to see Dr Allen Wallis, who is the Director of the Cabinet (Nixon) Committee on price stability. He gave me a copy of their 'preliminary conclusions' which are nothing but an endorsement of the present Administration policy as stated to Congress – it was a most disappointing document and I cannot imagine why they produced it at all. Wallis comes from Chicago and seemed very much a member of that school as he was arguing that the State should do nothing except improve the rules of competition and that the Fed. should increase the money supply by 3% a year as this was the proper rate of growth, and do nothing more. He obviously thought my ideas on wage policy were dangerous and indeed said that if the Government told employers and workers what they ought to do this would be far worse for the economy than inflation. But the report was not even a good exposition of extreme laissez-faire views and I can only suppose that he was a bit out of his depth. Kit McMahon (my man in Washington) said that he thought the explanation of the report was that Nixon wanted to be nominated, hence the very orthodox Administration line: if nominated he would want to be elected and would become more liberal.

I had a quiet weekend. Denis came on Monday and he and I and Arnold France and Cromer have been paying a lot of calls. On Monday night Geoffrey Wilson gave a small dinner for me and asked Arnold (who was staying with him), Dick Bissell, John Leddy, who is now the man in State Dept concentrating on Aid, and T. Wood, who is Research Director for the Draper Committee which is investigating military and economic aid programmes. We had a very good evening, almost like one in the old days, with everyone talking quite freely. Their ideas were not very different from mine and I think we all felt that we would have to bid more money and to get more co-ordination for a longer time than our present ideas implied.

They asked me how the potential donors could be co-ordinated and wondered if it could be done in OEEC. I was a bit doubtful about this but I don't know how it could be done – maybe there could be informal meetings under an OEEC church. I also thought that the IBRD was not much use to co-ordinate the donors though perhaps it could co-ordinate the plans. But I thought that the first thing was for the President to make a speech on the lines of Marshall's speech, saying that the rich countries would see the poor ones through if both sides were willing to sit down and agree plans as was done under the Marshall plan. It would also be necessary to find a large international staff: and to be willing to give no aid to countries that were badly misusing it. All this sounds very dry and sketchy but it really was a good evening and achieved one of the things I had come to Washington to talk about.

We had a rather unsatisfactory meeting at the State Dept with Jim Mason [?] who is Dillon's deputy on the economic side. He had just come back from three weeks' leave. We talked a bit about India: and our credits for Russia which they don't like: and the oil situation where they say that Venezuela is trying to get a 75/25 split on oil instead of 50/50 and that a serious situation is coming up, especially since there is now a big glut of oil.

Thursday, July 9th

The rest of our time in Washington was with the Fed. – where we lunched on Tuesday and talked about inflation and the balance of payments, which Bill Martin thinks are even more connected than they are – but he said it did not make sense for the US to lend Pakistan money to buy a German steel plant when the Germans then collected in US gold – and the Treasury which did us very well as we had two meetings and lunched on Wednesday.

The new Under Secretary, Repton, is a great improvement on poor Tom Coughran and he talked quite intelligently about the Indian problem, which Denis Rickett is trying to get looked at and which seems to me to be a type of underdevelopeds generally. George Willis, who is now said to be a power in the Treasury because he is the only senior survivor of the old régime, is very much opposed to looking ahead or sending an IBRD 'wise man' to India, because it would (a) encourage them to be extravagant, (b) suggest that we had a commitment. We pointed out that *not* talking to them would not prevent either of these from happening. Anderson had a good idea, that we ought to have a central register, perhaps in IBRD, for all loans, credits and trade credits to these underdeveloped countries. He said they often get trade credits for long-term projects where they had been unable to get loans.

We also saw Per Jacobsson and Southard, to talk about Article 9 and the GATT meeting and non-discrimination. All this will come up at the Bank/Fund meeting in September. The UK Treasury officials want to give up all discrimination and move to Article 8 as soon as we can:[9] our trouble is our Ministers who are nervous about removing discrimination (which is now protective not balance of payments) before an election. Southard of course wants this, but to our surprise he wants to go slow on what the new position on annual consultations will be, and therefore to go slow on Article 8 generally – because he does not like the idea of IMF consultation about the state of the US. I don't know if this is dignity, or nerves about the balance of payments.

Ottawa was quite interesting. N. Brook, strongly backed by R. Makins, had suggested that the time had come to end these regular meetings of senior officials on the economic side [the Anglo-Canadian Continuing Committee], initiated I think about 1947, when things were very different. And I had felt that they were becoming very routine affairs, that the Canadians were becoming far less imaginative and indeed far more concentrated on their own narrow interests than they had been, and were almost disingenuous in support of them, and that a lot of time was taken by the recital of grievances about particular tariffs, quotas, etc., on both sides.

However this meeting turned out to be a good deal better than some of the recent ones. Partly because the UK is now in so much stronger a position than she was and has made so much progress towards non-discrimination, etc. Partly because we had got a certain amount of initiative both from the European and our Washington talks. And finally that Diefenbaker is obviously an extremely difficult and uncertain factor so that the level of political life in Canada has been somewhat debased. Anyhow it was a meeting in which it was clear that we had recovered the international initiative and it was very interesting to discuss the problems of the future on that basis – though I could not get any spark out of them on international development other than that they were not likely to do any more than they are doing now.

I got back on July 5th and have been fairly busy on my talk [i.e. Presidential Address] to the Royal Economic Society which I gave this afternoon on 'Reflections on the Practical Application of Economics', in which I discussed mainly the little use that economics was, other than as a training in practical affairs, because our models were no good and economists disagreed so much on practical issues. It is a relief to have it over. I did not really allow enough time to get it ready, particularly as I had not expected to go to the US and Canada when the time was fixed –in the end Downie did a good deal of the final draft based on my original – it was a pity as his bits did not sound like me.

Nothing much on the home front while I was away – all the indications have remained good and production is definitely rising.

Tuesday, July 21st

I saw the Chancellor several times last week. He is still worried lest we should have a boom, or a balance of payments crisis, or both. I do not think there is any danger at present but we might have a private investment boom if the Conservatives win the election. I wrote a note on my visit, laying a good deal of stress on the US concern about their balance of payments, and the Chancellor has circulated this to the Cabinet.

We also had another drive on non-discrimination, largely based on the idiocy of discriminating against US and Canadian goods at this juncture, (a) our own balance of payments so good and the US so weak, (b) our exports to the US growing fast and a lot of their exports to us still on quota, (c) external convertibility and yet French and German goods given preferential treatment over US and Canada. The EPC took our paper and decided to think about it again in September but the Chancellor was not satisfied and has taken it to Cabinet. He is finally aware of the problems and also of his own position at the Bank/Fund meeting in September.

R. Makins drove all this along very fast to the indignation of Proctor and Winnifrith who were asked to agree papers for EPC the evening before they were to be *taken*. As they quite rightly said, if anyone but the Treasury had done this, the papers would have been deferred either by the Cabinet Office or by Ministers themselves. However it is a good thing to drive things occasionally.

Returning to the Chancellor's worries, he has tried to get a cut in the 1960/61 public investment programme which is up by the £200 mn added in 1959/60 and by another £60 mn or so of its own. He thought it better to keep it down a bit and in all the circumstances I thought it better to agree with him though this is on hunch, since all the present forecasts suggest that we shall still be rather slack next year. The July unemployment figures show a decrease *after* seasonal correction of about 8,000 so the pace is slackening. But I am more impressed by the failure of employment to grow than by the run-down of unemployment. However we now have full or over-full employment in London and SE England so it does no harm to be a bit quieter. It looks as if unemployment in October will be about 400,000 which I always said it would be though to be honest I did not think employment would have stayed so low. This was just what the Chancellor wanted from an electoral point of view and even the PM does not seem to mind. But it is a bit of good luck and the Chancellor may well think we can run it a bit closer to fine limits than we can.

I had lunch with E.P. on Friday and he told me that Roger's appointment to the AEA would be announced soon. Frank Lee had told me in Ottawa that it was settled and Oliver Franks told me on Friday night (he drove me to Oxford after a dinner) that it was coming. So much for secrecy. Then yesterday afternoon Roger himself came in and said that it would be announced on Wednesday morning, July 22nd. He talked very freely, told me that he *had* been promised the FO in writing when he came to the Treasury but that the PM had urged him to go to AEA as they could not think of anyone else whereas there were three or four people who could do the FO. (This is true, there must be at least four who would do it better than Derek Hoyar Millar.) He said he was very uncertain but had gone on the rule to go where he was told to go unless there were strong personal reasons against it. He had not wanted much to come to the Treasury, did not mind leaving it, and thought they ought to be able to handle their own problems, i.e. he felt little responsibility for the staffing question. I said that I was very sorry he was going as I thought that he had done very well here and I was worried about his successor. I did not think that T.P. would be up to it. He rather agreed and indeed volunteered that he had thought little of recent appointments as Permanent Secretaries. He said that N.B. and presumably the PM and the Chancellor had all agreed *not* to appoint a successor till after the election – the change at AEA is not until January so R.M. [is] here till Christmas – incidentally this suggests that October is fixed, and I saw a Minute from M/Lab. to the PM about the unemployment figures *which would be before the public* during October, i.e. the September count.

The US balance of payments forecast for 1959 has just been revised from a deficit of $3 bn to one of $4.5 bn so the whole thing is becoming more urgent. We are having a talk about all this at Denis Rickett's working party on Friday: Downie has written a paper on Reserve Currencies asking if we and the US ought to agree to hold one another's currencies if needed. The trouble, apart from it being a bit of lion-and-mouse, is to keep the two purchasing powers more or less the same, i.e. to keep costs in line. Otherwise one or the other might have to change the exchange rate. Perhaps this could be got over by exchange guarantees, upper limits and frequent discussions. It still seems very queer to me that the UK is temporarily in such a strong position but I can't think [but] that the US will put themselves right and in the process we are almost certain to be weakened.

Wednesday, July 22nd

I saw N. Brook this afternoon. He agreed that there was no point in winding up the UK/Can. Continuing Committee. He also said that it was definite that no appointment would be made to the Treasury till after the election and that he hoped I would let this be known. He reminded me that *his* appointment to the Treasury had been announced before the election in 1951 and had been reversed by Winston and pointed out that this was a good precedent for not doing anything now.

We have just done a mid-year economic assessment for the Budget Committee. It is a bit more bearish than the May one and certainly implies that we need not think about tightening up yet a while.

Thursday, July 30th

The House of Commons rises today and it seems unlikely that it will meet again, at any rate for serious business, before the election. The last few days have been mainly concerned with debates on African affairs (Hola and Nyasaland) which many people think are likely to damage their prospects. I had lunch with Clem Leslie yesterday but he did not think this very probable and on the whole thought the Government would get back fairly easily. If they do, it will be an extraordinary achievement for the PM since he took over at a very bad point, we have never recovered the losses from Suez, and he was deeply involved at that time.

Even more than his own achievements, however, has been done by the inability of the Labour Party to present a coherent image of themselves to the public, which I think stems very largely from their failure to adjust themselves to the changes brought about in economic life by full employment and the welfare state. The ordinary working man does not think that he is downtrodden or exploited and I think is more afraid that he will lose what he has gained than that the Conservatives will prevent him from going on to new fields. Thus the idea of social justice, which was the driving ideal of labour, has ceased to get the powerful reinforcements that came from the mass of the electorate feeling that social justice would improve their own sad lot. This has also removed much of the charms of nationalization, as at least Gaitskell realizes very strongly: but for internal reasons they cannot drop it and are driven to somewhat equivocal attitudes.

The assessment of the economic situation which we did last week was taken by the Budget Committee yesterday and has gone to the Chancellor. It takes the view that the main stimulus from HP must now begin to operate in the reverse direction, i.e. the creation of new debt will be at a decreasing rate, and that the biggest Budget effects were felt in June–July. Hence the main stimulating factor will be the growth of public investment, which has so far lagged a good deal behind our expectations. (In the 1st quarter of this year it seemed to be still *declining* – so much for the PM's Committee.) Until there is an increase in wages or exports or private investment, things will stay with only a gentle expansive effect (at most the long-term rate), wages moving very slowly, prices stable, productivity probably increasing as the numbers employed are hardly increasing at all. The BC endorsed this but recommended no change in policy either way.

Cabinet took the public sector investment programme this week.[10] The Chancellor had said he might have to make some cuts in the 1960/61 programme if things got tighter in the autumn. He is afraid that there will be a private investment boom after the election but if so it will come fairly slowly. R.A.B. told him that he had the smell of expansion going too far, and he asked me if I was sure that we were not going to have another 1955! I wrote him a long note comparing the two years and saying there was very little resemblance between them. The only thing that is at all mysterious is the very sharp increase in bank advances, which I am now having looked at in the Economic Section.

The Radcliffe Committee Report was or is to be signed today and W. Armstrong has a copy and has sent round a summary. It is more or less what we had been expecting. Monetary policy must be looked at as part of a general economic policy which includes fiscal measures and direct controls. It should operate on the structure of interest rates. The 30% liquidity ratio should be made legal and variable at will.

The most interesting structural recommendations, which had been foreshadowed to me, are that the Bank should not regard *any* of its functions as apart from the Treasury, and that there should be a Committee with the Chancellor in the Chair, four from the Bank, four from the Treasury and two from the Board of Trade, which would consider proposals about monetary policy before the Chancellor is asked to approve them. Changes in Bank Rate should be by direction; there should be a 5th Executive Director of the Bank, the Head of the Bank's economic intelligence division! Roger Makins wants to have a preliminary talk about all this, this afternoon.

Tuesday, September 1st

I was on leave from August 21st until yesterday. The most interesting event since I wrote last was the Radcliffe Committee Report which I have already outlined very briefly. It is rather a curious document from the point of view of its analysis as it goes into great detail about financial institutions generally from the Government and the Bank of England right down to building societies and investment trusts, most of the bodies concerned being of the kind which most economists would regard as financial intermediaries rather than parts of the *monetary* system. The general thesis seems to be that all these bodies can be sources of funds if people want to borrow from them and there is no clear distinction between a body which can add to the money supply, like the Government, or the cheque-issuing banks, and one which can turn its assets into money. If they had said that this was because, under the British system, anyone who wants to realize securities can set up forces which in the end will compel the Bank of England to provide money, it would have been more intelligible. But this analysis is not of any great significance to the conclusions, which are that monetary policy is not a very important determinant of economic events, that if it is used in ordinary times it should be done by changing interest rates, and that the national debt should be managed with this in view. However they do not want violent changes in interest rates. They *do* want the 30% liquidity ratio to be made explicit and to be varied if need be.

All this suits me very well as I have never thought that much reliance could be placed on money as an instrument of control unless (a) in a boom you were prepared to make it very dear indeed – when in any case it would primarily hit investment, (b) in a slump you were prepared to make it very cheap indeed, when it would lay up trouble for the future. I have also felt that we must be much less worried about interest rates (again if we wanted to use monetary policy) than we have been until recently. And that it ought to be quite clear that we *could* control the supply of money if we wanted to: at one time it was impossible to get the Bank of England even to admit that it was their responsibility to control the money supply.

I am a bit more doubtful about our taking powers to control *all* sources of liquidity, as they recommend – and that we should only use control of advances, of capital issues and of HP in emergencies. However, it may be that now we have got the economy under control we need not let it get out of hand again.

The recommendations about the relations between Treasury and the Bank of England suit me very well as they want the primacy of the Chancellor to be clearly recognized and major decisions only taken on the advice of a new Committee – Governor plus three from the Bank, four from Treasury, two from Board of Trade. Not that I want the Board of Trade to be mixed up in it – and I think we shall probably be able to avoid this.

Generally speaking, the Report suits me very well and endorses all the things I have stood for in recent years – and it is a very common-sense sort of document in its attitude, whatever is thought of its analysis.

It seemed clear when we read it that the recommendations about the Bank of England would be the ones to get the headlines as these clearly reduced the Bank's importance and especially that of the part-time directors. The Governor did not like this at all and took it (as he should have done) as an expression of some lack of confidence.

We all felt that it would be a pity if too much was made of this and O. Franks came to see me in Oxford on August 7th – he and Bill Harcourt were getting slightly cold feet. We agreed that he should write to the Governor to urge him to use the time between when the Press got the Report (August 17th) and publication (August 19th) to let it be known that he welcomed the Report and took these particular recommendations as being logical developments of current practice rather than anything very revolutionary. I was to urge the same thing from my end and also to use any influence I had with the newspapers to get them to take the same line. All this was duly done and the Governor replied rather ungraciously to Oliver but at the same time accepted the view, and Makins and Armstrong urged the same thing on him and he said he would. I saw a number of financial writers and made a few guarded remarks to them. Anyway the upshot of it all – or perhaps it had nothing to do with it – was that the reception played down the bits about the Bank a great deal and it all went off as smoothly as possible. In fact if anything it has been overdone. However Roger Makins accepts that there will have to be some sort of Bank/Treasury Committee and he says that the Governor accepts this also. We are going to talk about it next week.

But I think it is very likely that the election will be in October and that there will be no debate until after that.

Today I was given the draft of a speech for the PM to make in his constituency when he is renominated by the local Tories and I can hardly think that this is just being forethoughtful. The August unemployment figures show quite an increase due to school leavers – but the September ones, which will no doubt be the ones on which the election will have to be fought, cannot be all that better and we can't rely on any improvement after that with the seasonal factors the other way. In fact my people think that the pace of expansion will slow up from now on, though I think it is likely that private investment in manufacturing industry has now turned the corner. It seems almost certain that there will be no balance of payments difficulty as the reserves were still rising in August, so we have got over the 'odd year' complex – I think the last real 'odd year' was 1951 though one could make a case for 1955 but lots of people think that it is the other way and 1953 was a freak.

Finally, to come back to the elections, the President is here and has made it fairly clear that UK/US relations are still pretty special and he and the PM did a television interview from No. 10 last night which will have, I should think, a good effect on the public. All the recent polls seem to show the Tories well in the lead – a combination of the good economic position and the bad self-projection of the Labour Party, plus no doubt a bit of credit to the PM in international affairs. So I think the odds are very strongly on the Government. R.M. was talking to me yesterday about who the new Ministers will be – he wants Lennox-Boyd to go to the FO and the Chancellor to stay here. I certainly hope that he will as I do not like the prospect of Macleod who is I suppose the most probable alternative. R.A.B. will be a problem as I think he wants the FO where he would not be good – nor would the PM like him there.

I had lunch at Rothschild's today: one cannot help feeling a bit romantic just as I did when I lunched at Morgan's in New York. The present man, Sir Edmund, showed me all the family pictures and some of the documents, e.g. a letter from No. 10 in 1815 asking Rothschild's to collect gold wherever they could on the Continent up to £600,000 to pay the Commissary General in France. But I did not think Sir Edmund had inherited much of his family's flair unless he was concealing it very carefully. All the talk at lunch was on a highly trivial level, mostly contributed by an aged diplomat called Sir R. Leeper who used to be Argentine Ambassador and is now with de Beer's and whom I rather liked. But our host had nothing to say either on finance or on literature. He had looked everyone up in *Who's Who* beforehand as I suppose most intelligent people do, but got them somewhat wrong all the same, e.g. he said I was the chief statistician, no doubt a genuine inability to see any difference, but if I had cared, not very wise. I think these old houses are gradually losing their position, naturally enough with so many other larger bodies coming on the scene.

Nothing much has happened while I was away, in fact it must have been the quietest August since 1939 with only Radcliffe to ripple the surface and no one sent any messages much less recalled.

Now we are starting to get ready for the Commonwealth Ministers on September 22nd to be followed by Bank/Fund in Washington, beginning on September 28th.

Tuesday, October 6th

I am on my way back from the Bank/Fund meeting and the general election is in two days' time. The polls have showed that the apparent distance between the two parties has been diminishing rapidly but I still think that the Conservatives will win. I suppose that the very little difference between the policies of the parties means that as the actual election is nearer, the difference in votes gets less but I am slightly surprised that it now seems so even. I have been away from England since September 25th so am a bit out of touch with developments.

The announcement of the election date was very quietly done – most of us thought it would be October 22nd but as the polls showed more and more lead for the Government and the visit of the [President] went so well, I think the PM began to push it and the Chancellor dropped a few hints in the last few days. He got me to look at bits of his speeches to see if his arguments were logical or his facts correct but Ministers are nearly always very good about this and try to stick to the idea that Civil Servants don't help them in clearly political matters. Of course between elections it is very hard to draw the line and indeed politicians out of office are very conscious that they have not got the help of the Civil Servants.

The pressure of work fell away a good deal with Ministers trying to be out making speeches, etc., all the time but there was a good deal of discussion of the briefs for the Commonwealth Ministers' meeting and also the briefs for the Radcliffe Report. The Commonwealth Finance Ministers (to which I did not go) turned out to be a very workmanlike affair owing to the collective briefing which had taken place. There always has been some on balance of payments prospects but it is a number of years since there was any concerted action on these. This year there was an enormous brief on the Common Market/EFTA question where the Australians and New Zealanders had been very critical because their interests were as they thought damaged, while the Canadians were largely against it because it was moving away from multilateralism. However the treatment at the meeting seemed to be reasonably favourable, at any rate we are going to go ahead. There was also a better discussion than usual about development since it had been proposed that there should be a Commonwealth Development Bank and we had to discuss IDA in Washington. Having these concrete things to do is always good for any meeting and reading the Minutes afterwards I felt that the meeting (really the first of what is supposed to be a more formalized body and with more secretarial work than in the past) had been rather encouraging. It is getting an enormous body as more and more Colonies get independence but I think the new people rather enjoy themselves.

We laid on an NIF exercise to give a new Chancellor, if there should be one, the latest appreciation of the economic situation and the rest of the Treasury produced a long list of things which Ministers would have to attend to after the election. We also read the Party Manifestos but the only conclusion of any importance was that Labour would almost certainly have a big above-the-line deficit in their next Budget. As they say they can pay for all they intend out of the expanding economy this is logical enough. It is hard to say how much slack there is in the economy but Wynne Godley thinks quite a bit as he thinks the stimuli are now slacking off and investment not growing fast enough to take its place. Unemployment seems to be fairly stable after seasonal corrections. The most difficult thing to understand is the steady growth of Bank advances – it was easy to see why personal loans, HP finance and so on which were caught by the squeeze should expand but it is both wider and more persistent than that and this at a time when profits must be increasing and investment diminishing so liquidity high. Industrial production now seems to be about 6% above what it was a year ago and in general everything going smoothly – though the US balance of payments will cause us trouble before too long, I think.

When we came to look at Radcliffe more closely we did not like it so much though the general pattern still seemed very suitable. We decided that the Government in the first debate should reject the idea of an 'emergency' during which you would use all sorts of things you had forsworn at other times – that we should reject the proposal that local authority borrowing should be all from the Treasury – and that we should deal with the bits about the Bank of England in a friendly but somewhat vague way. In the later stages we had a meeting with Mynors, O'Brien and M. Allen and they agreed all this but Mynors seemed to be still smarting from his wounds, which considering the Bank did so much to pick the members shows how independent we can be.

The IMF/IBRD meeting was interesting. The Chancellor decided that no Ministers should go so R.M. led the team. It was a frightful grind as I was at meals all the time as I suppose the others were and so many people wanted to see me that I had very little time even to go to the sessions: though that matters little since all the speeches come round more or less as they are made.

By far the most interesting bit was the speech by Anderson on the Fund, in which he showed that they were worried about their balance of payments, intended to correct at least a good deal of the gold loss, said the imbalance was due to other industrial countries not financing their surpluses, and called on them to share the burden of aid to underdeveloped. We were told privately that they intend to tie at least the DLF (Development Loan Fund) money to US exports in future. I made a rather careful study of the speech which was especially interesting since we had used the argument that surplus countries should finance their surplus, in connection with Germany in earlier years, and had not got much encouragement from them. It has been clear for some time that they would have to do something and the worst things would have been to cut down on aid and to restrict imports. We will have to try again to persuade Ministers on what is left of discrimination. I don't think we can do a great deal more on aid though we could do some. The Germans realize that they will have to do more. However the US propositions, which implied (a) that present reserves were satisfactory, (b) that the size of the addition to reserves was the right measure of what extra could be done on foreign aid – were not ones we could accept and we got R.M. to make the points, in as friendly a way as possible, to Anderson. It is a pity about tying the DLF loans but there is still a good deal not tied – the main danger is that this may start a competitive process. I could go on at length on all this but I think we will hear a good deal more about it –although Kit McMahon says that the latest US forecasts show their exports rising rather fast.

The IDA got through in a general way without much trouble, as Bill Martin said, 'unanimous approval with whole-hearted reservations'. I think the Managing Board of the Bank will draw up a very loose set of rules in the end. The main trouble at base is how to make 'soft' loans or grants without offending those who don't get them.

Anderson suggested to R.M. two other things we have often suggested: (a) that there should be regular US/UK consultation – we forbore to remind him of my trip in 1957 and stressed that the arrangements should be very informal; (b) that we needed a bit more consultation between developing financiers. Erhard took this up publicly in his speech and Gene Black gave a dinner on Saturday for the donor countries – the 'blue chip' directors as it was said. We tried to get a bit further on India and I had a long talk to B. K. Nehru at a dinner at the Embassy. One of those occasions where one drinks a bit too much, gets carried away, feels very doubtful in the morning if one has not gone too far, and then finds by inquiry that one didn't really drop any bricks and that the recipient is as well aware of the nuances as oneself. I suppose the process of carefully analysing anything one is told at a dinner party goes on in practically all diplomatic circles. The two problems are to judge how much the person who spoke really liked you, and to what extent he spoke under a sort of general instruction. The main use of them I think is to give one an idea of how solid a position really is.

Note. Radcliffe. G. Wilson's dinner. Butler.

Thursday, October 8th

The note was to remind me to finish. On Radcliffe, the main reaction is that all the Central Bankers disliked it for obvious reasons, (a) it played down the importance of money, (b) it stated that Central Banks should be under the Government in matters of policy. On (a), I pointed out *ad nauseam* that Central Bankers themselves were always saying that money could not do much if fiscal policy went the other way and that Radcliffe had put the onus where it belonged. But they said that you couldn't rely on Governments and that monetary policy would have to do most of the work and it was a pity to reduce its status. (b) followed from (a), since if you start with the view that Central Bankers are more likely to act for the good of the country than Governments, it follows that the more independence they have the better. I said that if the Committee had tried to give the Bank more independence, the result would have been to have Parliament make it clear that this was not acceptable. They said this was all right for the UK but this would not be understood and everywhere else Finance Ministers would quote Radcliffe against their Central Bankers and in support of their profligacy. I did not even try to discuss the Report with Win Riefler as I am sure he regards it as practically a wicked document. An incidental result is that Alec Cairncross, whom Per Jacobsson wanted to get hold of as a sort of Chief Adviser, may have become unacceptable simply because he signed the Report. Talking of the IMF, I met Merle Cochrane the Deputy to Jacobsson at a dinner party on Saturday night and found him a delightful person, full of reminiscences about pre-war and early post-war personalities in the field of international money and finance. I do not know how influential he is but Bill Lacy told me that he is extremely influential in the State Department. I must try to see him when I am in Washington again.

Geoffrey Wilson gave a dinner party on Monday to enable Henry Phelps Brown (now economist on COPPI) to meet a number of US official economists interested in wage and price questions. Wallis and Eckstein whom I had met in June were there, also Henry Wallich of the Council and Win Riefler. But the most interesting thing for me was to have a chance of talking to Roosa of the Fed. of New York, about debt management particularly in London. He seemed to me to be the only man I had ever met who felt more or less as I did about these things. I went to see him in New York on Monday but was rather too hurried. However it was very encouraging and I must now do my best to get my ideas put into practice, i.e. to find a long-term rate that will cause long debt to be held and to get it sold by letting the market rise very slowly, relying on an occasional extraneous event to bump it back to the proper level for keeping it held. What Roosa called the staircase movement 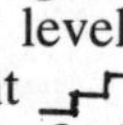 though it is really a saw tooth 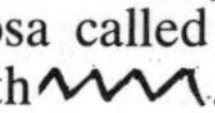. The main problem is to find out where the base line is and that depends on the price of equities and the growth of inflation.

After I saw him I went to see a man called Butler who belongs to the Chase Manhattan Bank but who is said to advise Nelson Rockefeller on economics. I still think Nelson Rockefeller has a good chance of being the next President and it would be interesting to meet his potential future adviser at this stage. I thought he was a very intelligent and sensible man but it was a slightly tricky interview as he was either suspicious of me or a bit nervous. Anyway he was very sound on wages. The dinner for Henry Brown by the way was not very successful from his point of view as he was too shy or cagey to talk freely or ask the right questions. But I think these dinners are very good things, getting the US side together on a neutral ground and with the onus of showing themselves to be world conscious.

The flight back was uneventful and of course everything very quiet here. Bryan Hopkin has done a very good appreciation of the economic situation and problems in case there is a new Chancellor. The polls have moved back a bit towards the Conservatives and my own guess is that they will have a majority of 20–25. This is a bit small for comfort and I would doubt if the Government would go its full term or if it could win a fourth time. However it will be very extraordinary, given the tendency to give the other man a chance, if they win at all. It will be prosperity and all those motor cars for the ex-working man that will do it if anything does.

Wednesday, October 14th

Like everyone else, I was quite wrong about the election – I did not dream that the majority would actually go up by nearly 40. Well not everyone else as a great many people bought steel shares like mad on the last two days (7th and 8th) which would not have been very sensible if they had expected a reduced Conservative majority – the big increase means that Labour will hardly be able to renationalize steel, if they do it [at] all, at the old sell-back prices which they had more or less promised to do if they won this time.

The swing was very closely related to the incidence of unemployment and recovery 1957/59 and one could argue that it was Thorneycroft who won the election since if he had not committed the Government to such restrictive measures it would not have been possible to stage such a sharp recovery! But more fundamentally, I feel sure that this is the first effect of the prosperity of the working classes getting motor cars and refrigerators and so on and thus regarding themselves as privileged. It certainly creates a problem for the Labour Party. The extreme left did very badly; Mikardo and Michael Foot lost their seats. This ought to bring Tony Crosland to the front, who has been trying for a new look. He had a very narrow squeeze at Grimsby, only in by 101. I am very glad he is back as he will be needed and he is clearly one of the best of the younger men.

Personally I am sorry as I felt very much opposed to the Government because of Suez and more recently from the way they handled the Devlin Report on Central Africa and Nyasaland. On the economic side I am on the whole glad as I think Labour has not settled its ideas enough and this gives us a chance to consolidate recent progress. But apparently foreign affairs had very little effect on the result.

The Chancellor is back and I saw him on Monday. You would not think there had been an election at all. He was worrying about the September trade returns and about whether he would not have to put up taxes in the next Budget, and thus appear to have done a R.A.B. on the electorate as in 1955. The trade returns are really quite good and I see no prospect whatever of having to put up taxes. The big problems are going to be on the wages/Trade Union relations front and the effects of the US cutting down their external deficit. I have written

Roger Makins a Minute on the labour problems saying that Ministers ought to make up their minds if they want a policy.

The Ministerial changes have just been announced and as far as I am concerned they are really all good ones. The most important from my point of view is that Reggie Maudling has gone to the Board of Trade – I was afraid Macleod might go, on his way to the Treasury, and I do not trust him. This must at least improve Reggie's chances even though Macleod has gone to the Colonial Office. Eccles is somewhat demoted, to Education. Sandys is somewhat demoted also, to a new Ministry of Aviation. Watkinson has gone to Defence: I am glad he is out of Transport and my own feeling is that Marples has done well at the PO and ought to be moved up, though I fear few in the Treasury would agree with me. Mills has left Power and become a sort of Cherwell, Paymaster no doubt to advise the PM.

In fact so far as my side is concerned, the new Ministers will be a better bunch on the economic side than the old ones. I do not know Heath who is going to Labour. I don't know what price we shall have to pay with my non-favourites going to other places except that Education is not likely to suffer much but it is very odd to think of Watkinson at Defence – he could not be worse than Sandys in my view. I don't know what Macleod will be like at the Colonial [Office].

Edwin Plowden is the Chairman of a new Committee on the control of expenditure which was set up towards the end of the last Government. He insisted on me being on it and it had its first meeting this morning.[11] I know most of the members – three outsiders John Wall, Jeremy Raisman and Sam Brown. Also Padmore and France from the Treasury. Dame Evelyn Sharp, Henry Hardman and a man called Sam Way from Supply. Incidentally the M/Supply is going to be abolished. I suppose Sandys will get the aircraft side as he is to be the Minister for the new Ministry of Aviation but I don't know yet where the rest will go. Not to mention Bill Strath (the Permanent Secretary).

The Committee will be a very interesting one but I suppose we shall have to work very hard for three years or so. I do not expect to be in the Treasury all that time myself.

Thursday, November 12th

Things settled down quite quickly after the election and as far as Treasury work is concerned there might never have been one, except that we have Edward Boyle back now as FST, of which I am very glad, and a new man called Barber whom I hardly know as EST. I am glad that Simon was promoted and also, really, that we have lost Erroll whom I liked very much but who did not seem to be quite up to it here. It is really quite significant of the Chancellor's outlook that he has managed to get Boyle, whom he has wanted ever since he arrived, and who must be the most radical MP in the whole Tory Party and on most issues indistinguishable from the right-wing economists of the Labour Party. He obviously is on good terms with them and even T. Balogh approves of him.

The Chancellor is still worrying a good deal, partly I think because he is a natural worrier, and partly because he feels that the better we do, the more risk there is of things getting worse and thus he being the man that let us slip. It is not necessarily true in economics that the better you do, the more the risks, since many of the processes can be cumulative and God is on the side of the big battalions. However no doubt some things, e.g. the balance of payments and the stability of the price level, *can* get worse and to be fair to him he worries most about these. He has made or is just going to make several speeches (the Debate on the Address last week, Mansion House and NPACI this) in which he harps mainly on the need for exports and for price stability and wage restraint, and he has practically got the new Wages Policy Committee round to the 'guiding light' which to my mind has always been the primary object to go for. It will be attacked and will need a bit of spelling out but at least it is a policy that has a chance of success whereas so far we have not had one. As a first step he is thinking of talking to employers' organizations.

The economic situation generally continues to go well. The Civil Service is now very busy speculating about who will take Roger Makins's place at the Treasury, when he goes at the end of the year. The obvious candidates are Frank Lee and Tom Padmore, but Frank is not much liked at the Treasury and by some Ministers, and Tom is not quite strong enough. Edwin P. suggested to me this week that *I* might be a candidate, but it would be very much avoiding two evils than choosing a good if I were. However one cannot but be a bit disturbed even at the idea; I might have expected it if Labour had got in but I certainly didn't with the Tories. However Edwin would hardly have mentioned it if it had not been at least some sort of a starter.

Thursday, November 19th

Frank Lee told me yesterday that *he* had been told definitely that he was to succeed Roger Makins, so I was not left disturbed very long. I felt a somewhat cowardly relief about this, partly because I felt that Frank had a very good claim and partly because I don't think I am at my best under very heavy administrative pressure. It is very hard to know what one really feels but at least I can say that any disappointment I felt was mixed with relief. Frank said, of course, as he has often done in the past, that he would have to rely on me for advice and ideas, but he has plenty of his own and has always wanted to operate on the widest scale. He is rather under the influence of people like Dennis Robertson and Lionel Robbins who attach too much importance to money and are too deflationary at heart to suit Ministers. However this is about the best time since 1939 to have such ideas and I myself hope that we will not let ourselves get too over-employed again. The Chancellor thinks of little else than the menace of returning inflation so he will find Frank fairly congenial on this. But we shall have to see how it goes in a more general way.

Monday, November 23rd

The November unemployment figures have just come in and show that the total is flattening out, just as we thought it would. From January to June it dropped by over 110,000 and from June to November less than 25,000 (after seasonal correction). The October trade figures were very good so the Chancellor can't find much support for his gloom. But I have to see him later today about next year's Local Authority housing which I think he would like to cut a bit to be on the safe side.

The Radcliffe Report is to be debated on Thursday and we have been doing a bit of work on the speech. William Armstrong is really very good and it is a great relief to have him there. The Government is going to turn down the recommendation about Local Authority loans and to reject the concept of 'emergency' (I am sure this is right and I feel inclined to tell Harold Wilson to do the same). They are accepting in a modified way the recommendation about Bank Rate and saying that they will achieve the result the Committee want on co-operation between Bank and Treasury by getting the Bank to send people to Economic Policy Committees (it will be the BC, the Steering Committee and EPB), but won't have a special monetary committee. I think all of this is about right, and in fact we are on much better terms with the Bank than we used to be and will be better still when the Governor goes, if he still intends to go next year. Bill Harcourt is the most likely successor but he is very much down now because his wife died a few weeks ago and she was a great prop to him.

When the first draft of the speech was made it had almost nothing about the central part of the Report, saying that it was the general state of liquidity that mattered and not the quantity of money. As the Treasury evidence had gone quite a way on this, I was very anxious to be at least slightly communicative, and Jack Downie wrote a beautiful passage for it, which Wm Armstrong and Tom P. both accepted. However the Governor did not like it, and wanted to say nothing, so I have had to boil it down quite a bit. I hope, however, that we will keep at least what I have done. The Report has been heavily criticized on this, partly through ignorance, partly prejudice by Central Bankers and partly their own fault through not very good drafting. Jack's passage went a long way to get it into a better perspective. The Labour Party is going to press for the acceptance of the recommendations about Local Authority loans and the relations with the Bank but I think the Chancellor goes a good deal of the way except on Local Authority loans.

Everything is quiet on the economic front; prices still steady and wages very slow to move. I have written to Philip Morris to ask him again if he won't try COPPI – it is now agreed to go on with it if we can get a good Chairman.

Roger Makins told me this morning about Frank Lee; it will be announced tomorrow. He says Richard Powell is going to the Board of Trade which is a very good idea, and Eddie Playfair to Defence. I have always liked Richard Powell and thought well of him though I have not seen him much lately – we used to do Economic Conditions in War together. It would have been hard to get anyone better. Roger says R. Maudling is a bit wild but I don't think he is really.

The EFTA Convention is at last signed after a compromise on fish fillets. It only shows how mad Ministers can get on protectionist issues that they were nearly ready to wreck the whole negotiations for a few thousand tons of fish. We are getting into a more sensible position on future trade policy as a result of various meetings and discussions. We will now (probably) try to make GATT a bit more of a reality and get tariffs down all round. Meanwhile Otto Clarke thinks trade will go out of fashion and that all the heat will be on Development. I have been pressing this view for a long time but I doubt if all that much will happen. The US seem to be wanting to use OEEC rather more as a co-ordinating body and think they might become full members.

Wednesday, November 25th

It took quite a long while to persuade the Chancellor to agree to 115,000 Local Authority houses even though he must have known that he would lose it if it went to Cabinet, if only because the Queen's Speech had been very forthcoming on housing. I suppose he wants to feel as safe as possible. I think that we have been quite right in saying that the rate of expansion is slowing down – the November unemployment, the HP debt statistics, and yesterday the latest statistical report from the Board of Trade, all confirm this.

Frank Lee's appointment was in the papers yesterday and R. Powell's this morning – Eddie Playfair to Defence and a man called Way whom I have only met recently at Plowden's Expenditure Committee to the War Office. There was very little comment on any of these moves, an extraordinary tribute to the *éminence grise* character of senior Civil Servants. I remember in 1947 when Edwin was made Chief Planning Officer, although the papers were very restricted on newsprint, there was a great splash. But all this is very naïve of me since no one thinks that the space given by newspapers is related to the importance of the subject, assuming we know what that is.

I had lunch yesterday with Maurice Green of *The Times* and, after telling him I thought all was quiet on the home front and would be till we got into the wages struggle, I began to speculate on the next ten years or at any rate the next period – on the lines that we really were over the crises that could by any stretch be called post-war, that it was likely that the atmosphere would be less inflationary, and hence that there was a good chance that business would be more competitive, more pressure on prices, and profits harder to get. He said that in the last eighteen months conditions in the high-class newspaper world had become 'more stable, more profitable and more competitive'. By this he meant that both circulation and advertising revenue for the group (which he said was *Times, Telegraph, Guardian* and to some extent *Financial Times*) were rising, but that they all had to watch one another closely to see that nobody got far ahead with the quality and range of the writing.

Hence it was more competitive in content which had led to much more competition for the better writers, reporters and so on. I have thought that we have never been too certain, until last year, that we had really got the excess demand out of the system, and also that the community of entrepreneurs and potential entrepreneurs had not got adjusted to the profits obtainable under full employment. If I am right, there will be more entrepreneurs, so to speak and hence more competition for that kind of ability. This is seen already in the wild competition for good executives and technicians compared to before 1939.

The wages front continues to move slowly but Fords and ICI have given rather substantial increases (though Paul Chambers denied it for ICI to the Chancellor) and today the engineers have been reported to have offered 1½ hours off the 44 hour week with no loss of pay. I suppose we can stand this as a pattern but not all that much more.

The Chancellor is now seeing all the employers on December 7th.

Tuesday, December 1st

The Radcliffe Report was debated in the House of Commons on Thursday (Nov. 26th) and I went to listen to the Chancellor and Harold Wilson. That is really the official end of the story, since although we will no doubt be struggling with debt management and interest rates for a long time, they will be in the context of the day's work. I think the announcement of the Committee was made in the Budget speech on April 8th 1957 so that we have been occupied by it for about 2½ years. It is unfortunate that the papers took the line that the Chancellor was turning all the recommendations down flat which is far from the case – he really accepted them in substance if not in form, on everything but Local Authority borrowing and the concept of emergency. It is true that he said he thought the Committee had perhaps underestimated the part that monetary measures could take but he couldn't say any less without exposing the Government to a violent attack *re* both the Butler and Thorneycroft policies. Anyway I told Wilfrid King that I thought the Press made it out to be a far more sensational difference than there was.

I got a note from Sayers this morning (I had written to him when the Report came out to say that I thought it was a very helpful document) and incidentally he said how much my letter had comforted him so I was able to reply and make the same points.

It is very sad for the members of the Committee that the Report has been taken so badly by Central Bankers and right-wing Tories everywhere. It is partly their own fault for putting what they had to say about liquidity in a form which implied that money did not matter. After all you can only spend liquidity when it is in the form of money. But the emphasis was in the right place as I hope will appear when the evidence is published. Apart from this, there can be no doubt that the preparation of the evidence for the Report, plus the Bank Rate Tribunal, plus the Report itself, have transformed the scene in

London. The part-time Directors are now plainly advisory only – the responsibility for the Bank Rate is seen to be with the Chancellor – and in fact the Bank is being far more open with the Treasury than it has ever been before, a relationship which will no doubt be confirmed by the next Governor, unless Oliver Franks and Bill Harcourt are both under suspicion because they signed the Report. (Incidentally a lot of people seem to think that *I* will be the next Governor which would surprise me even more than it would have if I had been the successor to R.M.) I suppose all this gossip means that my name has at least been on the list for both appointments. I still have no idea when the Governor will go.

The Chancellor sent for me this morning and I had a chance to have a general chat. He is worried about the loss of reserves and the increase in imports and seems to be thinking that we ought to check expansion just to keep down imports. It is hard to get him to see how impossible it would be to defend (even if it were sensible) a policy of restriction just to reduce imports. He also thinks that we are expanding too fast, although the latest figures are wonderful since industrial production is now estimated at about 114 and employment still only about 1% above last year. I managed to get him to give me a sort of line for the brief he wants for his meeting to tell the employers to cut prices on December 7th. He is even toying with the idea of removing individual resale price maintenance – nobly supported by E. Boyle and the new EST Barber who has made a very good start.

The main conversation, however, was about whether we should put Bank Rate up. I had already suggested to R.M. that we should have a meeting with the Bank on this, in order to establish a precedent for the new order. The reason of course is that rates in New York and Bonn are now above the London ones and we are beginning to lose balances on interest considerations. The Chancellor seemed to think it would be a good idea to have a Bank/Treasury meeting but he is anxious to put the rate up and told the Deputy (the Governor is in America) to be thinking about it. I don't think it would be a very good idea particularly since we are still trying to stimulate private investment and it would rouse evil passions if we said we had to do it because of rates abroad; though not as bad as if we said we had to cut production to restrict imports. I had a talk to William Armstrong about this – he is really a most sensible man and is much against it, though he would like to jerk the long rate up a bit as he is not doing too well on funding.

Dillon, the US Under Secretary of State, is to be here next week. The whole of our policy on EFTA, EEC and FTA is in a frightful mess and I feel sure I will have to take a bit more interest in it. Harold Caccia has suggested that we should go for a FTA including the US and Canada. This would be wonderful but I don't suppose it is a starter. Anyway it is no good our trying to persuade Dillon that the FTA is the only thing to go for, when he is worried that it will be discriminatory against the US.

Tuesday, December 8th

The Chancellor got into a state of acute nerves about reserve losses and tried to persuade the Deputy to put the rate up last Thursday or if not to send for the Governor. After the Steering Committee that afternoon, R.M., Denis R., the Deputy (H. Mynors) and I had a talk about it and we all agreed that there was no case for acting at present, nor indeed until the reserves have come under much more strain. The internal situation was such that we could hardly say it needed restraint, particularly when the election was largely won on prosperity. Overseas, we couldn't object to the US taking steps to safeguard their position, and though we might not like what the Germans were doing, their position was more inflationary than ours. In these circumstances a move would look like panic. We dictated an agreed note to the Chancellor forthwith. Mynors showed more strength of mind than I have seen him display in the past – he said he would not send for the Governor unless Roger wanted him to, and would not put the rate up unless he were given a direction, which would have to go to the PM.

The Chancellor was in such a state that he went to see the PM on Friday taking R.M. with him but he did not get much change there and indeed the PM told him there was nothing to worry about. The Chancellor seems a lot better this week, and the pressure on the reserves has relaxed.

Oliver Franks came to see me last week to say he had been offered the Headship of some Oxford College (he didn't say which and I don't know – *I* was asked to be a candidate for BNC but I doubt if he would go there – it might just be Balliol) and that this was very attractive to him but he wanted (a) my advice, (b) did I think he would be summoned before long to some great task, i.e. the B/E. I was rather surprised that he was so attracted and I don't really know why. Anyway I said it was a matter of personal preference though I could see that it might be pleasant if one had had enough [of] public affairs. On the other question, the only things I could think of were the Bank, on which he knew what I thought, and the possibility of an OEEC with the US and Canada in, which seemed to me very far away. But I would see if I could find out any more.

After a good deal of thought, I decided to consult N. Brook who is more discreet than anyone else. He told me, as I expected, that there were no great openings going and also that the Bank Court had already recommended Harcourt to succeed Cobbold. I did not even know that the Court made recommendations, much less that they had already. Norman also said he would snoop around a bit. On Friday he told me he had done so – Oliver would always be a candidate for any important job but he thought he was far from the favourite for the Bank. So I told Oliver on Saturday that I thought this – he was a bit disgruntled although he must have known since the election that his chances were poor. He told me that it was rather sad that the war had thrown up a small number of people like himself, Edwin and me, who were very good at public affairs. But now we were a dying race and no steps were being taken to see if there are any similar animals available. I think there is something in this, especially since the intake for the Administrative Class is a good deal thinner than it used to be, the result of full employment causing employers to compete for good management material.

The Chancellor has been considering more steps in his anti-price, anti-wage campaign and a week or two ago he arranged to meet all the employers' organizations, and I had been writing him a brief on this. The meeting took place yesterday and R. Maudling and Heath, the new Minister of Labour, were there, also the EST and me. It went off very well and gave me a sense that we were at last on the move. What a contrast to those awful meetings under Eden in 1956 – in case I did not say so at the time, they now in retrospect seem quite ghastly to me. This time the Chancellor has studied it all very carefully and has a clear idea of what he wants to do. He read out my piece and then there was a general discussion.

The most interesting things were: (a) the FBI said that they felt that this could only be handled from the long-term angle, between employers and workers. They wanted to start to sound the TUC, if Ministers did not disapprove. Heath said he would think this over. Maudling obviously felt it was a new development. (b) The Chancellor, when asked *how much* he thought we could stand, said 2½%, or at the very outside 3% p.a. So the 'guiding light' is launched at last. The employers felt that this round would be settled at 4½% covering an 18 months' period. (c) The Chancellor said he did not want *any* freeze but that people ought not to make 20% increases in dividends and expect the Trade Unions to put up with 2½%. Heath spoke quite firmly on this and also produced the production–employment figures to show that there was room for price cuts. A number of misconceptions came up also, which the Chancellor is going to pick up in a speech to the Nat. Liberal Forum tonight. Altogether it was quite a good meeting and it had a good press today, especially a leader in *The Guardian*.

NIF has just finished its preliminary look at 1960 – it is fairly clear that there will be no need, and no case, for anything one way or the other in the Budget. But I fear that Frank Lee will not take the same view.

Monday, December 21st

I can end this volume[12] on a pleasant note in describing the dinner which the Governors and the Court of the Bank gave for Roger Makins last Thursday. I think that they normally only have dinners on a few formal occasions every year and this must be an unusual if not unique event. As the Governor made clear in his speech, it was a sort of demonstration of appreciation for all the help Roger gave them in the troubled weeks of the Bank Rate Tribunal and of Radcliffe. Almost the whole Court were there and otherwise T. Padmore, D. Rickett, W. Armstong, L. Rowan, Bill Harcourt and Guy Thorold. We were received by swarms of tall footmen in their plush livery and had sherry in the ante-room and dinner in the Court Room, which was comfortably filled but with plenty of room. One large table with a white cloth and a good deal of silver, nearly all bought by the Bank because it was [founded] around 1694. They do not have the custom of getting presents from retiring members. A very good but not elaborate dinner which reminded me of Sitwell's description when he was the Guards Officer on duty. All the servants have learned one's name for the occasion and whisper in a friendly manner when they offer you anything. In fact it was rather like dining in one's own College.

The Governor made a little speech about how much their safe survival owed to Roger, and he replied pleasantly. I sat between the Governor and Cadbury – the former much more talkative than I had ever known him before and making slightly malicious sketches of his colleagues. Afterwards we stayed at table and the hosts moved around – I talked to Bicester and Babington-Smith. About 9.45 the Governor began to edge us out and it must have been all over about 10. And it was really extremely well done and most enjoyable. Tomorrow night I have to dine with the PM to say goodbye to Edwin Plowden.

Friday, January 1st 1960

Dinners
The Prime Minister

The Prime Minister gave a dinner party at 10 Downing Street last night for Lord Plowden. The other guests were:

The Marquess of Salisbury, Mr Derick Heathcoat Amory, Viscount Hailsham, Lord Mills, Mr Reginald Maudling, Sir William Strath, Sir Robert Hall, Mr T. J. Bligh.

I went to a small dinner given by the Prime Minister for Edwin Plowden on December 22nd. I gathered that it was the first time Salisbury had been in the house since his resignation. It was a very pleasant affair – I knew everyone, though Salisbury and Hailsham only because I used to brief them for economic debates in the Lords. However at dinner I talked nearly all the time to Reggie Maudling, mainly about the economic situation. He wants to get rid of individual Resale Price Maintenance, but Mills (who was on my other side) was strongly against it.[13] The PM and Salisbury made very nice little speeches and Edwin replied; he was much more affected than he had expected to be and sounded it – he had lunch with me yesterday and said he was covered with shame at his performance but it was rather charming in practice.

After dinner, to my great surprise, the PM seized me and took me into a corner and talked tête-à-tête the rest of the evening. He began on the Memorandum he had sent us about the possibility of a Bank Rate change, which we had thought very sensible and timely as it agreed with us rather than the Chancellor, so I told him so. Then he went on to give me a detailed account of the Summit meeting from which he had returned that day.[14] He was obviously extremely pleased with himself and felt that he had reached a close understanding with de Gaulle, who had asked him to tea with Madame de Gaulle which is quite a thing in France, the opposite of what it would be here. He said that he had agreed to de Gaulle's request for occasional tripartite meetings on world affairs, against the advice of his officials, and de Gaulle (wrongly) attributed this to the PM's intervention. The result was that de Gaulle had agreed to give his people instructions to be accommodating on the Six and Seven problem. I said that this would depend on what we had to throw into any compromise – the trouble is that we aren't willing to abandon tariff autonomy, or Commonwealth free entry, or any agricultural protection and it is hard to see how we can have a FT Area and keep all these. Anyhow it was a very interesting as well as a pleasant evening.

Roger M. left yesterday and Frank Lee starts on Monday so we shall soon see what happens. Meanwhile Edwin has gone to Brit. Aluminium and is out of the machine for the first time since I met him in 1947. I feel that times and people are now changing quite markedly and there will soon be a new lot of people at the middle. T. Balogh told me that E. Boyle told him that I was the runner-up for the Treasury job but I think I honestly feel glad that I did not get it.

We go into 1960 in quite a healthy position. But the Chancellor continues to think that we are in far too much of a boom and that we ought to restrain it in some way and wants to start with Bank Rate. So far we have held him off. I told him that we would also have a chance in the Budget but he did not like that much! We ourselves (I mean the Economic Section now) are rather uncertain because the expenditure side of the National Income accounts does not add up to the total income generated by the production side; the most probable thing is that stocks have gone up more than is recorded but if it is something else it is quite important.[15]

Tuesday, January 12th (Paris)

Frank Lee's first week went very well as far as I was concerned, as he seems to be quite clear that he wants to discuss all major economic questions with me, and a good many other that R.M. didn't. An early example was the successor to the Governor. He told me that he did not think Harcourt was up to it and when he dined with the Chancellor (which they did, alone together) on Wednesday, he raised it and got the Chancellor to agree (a) that Harcourt was not necessarily the best candidate, (b) that Frank should be authorized to discuss it with me and make a submission. He wants Oliver and as I do too it makes it fairly easy to work together. I thought I had better get hold of Oliver at once and tell him that the door was not so firmly closed as I had thought, which I did at once. He told me that he had not yet made up his mind about the other offer (to be Head of some Oxford College or other) and he took my news on board though in a very restrained and indeed gloomy way. Frank thinks that neither the Chancellor nor the PM feel exactly warm about Oliver and I have thought for a long time that the Tory Party would not be keen. But who can they get? We both thought Parsons would be the best of the present Bank staff but he is almost unknown outside a rather narrow circle.

We also had some talk about Bank Rate. The Governor has come round to the Chancellor's point of view and I feel I have exhausted my credit in getting any decision prolonged so long. So it is very likely that we will move in the next week or two, and present it as a moderation of the forward speed and not a check or a reversal. The PM does not sound too keen and sent a telegram from Shannon saying he hoped that we would not do anything while he was away.

Meanwhile the arrangements for the Paris meeting, at which the ideas were being explored which had been mooted in the communiqué after the Western Summit, were going ahead. A tremendous lot of writing of papers and exchanging of telegrams went on over Christmas with most of our end being done by Otto Clarke. Frank Lee spoke to Denis and me about it and there was a slightly painful scene as Denis brought out the worries he had been feeling about all this being in Otto Clarke's division and not in OF. The immediate occasion was the US idea that aid to underdeveloped countries should be discussed in a new Committee under the new body,[16] and as we have painfully got a Development Policy Committee going with Denis in Whitehall, he felt it would be too much to bear to have all this co-ordinated with Otto.

Frank told us (what I had already gathered from Edwin) that Bruce Fraser was going to the Ministry of Aviation and that Otto was going to take his job in charge of Supply Services and A.France take Otto's job. This will simplify things a bit as Otto has been getting too many things into his clutches and would be a difficult man – I am glad he is being moved although he has got a lot of things going that I approve of, especially the annual review of investment and the long-term survey of resources. But once he starts on anything he cannot stop himself from empire building and he takes ideas more for the sake of getting action than because of the particular content of the ideas. Anyway Denis nearly made a *démarche* on the lines that he ought to be a 2nd Sec. and have the co-ordination of trade and development under him. Frank very wisely refused to commit himself – he told me later that he did not altogether trust Denis. But the upshot of it all was that Frank himself was persuaded by the Chancellor that he ought to go to Paris – and as I had to come here anyway yesterday, to talk to R. Kahn's group about the causes of rising prices, I was to stay on for the further talks.[17]

I came yesterday and had quite a good talk with Kahn's Committee which seems to me to be quite a good one. It includes Bent Hansen, the Swede who wrote a very good book on inflation, de Wolff, who succeeded Tinbergen as head of the Netherlands Conjuncture Institute or planning agency, Milton Gilbert, a Swiss, Funelman and an American.

Since then I have been in fairly constant talks, but it is all rather a shambles. The real point at issue is that the US now want, or say they want, a forum to discuss the major economic problems for the world among the major countries. This is what we have been urging for years, though it must be admitted that we have generally said that there should be a UK/US forum rather than a wider group. However all attempts to get this going, since 1949, have come to very little, the most successful being the agreement to increase the resources of the Bank and Fund.

This is appearing in the form of a move to study the functions, etc., of OEEC with the idea that the US and Canada might become full members. But it comes at a time when the world is preoccupied with problems about the Six and Seven and the Free Trade Area. And the problems involved are all very delicate and complicated as nearly all countries feel jealous and suspicious if they think that others are plotting together to run their affairs for them. It is absurd that such large issues should be discussed at a meeting for which there was only about a fortnight's notice, including Christmas and New Year. Our delegation was collected and briefed in great haste with no clear ideas about what the issues were going to be. And it is all chaos in Paris. However the first meeting is taking place just now.

Frank Lee and I had a long talk this morning with the US – John Leddy, Tuthill and Repton – about the problems. This was very useful and it is certainly easy to have such talks with Frank. Their tentative ideas were:

(a) that the co-ordination of aid should be carried on by a self-constituted group, to set *itself* up here with the benevolence of the other countries meeting – the Group to be US, Canada, UK, France, Germany and Italy, and the Commission. The US would like to include Japan and possibly Australia but we got them to agree to leave the door open to this rather than to refer to it explicitly.[18]

(b) that trade problems (Six/Seven) should be remitted to an ad hoc Committee of the Six and Seven plus a representative of EEC plus a representative of GATT. The terms of reference to be very loose. UK Ministers had decided that as the price for our being co-operative about this meeting at all (how absurd to think in such terms when our basic interests are served by it) we should insist that there should be real progress towards a Free Trade Area. And at the meeting of the Seven in the British Embassy this morning, several of them made it clear that this was their prime objective. Personally I do not think a FTA is on the cards at all and in any case the US and Canada and Australia do not like it. However this proposal would do to keep the thing going. This is clearly going to be the thorniest of our problems.

(c) that the future of OEEC should be studied by three people appointed for the purpose, but reporting to the whole 20 countries.

We had a good deal of talk telling them what our difficulties were and suggesting ways to meet them. Basically I feel sure that US and UK interests are quite compatible if not very much the same. But our preoccupation with a Free Trade Area, and our involvement with the

Seven, needs a good deal of care and I am afraid our Ministers still have a long way to go before they realize that a FTA is objectionable to the USA. I have been convinced, at any rate since the OEEC meeting last October (or November) of the Economic Policy Committee, that the only way we could get out of our troubles was by agreeing that the tariff reductions to be made both by the Six and by the Seven this year should be extended not only to one another but to all members of GATT, it being made plain that they expect equivalent concessions from the others. This was what van Lennep put to me at McCarthy's lunch and I tried to sell it in London, without much apparent success. But just before I left for this meeting, Frank showed me a letter from Richard Powell (who succeeded him at the Board of Trade) saying that the President was now prepared to back this with his colleagues, the condition being that it was only for 18 months and would be withdrawn after that if equivalent concessions had not been made. This was most encouraging to me.

Wednesday, January 13th

I am writing this in the lounge at Le Bourget where there is a delay on the flight to London because of snow there. I decided to come back this evening, mainly because proceedings in Paris, which were never orderly, have moved into that frenzied state when people are trying to agree some compromise solution behind the scenes and against the clock. But also because the PM sent the Chancellor a cable from Accra asking what he thought about the UK economic position and obviously designed to discourage any more on Bank Rate at this time, since he ended up with a plea not to check recovery in investment when it was only just beginning. As the Bank was thought to be weakening but the Treasury is hardening, it seemed that we ought to make very careful preparation and I am going to start this. It will presumably be thrashed out on Monday and a cable sent to the PM and then we must see what he says.

Dillon spoke at the meeting at 5 last night and there was an almost immediate adjournment to consider his speech, which the Chancellor read out to us (there were only two copies available) at a UK Del. meeting about 6.15. The speech was very good, especially in its treatment of OEEC as something to be adapted and broadened rather than to be superseded by some other body. But the resolutions were not very good and after dinner we spent a good deal of time on redrafts, which were then discussed at a meeting of the Seven at 9.45 this morning. No one seemed to mind much about the Development procedure except that the Portuguese were most anxious to become a member. There was some criticism of the US draft for the study of the successor body to OEEC and especially the idea of 3 men. But we thought that the US proposal was really that the 3 should do the secretariat and preparatory work and report to the 20, rather than that they should try to impose anything.

I feel a good deal clearer than I did on all this, as I had not realized that Monnet was trying to kill OEEC altogether. This is no doubt because it stands for an alternative to the European Community on which Monnet has increasingly set his heart. The odd thing is that Monnet certainly does not represent all of French opinion and (unless France was clearly to dominate the Community) does it represent de Gaulle? However Monnet and Marjolin have a good deal of influence with the US and they have been plugging the idea that the Community is the best hope for a strong Europe (in the defence sense) and the best instrument for Atlantic co-operation. What I had not appreciated at all was that they are carrying on a whispering campaign against OEEC on the ground that it is useless, inefficient and expensive. This has made the Scandinavian countries very angry as they like OEEC and dislike the EEC. So there was a good deal of discussion both about the exact way in which the references to OEEC were to be made, and how dangerous to have three men unless you were sure who they were going to be.

Thursday, January 21st

The Bank Rate was increased to 5% today. I came back from Paris on Wednesday night (13th) and wrote an appreciation of the situation which we discussed on Friday and gave to the Chancellor over the weekend, and we had a meeting with the Governor and Deputy on Monday afternoon. The latest indications were that the boom was picking up, as there was a big change in the Board of Trade survey of private sector investment, and a lot of new and large wage claims. So there was not much difference of view in the end, though I said I thought we were moving a bit early and the Chancellor that we were at least a month late and the Governor that the timing was just right.

We had rather a difficult incident about Press guidance – the Bank showed us a bit of paper they intended to use which we did not like and we redrafted and took the Chancellor's instructions – he took a lot of trouble and agreed our line with a few changes – and then Frank Lee and I agreed it with the Deputy and indeed conceded two changes to him. But when the Reuter report came out, they had kept two bits we wanted to delete and left out three bits to which we attached importance. It seemed to be either a mistake in that they had got the bits mixed up! or deliberate impertinence. Frank was very good and first rang them up and then sent them a formal expostulation. It was all rather sad as up to that point we had worked together better than I can ever remember in the past.

Philip Morris has turned down COPPI and Frank and I saw Lord Heyworth to ask him if he would do it. He was flabbergasted and has gone away to get over the shock – he said he had thought that judicial qualities were just the ones he did not have.

Friday, February 5th

Still no answer from Heyworth – he sent for me last week to ask about the work on COPPI, and was kind enough to repeat the offer he made several years ago, of an advisory job for me with Unilever if I left here. I should think I will want it fairly soon, especially as Edwin wants me to do the same for him with B. Aluminium and presumably Tube Investments.

The Bank Rate went off all right though there was some scepticism about the Bank of England saying that it was all due to the internal situation.

Friday, February 12th

Heyworth is now inclined to take on COPPI but says he could not start before September. It is a question of whether we can wait so long – Frank Lee is coming round to the view that (a) we can't, (b) it will be very hard to get anyone else therefore (c) probably better to wind it up. I am rather near that myself, though I think it could be useful. But these terrible delays over the Chairman tend to discredit the whole enterprise.

At present we are under the threat of a rail strike. The NUR have got themselves into a quite indefensible position; one would hardly have thought this possible. They have a promise to make any preliminary concessions after Guillebaud reports retrospective to January 11th. And they would have had an increase now, if the other two Unions had not insisted that the agreement they had all made to wait for Guillebaud, should be honoured. So they are preparing to strike (a) in breach of an agreement, (b) because they won't wait a fortnight for (c) just as much in total as they could get now.[19]

Faced with all this, Ministers are still split, with the Chancellor, Mills and Maudling wanting to hold out, and Butler and Heath to surrender anyway. I am afraid Frank Lee is more or less a surrender man, to my great surprise, while Tom Padmore wants to fight it out. It will have a very bad effect on all our negotiations if the Government give in over this one, when by an extraordinary chance the NUR are on such a bad wicket and have practically no public support.

The NIF Report, preparatory to the final Budget judgment, was finished early this week. The general outlook seems a good deal more inflationary than it did three months ago – of course the increase in Bank Rate was foreshadowed by preliminary thoughts to this effect – and it now looks as if we shall try a bit of deflation all the way round. The Chancellor is getting into a frame of mind when he will agree to put up some taxes, and the Treasury is trying to get itself into a state when it will press the Bank heavily to introduce the Special Deposits scheme. I doubt if the Bank themselves are in the state of mind to introduce it so it will depend on the Chancellor. I have been writing a note for him to give to the PM as soon as the latter gets back. Frank brought Richard Powell into a general discussion on deflation, which is rather better than trying to bring him on to the Budget Committee from which Frank himself was dropped when he succeeded John Henry [Woods] – or soon after – as Permanent Secretary on the Board of Trade.

Friday, February 26th

All the tendencies before noted have been developing in the past fortnight. We have had long talks both about the Budget and with the Bank of England about special deposits and so on, and with the Board of Trade about reintroducing Hire Purchase controls. The Chancellor thinks he can persuade the PM to having £100 mn or so more taxes (to include profits tax which won't actually be collected until 1962, but which I think would have an immediate deflationary effect). The Governor before he went to Australia was disposed to argue that it was Government expenditure which was the trouble (ignoring altogether the very sharp increase in advances for over a year) so why should the Bank do anything? But since he went off the Deputy has been much more reasonable.

The Board of Trade do not like to reimpose Hire Purchase controls but as it is clear that we cannot get legislation to control Finance Houses which take deposits and anyway they could get round it, it seems as if Hire Purchase is all we could do there. R. Powell has been coming to the talks and has been quite helpful. It is rather refreshing to do this sort of exercise with the Chancellor who is always pressing us to be *more* deflationary than we think right, just as Treasury officials are always pressing the Bank of England to exercise *more* control over the monetary system than they want to do.

There was quite a flurry on Wednesday as the Bank suddenly stopped supporting the gilt-edged market and let prices fall by about a point. They did this partly because the Clearing Banks were heavy sellers and they did not want to take so much stock, and partly because we had been pressing them to get interest rates up in the interests of funding. The Bank put out some press guidance but denied next day that this had any policy significance. Nevertheless it has started a good deal of speculation. If the outside world knew what went on between the Bank and the Treasury they would be startled (at the doctrines held by the Bank and especially at the absence of any clear thinking). I have been a bit disappointed lately that the good effects I had hoped for from Radcliffe have been getting less – but I suppose they move a bit.

Frank Lee is still doing very well but he talks too much and this makes the meetings which he takes go on too long.

I am going to Washington for the Development Group Meeting on March 9th.

Friday, March 11th (New York)

The week before I left London, which I did on March 6th, was mostly marked by a rather difficult time with the PM. He wrote a long memo to the Chancellor saying how devastating it would be to have to check economic activity just when it was getting started, and what fools the Tories would look, and so on. He would not mind some action with the banks, and perhaps Hire Purchase, and perhaps some tax to cover any concessions that had to be made but it must not be presented as a brake. Then the Chancellor and Frank and I had to go and see him, but we did not make much progress as he talked rather frivolously and said that such important issues must go to Cabinet – to which we agreed – so then I drafted a paper very quickly and it was taken by an ad hoc meeting of Ministers specially selected: Rab, Heath, Eccles, Maudling and Mills I think, but there may have been one or two others. They did not agree and then I had a talk to Fred Bishop who is still acting as the PM's counsellor and told him there was really very little in it and it would be tragic if it were magnified into a row (since the Chancellor is quite capable of resigning on it). So Fred said it would be best if *I* saw the PM. But next day he rang to say that the PM and the Chancellor had had a long talk and were more or less reconciled. That was the last I heard. I don't think there is much in the figures between them but a long way in their approach. The Chancellor wants to present whatever he does in a way which will give the country a bit of a shock and the PM in a way intended to make it all seem part of a continuation of expansion.

I have just been to Washington for the first meeting of the Development Assistance Group (DAG) which was set up in Paris in January and which was foreshadowed at the dinner Geoffrey Wilson gave for me in Washington last year [entry for July 1st]. It has gone extremely well and I think is properly launched though it is a pity that the Portuguese and the EEC are represented on it.

I came with Denis Rickett, and Eugene Black, who had been giving a lecture in Oxford, was on the same 'plane. We have had a most hectic time. We left London last Sunday (on my 59th birthday!) in the afternoon and got to Washington in time to have dinner with the Cromers with whom we stayed. On Monday we spent most of the morning talking to the Ambassador and he gave a lunch for us to meet Dillon and Anderson and Sam Waugh of the Exim Bank and a man called Riddleberger who is head of the Economic Co-operation Agency. We talked a bit about the meeting but didn't get very far and then in the afternoon had a long talk to Ed Martin who was to lead the US Delegation and Repton of the Treasury.

As it was the very first meeting it was all a bit uncertain and a good deal of the discussion was about the status of the IBRD and of OEEC at the meeting. We wanted them there as much as possible and the State Department were afraid that if they came other organizations would come. Apart from these protocol questions we did not get very far.

On Tuesday we spent the whole day doing what one might call normal Treasury business, starting with Per Jacobsson of the IMF. We intended to discuss with him the question of better use of the IMF especially of its gold. However we did not get far with this as we got at once into a somewhat heated discussion of the German position. Per said: (a) the Germans were perfectly right to be trying to deflate to stop their price level rising, (b) we need not worry about their balance of payments surplus because it would inexorably raise their price level and bring it back into balance. I said I was so glad he felt so cheerful and that we didn't share his feeling. The big gold losses from the US especially to Germany and Italy would drive the US into various undesirable practices and the UK was already in some trouble which would probably get worse.

The rest of the day we saw Repton again (this time in the Treasury) but talked mainly about DAG: Saulnier of the Council of Economic Advisers who was obviously nervous about the prospect for the US economy where they are afraid of recession in an election year, and a man called Paarlberg who has replaced Hauge as the President's Assistance on Economic Affairs. He was mainly concerned with trade questions and said that the US expected concessions in the GATT negotiations to compensate them for the very liberal policies they had adopted in the past. They are perfectly right to feel like this but I don't know what they will get.

On Wednesday the meetings began and they lasted all that day and Thursday and Friday. I think that they were very successful for the first meeting of a new organization where there had been no agreement about the agenda beforehand. The great thing was that all the different points of view got an airing and the underlying differences of opinion were expressed. And it was abundantly clear that the definition of Aid needed to be gone into carefully since some countries included short-term export credits which we and the US did not regard as Aid at all.

The US was mainly concerned to get an increase in the total. We were mainly worried about the effect of the US deficit and the German and Italian surpluses on the balance of payments and rather stressed these points, which the US also made. We also said a good deal on tied loans and on the tendency to increase the period of ordinary export credits under the guise of Aid. The Canadians, who only make grants tied to Canadian goods, were rather on the defensive as they do not do very much. I don't think anyone else had a strong point of view and they were mostly rather defensive also. The Germans are trying to move from short export credits to loans of 12–20 years: they talked a good deal about the difficulties they have in organizing the operation at all (no capital market, political difficulties in using the Budget) which are really technical problems if they really want to do what they say. The Italians said that they were still a poor country and I pointed out that it was a great luxury to invest in reserves if this was the case.

Tuesday, May 31st

This must be one of the longest spells without any entries, in the whole series of these diaries. Like so many of the entries, it is written in an airplane – at present on the ground at Sydney, Australia, waiting to take off for the UK. I have been on a fortnight's visit, as I was asked by the University of Queensland to be the guest of honour at their Jubilee Celebrations and to give an address and receive an Honorary DSc. After my Indian and Polish experiences, I thought it well to get an undertaking from Frank Lee and the Chancellor that I would *not* be recalled. I came and am returning in one of the new Boeing jets which only take about 35 hours including stops – it still seems a bit extraordinary, we hopped along and stopped at a lot of places for 3/4 hour and did about 500 miles an hour in between. Australia seems to have become much more prosperous since 1954 and the face of the land is markedly better – the rabbits all gone and soil erosion much better understood and also the kind of grains to use. The celebrations went off very smoothly and I took the opportunity to speak on the Control of Economic Conditions, treating it more from a biological point of view than an economist's – it is the first beginning of the subject I would like to write about one day, the difficulties in a democratic country when the standard of living gets so high that there is no need to struggle. I must say that in England and Australia they don't seem to have lost the competitive urge among those people who would have ever had it. But I think there are grave dangers all the same, that people will vote for an easy life and politicians give it to them in order to get elected: and with the Russians and Chinese still in a militant and centralizing mood, we have a long dangerous period until their standard of living has removed their aggressive urge.

This morning I have been at the Commonwealth Bank or rather the Reserve Bank as it has now become. Coombs [The Governor] is in England but I met Phillips the Deputy Governor and several others and had a long talk about the problems of Governments and Central Bankers in controlling the economy. Everyone has the same sort of problems – they do not seem to have quite as much contact with the Treasury as the Bank of England has but I think the pressure is from them to get more out of the Treasury and not as with us. The difference between Coombs and Cobbold. Their main complication is that the division of powers between the States and the Commonwealth is unsatisfactory and uncertain.

Since I wrote last we have had the Budget and the first use of Special Deposits. The Budget was in the right direction but not nearly far enough, it was too difficult to get an increase in taxes on the scale required especially as Income Tax and Purchase Tax had both been lowered last year. However we got Profits Tax put up and something on tobacco so at least the idea was clear. Owing to the fact that the Chancellor had been afraid that it would be too severe a shock, there was an unusual amount of preparation of public opinion and hardly anybody expected an easier Budget while the experts mostly expected, and some at least would have liked, a sharper one. In spite of all this, the Conservatives did not like the Budget and were somewhat horrified at the measures when they actually heard them: this may have helped in getting them to think that Government expenditure can't go up without the prospective field for tax reductions going down, but the Chancellor had little but silence from his own side and a good many cheers from the Opposition who liked all the tax avoidance measures proposed. But the debate went off smoothly enough and at the end there was a sort of agreement that it was not too bad a Budget although the Government was to blame for letting expenditure grow; they had forgotten all the election promises and indeed performances.

However the balance of payments figures were not too good, imports running high and exports not going up fast enough; and unemployment kept dropping gradually and the tightness of the labour market in the S. and Centre getting worse. So I was very anxious to do some more and the Chancellor even more so, and the Bank less troublesome than might have been expected, though they were very keen to do what Radcliffe proposed and control lending institutions as well as the Clearing Banks – they would have been satisfied with Hire Purchase Finance Houses but we couldn't do it without fresh legislation. Bank advances rose very sharply in April and in the end there wasn't much trouble in getting 1% Special Deposits and some control over Hire Purchase terms – once more the build-up was almost too good and many papers said it wasn't enough. Before I left I pressed strongly for another 1% Special Deposits, unless the increase in advances in August was very small – I gathered from a *Times* I saw in Brisbane yesterday that the increase *was* small and no action was taken last Thursday but I will have to wait until tomorrow to find out what has been happening. My feeling is that we haven't done enough yet and that the economy will stay pretty tight for some time yet. NIF was doing an exercise when I left so I will know more about it shortly. But I shall be surprised if we do not have to pull in a bit yet.

Frank Lee and the Chancellor had been pressing me for some time to draft a statement that might be made on Wages if it were ever agreed to try the 'guiding light'. I managed to do this just before I left and got a good deal of help from Downie and Hopkin – the latter actually did the final draft. It was circulated to senior Treasury officials about 2 1/2 weeks ago and no doubt we will be talking about it. Frank Lee is a deflationist rather than an exhorter but he must be getting a good idea by now about how hard it is to get as much deflation as would be needed to be sure of steady prices. The wage situation is still fairly well under control but we are just approaching the open season for Trade Union Conferences and the formulation of new claims so we will be in a new round by the autumn, and I will be surprised if it is not started on a high figure and against a background of boom and very low unemployment. The appointment of Heyworth and Harold Emmerson, to replace Cohen and Howitt on COPPI, was announced in the middle of May. They won't be able to start work until October as Heyworth has a lot of unwinding of his Unilever activities to do.

All the flaps about FTA and Common Market are still going on and although our policy is to go for an all round reduction of tariffs in the GATT negotiations, I don't think Ministers are quite ready for it or indeed that they have any idea of what is involved.

The Plowden Committee agreed its first Report, concentrating almost entirely on the need for Ministers to have a long-term review every year and to take decisions about Government expenditure on the basis of this. With some difficulty, I got them to say that there should be a study of the prospects for variations in Government investment as a means of control – we were all in favour of making tax changes rather than short-run changes in Government current expenditure. But I feel a bit suspicious of all this because Otto Clarke is deeply involved in it all. He writes all the papers as if no one had ever thought of reviews of investment or expenditure before his time.

Finally, I told N. Brook just before I left that I still wanted to retire fairly soon. He was very affable but we did not have time to go into details. Everyone seems to think that the Chancellor is going shortly but I shall not believe it till I see it. No progress whatever has been made as to who will succeed the Governor.

Tuesday, July 12th

The main work in June was to tighten the economy a bit. When I got back I found that there had been no disposition to act on Special Deposits, which I had wanted, and we spent most of the month arguing about what should be done. The Governor finally came to the view that Bank Rate must go up and he would reluctantly add 1% to the Special Deposits but he felt very bitterly that we ought to do something on the Finance Houses too, although the joint Bank/Treasury study showed that it would be almost impossible to do anything either logical or likely to be effective. I wanted to start with Special Deposits and use Bank Rate, probably early in July. The PM was against anything at first and Mills also, feeling that we would just make another recession. I went to two meetings in No. 10 and rather a grand one in the PM's room in the House of Commons, consisting of him, the Chancellor, the Foreign Secretary, R.A.B., the Governor and me. That was on June 21st and we agreed to do both Bank Rate and Deposits.

Rab told me afterwards that it was a sham battle as he and the PM had previously agreed to give the Chancellor what he wanted, and I was to tell the Governor this! Presumably he wanted the Governor to know that he (Rab) took no notice of his advice. The next day the papers had figures showing that bank advances had hardly risen at all, rather bogus as the Nationalized Industries had repaid £12 mn and there was a strong seasonal movement downwards. However the Governor would not point this out as he wanted to prove that the banks did what he told them. The PM got on to this and decided to have another meeting on the morning of Thursday 23rd when the announcement was due to be made at 11.45 a.m. I was dining in Oxford the night before and was telephoned for a meeting at No. 10 at 9.30 a.m. However my train was so late, and the traffic in London so bad, that I did not arrive until 9.50 when it was all over and decided as we wanted.

The announcement itself was a bit of a surprise to everyone but it went off quite well and the Labour Party did not ask for any special treatment, just put down for a Debate yesterday, July 11th, which went off extremely quietly. In fact H. Wilson in his speech was just as pressing on the need for more exports as the Chancellor had been. The Chancellor, who seems to have got it very clear in his head, was quite firm about the need to adapt the economy to the changing situation and I think this is pretty widely accepted by now. One Labour member said that he *did* accept it, but why was there always expansion just before an election and austerity soon after! The Chancellor said it was because the prospect of a Labour Government checked all confidence and when the Conservatives were returned there was such relief that a boom began. There is just a grain of truth in this though of course the Government tends to overdo the stimulus.

It seemed increasingly clear that the Chancellor himself was going and finally Frank Lee told me about a fortnight ago that he *was* and that Selwyn Lloyd would succeed him. R. Maudling also told me this last Thursday, July 7th, after the meeting of the Royal Economic Society. Frank made an appeal to me to stay for another year until next summer, to get Selwyn into the job. I think this is too long but I might stay until the Budget. I do not much like the idea of Selwyn Lloyd as I think he is rather a weak man and too much under the PM's thumb. Incidentally the PM told me in the corridor of the House yesterday that he now thought we were quite right to make the changes, presumably this is because they have gone down well. But one never knows. I sometimes think that he regards it as his duty as PM to stir things up a bit just to make sure that people have considered very carefully what they are proposing.

We went to Bonn last week for the second meeting of the DAG. It felt very queer and rather unpleasant to be in Germany again, where I have not been since 1932. The meeting was rather a waste of time, as the Germans studiously avoided saying anything concrete and a great deal of time was spent on useless interventions by various members. The only useful part was a discussion of the need for better statistics and the agreement to make use of OECD and IBRD for this. These two bodies (OEEC really as it is not OECD yet) were only allowed in on sufferance but it was clear that they knew far more about it than anyone else, and the Bank has far more funds than any member except the US. It annoys me very much that the EEC should be a full member and IBRD treated so shabbily.

Monday, July 18th

We took the balance of payments paper at the Steering Committee last week. The prospect is rather gloomy, more because our foreign lending and Government spending abroad have gone up so much, than anything else. However my hunch is that the UK economy is on the turn and that we will do better from now on than the forecasts show – the main danger, I think, is that we shall lose too much of our car sales to the US but the manufacturers still profess themselves to be very confident. The Hire Purchase regulations, taken with a bit of a run-down in purchases of consumer durables anyway, have begun to take some of the edge off the boom and I suspect that stocks will begin to be a negative instead of such a strongly positive factor from now on. The main fear I have is that our next wage round will be too soon and too large.

Denis Rickett and I had a talk to Per Jacobsson this morning. His main purpose was to persuade us to move to Article VIII of the Fund Articles – we had thought there was no hurry because the French want to wait till November or December but he is trying to get a concerted move before the Bank/Fund meeting on September 26th.[20] Our Ministers are not so keen on it but it was left that we should talk to the French and find out if they still want to wait. If so, it will suit us. We also went on with our talks, begun in March, about international liquidity, etc. He is quite confident that the influx of money into Germany is driving up their costs, while the steps taken in the US will hold theirs down, so the forces making for a new equilibrium are hard at work. We still feel far from confident about this and even if the forces are working that way (which is arguable) there is a long way to go and not all that much time. Incidentally, a lot of Germans do not share his complacency which I think he gets from Blessing. They have started to talk about revaluation all over the place and do not attempt to conceal the fact that Ministers and officials are very much split about it. At a dinner I went to in Bonn, Spindler one of Etzel's senior people said all this to me, and it was said to D. Rickett at last week's meeting of the Anglo/German Economic Committee. The trouble is that the party in favour of revaluation only seem to be thinking of 7½% or so which I do not think would have much effect.[21] It is true that German wages are now rising rather fast. And the Central Bank has just made a 10-year loan to IBRD. But I still think that a good deal more needs to be done.

VI

Selwyn Lloyd's first year,
27 July 1960 to 21 April 1961

Selwyn Lloyd, who had been Foreign Minister since 1955, was Hall's eighth and last Chancellor – the fourth in four and a half years. Hall had no very high opinion of him but there were no marked disagreements.

Many of the concluding entries relate to efforts to persuade Oliver Franks to accept appointment as Governor of the Bank of England. Franks refused and Lord Cromer was appointed but did not take office until after Hall had gone.

Discussion of the West German surplus and a possible revaluation of the Deutschmark (entry for July 18th) continued and a 5 per cent revaluation was finally made in mid-March 1961 (entry for April 2nd).

There is a sense of unfinished business in the concluding entries with their references to talk of economic growth and planning (the National Economic Development Council was created in July 1961 to pursue these subjects); to surtax concessions in the Budget (which bedevilled efforts later in the year to establish an incomes policy); and to the two tax regulators in the Budget, one of which disappeared without trace while the other was brought into use in July immediately it was on the statute book.

Thursday, July 28th 1960

The Ministerial changes were announced last night but by then so much had been leaked out that there were few surprises. I was a bit surprised that D. Sandys was put to CRO as I do not think such talents as he has are right for that. Also, though I knew that Thorneycroft and Powell were coming back, it surprised me that the PM was willing to take them in and risk them resigning again. Thorneycroft may be chastened but I do not think anything would change Enoch Powell. However I have increasingly the feeling that there is very little to stop the PM doing whatever he likes – I had lunch with Edwin Plowden last week and he summed it up by saying that the PM and Norman Brook are running the country and no one in a position to stop them. I think the Treasury can stand up to the PM a bit though he is very pertinacious, but I do not expect to get much help from the new Chancellor. R. Makins lunched with me on Monday and was very bitter about him – said he had no courage and had let him (R.M.) down badly on a number of occasions. Otherwise both Edwin and Roger seemed fairly cheerful and Hitchman told me at still another lunch that Roger was doing very well at AEA though it was a bit awkward to be having to cut down now. They have over-expanded I think on research, and certainly on commercial power when interest rates have moved sharply against them, and I think their calculations about plutonium prices have turned out over-optimistic. However I still feel that all their investment was the right thing to do, and indeed I expect it to pay off ultimately.

Yesterday the EST, FST, Frank Lee, T. Padmore and I had a lunch to say goodbye to the Chancellor. It went off well and was technical and professional to the end as we talked most of the time about how long it would take to educate the Conservative Party to accept a capital gains tax.

I am very sorry he is going, quite apart from misgivings about his successor. He was personally a very 'nice' man, easy to get on with and completely reliable and ready to support and defend his staff. He was very well informed on economic matters when he came and he worked very hard at them and at the end was better informed, and able to see things as a Government economist ought to see them, than any other Chancellor in my time or I suppose in history, since most of them were pre-Keynes. Of course Gaitskell was very good but he was not here long enough, and our own system of reporting and analysis was less well developed: and Gaitskell spent too much time on economic discussion from an academic point of view.

The Chancellor was popular in the country and the House of Commons, a good speaker and a man of firm but enlightened convictions. His two main disadvantages were (a) he was rather a slow worker and would not concentrate on more than one thing at a time, so he was always in danger of being snowed under by work and holding up the business, (b) although he had plenty of courage, he was far from being a born leader and he found it very difficult to persuade his colleagues to do things that they did not like. He had too much of a sense of being one of a team and too little that he was one of the High Command and had the duty of insisting. However he was ahead of everyone else in the Treasury in wanting restrictive measures as early as Christmas 1959, so perhaps it does not befit me to say this of him, except that I was not the Chancellor. He told me yesterday that he had been in office for nearly ten years and felt this was quite long enough and that he detected in himself all the signs of mental weariness and indecision of which he was afraid; that he had told the PM he would be the 12th man, available for any emergency; but that short of this he wanted at least 12 months' rest. He has accepted a Viscountcy so he has made sure he won't come back to the Treasury.

His departure almost certainly weakens the composition of the Cabinet though it is hard to say what the influence of Thorneycroft will be. In official circles, it is thought that Lord Home [Foreign Secretary] will tend to be as much of a stooge to the PM as his predecessor was thought to be, but that Heath [Board of Trade] has a good deal of influence. I do not know much about Hare who is going from Agriculture to Labour. Broadly speaking, I should think that Macleod, Heath and perhaps Hare are the younger men now marked out for the future – I do not know about Sandys or Watkinson, in neither of whom I have any confidence. Unless some accident removes the PM fairly soon, I should think R.A.B.'s chances of the succession are now dim: and that Selwyn's will depend on how he does at the Treasury. I am to have my first interview with him tomorrow.

We had rather an interesting last day. The July figures for bank advances showed a very large rise even allowing for seasonal corrections and I was particularly annoyed because the Governor, at the meeting with Ministers on June 21st, had claimed that the June figures showed that he had the banks under control, and very nearly wrecked the operation for this piece of personal vanity, belied by the statistics of the Bank itself. So we had a meeting yesterday morning and in the afternoon persuaded the Chancellor as almost his last act to write to the Governor expressing alarm at the figures and pointing out that the banks could not expect any help from the Government if they got into difficulties with their liquidity ratio in January and February of next year.

I rather imprudently said it was a good time to send such a letter as the Chancellor would not be here to take it back again if the Governor brought it, as he had done once before when I got Stafford to send a letter asking if the Bank of England considered themselves responsible for the level of bank deposits! The Chancellor, a gentleman to the end, thereupon sent it by special messenger to give the Governor a chance to bring it, though he said he would refuse to let it be returned. Fortunately the Governor was taken up with the première of a film about the Bank of England (to which Frank, W. Armstrong and I went) and he did not read the letter till after 6. He then rang up Frank to protest and said it was an intemperate letter and that he did not accept a lot of the implications but that he would speak to Frank about it tomorrow (Friday) and later to the new Chancellor. So it is a sort of victory for the Treasury, since it is now on the record.

It is one of the great disadvantages of monetary policy, compared to fiscal policy, that if you change the taxes the Revenue Departments will go out and collect the money and be very unpleasant to the taxpayer if they do not get it. But if you try to tighten up on the money side, you get the Bank of England falling over themselves to soften the blow and make all sorts of excuses for the bankers that they probably would be ashamed to make for themselves. The financial world would be astonished if they knew that the Bank of England, unlike most central banks, is always trying to be easier in their monetary policy than the Treasury. Of course the Bank of England always want to be more austere on Government expenditure than the Treasury, though even the latter want to be more austere on this (or on taxes) than Ministers will let them be. But all other Central Banks must have the same experience.

Nothing has happened yet about a new Governor except that D. Eccles is trying to get the job. Selwyn Lloyd told Frank that he felt aggrieved that it had not been settled before he came as he knew nothing of the personalities involved.

The Governor wants Per Jacobsson to give up the IMF – which he has to do unless renewed – so that Coombs can get it. This would be a very good move and it is a most remarkable tribute to Coombs that this should be so, as his ideas are far more enlightened than Cobbold's.

The only other matter of note is that Alexander Sachs, an unorthodox but influential American economist, came to see me on Tuesday and told me he felt fairly sure that there would be a dollar crisis in the next twelve months, mainly because of speculative movements helped by the interest differentials – he wanted to get a scheme going for

Central Banks to hold one another's currencies to avert such crises. We have often toyed with this idea, and everything Sachs said fitted in with our ideas except that he felt it was more urgent and more dangerous than we do – I can't think that those who have left so much money in the US would take it to Europe with political conditions so disturbed, unless they expected a change in parities in the *immediate* future.

Friday, July 29th

I saw the Chancellor for about 15 minutes this morning but I do not think we made any impression on one another. He asked me a little about the Economic Section, and about 'how soon we were going bust' and what the Germans might do to improve the position. Otherwise he only said twice that he knew nothing about the job and would need all the patience and understanding we could give.

Frank Lee told me that he had discussed the fracas with the Governor and also the possible next Governor and that the Chancellor had repeated that it was a shame that the decision had not been taken before and that he would have to wait some time. But he said he did not think much of Harcourt, and was personally well disposed to Oliver. I had hoped that he might give me a chance to mention it but it was a very short and formal interview and no chance of anything like this.

The (new) Chancellor asked a day or two ago for a guide to economic statistics which was sensible of him – we have been doing this. The monthly Economic Report which we do for the Chancellor and EPC and the Planning Board is gradually becoming a useful document and he may find this the best guide. Economic statistics are gradually improving though there is still a long way to go. But we have been much more successful in getting figures seasonally corrected than we expected to be. Hopkin and Godley are first class at all this: and we have been helped by the competitive pressure of the National Institute.

Tuesday, September 20th

August was a quiet month with people going and coming from holidays and the Chancellor hardly in at all. We have been fairly busy since then, getting ready for the Commonwealth Economic Consultative Committee, i.e. the Finance Ministers, which is the successor to the annual or so gatherings – it is now in session and Heath made a long speech this afternoon setting out our present thinking about relations with Europe, which went in a tentative way further than we have gone before towards impairing Commonwealth free entry. We are also getting ready for the Bank/Fund meeting in Washington next week and having a constant look at the economic position.

The Governor was much shaken by the ex-Chancellor's letter and spoke sharply to the Clearing Banks and their August advances were actually down. The unemployment for September confirmed that the labour situation is flat and the August trade returns were a good deal better than the very bad ones for July. Meanwhile there is continued talk about how to stimulate exports. I feel that the world position is very shaky because of the imbalance between the US and Europe, especially Germany, and that it is hard to diagnose our own position in such circumstances. However if I am right in thinking that the economic climate here is changing, no doubt our balance of payments will begin to change also.

I have now seen quite a lot of the new Chancellor and he is not doing at all badly. He is certainly quick at reading a brief and asks pertinent and sensible questions, and so far he has shown more firmness than I expected. I have a curious sense of suspended judgment about him but most of this may be due to the foreboding with which I heard about his appointment.

He has shown quite unexpected firmness in one way and that is about the successor to the Governor. The PM, who sends out Minutes all the time, sent one last month saying how badly the credit squeeze was working and how bad were the relations between the Bank and the Treasury and the Clearing Banks and that we must certainly take the opportunity to get rid of Cobbold on January 1st when he had said he would go. About a fortnight ago, Frank Lee told me that Oliver's chances had improved a good deal, and last week he said that the Chancellor definitely wanted Oliver and he (Frank) hoped that if he were sounded he would not make a lot of conditions as he did when he was offered the Washington Embassy. I had to see Oliver at the weekend about a speech he has to make to some investment bankers in New York on October 5th (I have half written it, on the transfer problem not being a problem between developed and underdeveloped but a symptom of imbalance among the developed) so I took the opportunity to tell Oliver that it was more alive than had seemed likely during our earlier talks and (a) he had better think about what he would say and do if he were asked, (b) as it was so controversial, he had better be fairly keen if asked.

Then yesterday morning, to my great surprise, Frank told me that the Chancellor had made up his mind and wanted to see Oliver at once, to make sure that if he (the Chancellor) ran him hard, Oliver would take it if he were successful. So Oliver was summoned from hospital meetings in Oxford and he and I were dinner guests of Paul Gore-Booth's later and he drove me back afterwards and was obviously extremely pleased. He was anxious to know what the salary was (nobody knows) and how long the hours were but otherwise was only concerned to be sure that he was being asked as the Chancellor's candidate, not as one of a short list.

It was all rather extraordinary when one thinks that at about this time last year he was somewhat doubtful, and from then until the change from R. Makins to F. Lee, his chances got worse and worse. It is really due to two things: (a) Amory, and I suppose other members of the Cabinet, did not like Bill Harcourt so it was not settled for him as the Governor and Court would have liked, (b) Frank Lee was determined to get Oliver and now he has succeeded. It is a wonderful change and I think everyone in the Treasury will be pleased (if it does not come unstuck). The Governor won't like it and the Deputy perhaps will be a bit prickly but in nine months' time everyone will be saying what a good thing it is and the relations between the Treasury and the Bank will be transformed.

Wednesday, September 21st

I had lunch at Unilever's yesterday and more or less arranged to act as a consultant to them, one day a week, when I leave here. Today I lunched with Edwin and confirmed that I would do the same for Tube Investments. I have told Frank Lee that I think of going next April, after the Budget.

I had a long talk with Lord Heyworth this afternoon, about his new job as Chairman of COPPI. We are sending Michael Stewart as Secretary. After this we talked for about an hour on the unsatisfactory relation between economists and business men, where his ideas are very much the same as mine. He told me quite a lot about how bad the LSE Business School had turned out to be because Arnold Plant had the wrong temperament, and also that at Nuffield (where he is a Visiting Fellow) it hasn't worked because Andrews is not the right man either. But he spoke very warmly of the good job Noel Hall had done at the Admin. Staff College at Henley. He had discovered how to let business men teach one another. Noel is going to be Principal of BNC, a job I was more or less offered a year ago. I never thought much of him and was interested that Heyworth, who ought to know, said he had been so good.

Heath gave the Commonwealth Finance Ministers our exposé of the European Trade problem yesterday; he was quite frank in explaining the UK problems and I gather that it went down fairly well though it does not get us any further except that we can now start conversations with the Six without the Commonwealth being worried that they did not know the score. I think there are two problems: (a) to convince the Six that we really want to make the Community a success, (b) to negotiate the countless difficulties on the basis of getting a compromise. So far the French have been very difficult and I don't think they really want us but all the others do.

Wednesday, October 5th

We have just finished a week of the Bank/Fund meeting, and three days of the DAG, in Washington, and I am going to spend two days in New York before returning to England. The only thing that was really interesting at the Bank/Fund meeting was the relation between the UK and US balance of payments deficits and the German surplus. We had persuaded the Chancellor to make rather a strong speech pointing out that a main purpose of the Fund was to deal with just this situation and that it would be very bad for the world if it were not dealt with. It sounded quite well but of course did not make nearly as much of a splash as we had expected – a main trouble is that if one says too much, it starts speculation about exchange parities. We had first exchanged ideas with the US who had agreed that it ought to be taken seriously. Anderson in his speech was more practical and did not treat it as an example of a general problem but he was more explicit against Germany. Per Jacobsson in his opening address also spoke of the need for something to be done and seems at any rate a bit less complacent than he has been so far.

The Germans were very disappointing as they said that revaluation was out of the question and that they were too poor to do all that much more on Aid, though they were trying. I had a long talk with Emminger who was or appeared to be completely frank with me and asked what I myself would do. He agreed with my analysis and said that if it were only a question of the best course technically, he would certainly want to revalue. However it was out of the question politically (presumably because Blessing was against it and he had the ear of Adenauer). Emminger said that they ought to do more on Aid and would do so but he himself did not think that this would do the trick because their prices were so low and all that they gave in Aid came back to them in the form of more export orders. I forgot to ask him about US military expenditure in Germany, which could make a big difference to the position and create no problems. Anyway he said that it was getting very hard to hold the currency down against the stream of foreign exchange, supplemented by high interest rates. And the internal position was one of such severe pressure on resources that it would be impossible to prevent costs and prices from rising. So in effect they would inflate themselves into balance, a result that will produce results very similar to revaluation but in a much more damaging way and not creating the book-keeping problems which Abs wrote so much about. Emminger was quite gloomy but I hope he is right and that it won't take too long. Incidentally the Italians made a most virtuous speech at the Fund saying that as they had such increases in their reserves, they intended to act as a good creditor and keep interest rates down, money plentiful and imports free.

In his summing-up speech Jacobsson again mentioned the problem. It is something that we and the USA now see eye to eye and Per Jacobsson coming round: but it has taken a long time. If the Americans had listened to us two years ago instead of implying that the Germans should be an example to the profligate, it would have been a little easier though I suppose the Germans would still have played it all very slowly.

I talked to everyone I could on the lines that the US balance of payments was a function of what other people were doing as well as of what they themselves were; and also that I did not think that there was much danger of a flight from the dollar on a serious scale (I don't really, because I cannot think they could lose nearly as much gold as they can still afford to do), but that the main trouble would be the pressure on the US to increase tariffs, reduce foreign aid and so on. Since they could not go on for ever with a deficit on the present scale, they would have to do something. It was unreasonable to expect them to devalue when they had a big current account surplus and it was very much in the interests of the world that they should be helped to continue their present policies. I said this to a group of US journalists, to Aschinger of the *NZZ* and to quite a lot of economists and bankers. Probably everyone else is saying it too but I feel I am clearer and more urgent about it than most of my listeners. Nothing else very interesting happened at the meetings. IDA is now practically in existence and will soon have to make up its mind about how soft its loans are to be and who is to get them – I rather hope they spend their first billion dollars fairly quickly though I was a bit shaken by the discussion at DAG on Technical Assistance, of which more later.

I had wanted during this trip to find out three things. First, who was likely to win the Presidential Election, second which economists would be advising the new President and who his Secretary of the Treasury would be, and third, the prospects for the US economy. I got a fairly clear view on the third of them but extremely little on the other two. R. Anderson made a very optimistic speech in the first half of his address to IMF, about how the US was poised on the verge of expansion, but I do not think that many of his hearers believed him. I think that they are going down gently now, and will have a mild but clearly established recession in the first half of next year. But the inventory position is improving and state and local expenditures are rising, and whichever of the candidates becomes President, Federal spending will rise – so I don't think any recession will be deep or long.

On the President, there seems to be a completely unanimous view that no one knows who will win. This is because a lot of the voters are still undecided and no one can say what will decide them. All the poll takers as well as other experts say the same. On Tuesday night Lord Cromer (HE)[1] gave a large dinner party and afterwards we all watched the two candidates in their first joint TV appearance. Most of the American watchers were Republicans and thought that Kennedy did better – mainly because Nixon seemed more on the defensive and agreed with Kennedy much more than Kennedy with him. This later seemed to be the general view and even affected some marginal voters. But I thought both of them were so anxious to seem well informed, quick but also pleasant and easy, that it was very hard to choose between them. And indeed I felt that it would have been wiser if they had been less glib and seemed to think more about what they were going to say.

Finally, it was equally difficult to say who would be the Secretary of the Treasury of either person. Nixon is said to be 'lone wolf' who hardly commits anything to anybody – it is curious that he should have been nominated if so, but he was the Vice-President and is clearly very able. Kennedy is said not to have made up his mind at all because he thinks he ought to have a good sound man to avoid any suggestion that he is going to be profligate and the dollar devalued – but the good sound men in that sense are mostly Republicans.[2] I got perhaps a little light on their economic advisers. Paul Nitze gave me lunch and brought Archibald Cox, a Harvard lawyer who is now head of the organization writing speeches for Kennedy and he told me that Samuelson, Galbraith, Seymour Harris and Walt Rostow were the main advisers. I went to Cambridge for the weekend and had a long talk to Samuelson and I got the impression that he rather hoped to be advising Kennedy if he won. Paul Nitze and Dick Bissell both felt the same. So it might be Paul on economics and he would not be a bad Chairman of the Council. I think there is little doubt that Kennedy will have some very good advisers but there is more gloom about his Cabinet, not only the Secretary of the Treasury but the Secretary of State who is said to be more likely to be Chester Bowles than Stevenson.

I saw a good many people but nothing very noteworthy happened. Robert Marjolin talked to me about Sixes and Sevens, mainly to say that he thought no overall negotiation was feasible at present, because if we got any concessions on agriculture the Germans would want them, and if the Germans got them the French would withdraw from the Rome Treaty because the French farmers would withdraw their support. He was inclined to urge the same sort of things as he did last year, i.e. negotiations on particular groups of commodities, but this time also spoke in favour of a general effort at tariff reductions in GATT. It seemed a bit melancholy. I think it must be a frightful strain to be completely committed to the cause of European unity when de Gaulle is so unpredictable. The latest stories are that he has terrified Adenauer because he *wants* the US to take their troops away from Europe and Europe to organize its own defence – under French generals. This in turn may be frustration that he cannot set up his three power group of US, UK and France.

Friday, October 7th

I have just spent two days in New York and had a long talk with Bob Roosa at the Fed. where I later lunched. I think he is a most congenial man to talk to about monetary policy and indeed economic policy in general. We discussed how things have been going in the UK and I think he feels that we have been doing very well. He is rather worried about the US because they have too rigid a framework for their monetary policy (because of the debt ceiling). But he thought there were a lot of other rigidities including the rates which could be paid on time and savings deposits and the rates charged by the banks. He was also a bit worried by the losses of reserves and would be very glad if we could lower our Bank Rate which I think we ought to do while keeping the long-term rate up. We had a talk about Germany on which we saw eye to eye.

I also saw Elliott Bell [Director] of McGraw-Hill and [Editor and Publisher of] *Business Week*, and Howard Whidden who deals with world affairs for him. We had a good talk about Germany, etc., where again I felt that I was preaching to the converted but put it a bit more clearly – and about the US internal situation. They think the recession started four or five months ago but otherwise felt as I do. I asked Bell about the Secretary of the Treasury and he said that Kennedy would need a strong man but could not easily find one – he said Frank Pace had been suggested, who used to be Secretary of the Army, I think, and then Director of the Bureau of the Budget. He felt that if Bowles were Secretary of State and Pace of the Treasury it would not be a very commanding team! I asked him if *he* were likely if the Republicans got in and he said no but he might possibly go to the Fed. Reserve.

Monday, October 10th

I saw O.S.F. in Oxford last night and we exchanged gossip about the US – more or less agreeing. I then asked him where he stood on the Governorship and he said (a) he had not been thinking about it (which I do not believe), (b) that he now wanted to see Cobbold and ask him various questions. This is reasonable enough but I wish he would not pretend to be so coy.

Wednesday, October 19th

After the above talk, Oliver wrote to Frank Lee saying that he was really quite unable to make up his mind and had to talk it over with Cobbold. This was very awkward as the PM did not want to tell Cobbold that he had decided on Oliver unless he was sure Oliver was a runner. On my advice Frank wrote a slightly cool letter to Oliver saying it was all very difficult. I was not surprised in Oxford that Oliver rang me up and asked to see me which he did on Sunday (16th). He said he wanted my views on the advantages and disadvantages of the job, which I put to him as best I could.

Cobbold got Hanbury Williams, Hambro and Basil Sanderson to see (a) Amory, (b) Selwyn Lloyd, (c) the PM himself this week, to say they did not want Oliver and would like either Harcourt *or* Cromer *or* Mynors better. Fortunately none of them are very impressive and they only hardened the minds at least of Lloyd and the PM. I think it will be a good thing for Lloyd to have made a strong and somewhat unorthodox appointment. He continues to do better than I had expected him to do and he takes quite a firm line about the economy. At present we are having a lot of discussion about whether to put Bank Rate down or not.

Friday, October 21st

Yesterday was full of incident, beginning with a discussion with the Chancellor about Bank Rate, going on to the free market price of gold rising to over $39 an ounce, and ending with the Mansion House speech. On Bank Rate, the Chancellor, and on the whole the Treasury, do not want to move unless the Germans do, at any rate for some time. It will be difficult to do so without giving the impression that we are letting up on the home market and there is a good deal of pressure which we want to resist, to ease on the Hire Purchase regulations. But in present circumstances it raises some nice technical points. We are funding quite nicely and so the supply of Treasury bills is getting less at a time when they are very attractive to non-market holders because of the high yield. To keep the market in the Bank therefore would compel us to issue more bills than we need to do and therefore to stop funding which would probably cause the long-term rate to fall which is in general the opposite of what we want. As we are to talk to the Governor on Tuesday we need to get our own thoughts straight and mine are very far from clear.

I have been nervous for some time about the dangers inherent in the US balance of payments and the flurry on the London gold market was the first obvious symptom – due I think to orders from the Continent to buy gold 'at best' since it is hard to think anyone in their senses would pay $39 at present. This is supported by the fact that the price fell sharply this morning, though it is still well above the shipping point if Central Banks were willing to sell gold on the market, which I trust they are not except for small quantities from the Bank of England. The Bank have sent Parsons, who was in Montreal, to New York and the Chancellor sent Anderson a telegram asking if we could do anything and if so would he get a message to Parsons at the New York Fed. I think we ought to make up our minds what to do in various contingencies of this sort, and had a long talk to Downie this morning on the basis of which I will write a paper. We thought:

(a) make sure no Central Bank would sell gold to any market;
(b) concert with the Fed., Bank of England, Bundesbank and Bank of France, to hold all dollars that we get;
(c) make it clear that we did not intend any devaluation of the dollar.

It *must* be against the interests of W. Europe that the US should either devalue, or (which they will certainly do first) cut down on foreign aid and military expenditure and put up their tariffs.

Meanwhile H. Wilson is going to stand against Gaitskell as Leader of the Labour Party which I trust will not do him any good. He made a bad guess in 1951 and I shall be surprised if this is not another.

Friday, October 28th

It has been an awful week. The Governor more or less talked us all into a Bank Rate move, hinting that the Germans probably would. But he agreed that we should put most of it down to international conditions and he was quite firm that there ought to be no change unless we stood firm on no other relaxations. R. Maudling wanted to relax the Hire Purchase regulations because of the pressure on him from motor car and television manufacturers. However he was persuaded.

Oliver spoke to me over the weekend and said he had talked to the Governor and all well there, but that he felt 'sick, miserable and uncertain'. This was the first time I had ever felt doubtful about him. He then came on Tuesday – the last day – and told the Chancellor he would not do it. The PM saw him that night and tried to persuade him. He asked for a day and on Wednesday came to see Frank and talked at length about how the job did not appeal to him because he did not much like 'finance' – if it had been US relations, or European, or with underdeveloped countries, it would have been different. Frank politely said this was all bogus. Late on Wednesday Oliver asked for another day, and Frank asked Edwin to speak to Oliver. Edwin thought he had persuaded Oliver but nothing happened yesterday. Then this morning the PM got a letter from Oliver finally refusing. It is a frightful blow. Cromer seems the most probable candidate now, though I would have preferred Harcourt. The Chancellor does not want him and neither does Frank.

Tuesday, November 1st

Everyone is still bewildered about Oliver's decision which is very hard to understand psychologically.

The Chancellor was so anxious to get on with it that he telephoned Cromer in Washington on Sunday and asked him to come at once, and as soon as he got off the 'plane yesterday (Monday) he was whisked into the Chancellor's office and offered the Governorship stone cold, with no warning at all. But of course the Governor and Court had been plugging him ever since they knew they could not have Harcourt. I saw Cromer in the afternoon and as I expected he was worrying about whether he could do it. I told him I felt sure that he could. He is seeing Cobbold today to find out what sort of a job it is and going back on Wednesday to discuss with his wife and reach a decision. I imagine that he is likely to take it. Frank Lee has still not got over the shock caused by Oliver's refusal.

On gold, Parsons had a long talk last week in Washington to Anderson, Martin and all their staffs. It seems to have been much more intimate and friendly than usual and they agreed that we could intervene in the market at our discretion and earmark gold in New York against the dollars we get. But I hope we won't intervene too much, or earmark dollars too much. I have written a paper to say so.

Sunday, November 20th

Cromer did not take very long to make up his mind. *The Times* had rather a cold article about him but most of the other papers were all right. Wilfrid King rang me up and said his reaction was the same as *The Times* but he wanted to know what I thought: I said I thought Cromer would probably be very good, etc., and as a result *The Economist* had rather a nice article, more or less what I had said! Everyone is still mystified about Oliver. Edwin Plowden told me that he thought, on the last night, that he had persuaded him to accept.

Meanwhile my own affairs are now well under way. Frank Lee saw Alec Cairncross at lunch today and offered him this job and he came to see me this afternoon and seemed to be delighted, as he ought to be. I advised him to get the staff position a bit clearer before he accepted, as this had been the biggest headache I had had all my time and it would be a help to him to have it all down on paper as a starting-point for later negotiations. I have always felt very irritated and frustrated on this, not because the people I deal with are not nice enough but because it is the only Treasury relationship of a buyer–seller kind and they naturally feel that they must keep their end up while I feel that the efficiency of the Section should be the criterion. Alec does not know if he can persuade Glasgow to release him by next April but I should think that he could and I am determined to go then anyway. Actually, with the Budget over, Bryan Hopkin and Downie could carry the thing for several months if necessary.

The American elections have come and gone and all the people who said they did not know who would win have turned out to be right. According to the *Manchester Guardian* today it is still possible that Nixon will get in, on a complex series of hypotheses, but it sounded a pretty remote chance. There is as much speculation as ever about who will be the Secretaries of State and the Treasury: but Eric Roll told me over the weekend that he had heard that Paul Samuelson had been offered the Chairmanship of the Council of Economic Advisers (which I thought might happen from the way Paul spoke to me) and had turned it down which I find rather surprising if it is true.

The dollar is in rather an easier position since the election, which seems to mean that a Kennedy victory had been heavily discounted. The US balance of payments has improved so much that it is only outward speculation that is now straining it. Meanwhile our own position is still a difficult one, and I have done a paper which the Chancellor is putting to his colleagues. The Bank Rate reduction went quite smoothly by the way, it just shows that if you have a coherent story and tell it the papers will accept it.

The troubles are threefold:

(a) Production is steady and has been for six months or more, but employment has increased and labour got shorter all the time. So we are moving into another 'stagnation' period.
(b) A lot of wage demands are in the mill and it looks as if this round will be more expensive than the last two. Prices are now beginning to rise and will continue to do so.
(c) Imports obstinately stay high and exports – low. All our calculations suggest that stock-building is high and won't last but I wish

the imports would turn. And the failure of exports to do so, in spite of less pressure here and of the Germans being rather (or very) inflationary, is very disappointing and suggests that we have become less competitive since 1956. Although unemployment is low, it isn't as low as it was then.

The Chancellor removed some general questioning from my papers and put in some rather weak stuff of his own at the end. Marples sent for me last week and said he was very worried about our position and I urged him to take the occasion of the Chancellor's paper to put in one of his own, more or less saying that we don't work hard enough which I am coming to think is the basic trouble. Of course lots of men work hard and lots of managers are efficient but I feel that too many are not and when anything goes wrong they come rushing to HMG for help. I had thought that if we started to tighten up when unemployment was still about 1.8% or so, we would not run into such pressures as we have done but it seems clear that we ought to have aimed at a higher figure.

There is a great deal of discussion about growth and why we lag behind most advanced countries; it is very hard to disentangle all the possible causes but when this is all done we are still left with an element which suggests that there is something wrong with the UK. At least some of our investment must be producing very little – for instance, in coal, output per man-year fell between 1953 and 1959 although there was a great deal of investment.

There has been a lot of talk in the last two weeks about Hire Purchase, stimulated mainly by the contraction in the motor car industry. Television is also down a good deal but it will stay down. The Governor wants to reduce Bank Rate but R. Maudling wants to ease up on Hire Purchase and says he can't hold it if we lower Bank Rate and probably not even if we don't. We had a long talk with the Bank of England last week and were more nearly together in our views than I can ever remember: partly because the Treasury made up its mind the day before and Frank went and told the Governor just what *we* thought. Somewhat to our surprise, he said he did not want to do anything to ease things for the Clearing Banks until February at the earliest. He must have been so stung by our letter in late July that he is determined to show he is a strong man. The monetary position is very odd since the Banks are being very much squeezed on liquidity and are therefore competing hard for Treasury bills and making it difficult to keep Bank Rate effective – it is a predictable result of a situation in which the short and long rates are too close together for the appetites of the public in relation to the amounts of stock and bills available. And I doubt if we *can* hold the market at Bank Rate unless we are prepared to unfund, which would be contrary to our general policy. But it is so new a situation that none of us quite know where we are.

There has been a flurry about a bid for Ford's UK by Ford's USA which has caused a great deal of bad logic and bad argument but I am glad to say that the Government has been quite sensible and today said they were going to permit the transaction. The argument I liked least was that of City journalists who say that 145/6 [£7.27½] is too little for a share that was standing in the market at 91/- [£4.55] the day before the bid. If they are right now, then they must think Ford has growth possibilities far above any other British stock – for otherwise it would pay to get the 145/6 and put it in other growth stocks which are still at prices more like 91/- for Ford.

Friday, December 9th

The Cabinet took the Chancellor's paper and also two by R. Maudling, one on exports and one on reducing Hire Purchase terms a bit. There was not any very useful discussion, particularly about the long-term issues: but there was hardly any pressure for easing up at home. Both the Chancellor and R. Maudling have made speeches to this effect. Yesterday Bank Rate was reduced to 5% – the Chancellor and the Governor both wanted this mainly on international grounds and the Treasury agreed as long as it meant no weakening on the home front. On this occasion our publicity was so good that no one at all took it as a sign of good cheer. The general employment position is still pretty tight and although there is a lot of short time in cars, and real trouble in making TV sets, the Government is under no pressure.

We have had the NIF and B. of P. Reports and also a good deal of talk about imbalances, ending with a general discussion in Frank Lee's room this morning.

Thursday, January 5th 1961

I heard yesterday from a friend in Oxford that O.S.F. had told his friends in Worcester (College, Oxford) that he would accept if he were asked to be Provost. I said I was a little surprised by this as I had understood from him that he had refused an Oxford Headship recently (my friend said this was BNC) and did not think Worcester was such a catch. She said that it was thought that he would try to remain Chairman of Lloyds *at the same time*. I thought this would be extremely unusual (as I am sure it is) and would the College and Lloyds agree? She said (a) Worcester were very poor and could not pay a decent salary, (b) Oliver had just resigned from his Oxford Hospital Boards and it was thought that this was to give him time, if he were elected, to run the College Friday to Tuesday and the Bank Tuesday to Friday. She added that it was far from certain as some of the Fellows of Worcester did not agree with this choice.

I had already heard from a different source that he was being approached by Worcester and this lady was in a position to know about the Hospital Boards and probably about Worcester too: all this was given to me in strict confidence. It is probably correct and would check with what has happened already though it does not make me any less surprised: particularly since one of the reasons he gave for not wanting to be Governor was that he did not want to give up the hospital work although I thought it was clear that this would not be necessary.

There have been no changes at all in the economic position but the Board of Trade think the December trade returns may be better: the engineering unions settled for 4½% which was a quicker and cheaper settlement than M/Labour had expected. All the New Year appreciations conform more or less to ours in analysis but they are more in favour of reflation at home than the Treasury is. The Budget Committee has taken the preliminary NIF Report and told the Chancellor that we must concentrate on exports and investment. The Chancellor and the President of the Board of Trade have been quite firm so far in making no concessions on Hire Purchase and the Bank in making none on Special Deposits, and all this seems to be accepted.

The Prime Minister has agreed to a visit by officials to Washington, if they will have us, in February and the present idea is that we should have a UK/Canada Continuing Committee first as a cover story, and that Frank Lee, R. Powell, D. Rickett and I should then filter into Washington. Kennedy has made what I think are very good and courageous appointments to his top jobs, and to my great pleasure has made Bob Roosa of the NY Fed. the Treasury Under Secretary for Monetary Affairs, to handle debt, etc. I like him very much and think he is very able. The Chairman of the Council of Economic Advisers is someone I had hardly heard of called Walter Heller from Minnesota U. He is a tax expert and Nicky Kaldor told me that he knew him quite well and thought highly of him. He is a Keynesian and according to Nicky admires his expenditure tax! His main contribution is the sensible one that if there were no tax exemptions general tax rates could be lower. A number of people say that Paul Samuelson was offered the job and refused it. Arthur Burns came to see me last week and said he was very sorry if this were so. He thought Heller was a bit lightweight for the job and said he would nevertheless have to carry the load – even if Kennedy thought now that he could go on consulting his Harvard friends, once he was in the White House, he would be too busy. Both Paul Nitze and Archibald Cox, with whom I lunched in Washington in October, have got jobs. I am glad that Paul has as he is a very able man and has been preparing himself for this for a long time.

Alec Cairncross has now settled most of the outstanding points and an announcement is to be made the week after next – it is high time as a great many people know about it already. So my time is now rapidly coming to its end and I suppose that I will miss it very much but I do not find the job very exciting now so I expect that my subconscious is making the necessary adjustments for me.

One thing that would be interesting is to work on a policy for growth, which has been anathema since about 1951. It is now getting into the air again, partly because of the almost continuous comparisons which are being made between ourselves and the US, and various other countries like Russia, Germany, France, Italy, Japan. The FBI had a sort of symposium on economic matters recently and almost said that the Government should have a plan, and the demand expansionists led by Roy Harrod are always plugging it. There are a lot of difficulties, of which the main one is the upward drift of wages and prices with full employment and the adverse effect this has on the balance of payments. It is also true that both employers and workers in the UK are too lethargic and restrictionist in their attitude. But it would help if the Government would think about it and we are now trying to get them to, for instance the Planning Board has asked for a paper about it. After ten years, the Conservatives are less worried than they were about the word 'planning'.

Thursday, January 12th

The news about Cairncross apparently leaked out to a Glasgow paper on Tuesday (Jan. 10th) and so it was decided to make an announcement yesterday which was done in rather a rush. I was sorry as I had intended to warn several people besides those who knew already. I told all my staff apart from Downie, Hopkin and Turvey who knew already. It all passed off quite smoothly, several papers rang me up but naturally were more interested in Cairncross than me. I had a very nice letter from the PM. At a party last night a man from Lombard Banking asked if there was any chance of my seeing their chief, a man called Knight. I don't want to say anything about my new occupations until I have got rid of the present one, if this can be avoided.

Dillon has agreed to our going to the US and unless he changes his mind when he actually takes over at the Treasury, we shall go in the week of February 19th. So far the dollar and the pound have got on all right this year but there is a long time to go.

We had a talk about growth before the Planning Board and decided that we ought to recommend Ministers to have it properly studied. There was not time at EPB to do more than begin on the subject and the Board is going to have another meeting to discuss the paper properly at the end of January. We had a Budget Committee on Tuesday to think about things that might be in the Budget. On present form we don't think there will be any net reductions but we are waiting month by month both for the unemployment and the trade figures and I feel that both will begin to move fairly soon, in fact I will be surprised if this month's figures do not show some improvement in the balance of payments and the first real increase in unemployment since they both began to flatten out last year.

Friday, February 24th

In the end I did not go to Washington, as Dillon said he hoped that we would keep the party small and Cromer wanted the Bank to be represented. So Lee, Rickett and Parsons went, which was obviously sensible. However I felt rather sorry, particularly since the visit was given a good deal of publicity (Frank *likes* it and got the Chancellor to announce the visit in the House), so that any damage that could be done that way was done: and in the end about a dozen attended on the US side, so that not only our three went, but also Pitblado who has replaced Cromer, the Bank of England man in Washington, my own man there (Kennedy) and Fred Atkinson whom we had sent to compare balance of payments forecasts. This latter exercise has gone very well as we have exchanged views with the Germans and French as well and everyone concerned thought that it was a very useful exercise.

The talks were extremely interesting and though we didn't agree on all points, especially that they are not very keen on a German revaluation, there was a general feeling that we were both under strain, and that it was in both our interests that neither the £ nor the $ should weaken. It was also agreed that there should be a continuance of the talks, and that perhaps we should try to bring the French and the Germans in.

Everyone was very much struck by the energy, liveliness and high quality of the new US team, which qualities have affected the remaining top people from the last Administration. But it is also likely that Kennedy will have a difficult time with Congress, which is more reactionary than the previous one, unless Kennedy can get a very strong public opinion behind him. On the US outlook, their present expectations are that revival will be rather slow and unemployment a problem for some time. This may be because Kennedy is nervous about unbalancing the Budget too soon, after everything Eisenhower said on the subject.

At home we are now deep in the Budget preparations and it looks as if we will have a sticky time. My expectations on unemployment have turned out to be quite wrong and our first NIF forecast too optimistic. The main reasons are that private investment seems to be expanding much faster on recent surveys than on the earlier ones: and that the Chancellor eased the Hire Purchase regulations (without consulting me, I may say) on January 20th, which has encouraged a turn-round that was taking place anyhow. So as between 1960 when Hire Purchase was pulling us back, and 1961 when it is pulling us up, the change is quite marked. We think therefore that the Budget should take away more than it gives. The Chancellor is most anxious to ease up on surtax and does not like our advice at all. However he seems to be coming round and may agree to put up a few taxes this year and make the surtax changes only in relation to income earned after the Budget which would not pay tax anyway until January 1963 – he could put up profits tax to bring in some money at the same time. Frank and I are to have a go at him on Monday on the general objective of the Budget. It is awkward on timing this year, since the obvious day is April 11th. But the PM is going to the US on March 24th and won't be back till Sunday, April 9th. So unless he can be squared completely beforehand, it is taking a risk and he himself would like the Budget deferred until April 18th.

My own arrangements are well in train and I shall be leaving in the middle of April: I want to visit the US before I go. I have been to a general meeting of Unilever Managers to hear a review of last year. Edwin P. talks to me quite freely about his problems at Tube Investments which seems to be a one-man show at present under the Chairman's (Stedeford's) personal supervision, and just the opposite of Unilever which spends much thought on how to keep the organization informed and co-ordinated. I have been asked to be the UK Representative on the Commonwealth Economic Committee which will give me a foot, and an office, in Whitehall but not much work.

The other main developments have been connected with growth, which is certainly very much in the air. After the first Planning Board talk, two more were arranged. And we had a useful talk with what is called the interim Committee of NPACI, with both the TUC and the FBI represented (plus ABCC and NUM). This was more down to earth than the Planning Board and gave us a chance to put some of the Government's difficulties more clearly. Ministers and Parliament are much more interested than they have been ever before and some quite good speeches were made, especially by Tony Crosland, in a Debate on the Economic Situation which took place on February 6th and 7th. The Chancellor, who had been making far too many speeches, had not done his homework and put the speech together in bits and pieces on the morning of the Debate. The result was that he spoke very badly. I am not much impressed by him so far and the Office tells me that he is very weak in resisting demands for increased expenditure. He is erratic and can do quite well but I shall be surprised if he turns out to be a good Chancellor.

The Government has been putting up social service charges and has roused the Opposition who are making Parliament quite lively, with all-night sittings, constant points of order and so on. I would have thought that this would unite them but T. Crosland says that Hugh Gaitskell is not handling the defence issue at all well so that it is not having the effect it might have.

Thursday, March 2nd

I think I may have to go to Washington with the PM next month. He asked for me. Frank Lee was rather anxious to go himself but the Chancellor was quite firm that he did not want him to be out of the country for a week or so just before the Budget. There is rather a difficulty about the Budget and the PM himself, since the Chancellor is doubtful whether he can both make up his own mind, and clear it with the PM, before the latter leaves for the West Indies – before he goes to Washington – on March 24th. The PM is not due back until April 9th and the Budget was to have been on the 11th. For a while it looked as if it might be moved to the 18th but now it looks like the 12th. Even that gives us far too little time if anything remains to be settled by the 9th.

We are in the thick of discussions now and Frank and I had quite a good talk about the shape of the whole thing and the need to take away more than we gave. Since then there have been a lot of detailed discussions and the range of starters has been narrowed and one or two approved. The principal problem is about the Surtax – whether to let any relief run till 1963 before anyone gets it, whether to have an increase in profits tax to pay for it, how to treat unearned income when you want to operate mainly or wholly on earned. The Chancellor seems determined to make a splash here. But on the whole he has been rather better this week.

Meanwhile we are in the middle of the Economic Survey and have started to write the Speech, but I do not feel particularly worried about either of these.

Sunday, April 2nd

I am now on my way to Washington where I am to have some talks with US officials tomorrow and Tuesday, before the PM arrives (on Tuesday night) for his talks on Wednesday. I have been having a very hectic time, going to meetings to get the briefs ready and also working on the Budget and doing a little to get things ready for my departure. But I had to go to Paris on March 23rd and 24th for a meeting of the Economic Experts, and the first three days of last week were taken up by the 4th DAG meeting in London. So I had the feeling that I wasn't really doing anything properly.

The new balance of payments figures are out and don't seem to have caused much stir. They were very discouraging to me since I felt that all my judgments in recent years had been based on somewhat false views of the actual situation. It is always an obvious problem in this job, to know where one is at a given time. But this radical write-down of our foreign earnings goes much deeper than that since it happened well after we ought to have known as much as could be known for practical purposes about the past.[3] Of course our monetary position is unchanged but the fact is that we were getting more inward investment and thus investing much less net abroad, than we had supposed.

I feel that we ought to have had a more austere policy basically, in fact it is the last example of the state that we have really run the economy too full ever since I came to this job. Although Ministers have all along put an enormous amount of pressure behind high employment, and also there has been this continuous pressure to lower taxes so that the best one can do in bad years is not to lower them – one can hardly ever raise them – still I feel now that we ought to have put more weight than we did on the need for deflation from the beginning – then we might have got on to a base where we could have moved more or less as we have done but with the whole position under less pressure.

The March gold figures will show a substantial loss; I don't know exactly as they were changing every day and I left the office on Thursday before they had closed down, but I would guess about £70 mn or so. It could have been made almost anything as the Germans and Swiss have lent us a great deal of money – they have a gold guarantee under EMA but all the same they have behaved very well. I have been pressing to show as big a loss as we could without starting a panic: I suppose one can't predict the figure that will do that. But everyone knows we have lost a lot. The Central Bankers' meeting at the BIS in Basle made a very useful statement that they would co-operate over the exchanges and they are really behaving very well.

I ought to have begun this by recording that all the movements were set off by the DM Revaluation in mid-March – it was a small step [of 5%] in the right direction but seemed to make speculators suddenly aware, in a way they had not been practically aware before, that exchange rates could be moved. However I was rather pleased: it was a step in the right direction and we were so vulnerable with the enormous build-up of NSA sterling balances last year, because of distrust of the dollar and our high Bank Rate, that I wanted the movement to start. It was inevitable and we wanted a few trial runs. Of course the publication of the figures may stir things up a bit in itself, but I think we have now enough resources and friends to ride it out.

There has been a great deal of discussion about how to make the IMF more suitable to present conditions – the main drawings have always been in dollars but here too the Germans have been very helpful and agreed to lend the Fund quite large sums in DM if UK or USA wants to draw. So it is all a bit more rational than might have been feared and in fact rather encouraging. This is one of the things the PM will want to talk about.

He has been convinced for a long time that the real trouble is a shortage of international liquidity and Harrod has pushed him far too far. Failing an increase in the price of gold, which he has at last accepted is out for the US, he wants whatever scheme will most increase the credit-creating powers of IMF. The favourite is Triffin and I gather that the new Council of Economic Advisers back it and has taken on T. to advise them on international economic affairs.[4]

Meanwhile the Fed. Reserve has set up a group of Central Bank foreign exchange experts to consider all this sort of thing. I expect to get involved in arguments, perhaps between Kennedy – Macmillan and their advisers, rather than between K. and M.

The Budget has not given a great deal of trouble once we managed to persuade the Chancellor that he ought to end up with a larger surplus. He is going to do a really big operation on earned income for Surtax – too big I think when nothing is being done about capital gains – but to offset it by profits tax which most people will regard as rough justice. He is also going to introduce, if he can get his colleagues to agree, *two* economic regulators: a surcharge on all indirect taxation and a flat tax on employees, using a supplement to the insurance stamp. But the Minister of Pensions, Boyd-Carpenter, is against this. The Speech is now in its fourth draft and is beginning, as usual, to look all right.

The Experts Meeting in Paris went off all right and, as I have said earlier, the Germans seem really anxious to help now. I think their surplus is going to diminish, and our own balance of payments is now improving, with exports rising and imports falling or seem likely to do so. We also took the independent group of economists' report on 'The Problem of Rising Prices'. R. Kahn was the Chairman and he has done a first-class job which will probably make quite an impact, since it really accepts that there can be a cost inflation as well as a demand one.

The DAG meeting was very interesting because the US is now taking a strong lead. The President sent a long message to Congress about Aid, and besides a lot of ideas on their own front which will be quite a change, he proposed a stronger international effort, working on OECD which is to replace OEEC and with DAG becoming the Aid Committee (DAC) of the new body. These ideas were floated off at the London meeting [of the DAG]. They will be very difficult to get off the ground in any adequate way, but it is a great thing to have the US really taking an initiative at last. No doubt this will be another subject for the President and the PM to talk about. The PM is a bit out of date on American thinking and I suspect not only on the Aid front. It is wonderful to have Washington so advanced and intellectual in their thought, after the long period in which ideas were really suspect by the Administration.

Wednesday, April 5th

I have spent two days talking to various officials in Washington and ending up with a late session last night with the PM, Lord Home and Harold Caccia. The change in the Washington atmosphere to which I referred at the end of the last page is quite extraordinary and impossible to convey unless one were to set out rather carefully the later Eisenhower atmosphere with which it is contrasted. But I suppose basically the Eisenhower régime was almost an anti-intellectual one, distrustful of men who are likely to have new ideas, inclined to be angry at those who could think faster than they could and who were too much given to pressing things to their logical conclusions, holding to tenets which they held dogmatically and were angry at anyone who questioned them. So that even their academic characters were drawn from those who were nearest to their own dogmas and who were prepared to make extensive use of intellectual scepticism to refute inconvenient ideas in what could appear to the Administration to be their own language. Now the place is swarming with enthusiastic young men drawn from the brightest of those at places like Harvard and MIT, who are all positively encouraged to be as bright as possible and look at things from all angles. This has encouraged those who remain over from the last Administration, and who presumably cherished ideas that they had better keep to themselves, to come out into the open with them. So all sorts of metaphors of the general family of new brooms [that] are sweeping through ministry corridors and so on have become appropriate. Of course I have been writing a poetic rather than a literal description: there were bright men in the last Administration and no doubt stupid ones in this – including of all people George McGhee, in of all places the Head of the Policy Planning Division of the State Department, an appointment impossible to understand.

I started on Monday with Heller, the new Chairman of the Council of Economic Advisers, whom I had never met before. He spent most of the time explaining that they would not get the level of employment up quickly enough because the President had decided that politically it was impossible to get the country to accept a really unbalanced budget without a lot of education away from Eisenhower ideas. He was doubtful whether they could make much impact on the position before late 1962. He then got on to Triffin, whom he has taken on as a technical adviser to the Council which is causing him a lot of trouble. He says he cleared it with Martin, Dillon and Roosa but all the same they regard it as a sort of flag of defiance; and I should think rightly so, since Triffin is determined to get something like his own plan and I felt that the Council would be backing him up. Later on when I saw Bob Roosa he got quite heated and said it must be made clear that if Triffin was a member of any US Delegation it was in the capacity of technical adviser and with no authority to speak on matters of policy.

The most interesting thing about the talk with Roosa was that he gave me an early sight of a paper the US is putting to the Economic Policy Committee in Paris on April 18th, calling for the establishment of a number of working groups to further the work of consultation and 'confrontation' about economic policies of OECD.[5] They clearly are very anxious to make a great deal of it and these two initiatives – at DAG and now this – are the clearest proof that at present they intend to put a lot of drive in it. This is all going to be a very difficult undertaking: they want senior officials who are close to top policy levels to go, and for the groups to be restricted and yet to keep the non-member countries informed. It is very hard to get restricted groups anyway since the countries excluded are jealous: but if the groups are large the work is useless. However it is all a good sign, though in the end we shall have to get back either to bilaterals, or to some form of 3 or 4 or 5 power consultations. Incidentally, the Governor told me just before I left that the US idea to have discussions among Central Banks about how to support one another's currencies, make more use of IMF, etc., had got off the ground and Martin had proposed terms of reference. Martin himself told me yesterday that Coombs of the NY Fed. had gone to Europe to sell the ideas finally to Germany, France and Italy who were to be the other participants besides UK and US.

It became very clear during my various talks that a good deal of pressure would be needed if the IMF were to get powers to borrow all the Deutschmarks, etc., that it might need, in time to lend them. Jacobsson is playing it slowly and the French are being very difficult and doing their best to stop other European countries by bringing pressure to bear through the Six. One often gets the impression, listening to the Germans, that they are very anxious to meet us in the various things we want to do in Europe: but that Adenauer will listen in the last resort to de Gaulle. However I think that the French lower down the line are also capable of pushing the Germans and all their other partners about, though there may be a residue of memory that, when things were taken to the top, de Gaulle prevailed. But Emminger was very forthcoming when Jacobsson first put his plan forward. De Largentaye, the French member of the IMF Board, had been told in advance but had forgotten this and he cabled back that this was a Jacobsson–Anglo-Saxon ramp which they were trying to put across. And Emminger told me that he had a very difficult time with the French at the Committee on monetary matters, etc., which the Six have set up.

Frank Southard and I talked about the need to hurry up the French and said that it was very dangerous that Triffin was here, since he wanted the Fund to take voluntary deposits as a first step. This would be equivalent to giving gold guarantees by the US and the UK through the Fund and would not suit the UK. He also said that they would have to go to Congress about this and it could be very difficult. So he thought that Triffin and through him the Council would be pressing for something that we would be very doubtful about and that would delay what we really wanted. I managed to get this over to the PM in the evening which was a great relief. Otherwise the most interesting thing about the talk with him was on the Six/Seven problem where he asked me what I really thought and I replied that I did not think we could get in unless we did so on a political basis but that if we were willing to do this we would not find it insuperable to reach some agreement about our two major economic problems, i.e. the Commonwealth free entry and our system of agricultural support.

Sunday, April 9th

I am now in Cambridge, Mass., where I came on Friday evening. The talk between the PM and the President on Wednesday morning was about economics for the first hour and I sat on the PM's right for this and was opposite Dillon who was next to Kennedy so I was able to see him operating in detail. He was obviously inexperienced in these international matters but struck me as a man of very strong will and also of great self-control. He said very little and did not allow his face to show what he thought of what others said: and left nearly all the talk to his aides without even endorsing what they said. The only exception to this was where it was a matter of troubles with Congress, e.g. German acts on Hong Kong cotton, where he spoke up very clearly to stress that he *would* have trouble if nothing were done.

The talks went fairly well on this point. The PM said that we would lose the cold war unless we acted more coherently in the West, and illustrated this mainly with the need to reach a European solution on Six/Seven and the need to remedy the current imbalance and overhaul our monetary and other institutions. He actually mentioned Triffin and Harrod but in a very light way. Dillon spoke up very well, said that on these matters (except Six/Seven) we were in very general agreement and that we ought to concentrate on what we could do in the Fund now and have preliminary talks between ourselves about further steps. The PM took this cue very well and said that we must not allow the fact that we could not get everything to be an excuse for doing nothing. I was much relieved and so was Dillon – for reasons which I will explain, this was a very useful agreement for them and as the President did not dissent, and Heller who was there said nothing, it was taken by all to be a settled thing.

On Europe, the PM was very eloquent and shifted the UK position quite a bit compared to anything I had heard before, or indeed than I thought was agreed, by the Cabinet or anyone else. The gist of what he said was that it was an American as well as a UK interest that the UK should be a full member in the political sense of the Treaty of Rome. Otherwise the desire of the French to put an end to 'Anglo-Saxon domination', and the deep desire of the Germans to show that they were strong and independent again, would lead in the end to a Third Force. But the PM wanted to know if the US agreed. He said that the French wanted the UK in but on Third Force lines whereas he (the PM) would never agree to anything that weakened the US–UK entente.

I had a bit of trouble on Thursday when I had lunch with Heller. It had just dawned on him that the agreement to go slow and on a bilateral basis, on the longer-term plans for the IMF, would alter the ideas he had had for taking Triffin to Paris for the EPC meeting and making a start there with plans for a new international currency. He left me after lunch for a meeting with Roosa and Ball to try to sort it out but later that evening Roosa telephoned me to say that it had been settled and that *he* was pleased. I think it was agreed that Triffin should be regarded entirely as a technical adviser.

The PM made a very good speech at MIT on Friday evening and though he did not say anything he hadn't said to Kennedy – inevitably indeed less – he got his point across that we needed to pull our socks up and co-operate much more and reform our machinery, if we were not to lose the cold war.

I have had some very interesting talks in Cambridge, especially with Paul Samuelson who is consulted by the President a great deal. He told me that *he* had suggested Roosa for the Treasury and thought him the best of the younger central bankers in the world. He obviously nominated Heller and the other members of the Council of Economic Advisers as well. He was a bit worried about Triffin. I told him I thought it was essential that Roosa (about whom I shared his opinion) and Heller should get on together and that it would be a pity if fanatical characters should give them both too much to do in tidying up afterwards, just the experience I had had in the early days of the Section. It is clear that the President is encouraging people with new ideas to go to Washington and to give voice to them, and also that he is using his own staff to keep a watch on Departments. This is said to be due to Schlesinger, who is himself in Washington, telling him that in Roosevelt's early days he found this essential.

Friday, April 21st

This is my last working day in the Treasury and I am going to a cocktail party given as a sort of farewell for me, in half an hour. I have had a most hectic time since I got back from Washington and it is a pity I have not been able to record more of what happened. We have had a Budget and Budget Debate, I have been to Paris twice, and we have also had an argument with the Governor about Special Deposits.

I got back on Monday 10th but apart from reporting on what the PM said on Europe, and my discussions in Washington about the US proposals on OECD, I did not do much but clear up papers and see my staff. On Tuesday night the Economic Section past and present gave a dinner for me which was very nice indeed and almost a moving occasion. The great bulk of all those who have worked for me were there, the main exceptions I think were Marcus Fleming, Nita Watts and Alan Day all of whom were out of the country, and Philip Watts who was held up somewhere. Anyhow they looked a very charming and intelligent lot of people. Downie and David Henderson made speeches, Downie especially making a few observations about how I operated which were rather new to me, and especially how plainly I showed it when a conversation was ended – though I knew I was good at this, and indeed one has to do it. Anyway I felt that everyone thought I had done a fairly good job and was sorry that I was leaving.

The Budget was more or less settled and there were only a few points on the speech. The Chancellor has been a good deal bolder than I expected but I still feel rather uncertain about him: I mean what is the strength of his character and moral feelings and so on. On Monday he delivered himself very well indeed, by far the best speech he has made since he came to the Treasury. The matter and indeed form had been worked over so often that it ought to have been good but different Chancellors speak it in very different ways, and he really gave the impression that he understood it all and he made the various points stand out though so many of them were essays rather than proposals – in fact I thought he made only one mistake, a lecture on business expenses which roused a good many expectations that were all deceived in the end. The Surtax proposals pleased his party enormously and he got a warm reception at the end: the Press described it as mildly enthusiastic but they have forgotten what has happened to some of his predecessors.

Note

I stopped there. Besides the Economic Section dinner, the Chancellor had a small lunch for me and the Bank of England a second-class dinner party with the Deputy Governor as host. I felt on the whole glad to be leaving the Treasury as I felt that although, after Bridges left, the Permanent Secretaries and the Chancellors always took my advice, I was not at all popular with the top officials. I suppose they felt I had too much influence. But they were a poor lot, and Rab Butler used to complain to me about them. When Bridges went, Ministers brought in Roger Makins as Permanent Secretary, and when he went, they brought in Frank Lee from the Board of Trade. When he got a stroke, they went over the heads of all the Treasury 2nd Secretaries to make William Armstrong Permanent Secretary and Burke Trend Secretary of the Cabinet – this must have been unprecedented.

Notes

1 *Butler's last years as Chancellor, 1 January 1954 to 20 December 1955*

1 The Friday Forum was a Treasury Committee under Sir Bernard Gilbert. The papers for 1953–4 survive in PRO T 230/261.

2 The balance of payments target is discussed in Cairncross, A. (ed.), *The Robert Hall Diaries, 1947–1953* (London: Unwin Hyman, 1989), pp. 261–2, 264–5, 279. It was first put forward in the reply to an OEEC questionnaire and later included in the *Economic Survey 1953*. By 1959 the target had been increased from £300–£350 million to an average of about £450 million a year in the early 1960s (Radcliffe Committee Report, para. 62).

3 Hall had been a Fellow of Trinity College, Oxford, and was succeeded by Anthony Crosland.

4 The Randall Commission on Foreign Economic Policy reported on 23 January 1954 in favour of reductions in US tariffs, waiving of the Buy American Acts under certain conditions, a three-year extension of the Reciprocal Trade Agreements Act and 'a gradual and controlled approach to currency convertibility'. Three prominent Republican members of the commission dissented either from the whole of the report or from nearly all parts of it and the proposals were shelved in July 1954.

5 For the record of the Washington discussions see PRO T 230/252.

6 The reference is to NIF(WP)(54)2 in PRO CAB 134/1060.

7 Whatever the figures available at the time, GDP in 1953 increased by 4 per cent. This was appreciably *above* trend and compares with an increase in employment of 0.6 per cent (on a mid-year comparison). There was very little reduction in unemployment.

8 For the Budget discussions in 1954, see PRO T 171/449.

9 The Civil Economies Committee under Lord Swinton had recommended in July economies totalling about £100 million of which two-thirds represented cuts in agricultural and food subsidies (C(54)232 in PRO CAB 129/70).

10 The Air Ministry had compulsorily purchased 725 acres (forming part of three separate farms) at Crichel Down in Wiltshire as a bombing range in 1940 and this had been transferred to the Ministry of Agriculture in 1950. It was subsequently equipped at high cost as a single farm and let by the Land Commission. The commission did not pursue offers to buy the land unequipped and was criticized in an official report as 'infatuated with the idea of creating a new model farm'. The Minister of Agriculture resigned and some of his officials were moved to other jobs.

11 These figures are much too low if they are in current prices and relate to a twelve months' period. The increase in GDP at 1954 prices was put in

1959 at £729 million, and in exports of goods and services at £250 million. Stockbuilding was probably about £50 million.

12 Hall was in Washington in September 1949 for the pre-devaluation talks with the USA and Canada and had been there for over a week before Wilson Smith arrived for the Bank/Fund meeting.

13 The papers are presumably in PRO T 230/253 (which has not been released).

14 The Economic Section's views on 'trade rules' are in PRO T 230/270.

15 Bolton later claimed that financial markets expected convertibility in September 1954.

16 The Economic Section made several estimates in 1954–5 of the balance of payments effects of removing dollar discrimination: one by Maurice Scott in April 1954 (in PRO T 230/342), a second by Christopher Dow in May 1954 (in PRO 230/281) and a third, in March 1955, by Alan Day and J. S. Sadler (in PRO T 230/28). The last of these drew on the work of no less than four committees which had been at work since the summer of 1954, and put the balance of payments effect of the removal of discrimination by the United Kingdom alone at £300 million.

17 Under exchange control regulations, tourists making journeys abroad could purchase only a limited amount of foreign exchange annually as 'travel allowance'. The limit had been as low as £25.

18 The Chancellor subsequently argued successfully for less subsidized housebuilding and more investment in roads, schools, etc., in C(54)344, 12 November 1954.

19 Ian Little's paper is presumably in T 230/356 ('Increase in coal prices 1954–58') which has not been released.

20 Hall's Sidney Ball Lecture on 'The place of the economist in government' appeared in *Oxford Economic Papers* in June 1955.

21 A reference to the Mau Mau rebellion in Kenya and the prolonged insurgency in Malaya.

22 At the Conservative Party Conference in October 1954 Butler could 'see no reason why, in the next quarter of a century, if we run our policy properly and soundly, we should not double our standard of living in this country'. The Economic Section's 'Long-term survey' is in PRO T 230/284–5.

23 I have not succeeded in finding the papers of this group nor of Burke Trend's working party on the power-station programme.

24 The first Magnox power station (at Calder Hall) opened in 1956; the Dounreay experimental plant was a fast breeder station.

25 The Report of the Court of Inquiry (Cmd 9352) included the following passage: 'The Nation has provided by statute that there should be a nationalized system of railway transport, which must therefore be regarded as a public utility of the first importance. Having willed the end, the Nation must will the means.' This implied that in the wage negotiations to follow, the railways should adopt an accommodating stance irrespective of the way in which labour agreed to be deployed.

26 Thus the forecast in March 1954 of a deficit of £380 million 'above the line' in the 1955–6 Budget had become one of 'a good-sized' surplus a year later without much change in taxation or in government spending plans.

27 As explained above, the previous forecast for 1955 was of a surplus of £155 million; this had now been revised to show a deficit of £70 million.

28 These views were repeated in minutes to Bridges on 10 and 18 February 1955 in PRO T 273/317.

29 For the arguments adduced and references to the official papers, see Cairncross, A., and Watts, N., *The Economic Section* (London: Routledge, 1989), pp. 310–17.

30 It took four Cabinet meetings in February and March to reach agreement that an increase in coal prices should be left to the National Coal Board and should not be such as to involve a conspicuous surplus that 'might sharpen claims for wage increases' (CM(55)22, 9 March 1955).

31 Indian exports of cotton textiles to the United Kingdom increased from 20 million yards in 1953 to 125 million yards in 1954 while Indian imports from the United Kingdom fell from 6 million yards to just over 3 million yards. Purchase tax on textiles was reduced in the April Budget and removed in May. India had raised tariffs on textile imports in 1953 but agreed to a reduction in 1954.

32 This group seems to have been a forerunner of Working Party No. 3, although differently constituted. It may have had the same membership as the group of seven economists referred to in the entry for October 4th 1953 which was asked to make a study of the economic situation for the Fifth Report of the OEEC.

33 Rowan's paper, 'External economic policy', 27 May 1955, is in PRO T 273/317.

34 The latest official estimates show a deficit on current account in each quarter of 1955. If there was a surplus in the second half of 1954 it must have been very small.

35 The views expressed here proved too optimistic. The credit squeeze had at first little effect on bank advances and even when the level of advances fell, the boom continued. Stockbuilding was higher in 1955 than in any previous postwar year except 1951.

36 Kaldor was a member of the Royal Commission on the Taxation of Profits and Income.

37 Hall to Bridges and Chancellor, 28 July 1955, in PRO T 230/384.

38 Hall to Bridges, 26 July 1955, in PRO T 236/3942.

39 The Cabinet, in its discussions on commercial policy in the autumn of 1955, was concerned mainly with amendments to the GATT, the admission to GATT of Japan and the difficulty of protecting British industry against Japanese competition because of Commonwealth free entry and the 'no new preference' rules. The papers referred to by Hall were taken by the Economic Policy Committee in October 1955.

40 The Budget introduced on 26 October increased purchase tax and profits tax by amounts estimated to add £113 million to revenue in a full year. This compares with cuts in the April Budget equivalent to £155 million in a full year.

41 The White Paper, *The Economic Implications of Full Employment*, CP(55)173, was discussed by the Cabinet on 22 November 1955 and was to have been published on 8 December but the Chancellor had second thoughts and asked on 1 December for some delay. It was ultimately published in March 1956 (Cmd 9725).

42 The Anglo-American Loan Agreement of 1946 (Cmd 6708) provided for a waiver of interest under certain conditions which were hard to interpret. The United Kingdom was never able to take advantage of the waiver and had sought without success to have the relevant clause amended.

II *Macmillan's Chancellorship, 20 December 1955 to 9 January 1957*

1 Two papers on 'The economic situation' were circulated by the Chancellor to the Cabinet: the first, C(56)7 on the economic situation on 6 January, and the second, C(56)17 outlining the economies to be made in government expenditure on 21 January. The first paper was presumably drafted by Hall, the second by Bridges. The economies proposed in C(56)17 were mainly on capital expenditure and were considered item by item by the Cabinet. A further paper, C(56)32 on 9 February, reviewed the state of play.
2 The reports of the Treasury Investment Committee are filed with the Budget Committee papers in PRO T 171. The report for 1955, TIC(55)12, is in PRO T 171/469.
3 The economies were announced in the House of Commons on 17 February 1956.
4 The papers on the suggested capital gains tax are with the Budget Committee papers in PRO T 171/469.
5 Apart from the increase in Bank Rate from 4 1/2 per cent to 5 1/2 per cent, hire purchase restrictions were tightened and public investment programmes cut. Initial allowances were restored in place of investment allowances which were suspended. These measures added up to substantially more restraint than was exercised by the Budget in April.
6 I have been unable to trace this paper.
7 The working party, at which Hall hints in his entry for April 5th, reported in June (entry for June 21st). It came down against a prescribed liquidity ratio except in emergency and also against an advances ratio, laying emphasis on business sentiment as a factor to be ranked alongside changes in interest rates and the stock of money. The papers of the committee are in PRO T 230/472 (and in C40/69 in the Bank archives).
8 The exchange of correspondence is in C40/69 in the Bank archives.
9 In the Budget speech on 17 April the Chancellor had referred to the lateness and inadequacy of economic statistics, comparing them to 'last year's Bradshaw'. He made a further statement on 1 August. The Economic Section had been pressing for quarterly national income estimates and these finally became available in 1957. The Economic Section's file on 'Improvements in the supply and presentation of financial and economic statistics', covering the period from February 1956, is in PRO T 230/364.
10 'The Egypt crisis and the British economy', EC(56)38 in PRO CAB 134/1217, 27 August 1956.
11 The position on the Suez dispute was that, after the nationalization of the canal on 26 July and a tripartite declaration by the USA, the UK and France on 29 July, a conference of twenty-two nations met in London between 16 and 23 August. A majority of eighteen supported a plan put forward by Dulles (with amendments by four other countries – Pakistan, Persia, Turkey and Ethiopia) for some form of international control of the canal. On 28 August, Nasser agreed to meet representatives of the five powers but discussions on 8–9 September ended in deadlock. The USA, the UK and France then agreed to form a canal-users' association, which was the subject of a second London conference on 19–21 September, although Nasser had already vetoed the proposal. The matter was referred to the Security Council on 23 September but on 29 September the Israeli army attacked Egypt and the UK and France issued an ultimatum the following day.

12 Devons, E., 'The wage–price spiral', *District Bank Review*, September 1956; also included in Devons, E., *Essays in Economics* (London: Allen & Unwin, 1961).

13 An interim report on Plan G (the proposed Free Trade Area) had gone to the Cabinet on 17 July 1956 as an attachment to C(56)191 and the Economic Policy Committee had discussed the plan on 1 August. A supplementary report by officials ('Future commercial policy: UK initiative in Europe: Plan G', EA(56)70), was circulated on 31 August and was taken by the Economic Policy Committee (*not* the Steering Committee) on Monday 3 September along with a note by Gilbert, Chairman of the Steering Committee, entitled 'Future commercial policy: Plan G' (EA(56)79).

14 The Treasury inherited from wartime a portfolio of American securities which had at one time been pledged as cover for a dollar loan from the Reconstruction Finance Corporation.

15 In June 1956 the Texas Co. ('Texaco') offered £62.3 million (in dollars) for the Trinidad Oil Co. which did all its refining in Trinidad and supplied about 6 per cent of the entire British market in oil products. The bid created much controversy, nationalist in character, but was given government agreement.

16 The article was finally published in *Lloyds Bank Review*, April 1957, as 'The economist in Whitehall'.

17 This formula was what was later christened 'the guiding light'. Discussions on wage policy were taking place in the official Prices and Costs Committee which met under Bridges. Some of the papers of the committee are in PRO T 230/312.

18 'The economic situation', note by the Chancellor of the Exchequer, covering note by the Economic Adviser to HMG, 29 November 1956 (EA(56)92 in PRO CAB 134/1231).

19 The Budget Committee (BC(56)10M) recommended an increase in the petrol duty by a shilling (5p) a gallon and a rise in income tax from April 1957 so as to offset the expected worsening of the balance of payments (estimated at £200 million) if the Suez Canal were closed. Only the first recommendation was accepted and it was justified publicly, not on financial grounds, but as a temporary measure to conserve supplies of oil. In fact the effects of the Suez crisis on the economy turned out to be very small.

20 The Chancellor had appealed in May (see entry for May 15th) for what he described as a 'price plateau'. He invited employers to commit themselves to holding prices steady for a period in the hope that this would lead to corresponding stability in wages. Retail prices held steady between the second and fourth quarters of 1956 but other items, making up about half of consumer spending, continued to rise in price while wages and salaries also rose but at a relatively slow rate until the spring of 1957.

III *Thorneycroft's Chancellorship, 9 January 1957 to 6 January 1958*

1 The Governor's letter is in the Budget Committee Papers for 1957, PRO T 171/478. The paper by Macmillan on 'The state of the economy' (CP(57)4, 3 January 1957) was taken by Cabinet on 8 January, the day before he became Prime Minister. Eden, in his last paper to the Cabinet (CP(57)8, 7 January 1957), took exception to the opening sentence: 'The Suez operation has been a tactical defeat.'

2 No cuts of any size were made in investment.
3 There was a monthly meeting in Basle of the BIS at which central bankers met to discuss developments.
4 The six countries which had attended the Messina Conference in 1956 were about to sign the Treaty of Rome on 25 March 1957 and bring into being the European Economic Community. British ministers, while unwilling to join the Community, hoped to negotiate a free trade area (first mentioned as Plan G in the entry for August 30th 1956) that would include all the European members of OEEC but exclude agriculture.
5 These remarks were prompted by the submission of a paper on 'Statistics for economic policy' (EA(57)6) to the Economic Policy Committee on 31 January. The Steering Committee, which submitted the paper, had been much occupied with economic statistics throughout 1956.
6 Briggs Bodies were suppliers to the motor industry of sheet-metal components.
7 'The sterling area', EA(57)12, 4 February 1957, in PRO CAB 134/1231. The Economic Secretary showed a particular interest in sterling and submitted a note (EA(57)20) on 1 March and a memorandum on the capital account (EA(57)47) on 17 May.
8 The request to the banks to limit advances had been in force for nearly two years and they were increasingly reluctant to co-operate in dealing with inflation by a method that denied them the power to compete for business, especially when publicly financed expenditure kept increasing. For the Governor's representations see PRO T 233/1369.
9 Archbishop Makarios, Primate of Cyprus, had been removed in March 1956 to the Seychelles in the hope that this would help to establish more settled conditions in Cyprus.
10 A reference to the October Budget which increased purchase tax on pots and pans and other items and to the increase in the duty on petrol at the height of the Suez crisis.
11 The Treasury Investment Committee issued a report (TIC(57)5) on 8 March covering the period up to 1958–9. It then embarked on a long-term review which was not completed until February 1958 (TIC(58)9 in PRO T 234/88; see also PRO T 230/338).
12 'Wages, prices and the pound sterling', memorandum by the Chancellor of the Exchequer, 27 April 1957, C(57)103.
13 The minutes of the Makins Committee for 1957 are in PRO T 233/1404. The memoranda and drafts are scattered through PRO T 233/1404–14 and 1684–98.
14 A surplus on current account at an annual rate of about £400 million was forecast for the second half of 1957 and the first half of 1958. The latest official estimate puts the recorded surplus at £350 million, the highest total in the 1950s.
15 'Monetary policy and the control of economic conditions' in *Memoranda of Evidence to the Radcliffe Committee*, Vol. 1, pp. 92–9.
16 'Inflation', memorandum by the Chancellor of the Exchequer, 17 July 1957, C(57)168.
17 After a meeting with the Chancellor on 7 August Hall wrote a minute ('Deflationary measures') outlining the Chancellor's instructions (PRO T 233/1369) and a further minute to Makins on 9 August (PRO T 230/408). His 'longish minute' to Makins ('Further deflationary measures', 16 August 1957) is in PRO T 233/1369 ('The government's deflationary measures 1957').

18 Officials reported on 'Further deflationary measures' on 20 August (PRO T 233/1369) in response to the instructions given on 7 August and this was presumably the starting-point of the meeting on 23 August. The draft Cabinet paper referred to later in this entry and in the entry for August 28th was no doubt revised by the Chancellor before circulation as 'The economic situation' (C(57)195) on 7 September 1957.

19 The Working Group on credit control, with the Economic Secretary in the chair, considered papers by Robert Hall (18 September), Jack Downie (28 September) and Lionel Robbins (25 September) and a note by the Bank of England on 'The liquidity ratio and the floating debt'. It reported on 7 October (PRO T 230/337).

20 Hall regarded Q 1613, put to him on 24 October, as the heart of the matter and as justification in itself for holding the inquiry. Professor Sayers asked whether the choice between holding money and holding securities when the rate of interest is 50 per cent is identical with the choice when the rate is 2 1/2 per cent.

21 Nationalized industries, instead of borrowing in the market, were required to change over to borrowing through the Public Works Loan Board, in the middle of the credit squeeze of 1955–6.

22 'Debt management', *Radcliffe Memoranda*, Vol. 1, pp. 108–9.

23 A tribunal under Mr Justice Parker was appointed to investigate allegations of a leak before the rise in Bank Rate on 19 September. It heard extensive evidence, much of it sensationalized by the press, on what occurred in September, but no real evidence of a leak. The hearings provided the public with an unusually revealing picture of the practices and personalities of the City. The proceedings and minutes of evidence were published in January 1958 by the Home Office (see entry for January 30th).

24 'Some possible modifications in technique', *Radcliffe Memoranda*, Vol. I, pp. 38–42.

25 The letter organized by Sir Donald MacDougall carried the signatures of twelve distinguished economists of different political persuasions in the universities of Cambridge and Oxford and appeared in *The Times* on 29 October 1957. It dealt with the consequences of the fall in commodity prices then in progress.

26 The Public Works Loan Board raised funds on the central government's credit and was empowered to on-lend to local authorities and nationalized industries. This complicated the efforts of the Bank of England to fund more of the government's debt and gave rise to proposals that the local authorities should go directly to the market, as the nationalized industries had formerly done.

IV *Heathcoat Amory's first year, 6 January 1958 to 31 December 1958*

1 The problem of international liquidity (i.e. adequate reserves of convertible currency to allow the international monetary system as a whole to function satisfactorily) had been under discussion in the Economic Section over the winter of 1957–8 and was the subject of minutes by Downie and others (PRO T 230/398, 'External economic policy'). See also note 4 to Section VI, below.

2 This probably refers to BC(57)26 of 18 December ('The economic outlook: a preliminary appraisal') and BC(58)15 of 24 February ('Economic outlook

for 1958') which recommended a standstill Budget and a review of the position in June. By the end of March, while still counselling caution, Hall had begun to modify his position in 'Preparations for reflation' (BC(58)21, 31 March 1958).

3 Hall's draft on 'Flexible rates' was one of several documents annexed to a memorandum by Rowan on 'Exchange rate policy' which was submitted to Makins and the Chancellor on 2 April 1958. The other annexes included one by the Bank and one on discrimination. Makins, who had been rather in favour of floating, was converted (PRO T 230/373, 'The future of sterling').

4 The papers considered by the Steering Committee (ES(58)18 and 20, 27 and 28 March, in PRO CAB 134/1837) dealt with export credit and export credit insurance, but also referred to special loans and guarantees.

5 A Cabinet Committee on Wages Policy had been set up in March and the Chancellor submitted a short memorandum on wages policy (WP(58)5) on 20 May which may have been drafted by Hall.

6 'Imports of butter', ES(58)23, 1 May 1958, in PRO CAB 134/1837; also annexed to C(58)95, 3 May 1958.

7 A subcommittee of the Steering Committee prepared the ground for the Montreal Conference. Its papers are in PRO CAB 134/1841–4. Another subcommittee, appointed in July 1958, dealt with UK external investment (PRO CAB 134/1905).

8 T. L. Rowan, 'Convertibility and other matters', in PRO T 230/373. Hall did a note on 15 August with the same title suggesting that nothing should be done until after the Bank/Fund meeting in Delhi and that if it was decided to introduce convertibility it should be done quickly.

9 Hall to Makins, 9 September 1958, in T 230/386.

10 Hall was right in detecting a change in June to a much less steep climb in unemployment. The seasonally adjusted total reached a peak in November and the unadjusted figure peaked in January 1959 when the number on the register reached 621,000 (2.8 per cent).

11 The current account surplus in the first half of 1958 is now put at £218 million.

12 The Chancellor had already circulated one paper on wages policy (WP(58)12 in PRO CAB 134/2572) to the Wages Policy Committee in July and circulated another (WP(58)17), presumably drafted by Hall, on 6 November, which discussed the basis of current policy at some length.

13 'British Transport Commission', memorandum by the Minister of Transport and Civil Aviation, C(58)202, and 'Fuel and steel: effect of the recession', memorandum by the Minister of Power, 1 October 1958, C(58)203.

14 The European Monetary Agreement of 29 July 1955 left it to the United Kingdom to take the initiative in terminating the European Payments Union and establishing convertibility. By September 1958 the Chancellor judged that a move would be possible within the next six months and informed the Americans, the West Germans and the IMF. Official preparations were begun but there were hesitations in October (when the Cabinet insisted on 'the willing acquiescence of the French') and in November (when the West Germans argued for postponement until after the French elections). The Free Trade Area negotiations, which were suspended in November after French opposition, were a further complication and so, too, was uncertainty whether the French would devalue the franc in advance of convertibility. It was not until the French Finance Minister, Pinay, told the Chancellor at a NATO dinner that the

franc would be devalued, and encouraged him to move immediately after Christmas, that a final decision was taken. Continental members of the OEEC, other than France and West Germany, would have preferred to delay convertibility and continue the EPU for a further six months or more as a symbol of intra-European co-operation. For the full story see Kaplan, J. J., and Schleiminger, G., *The European Payments Union* (Oxford: Oxford University Press, 1989), ch. 17.

V *Reflation under Heathcoat Amory, 1 January 1959 to 27 July 1960*

1 The Budget papers for 1959 are in PRO T 171/4.

2 The (Ministerial) Employment Committee (see entry for November 20th 1958) met in 1958–9 under the chairmanship of the Prime Minister. The papers are in PRO CAB 134/1734–5.

3 Uniscan would have involved some form of economic integration with the Scandinavian countries, which showed no inclination to join the EEC. After the breakdown of the negotiations for a European Free Trade Area, the Swedes suggested that a group of European non-members of the Community might form a free trade area of their own and by 1960 a new EFTA had been established, including Portugal and Switzerland as well as the four Scandinavian countries and the United Kingdom (see entry for May 7th).

4 The Whitehall Dining Group, as it was later called, was a small private group of civil servants and business men (at first, business men who had served in government as temporary civil servants). The group, considerably enlarged, continues to dine together several times a year.

5 It was as a result of this initiative that *The Problem of Rising Prices* was produced by OECD in 1961.

6 Later figures show a rise in employment in the first half of 1959 by 200,000 and a fall in unemployment of 100,000 – much as one would expect.

7 The balance of payments on current account was in fact deteriorating steadily throughout the recovery, falling from a surplus of about £350 million in 1958 to a deficit of £230 million in 1960.

8 The reference is to Sir Donald MacDougall's *The World Dollar Problem* (1957) and to Geoffrey Crowther's *Balances and Imbalances of Payments* (1957) (Boston, Mass, Harvard School of Business Administration).

9 Under Article VIII of the Articles of Agreement of the IMF, members were required to refrain from imposing restrictions on payments and transfers for current international transactions without the Fund's approval. The only exceptions to this were the scarce currency clause (Article VII) and Article XIV which dealt with restrictions during a transitional period expected to last five years. But after ten years (i.e. in 1957) only ten countries, all of them in the Western hemisphere, had accepted the convertibility obligations of Article XIV. The IMF was naturally anxious to see countries whose currencies were already convertible move as soon as possible to the long overdue acceptance of their obligations under Article VIII.

10 The Chancellor's paper on public investment 1958–63 (C(59)131) was taken by Cabinet on 19 July 1959 (CC(59)47).

11 The report of the Plowden Committee was issued in 1961 as *The Control of Public Expenditure* (Cmnd 1432).

12 The Diaries were written in thick notebooks each of about 280 pages and a new notebook was started whenever one was filled up.

13 Resale price maintenance was ultimately abolished in 1964 on the initiative of Edward Heath, President of the Board of Trade.

14 A 'Western summit' meeting between President de Gaulle, President Eisenhower, Mr Macmillan and Dr Adenauer opened in Paris on 19 December 1959 and continued at Rambouillet on 20 and 21 December. A letter was sent to Mr Khrushchev inviting him to a 'summit' conference between East and West on 27 April 1960; and an 'informal' economic conference in Paris was proposed to discuss problems of trade relations and aid to underdeveloped countries. After further consultations the date for the 'summit' meeting was changed to 16 May and the invitation was accepted by Mr Khrushchev. Although Khrushchev came to Paris for the meeting, the U2 incident at the beginning of May led to its abortion.

15 Between the first quarter of 1958 and the last quarter of 1959 the national income had risen by 5 percentage points when measured from output data and by only 3.6 percentage points when measured from expenditure data.

16 The new body was the OEEC transformed by the entry of the United States and Canada into the OECD and the new committee was the Development Assistance Group (DAG).

17 'Kahn's group' of economists produced in 1961 the well-known OECD report, *The Problem of Rising Prices*. The members were William Fellner, Milton Gilbert, Bent Hansen, Richard Kahn, Friedrich Lutz and Pieter de Wolff. The reference to 'Funelman' should presumably be to Lutz.

18 The Development Assistance Group, of which Hall was a member, was set up as a result of the January meeting (entry for March 11th).

19 The Guillebaud Committee on Railway Pay was appointed in the spring of 1959 and reported at the beginning of March 1960. Meanwhile in February the government had promised a 5 per cent increase in pay 'on account' in an effort to buy off a railway strike. The committee concentrated on comparisons with pay in jobs thought to be comparable and concluded that there was a gap of about 10 per cent. They suggested that clerical and salaried workers should be given a rise of that order and the 'conciliation' grades one of 8 per cent.

20 For Article VIII see note 9 above.

VI *Selwyn Lloyd's first year, 27 July 1960 to 21 April 1961*

1 In October 1960 Lord Cromer was Economic Minister (with the rank of Ambassador) at the British Embassy in Washington. Before the month was out he had been offered the Governorship of the Bank of England.

2 The Secretary of the Treasury appointed by Kennedy after he won the election in November was Douglas Dillon, a Republican.

3 Balance of payments estimates are liable to revision long after the event. The revisions in 1960 were mainly to the estimates for net earnings from invisibles which were reduced for the mid-1950s by over one-third (the average reduction for the years 1954–7 was £125 million). For 1960 the current deficit was revised upwards from £150/£175 million to £344 million. By the 1980s this had come down to £228 million.

4 Robert Triffin was Professor of Economics at Yale University and had played a prominent part in the formation of the European Payments Union. In *Gold and the Dollar Crisis: The Future of Convertibility* (New

Haven, Yale University Press, 1960) he pointed to the danger of relying year after year on a persistent weakening in the net reserve position of the United States for a contribution to the growth of world liquidity. For nine years the United States had been in deficit by this measure, either adding to its dollar liabilities or suffering a continuing gold drain. As the dollar deficit was corrected, the world liquidity problem would reappear or be aggravated. Triffin did not, however, argue for a rise in the price of gold; and the increase in quotas in the Fund by 50 per cent made the warning of an impending shortage of international liquidity rather unconvincing.

5 These groups took the form of Working Parties 2, 3 and 4, of which Working Party 2 dealt with economic growth, Working Party 3 mainly with what might be called the conjuncture and Working Party 4 with the labour market.

Appendix 1: Summary of monetary measures, 1954–60

		Bank Rate (per cent)	*Control of bank advances*	*Hire purchase restrictions*
1954	13 May	3		
	3 July			Restrictions removed
1955	27 January	3 1/2		
	24 February	4 1/2		Restrictions reintroduced
	19 April		Budget assumes credit squeeze	
	26 July		'Positive reduction' requested	Restrictions tightened
1956	16 February	5 1/2		Restrictions again tightened
1957	7 February	5	Quantitative limitation	
	19 September	7		
1958	20 March	6		
	22 May	5 1/2		
	19 June	5		
	3 July		Control removed	
	14 August	4 1/2		
	15 September			Restrictions relaxed
	28 October			Restrictions removed
	20 November	4		
1959				
1960	21 January	5		
	28 April		First call for Special Deposits	Restrictions reintroduced
	23 June	6	Second call for Special Deposits	
	27 October	5 1/2		
	8 December	5		

Appendix 2: Main characters referred to

Allen, W. M. (Maurice) 1908–88 Fellow of Balliol College, Oxford 1931–48; Ass. Dir. of Research, IMF 1947–9; Adviser, Bank of England 1950–64; Exec. Director 1964–70.

Alsop, Joseph 1910–89 American political commentator and author; author (with brother Stewart Alsop) of column *Matter of Fact* (NY Herald Tribune Syndicate) 1948–58; sole author (Los Angeles Times Syndicate) 1958–74.

Anderson, Robert Bernard 1910–89 American lawyer; Asst. Attorney Gen., Texas 1932; Sec. of US Navy 1953–4; Dep. Sec. of Defense 1954–5; Sec. of US Treasury 1957–67.

Armstrong, William (later Lord) 1915–80 Private Sec. to Sec. of War Cabinet 1943–6; PPS to successive Chancellors of the Exchequer 1949–53; Under Sec. OF Division, Treasury 1953–7; Third Sec. 1958–62; Jt Perm. Sec. 1962–8; Head of Home Civil Service 1968–74; Chairman, Midland Bank 1975–80.

Birch, Nigel (later Lord Rhyl) 1906–81 Parly Under Sec. of State, Air Ministry 1951–2; Parly Sec. Min. of Defence 1952–4; Min. of Works Oct.–Dec. 1955; Sec. of State for Air 1955–7; Ec. Sec. to the Treasury 1957–8.

Bissell, Richard 1909– Assoc. Prof., later Prof. of Economics, MIT 1942–52; Asst. Administr., ECA 1948–51; Acting Administr. Sept.–Dec. 1951; Spec. Assist to Director, CIA 1954–9, Dep. Director Plans 1959–62; business consultant 1974– .

Bolton, George (later Sir) 1900–82 UK Exec. Director (1945–52) and alternate Governor (1952–67), IMF; Director of Bank of England 1948–68; Chairman, Bank of London and South America 1957–70.

Boyle, Sir Edward (later Lord) 1923–81 President, Oxford Union Soc. 1948; Parly Sec., Ministry of Supply 1954–5; Econom. Sec. to Treasury 1955–6; Parly Sec., Ministry of Education 1957–9; Fin. Sec. to Treasury 1959–62; Minister of Education 1962–4; Minister of State, Dept of Education and Science 1964; Vice-Chancellor, Univ. of Leeds 1970–81.

Bridges, Sir Edward (later Lord) 1892–1969 Secretary to the Cabinet 1938–46; Perm. Sec. UK Treasury 1945–56.

Brittain, Sir Herbert 1894–1961 Entered Treasury 1919; Treasury Officer of Accounts 1937; Under Sec. and Head of HF 1942–6; Third Sec. 1946–53; Second Sec. 1953–7.

Brook, Sir Norman (later Lord) 1902–67 Additional Sec. of Cabinet 1945–7; Secretary 1947–62; Jt Perm. Sec., Treasury and Head of Civil Service 1956–62.

Burgess, W. R. 1889–1978 Chmn, Exec. Cttee Nat. City Bank of NY 1948–52;

Deputy to Sec. to US Treasury 1953–4; Under Secretary of Treasury 1957; perm. US repres. on NATO from 1957.

Burns, Arthur F. 1904–87 Prof. of Economics, Columbia Univ. 1944–69; Dir. of Research, Nat. Bureau of Economic Research 1945–53; Pres. 1957–67; Chmn, Council of Economic Advisers 1953–6; Chmn, Bd of Governors, Fed. Reserve System 1970–8.

Butler, R. A. (later Lord) 1902–82 Under Sec. of State for Foreign Affairs 1938–41; Minister of Education 1941–5; Minister of Labour June–July 1945; Chancellor of the Exchequer 1951–5; Lord Privy Seal 1955–9; Home Secretary 1957–62; Deputy Prime Minister July 1962–October 1963; Sec. of State for Foreign Affairs 1963–4; Master of Trinity College, Cambridge 1965–8.

Clarke, R. W. B. ('Otto') (later Sir Richard) 1910–75 Financial journalist in 1930s; war service with Ministry of Production; Ass. Sec. HM Treasury 1945; Under Sec. 1947; Third Sec. 1955; Second Sec. 1962; Perm. Sec., Ministry of Technology 1966–70.

Cobbold, Cameron F. ('Cob') (later Lord) 1904–87 Exec. Director, Bank of England 1938; Deputy Governor 1945; Governor 1949–61.

Compton, Edmund (later Sir) 1906– Entered Treasury 1931; Under Sec. 1947; Third Sec. 1949–58; Comptroller and Auditor-General, Exchequer and Audit Dept 1958–66.

Cromer, Lord 1918– Man. Dir. Baring Brothers & Co. 1948–61, 1967–70; Head of Treasury and Supply Delegation and Economic Minister, Washington 1959–61: Governor, Bank of England 1961–6; Ambassador to United States 1971–4.

Crosland, Anthony 1918–77 Fellow of Trinity College, Oxford 1947–50; held various offices in Labour Government 1964–70; Sec. of State for Environment 1974–6.

Dillon, C. Douglas 1909– Chmn, Dillon Read & Co. 1946–53; US Ambassador to France 1953–7; Under Sec. of State for Economic Affairs 1957–9; Under Sec. of State 1959–61; Sec. of US Treasury 1961–5.

Dulles, John Foster 1888-1959 Member, Reparations Commission, Supreme Econ. Council, Paris 1919; Asst. Sec. of State at meetings of Council of Foreign Ministers 1945–9; negotiated and signed US–Japanese Peace Treaty; US Sec. of State, Jan. 1955–April 1959.

Emminger, Otmar 1911–86 Mem. Bd of Governors, Deutsche Bundesbank 1953–69; Dep. Gov. 1970–7; Governor 1977–9; Ex. Dir., IMF 1953–9; Dep. Chmn, Monetary Cttee EEC 1958–77; Chmn, Monetary Cttee of OECD 1969–77.

France, Arnold (later Sir) 1911– Entered Treasury 1945 after military service; Assistant Sec. 1948; Under Sec. 1952; Third Sec. 1960; Chairman, Board of Inland Revenue 1968–73.

Franks, Sir Oliver (later Lord) 1905– Fellow of Queen's College, Oxford 1927–37 and Provost 1946–8; Ministry of Supply 1939–45 (Perm. Sec. 1945–6); UK Ambassador to USA 1948–52; Chairman, Lloyds Bank 1954–62; Provost of Worcester College, Oxford 1962–76.

Gaitskell, Hugh 1906–63 Reader in Political Economy, University of London 1938; Minister of Fuel and Power 1947–50; Chancellor of the Exchequer 1950–1; Leader of the Labour Party 1955–63.

Gilbert, Sir Bernard 1891–1957 Entered Treasury 1914; Jt Second Sec. 1944–56.

Hall, Robert (later Lord) 1901–88 Fellow of Trinity College, Oxford 1927–50; Ministry of Supply 1939–46; Director, Econ. Section of Cabinet Office 1947–53; Economic Adviser to HM Govt 1953–61.

Hall-Patch, Sir Edmund 1896–1975 Ass. Under Sec. of State, Foreign Office 1944; Deputy Under Sec. 1946–8; Chairman, Exec. Cttee of OEEC 1948; UK Exec. Director of IMF and IBRD 1952–4.

Harcourt, Viscount 1908–79 Man. Dir. Morgan Grenfell & Co. 1931–68, Chmn 1968–73; Chmn, Legal & General Ass. Soc. 1958–77; Economic Minister and Head of UK TSD 1954–7; mem. of Radcliffe Cttee 1957–9.

Hauge, Gabriel 1914–84 Admin. asst to US President for econ. affairs, 1953–6; special asst to President for econ. affairs 1956–8; later, Chmn of Manufacturers Hanover Trust Co.

Heathcoat Amory, Derick (later Lord Amory) 1899–1981 Min. of Pensions 1951–3; Min. of State, Bd of Trade 1953–4; Min. of Agriculture and Fisheries 1954; and Food 1954–8; Chancellor of the Exchequer 1958–60; UK High Commissioner in Canada 1961–3.

Hitchman, E. A. (later Sir Alan) 1903–80 Under Sec. HM Treasury 1947; Deputy to Chief Planning Officer 1948–9; Third Sec. 1949–51; Perm. Sec., Ministry of Materials 1951–2.

Humphrey, George Magottin 1890–1970 President, the M. A. Hanna Co. 1929–52; Sec., US Treasury 1952–7; dir. of US coal and steel companies from 1957.

Jacobsson, Per 1894–1963 Mem. Econ. and Fin. Section, Secretariat of League of Nations 1920–8; Economic Adviser, Bank for International Settlements, Basle 1931–56; Managing Director, IMF 1956–63.

Lee, F. G. (later Sir Frank) 1903–71 Colonial Office 1926–40; HM Treasury 1940–4; Treasury Delegate to Washington 1944–6; Ministry of Supply 1946–8 (Dep. Sec. 1947–8); Minister at Washington 1948; Perm. Sec., Board of Trade 1951–9; Ministry of Food 1959–61; HM Treasury 1960–2; Master of Corpus Christi College, Cambridge 1962–71.

Leslie, S. C. (Clem) 1898–1980 Rhodes Scholar; Senior Lecturer in Philosophy, Melbourne University 1924–5; Publicity Manager, Gas, Light & Coke Co. 1936–40; Director, Council of Industrial Design 1945–7; Head of Treasury Information Division 1947–59.

Lippmann, Walter 1889–1974 American political commentator, editor and author; in 1920s assoc. ed. of *New Republic* and ed. *New York World*; later, special writer for *NY Herald Tribune* and other newspapers; Pulitzer prize special citation 1957.

Lloyd, John Selwyn (later Lord) 1904–78 President, Cambridge Union 1927; Min. of State, Foreign Office 1951–4; Min. of Supply 1954–5; Min. of Defence 1955; Foreign Secretary 1955–60; Chancellor of the Exchequer 1960–2; Lord Privy Seal 1963–4; Speaker of the House of Commons 1971–6.

Macmillan, Harold (later Sir, then Earl Stockton) 1894–1986 Minister of Housing and Local Government 1951–4; Minister of Defence 1954–5; Foreign Secretary 1955; Chancellor of the Exchequer 1955–7; Prime Minister 1957–63.

Makins, Roger (later Lord Sherfield) 1904– Foreign Office 1928–56; Asst Under Sec. of State 1947–8; Dep. Under Sec. of State 1948–52; British Ambassador to the USA 1953–6; Jt Perm. Sec. of the Treasury 1956–9; Chmn, UK AEA 1960–4.

Marget, Arthur 1899–1962 Univ. teacher of economics 1923–48; prof., Univ. of Michigan 1930–43; Chief Finance Dir., Office of Spec. Rep., ECA 1948–9; dir., division of international finance, Fed. Reserve Board, from 1950.

Marjolin, Robert 1911–86 Head of French Supply Mission in USA 1944; Director, Foreign Economic Relations, Ministry of National Economy,

Paris 1945; Joint Commissioner-General, Monnet Plan 1946–8; Sec.-Gen. OEEC 1948–55; Prof. of Economics, Nancy, 1955–8; Vice-Pres., EEC Commission 1958–67.

Martin, William McChesney 1906– Chairman and President, Export-Import Bank 1946–9; Ass. Sec., US Treasury 1949–51; Chairman, Board of Governors, Federal Reserve Board 1951–70.

Maudling, Reginald 1917–79 Called to the Bar 1940; Conservative MP 1950–74; Ec. Sec. to the Treasury, Nov. 1952–April 1955; Ministry of Supply 1955–7; Paymaster-General 1957–9; President of Board of Trade 1959–61; Chancellor of the Exchequer 1962–64; Home Secretary 1970–2.

Moffat, Abbot 1901–? Staff of US Dept of State 1943–8; staff of ECA, MSA, FOA 1948–53; staff of World Bank 1954–61.

Mynors, Humphrey (later Sir) 1903–89 Bank of England 1933–64; Deputy Governor 1954–64.

Nitze, Paul 1907– Vice-Pres., Dillon Read & Co. 1939–41; Vice-Chairman, US Strategic Bombing Survey 1944–6; Deputy to Ass. Sec. of State for Economic Affairs, 1948–9; Director, Policy Planning Staff, Dept of State 1950–3; Sec. of Navy 1963–7; Dep. Sec. of Defense 1967–9; Head of US Negotiating Team, Arms Control Talks, Geneva 1981– .

O'Brien, Leslie K. (later Lord) 1908– Bank of England 1927–73; Chief Cashier 1955; Exec. Dir. 1962–4; Dep. Governor 1964–6; Governor 1966–73.

Padmore, Thomas (later Sir) 1909– Second Secretary, Treasury 1952–62; Permanent Secretary, Ministry of Transport 1962–8.

Playfair, E. W. (later Sir Edward) 1909– HM Treasury 1934–46, 1947–56; Perm. Under Sec. for War 1956–9; Perm. Sec., Ministry of Defence 1960–1; Chairman, ICI 1961–5.

Plowden, Sir Edwin (later Lord) 1907– Ministry of Aircraft Production 1940–6 (Chief Exec. 1945–6); Chief Planning Officer and Chairman, Econ. Planning Board 1947–53; Chairman, Atomic Energy Authority 1954–9; Chairman Tube Investments 1963–76.

Powell, J. Enoch 1912– Fellow of Trinity College, Cambridge 1934–8; Prof. of Greek, Univ. of Sydney, NSW 1937–9; Parly Sec., Ministry of Housing and Local Govt 1955–7; Fin. Sec. to the Treasury 1957–8; Minister of Health 1960–3.

Rickett, Denis (later Sir) 1907– Fellow of All Souls College, Oxford 1929–39; Staff of Econ. Adv. Council 1931–9; PPS to Minister of Production 1943–5; to Prime Minister 1950–1; Economic Minister and Head of UKTSD, Washington 1951–4; Third Sec., Treasury 1955–60; Second Sec. 1960–8; Vice-Pres., World Bank 1968–74.

Riefler, W. W. 1897–1974 Member of staff, Federal Reserve Board 1923–35; Professor at Institute for Advanced Study 1935–8; Asst to US Ambassador in London 1942–4; Asst to Chairman of Board of Governors 1948–59; Sec. of Open Market Committee 1952–59.

Robbins, Lionel (later Lord) 1898–1984 Prof. of Economics, LSE 1929–61; Director, Economic Section of War Cabinet Offices 1941–5; Chairman *Financial Times* 1961–70.

Roosa, R. V. 1918– Rhodes Scholar 1939; university teacher of economics 1939–43; staff of Federal Reserve Bank of NY 1946–60; vice-pres. research dept 1956–60; Under Sec. for monetary affairs, US Treasury 1961–4; partner Brown Bros Harriman & Co. 1965– .

Rowan, Sir Leslie 1908–72 Ass. Sec., later PPS, to Prime Minister 1941–7; Perm. Sec., Ministry of Economic Affairs 1947; Second Sec. HM Treasury 1947–9, 1951–8; Economic Minister to Washington 1949–51, Managing

Director, then Chmn, Vickers Ltd. 1962–71; captained England at hockey 1937, 1938 and 1947.

Saulnier, Raymond J. 1908– Univ. teacher of economics, latterly prof., Columbia Univ., NY, from 1936; special adv. to Board of Governors, Fed. Reserve System 1950–2; consultant to CEA 1953; member 1955; Chmn 1957–61.

Southard, Frank 1907–89 Asst. prof., prof. of economics, Cornell Univ. 1931–48; Dir. office of internat. finance, US Treasury 1947–8; Special Asst to Sec. of Treasury and US Exec. Dir., IMF 1949–62; Dep. Man. Dir., IMF 1962–74; Hon. OBE.

Stassen, Harold E. 1907– Governor of Minnesota 1938–45; President, Univ. of Pennsylvania 1948–53; Director, Mutual Security Agency 1953; Director, Foreign Operations Administration 1953–5; special asst to President 1955–8; candidate for Republican Presidential nomination 1988.

Strath, William (later Sir) 1906–75 Ministry of Aircraft Production 1940–5; Ministry of Supply 1945–7; Central Economic Planning Staff 1947–55; Member, Atomic Energy Authority 1955–9; Perm. Sec. Ministry of Supply 1959, of Aviation 1959–60.

Thorneycroft, Peter (later Lord) 1909– Commissioned in Royal Artillery 1930; barrister 1935; President of the Board of Trade 1951–7; Chancellor of the Exchequer 1957–8; Min. of Aviation 1961–2; Min. of Defence 1962–4; Chairman of Conservative Party 1975–81.

Thorold, Guy (later Sir) 1898–1970 Ministry of Economic Warfare 1939–45; attached to UK Delegation to OEEC 1948; Head of UK TSD and Economic Minister, Washington 1957–9.

Trend, Burke St J. (later Lord) 1914–87 Entered Treasury 1937; PPS to Chancellor of the Exchequer 1945–9; Under Sec., HM Treasury 1949–55; Dep. Sec. of Cabinet 1955–9; Secretary 1963–73; Rector, Lincoln College Oxford 1973–83.

Waugh, Sam 1899–1970 American banker and government official; Pres. First Trust Co., Lincoln, Nebraska 1946–53; Asst. Sec. of State 1953–5; Dep. Under Sec. of State 1955; Pres. Ex.-Im. Bank 1955–6.

Wilson, J. Harold (later Lord) 1916– Secretary for Overseas Trade March–Oct. 1947; President of Board of Trade 1947–51; Leader of Labour Party 1963–76; Prime Minister 1964–70 and 1974–6.

Appendix 3: Members of the Economic Section, 1954–61

(Omitting those who left during 1954: David Bensusan-Butt, Christopher Dow, Miles Fleming, John Jukes, Joan Kelley and Maurice Scott.)

Atkinson, F. J.	1949–69 1977–9	(later Sir Fred; Head of Government Economic Service 1977–9)
Brown, Miss M. P.	1959–85	(Under Secretary, Treasury 1972–85)
Brunner, J.	1958–61	(later Sir John)
Day, A. C. L.	1954–6	(Professor of Economics, LSE 1964–1989, and Pro-Director 1979–83)
Downie, J.	1948–61	(Ass. Sec.-Gen., OECD 1961–3; died 1963)
Figgures, F.	1955–7	(later Sir Frank; Director of Trade and Finance, OEEC 1948–51; Deputy Director, Economic Section 1955–7; Under Sec., Treasury 1955–60; Sec. Gen. EFTA 1960–5; Dir.-Gen., NEDO 1971–3)
Franklin, M. D. M.	1952–5	(later Sir Michael; Permanent Secretary, Ministry of Agriculture, Food and Fisheries 1983–7)
Godley, W. A. H.	1956–70	(Director, Dept of Applied Economics, Cambridge 1970–)
Grieve-Smith, J.	1949–57	(Senior Bursar, Robinson College, Cambridge 1982–)
Hall, R. L.	1947–61	(later Lord Roberthall; Director 1947–61; Economic Adviser to HMG 1953–61; died 1988)
Henderson, P. D.	1957–8	(Professor of Economics, UCL 1975–83; Head of Economics and Statistical Division, OECD 1984– ; Reith Lecturer 1985)
Hopkin, W. A. B.	1948–50 1958–72 1974–7	(later Sir Bryan; Deputy Director 1958–65; Head of Govt Econ. Service 1974–7; Professor of Economics, University of Wales, Cardiff 1972–82)
Howell, D. A. R.	1959–60	(Sec. of State for Energy 1979–81; for Transport 1981–3)
Howell, Miss K. (Mrs Jones)	1945–60	(Secretary, National Institute of Economic and Social Research 1968–90)
Joseph, Miss M. W. B. (Mrs Hemming)	1940–3 1947–55	(Senior Research Officer, NIESR 1956–70)

Kennedy, M. C.	1956–65	(later Senior Lecturer, University of Manchester)
Little, I. M. D.	1953–5	(Deputy Director; Professor of Economics, Oxford 1971–6)
Mackintosh, A. S.	1957–61	(deceased)
McMahon, C. W.	1954–60	(later Sir Kit; Dep. Gov. of Bank of England 1980–5; Chairman, Midland Bank 1987–)
Neild, R. R.	1951–6	(Professor of Economics, Cambridge 1971–84)
Nove, A.	1956–8	(Professor of International Economics, University of Glasgow 1963–82)
Opie, R. G.	1958–60	(Fellow of New College, Oxford, since 1961)
Richenberg, L.	1955–7	(later in merchant banking and insurance)
Ross, C. R.	1952–5	(Dep. Sec. CPRS 1971–8; vice-Pres. European Investment Bank 1978–89)
Sadler, J. S.	1954–6	(Dep. Chairman, John Lewis Partnership 1984–9)
Scammell, W. S.	1956–8	(Prof. of Economics, McMaster University, Ontario 1970–87)
Stamler, Mrs H.	1954–6	(Senior Economic Adviser, Treasury 1974–)
Stewart, M. J.	1957–62	(Reader in Political Economy, UCL 1969–)
Troup, G. W.	1957	
Wannan, Miss G.	1956–8	
Watts, Miss N. G. M.	1941–55	(Deputy Director, Research Division, ECE (Geneva) 1959–64; Vice-Principal, St Hilda's College, Oxford 1968–81)
Watts, P. E.	1954–9	(Commercial Controller, Central Electricity Generating Board 1960–)

Appendix 4: Initials and abbreviations

A.	Anthony Eden
ABCC	Association of British Chambers of Commerce
AEA	Atomic Energy Authority
AEI	Associated Engineering Industries
A.L.M.	Abbot Moffat
A/P	Assistant Principal
A/S	Assistant Secretary
ASLEF	Association of Stokers, Locomotive Engineers and Firemen
BC	Budget Committee
B/E	Bank of England
BEA	British European Airways
BEC	British Employers' Confederation
BIS	Bank for International Settlements
BMC	British Motor Corporation
BNC	Brasenose College, Oxford
BOAC	British Overseas Airways Corporation
BOP	Balance of Payments
BOT	Board of Trade
BRMM	British Raw Materials Mission in Washington
B.W.G./B.G.	Sir Bernard Gilbert
C&AG	Comptroller and Auditor General
CEA	Council of Economic Advisers (US)
CEPS	Central Economic Planning Staff
Ch. Ch.	Christchurch College, Oxford
CIA	Central Intelligence Agency
CIC	Capital Issues Committee
COPPI	Council on Prices Productivity and Incomes
CP	Communist Party
CPRS	Central Policy Review Staff
CRMB	Combined Raw Materials Board
CRO	Commonwealth Relations Office
CSO	Central Statistical Office
DAC	Development Assistance Committee
DAG	Development Assistance Group
DLF	Development Loan Fund
DVC	Damodar Valley Corporation (India)
E.B./E.E.B.	Sir Edward Bridges
ECA	Economic Cooperation Administration
ECE	Economic Commission for Europe

ECGD	Export Credits Guarantee Department
EEC	European Economic Community
EFTA	European Free Trade Association
EIR	Earned income relief
EMA	European Monetary Agreement
E.P.	Sir Edwin Plowden
EPB	Economic Planning Board
EPC	Economic Policy Committee
EPU	European Payments Union
EST	Economic Secretary, Treasury
EXIM	Export–Import Bank
FBI	Federation of British Industries
FO	Foreign Office
FOA	Foreign Operations Agency
FRB	Federal Reserve Board
FST	Financial Secretary, Treasury
FTA	Free Trade Area
FT Index	Financial Times Share Index
G.(C.)	Geoffrey Crowther
GATT	General Agreement on Tariffs and Trade
GNP	Gross National Product
H.A.	D. Heathcoat Amory
H.B.	Sir Herbert Brittain
HE	His Excellency, UK Ambassador
HF	Home Finance Division, Treasury
H.G./G.	Hugh Gaitskell
H.M.	Harold Macmillan
HMG	Her Majesty's Government
HOPS	Home and Overseas Planning Staff
HP	Hire purchase
H.W.	Harold Wilson
IBRD	International Bank for Reconstruction and Development (World Bank)
ICI	Imperial Chemical Industries
IDA	International Development Association
IDAC	Import Duties Advisory Committee
IDT	Information Division Treasury
IMF	International Monetary Fund
IPC	Investment Programmes Committee/Iraq Petroleum Company
IR	Inland Revenue
ISI	Indian Statistical Institute
ITO	International Trade Organization
LCES	London and Cambridge Economic Services
LMH	Lady Margaret Hall, Oxford
LP	Lord President
LSE	London School of Economics
M.	Mahalanobis/Maudling
MEW	Ministry of Economic Warfare
MIT	Massachusetts Institute of Technology
MSA	Mutual Security Agency
N.	Richard Nixon
N.B.	Sir Norman Brook
NCB	National Coal Board

NEDO	National Economic Development Organization
NIs	Nationalized industries
NIESR	National Institute of Economic and Social Research
NIF(WP)	National Income Forecasts Working Party
NJAC	National Joint Advisory Council
NPACI	National Production Advisory Council for Industry
NR	Natural resources
NSA	Non-sterling area
NUM	National Union of Mineworkers
NUR	National Union of Railwaymen
NZZ	*Neue Zürcher Zeitung*
OCT	Overseas corporation tax
OECD	Organization for Economic Co-operation and Development
OEEC	Organization for European Economic Co-operation
OF	Overseas Finance Division, Treasury
O.S.F./O.F./O.	Sir Oliver Franks
OTCs	Overseas trading corporations
PAYE	Pay as you earn
PM	Prime Minister
PO	Post Office
(P)PS	(Principal) Private Secretary
PSA	Property Services Agency
PT	Purchase tax
P.T.	Peter Thorneycroft
PWLB	Public Works Loan Board
QM	*Queen Mary* (the liner)
q.r.	Quantitative restrictions
R.A.B.	R. A. Butler
RES	Royal Economic Society
RFC	Reconstruction Finance Corporation
R.M.	Sir Roger Makins
RSA	Rest of the sterling area
S.	Lord Salisbury/Saulnier
S.C.L./S.L.	S. C. Leslie
SE	South-East England
T.B.	Thomas Balogh
TDRs	Treasury deposit receipts
TGWU	Transport and General Workers' Union
TIC	Treasury Investment Committee
T.L.R.	Sir Leslie Rowan
T.P.	Sir Thomas Padmore
T.S.D.	*see* UKTSD
TUs	Trade Unions
TUC	Trades Union Congress
UKTSD/UK Del.	UK Treasury and Supply Delegation, Washington
UN	United Nations
Uniscan	Proposed economic bloc of the United Kingdom and Scandinavia
U/S	Under Secretary

W.	Washington
WEP	Working Party on World Economic Problems
WP	Wages Policy Committee
WPB	War Production Board (US)

Bibliography

Alford, B.W.E. (1985) *British Economic Performance 1945–75* for Economic History Society (London: Macmillan).

Arndt, H.M., Bensusan Butt, D.M. and Swan, T.W. 'An Appreciation of Robert Hall, 1901–1988', *Economic Record*, 1988.

Brittan, S. (1971) *Steering the Economy* (Harmondsworth: Pelican).

Cairncross, Sir Alec (1989) 'The United Kingdom' in Pechman, J.A. (ed.) *The Role of the Economist in Government* (Hemel Hempstead: Harvester Wheatsheaf).

Coats, A.W. (ed.) (1981) *Economists in Government* (Durham, North Carolina: Duke University Press).

Crowther, Sir Geoffrey (1957) *Balances and Imbalances of Payments* (Boston: Harvard School of Business Administration).

Devons, Ely (1957) 'The wage-price spiral' in *Essays in Economics* (London: Allen and Unwin).

Fellner, W. *et. al*, (1961) *The Problem of Rising Prices*, (Paris: OECD).

Hall, Sir R.L. 'The place of the economist in Government' *Oxford Economic Papers*, (1955).

Hall, Sir R.L. 'Reflections on the practical application of economics', *Economic Journal*, (1959)

Hall, Sir R.L. (1982) 'The end of full employment' in C.P. Kindleberger and G. di Tella (eds.) *Economics in the Long View: Applications and Cases* (London, Basingstoke: Macmillan).

Holmans, A.E. *Demand Management in the United Kingdom, 1952–58* (unpublished).

Hutchinson, T.W. (1968) *Economics and Economic Policy in Britain, 1946–66*, (London: Allen and Unwin).

Little, I.M.D. 'The economist in Whitehall', *Lloyd's Bank Review*, 1957.

Lowe, Rodney 'Resignation at the Treasury: the Social Services Committee and the failure to reform the Welfare State, 1955–57' *Journal of Social Policy* (1990).

MacDougall, Sir Donald (1957) *The World Dollar Problem* (Oxford: Oxford University Press).

Macmillan, Harold (1969), *Tides of Fortune 1945–55*, (London: Macmillan).

Macmillan, Harold (1971), *Riding the Storm 1956–59*, (London: Macmillan).

Marris, Robin 'The position of economics and economists in the government machine', *Economic Journal* (1954).

Pliatzky, Sir Leo (1982), *Getting and Spending* (Oxford: Blackwell).

Triffin, Robert (1960), *Gold and the Dollar Crisis: the Future of Convertibility* (New Haven: Yale University Press).

Official Publications (H.M.S.O.)

Home Office *Proceedings of the Tribunal appointed to Inquire into Allegations that Information about the Raising of Bank Rate was improperly disclosed, with the Minutes of Evidence taken before the Tribunal, December 1957*; 1958.

Ministry of Labour and National Service *Interim Report of a Court of Inquiry (Chairman, Sir J. Cameron) into a Dispute between the British Transport Commission and the National Union of Railwaymen, January 3, 1955*; 1955, Cmd 9352.

Ministry of Labour and National Service *Final Report of a Court of Inquiry (Chairman, Sir J. Cameron) into a Dispute between the British Transport Commission and the National Union of Railwaymen, January 3, 1955*; 1955, Cmd 9372.

Special Joint Committee (Chairman C. Guillebaud) *on Machinery of Negotiations for Railway Staff, Report*, 1960.

H.M. Treasury

Economic Survey 1953 (and later years)

Economic Implications of Full Employment Cmd 9725, 1956

The Control of Public Expenditure, Cmnd 1432, 1961

Report of (Radcliffe) *Committee on the Working of the Monetary System*, 1959, Cmnd 827.

Minutes of Evidence (to Radcliffe Committee) 1960

Principal Memoranda of the Evidence (3 vols) 1960

Council on Prices, Productivity and Incomes, *Reports* 1958–61

Index

Abbott, Douglas, Canadian Minister of Finance 7
Abbott, Mrs E. M., Treasury 156
Abs, H., German banker 247
Acheson, Dean, U.S. Sec. of State 201
Adenauer, Konrad, President, Fed. Rep. of Germany 195, 247, 249, 263
Agricultural policy 4, 29, 99; price review 60, 102; surpluses 6, 41; wages tribunal 120
Aid to developing countries 49–50, 130, 139, 143–4, 149, 187–8, 202–3, 212–13; co-ordination of 213, 227; *see also* Development Assistance Group
Aidenham, Lord, Chmn. Westminster Bank 33
Algeria 138
Ali Mohamad, Finance Minister of Pakistan 4, 18
Allen, W. Maurice, Bank of England 43, 66, 68, 99, 169, 212
Alsop, Joseph 12, 18–19, 26, 40–1, 47, 78, 159, 201
Alsop, Stewart 18, 78
Alternative techniques (of monetary control) 135–6, 139, 145
Amory, Derick Heathcoat, Chancellor of the Exchequer ix, xi, 30, 91–2, 94, 224–43 *passim*, 245, 250
Anderson, Robert, Sec. of U.S. Treasury 130–1, 151, 159–62, 185, 197, 203, 212–13, 232, 247–8, 250, 252
Andrew, Herbert, Board of Trade 189
Andrews, Philip M., Nuffield College 246
Arbitration 80, 153
Armstrong, William, Treasury 3, 5, 20, 51, 163–8, 170, 197, 208–9, 218, 221, 223, 243, 267
Aschinger, Swiss journalist 15, 248
Aswan High Dam 49
Atkinson, F. J., Economic Section 3, 12–13, 16, 37, 40, 66, 72, 103, 156, 171, 197, 258
Atomic energy 26, 75, 110; authority 26, 46, 125, 164, 173–4, 197, 205
Attlee, C. R. 109
Australia 3–7, 227, 233–4
Automobiles, *see* Cars
Babington Smith, M. J. 193, 224
Baird, J. G., U.S. Treasury 132
Balance of payments 22–3, 29–30, 33–4, 36, 42, 61, 85, 91, 102, 105, 117, 137, 147, 172, 192, 199, 201, 205, 246, 255, 257, 261–2; target 3, 197
Ball, George 265
Balogh, Thomas 61, 147–8, 174, 195, 216, 225
Bamford, Sir Eric, Inland Revenue 38
Bancroft, Ian, Treasury 58
Bank advances 37, 42, 65, 104, 126, 172, 208, 242
Bank of England 28–9, 33, 37, 42–4, 47, 68–9, 75, 96, 100, 112, 121, 126–8, 145, 179, 186, 208, 212, 230, 254; appointment of new Governor 140, 176–7, 188, 221–2, 225, 243–5, 250–3; part-time directors 145, 209, 221; relations with the Treasury 33, 42–3, 65, 69, 135, 155, 176, 231, 242–3, 245; Treasury Working Party 66–9
Bank for International Settlements 42, 77, 97, 261
Banking, Working Party on 127
Bank rate 29–30, 62–3, 65, 96–8, 126–7, 137, 147, 151–2, 169, 171–2, 179, 218, 221, 224, 226, 228–30, 236, 249, 252–5, 261
Banks, central, independence of 135, 213; commercial directives to 122, 124, 127; personal loans 171, 212; requests to 43
Barber, Antony, Economic Sec. to Treasury 216, 223, 241
Beales, R. G., Central Statistical Office 189
Beaver, Sir Hugh 155
Beer 188, 191, 194
Bell, Elliot, *Business Week* 249–50
Bernstein, E., I.M.F. 16
Bevan, A. (Nye) 19
Beveridge, Lord 111, 119
Bevin, Ernest xiv
Bicester, Lord, Director, Bank of England 224
Birch, Nigel, Economic Sec. to Treasury ix, 94, 97, 99, 107, 124, 134, 140, 143–4, 168, 179

Bishop, F. A., Cabinet Office and Treasury 7, 58, 232
Bissell, Richard, C.I.A. 12, 15, 133, 202, 249
Black, Eugene, President I.B.R.D. 10, 62, 197, 213, 232
Blessing, Karl, President, Bundesbank 175, 238
Bligh, Timothy, Cabinet Office 224, 247
Bolton, George, Exec. Dir., Bank of England 13, 47, 134
Bowles, Chester 249–50
Bowyer, Sir Eric, Perm. Sec., Ministry of Pensions 39, 58
Boyd-Carpenter, J., Minister of Pensions 261
Boyle, Sir E., Econ. Sec., later Fin. Sec., Treasury 58, 60, 64, 70, 75, 95, 216, 225, 241
Brand, T. H., Lazard's 58, 60
Brech, R., Unilever 79
Bridges, Sir E., Perm. Sec., Treasury xiv-xv, 8, 30, 36, 39, 44, 46, 50–1, 57–8, 60–1, 64, 69–71, 73, 75, 80–1, 99, 116–17, 154, 165, 167, 266–7
Briggs Bodies 100
British Aluminium 188, 195, 225, 230
  Association 111
Brittain, Sir H., Treasury 8, 43, 51, 69, 117, 119, 165
Brook, Sir Norman, Cabinet Secretary 5, 20, 24, 39, 58–60, 71, 80–1, 84, 123, 125, 154–6, 165–7, 170–1, 178, 200, 204, 206, 222, 236, 241
Brooke, Henry, Fin. Sec., Treasury 33, 86, 95
Brown, Sir Allen 7
Brown, Sam 216
Budget 8–9, 30, 34, 43, 56, 65–6, 86, 103, 148, 152–4, 156, 164, 172, 180, 185, 188–9, 191–4, 257, 259–60, 266
  Committee 8, 50, 55, 58, 94, 101–2, 152, 154, 176, 189, 191, 206–7, 218, 230, 257
Building controls 61, 96
Burgess, W. R., U.S. Treasury 11, 13, 40, 47, 111, 132
Burns, Arthur, Chmn., Council of Economic Advisers 7, 11–13, 19, 40–1, 47–8, 51, 66, 77, 82, 110–11, 256
Bush, G. 117, 136
Butler, Chase Manhattan Bank 214
Butler, R. A., Chancellor of the Exchequer ix, xi, xiii, xxi, xxii, 4–45 *passim*, 55–7, 61–71, 75–6, 80–2, 85–7, 91–4
  Home Secretary 95, 97, 107, 140–5, 153, 172, 185, 191, 207, 210, 215, 220, 230–2, 236, 242, 266–7
Butt, D. M. B., Economic Section 109, 156, 166, 171–2
Caccia, Sir H., U.K. Ambassador to U.S.A. 85, 111, 133, 161, 221, 262
Cairncross, Alec 46, 99, 108, 118, 214, 253, 256–7
Caliban xiv
Campion, Sir H., Director of C.S.O. 37, 70, 99
Canada, visits to *see* Hall, Sir Robert
Canal Users Association 74
Capital gains taxation *see* Tax
Cars, manufacture of 39, 198, 237, 255
Central African Federation 17
Ceylon 6, 78
Chambers, Sir Paul, chmn. I.C.I. 220
Chandos, Lord 193
Cherwell, Lord xv, 120, 216
Chilver, Guy and Richard 38
China 40, 174–5
Churchill, W. S. 19, 27–8, 31–2, 80–1, 92, 120, 206
Clark, William, Cabinet Office 68–9
Clarke, R. W. B. ('Otto'), Treasury 39, 46, 79, 125, 164–8, 170, 178, 189–91, 195, 219, 226, 236
Coal 10, 23–4, 26, 29–31, 44, 75, 93, 100
Cobbold, C. F., Governor, Bank of England 29, 33, 42–4, 55–60, 65, 69, 81–2, 91–7, 104, 116–18, 121–3, 127, 134–8, 140, 146–7, 152, 169, 177, 188, 209, 221–6, 229–36, 242–6, 250–1, 254, 263, 266
Cochrane, Merle, I.B.R.D. 214
Cohen, Edgar, Board of Trade 20, 75–6, 99
Cohen, Lord Justice 123, 129, 136, 147, 173, 189, 235
Collective approach *see* Convertibility
Committees: Anglo-Canadian Continuing 46, 48, 51–2, 107, 113, 204, 206, 256; Anglo-German Economic 238; Balance of Payments 68; Civil Economies 49; Colerain 260; Commonwealth Liaison 18; Development Policy 226; Draper 202–3; Economic Measures 132; Economic Planning Board 218, 257; Economic Policy (U.K.) 177; Economic Policy (O.E.C.D.) 263; Employment 178, 186, 207; External Economic Policy 10; Fleck 197; Guillebaud 230; Investment Allowances 173, 189–90; Investment Programmes 8; Macmillan 69, 99; Programmes 8, 21, 29, 36; Public Expenditure (Plowden) 216, 219, 235; Publicity 72; Steering 154, 159, 218, 222; Treasury Investment (T.I.C.) 8, 24–5, 57, 148, 163, 226; Wages Policy 173, 180, 217; World Economic Problems (W.E.P.) 36; *see also* Budget, Expert Group, National Income Forecasting, and Radcliffe

Commodity prices 4, 129, 148, 154, 165
Common Market 98–9, 112–13, 187, 193, 221, 227, 235
Commonwealth conferences 3–7, 148, 163, 172–3, 211; Development Fund 162, 211; Finance Ministers conferences 16–19, 78, 172–3, 211, 244–6; free entry 31–2, 44, 72, 159, 225, 264
Compton, Sir Edmund, Treasury 46, 66, 68, 82, 99, 104, 118, 127–8, 134–5, 139, 147, 152, 163–5, 167, 170
Controls 3, 8–9, 17, 34, 42, 147
Convertibility 3–4, 10, 13–14, 16–19, 21, 28–31, 34, 37–40, 42–3, 50, 78, 147, 169, 172–3, 180, 186, 211, 244, 246
Coombs, C., Fed. Res. Bk. of New York 263
Coombs, H. C., Commonwealth Bk. of Australia 234, 243
Conservative Party Conferences 21, 174, 195
Copeman, Harold, Treasury 177
Cotton industry 31–3
Coughran, T. B., U.S. Treasury 203
Coulson, John, Foreign Office 48, 119
Council of Economic Advisers 7, 12, 41, 110, 129, 132, 150, 233, 253, 256, 261
Council on Prices, Productivity and Incomes (C.O.P.P.I.) 116, 119, 123–5, 128–9, 136, 152, 158, 173, 180–1, 187–91, 218, 229–30, 235, 246
Cousins, Frank, Sec., T.G.W.U. 119
Couve de Murville 187
Cox, Archibald, U.S. lawyer 249, 256
Coyne, J., Governor, Bank of Canada 114
Credit, export 173, 203, 233; post-war 188, 192–4, 199; restriction of 28–9, 37, 42–3, 56, 59, 65, 101, 122, 127, 245
Crichel Down 9–10
Cripps, Sir Stafford xiv, 9, 18, 62, 104, 108, 193
Croft, Sir William, Customs and Excise Dept. 38
Crombie, Sir James, Customs and Excise Dept. 38–9, 46, 165, 194
Cromer, Earl of, Man. Dir. of Baring Bros. 180, 187, 202, 232, 241, 248–53, 257–8
Crosland, C. A. R., Labour M.P. 37, 192, 215, 259
Crowther, Sir Geoffrey, Editor, *The Economist* 21–2, 201
Customs and Excise 9, 39, 46, 191

Damodar Valley 8, 62, 160
Davenport, Nicholas 92, 124
Davis, J. S., Council of Economic Advisers 41
Day, Alan, Economic Section 75, 266
Debt ceiling (in U.S.A) 148, 249; management 128, 133, 171, 214
Defence 9, 24, 37, 59, 87, 91, 93, 101, 108, 131, 201, 259
Deficit finance 8, 12, 160
Deflation 59, 66, 87, 93, 96, 110, 122, 124–5, 131, 175, 231, 260
De Gaulle, Charles 195, 225, 229, 249, 264
De Largentaye, J. M. R. O., French Exec. Dir., I.M.F. 266
Deshmukh, C. D., Finance Minister of India 4, 18, 38
Devaluation 61–3, 66–7; of dollar 245, 251; danger of 85
Development Assistance Group (D.A.G.) 227–8, 232–3, 237, 246, 248, 262
Development Loan Fund 212
Devlin Report 215
Devons, Ely 73
De Wolff, P. 226
Diebenbaker, J. G., Prime Minister of Canada 204
Dillon, Douglas, U.S. Under-Sec. of State 130–3, 221, 228, 232, 259, 264
Discrimination, against dollar imports 14, 34, 44, 50, 172, 201, 204–5, 213, 221; in favour of Commonwealth imports 5–6; within Europe 187
Dividends 24–5; -stripping 156–7
Dollar problem 41, 50
Dounreay power station 26
Dow, Christopher, Economic Section xvii, 37, 103
Downie, Jack, Economic Section 37, 75, 96, 117, 127, 148, 156, 166, 170, 197, 204, 206, 218, 235, 251, 253, 257, 266
Dulles, John Foster, U.S. Secretary of State 19, 74, 76, 190, 195
Dumping (of butter) 158–9

Eady, Sir Wilfrid, former Treasury official 80, 117, 165
Eccles, David, Minister of Education, then President, Board of Trade 24, 91–2, 94, 99, 101, 187, 216, 232, 243
Eckstein, O. 202, 214
Economic advisers 114–15, 249; research unit 170
Economic Survey 130, 190
Economist, The 21–2
Eden, Sir A., Foreign Minister, then Prime Minister ix, xv, 10, 20, 28, 31–2, 37–8, 44, 57–61, 64, 67–74, 86–7, 91–3, 137
Egypt, invasion of 84; negotiations with 93, 95, 190; *see also* Suez
Eisenhower, General D., U.S. President 11, 41, 47, 49, 78, 138, 155, 160, 162, 195, 201, 210–11, 258, 262
Elections 29, 31–2, 38, 71, 185

Electricity programme 26
Emmerson, Sir H., Perm. Sec., Ministry of Works 199, 235, 247
Emminger, Otmar, Bundesbank 79, 82, 264
Empson, Sir Charles 109
Erhard, Ludwig, German Chancellor 213
Erroll, F., Econ. Sec., Treasury 186, 216
Etzel, Franz, German Minister of Finance 238
European Customs Union 92, 114
European Economic Community, *see* Common Market
European free trade 72, 112–14, 143, 148, 159, 161, 176, 180, 187, 221; *see also* Plan G
European Free Trade Area (E.F.T.A) 197, 211, 221, 225, 227–8, 235
European Payments Union (E.P.U.) 3, 11, 42, 102, 122, 170, 186
Evans, Sir John, Inland Revenue 20, 189, 194
Exchange control 74, 122
Exim Bank 48, 74, 109–10, 122
Expert Group (O.E.E.C.) 35–6, 66, 79, 162–3, 196, 261–2

Fadden, Sir A. W., Australian Treasurer 7
Fall-out 25–6, 176
Fascism 15
Family allowances 138, 140, 144
Federal Reserve Board 7, 48, 66, 79, 110–11, 121, 131, 150, 203, 261; Bank of New York 47, 109, 256, 263
Federation of British Industries (F.B.I.) 28, 67, 70, 223, 256–7
Figgures, Frank, Treasury, 46, 57, 70, 99, 167
Film agreement 75
Fleming, J. Marcus, I.M.F. 16, 266
Flett, Martin, Treasury 3
Ford Motor Co. 100, 220, 254–5
Forecasters, in U.S.A. 77
Forge, Waldo 120
Foot, Michael 215
France 15, 18, 121, 129, 131, 138, 149, 161–2, 181, 265
France, Arnold, Treasury 3, 33, 99, 112, 122, 139, 187, 202, 216, 226
Franks, Sir Oliver 9, 11, 20, 33, 55, 58–60, 76, 99, 104, 108, 116, 118, 121, 128, 139–40, 153, 174, 177, 188, 192–5, 205, 209, 221–2, 225–6, 241, 244–5, 250–3, 255
Fraser, Bruce, Treasury 164–5, 167–8, 171, 226
Free trade negotiations 246
Friday forum 3
Friedman, Irving, I.M.F. 16
Fuel efficiency 23
Full employment 23, 25, 66–8, 101, 171, 179, 192, 198, 206, 210–11, 215, 222–3, 257, 260
Funding 59–60, 97–8, 116, 128, 145, 152, 231, 251

Gaillard, Felix, French Minister of Finance 131
Gaitskell, Hugh, Leader of Labour Party 3, 17, 19–20, 34, 45–6, 62, 98–9, 107–8, 120, 157, 185, 188, 192, 195, 202, 207, 251, 259
Galbraith, J. K. 249
Gandhi, Mahatma 18
Garner, Sir J., U.K. High Commissioner, Canada 112–15
GATT 12, 18, 21, 28, 31, 76, 103, 113, 130, 197, 204, 219, 227–8, 233
Germany 19, 138, 181, 237, 249, 261; export surpluses 79, 82, 110, 113, 121, 124, 129–30, 151, 175, 196, 212, 233, 246–7
Gilbert, Sir B. W., Second Sec., Treasury 3, 8, 10, 16, 20, 26, 29–30, 36, 39, 43, 46, 50–1, 60, 63, 69–73, 79–81, 87, 116–17, 165
Gilbert, Milton, B.I.S. 226
Godley, Wynne, Economic Section 244
Gold Coast (Ghana) 78
Gold, earmarking of 251; market 250–1; price of 261; impending shortage in U.S.A. 77
Goonetilleke, Sir O., Finance Minister of Ceylon 6
Gore-Booth, Paul, Foreign Office 187, 193, 245
Green, Maurice, *The Times* 30, 58, 219
Grieve-Smith, John, Economic Section 13, 39, 77, 125
Growth, planning for 12, 256–7
'Guiding light' 80, 108, 146, 180, 199, 217, 223, 235
Guillebaud, C. 230

Hailsham, Lord 119–20, 145, 224
Haley, William, Editor, *The Times* 174
Hall, Sir N. F. 246
Hall, Sir Robert: early life xiii; role in 1949 devaluation and Robot xiv–xv; 'incoherent lucidity' xvi; introduces kinked demand curve xvii; helps to found National Institute xvii; knighted 3; visits Australia xxii, 3–7, 233–4; Canada 46, 51–2, 112–15, 204; Germany 238; India 52–4, 175–6; Paris 33–6, 66, 162–3, 226–9, 261–2; Poland 174, 178; United States 7–8, 11–19, 39–42, 46–51, 74–9, 107–12, 129–33, 149–51, 159–62, 200–4, 211–13, 231–3,

Hall, Sir Robert *contd.*
246–50, 260–5; of Amory 242; view of Butler 56–7; of Bridges 80; of Gilbert 80–1; of Macmillan 92; of Thorneycroft 143; of Selwyn Lloyd 237, 245; of Treasury colleagues 165–8, 193, 266–7; staffing problems 37, 41, 75, 123, 156, 173, 253; on duties of Economic Section 149; pay 117–18, 200; contemplates retirement 117–18, 155–6; offers to resign 122; retires 266
Hall-Patch, Sir E. 13, 62, 86, 193
Hambro, J. O. 250
Hanbury Williams, Sir John, Director, Bank of England 250
Hancock, Sir Henry, Inland Revenue 33–9, 58, 60, 165
Hansen, Bent 226
Harcourt, Viscount, Econ. Minister, Washington 13–14, 48, 71, 77, 85, 87, 99, 108–9, 129, 176–7, 188, 193, 195, 209, 218, 221–5, 244–5, 250, 252
Hardman, Henry, Dep. Sec., Ministry of Agriculture 216
Hare, John, Minister of Labour 242
Harris, Walter E., Canadian Minister of Finance 16–17
Harris, Seymour 249
Harrod, Sir Roy 98–9, 125, 179, 192–3, 257, 261, 264
Hauge, Gabriel, Assistant to U.S. President 3, 7, 11–12, 19, 40, 48, 77, 110, 130, 132, 159–62, 233
Head, Antony, Minister of Defence 94
Heath, Edward, Minister of Labour 216, 223, 230, 232; President, Board of Trade 242, 246
Heller, Walter, chmn., Council of Economic Advisers 256, 264–5
Henderson, P. D., Economic Section 123, 173, 266
Heyworth, Sir Geoffrey, chmn., Unilever 99, 108, 229–30, 235, 246
Hire purchase restrictions 16, 29–30, 60, 98, 106, 164, 168–9, 177–9, 192, 199, 231–2, 235, 237, 251–2, 254
Hitch, C. J. xvii
Hitchman, E. Alan 47, 112, 114, 117, 143, 241
Hobson, Oscar 120, 165
Hollister, J. B. 133
Hollom, Jasper, Bank of England 123
Home and Overseas Planning Staff (H.O.P.S.) 108, 173, 195
Home, Earl of, Foreign Secretary 242, 262
Hopkin, W. A. B. Economic Section xvii, 103, 123, 125, 129, 136, 147, 156, 171, 173, 177, 179, 215, 235, 244, 253, 257
Hopkins, Sir Richard, former Perm. Sec., Treasury 168
Housing 23–4, 29–30, 44, 168, 172, 189, 198, 219
Howitt, Sir Harold (C.O.P.P.I.) 123, 129, 136, 235
Hoyer Millar, J. R., Foreign Office 193, 206
Humphrey, George, Sec., U.S. Treasury 11, 12, 14, 15, 19, 40, 47, 85–7, 102, 130, 133, 160, 202
Hungary 96
Hutton, Maurice 77
Hydrogen bomb 9, 24, 40, 174–5, 200

Imperial Preference 6
Import Duties Advisory Committee (I.D.A.C.) 21
Import quotas 31, 205; restrictions 6, 12, 28, 73
India 18, 49, 139, 175; visit to 82–4
Industrial production 198, 212, 221
Inflation 10, 22, 28, 37, 43–4, 50, 59, 64, 67, 91, 95, 110, 140, 179, 217; cost 69, 117, 119, 145, 175; demand 117–18, 145
Initial allowances 164, 173
Inland Revenue 8–9, 20, 62, 173, 189–90, 192
Interest rates 59, 116, 192, 194, 208, 252, 254 *see also* Bank rate, Funding
International Bank (I.B.R.D.) 162, 185, 203, 237, 239; *see also* I.M.F. (annual meetings)
International Development Association (I.D.A.) 182, 211, 213, 248
International Monetary Fund (I.M.F.) 11, 28, 84, 110, 113, 121, 126, 151, 161–2, 173, 185, 199, 204, 212, 247, 261, 263, 265; annual meetings 11–16, 77–8, 173, 175–6, 204, 211–13, 246–50; borrowing by 263; credits to U.K. 13–14, 74, 87, 181, 199; future of 177; Article VIII 238
International Trade Organisation 21
Investment allowances 4, 58, 62–3, 79, 173, 189–90, 194; in Commonwealth 6; 'in success' 22–4; fixed 44, 73, 79, 122, 137, 152, 185, 192, 195; foreign 41, 151, 163, 169, 237; industrial 22, 137, 199, 210; long-term (inquiry) 108, 117; public 57, 59, 96, 122, 168, 172, 177–9, 195, 198, 205, 207, 217, 236

Jacobsson, Per, Man. Dir., I.M.F. 77, 110, 131, 204, 214, 232, 238, 247, 263–4
Japan 18, 227
Jay, Douglas, Labour M.P. 98
Johnston, Sir A., Inland Revenue 165, 199
Jones, Mrs K. xviii

Jukes, John, Economic Section 39, 77

Kahn, E. C., Treasury 45
Kahn, R. F. 101, 123, 226, 262
Kaldor, Nicholas 37, 192, 256
Katz, Sam, Fed. Reserve Board 112, 171
Kefauver, Senator Estes 78
Kennedy, John F., U.S. President 201, 248–50, 253, 256, 258, 261, 264
Kennedy, Michael, Economic Section 258
Keynes, Lord 36, 99, 119, 130, 160, 242
Keyserling, L. 110
Kindersley, Sir R. 134
King, H. 132
King, Wilfred, Editor, *The Banker* 55, 98, 220, 253
Kirkpatrick, Helen 78
Kruschev, Nikita 195

Labour relations 60, 70, 145–6
Lacy, W. S. B., Dept. of State 214
Laithwaite, Sir Gilbert 4
Lary, Hal 151
Leddy, John 202, 227
Lee, Sir Frank, Perm. Sec., Board of Trade, Min. of Food, then H.M. Treasury 20, 39, 44, 47–8, 50–2, 62, 71, 76, 112, 114–15, 164, 178, 205, 217–18, 223, 225–37, 241–6, 250–9, 267
Leeper, Sir R. 210
Lennox-Boyd, Alan 92, 210
Le Pan, Professor D. V. 52
Leslie, S. C. (Clem), Treasury 25, 58, 63–4, 92, 106, 119, 152, 193, 207
Lippmann, Walter 47, 78, 159–60
Liquidity, international 147, 149, 151, 161, 173, 238, 261; ratios 35, 65, 69, 116, 127–8, 135, 208, 243, 254
Lloyd, Geoffrey, Minister of Fuel and Power 23, 30
Local authorities 124, 139–40, 189, 212, 218
London and Cambridge Economic Service (L.C.E.S.) 10
Lusher, David, Federal Reserve Board 132

McCarron, Senator 19
McCarthy, Senator 19, 116
MacDonald, Malcolm, U.K. High Commissioner, Malaysia 4, 84, 180
MacDougall, Sir Donald xv, 120, 138, 173, 180, 187, 189, 191, 201
McGhee, George, U.S. Dept. of State 262
Mackintosh, A. S., Economic Section 156, 173
McLellan, U.S. Dept. of Commerce 48
Macleod, Ian, Minister of Labour, 68, 91–2, 144, 146, 157, 195–6, 216, 242
McMahon, C. J. Economic Section, xv–xvii, 77, 111, 132, 155, 202
Macmillan, Harold ix, 43–4; Chancellor of the Exchequer 56–86; Prime Minister 91 ff
MacRae, Norman, *The Economist* 68–9
Mahalanobis, Professor 58, 82, 175
Makarios, Archbishop 104
Makins, Sir Roger, Ambassador to U.S.A. 20, 40–1, 48, 51, 71, 75, 77–9; Jt. Perm. Sec., Treasury 81 ff
Marget, A. W., Fed. Reserve Board 112, 151, 161
Marjolin, Robert 46, 112, 229, 249
Marples, E., Minister of Transport 216, 254
Marris, A. D. 176
Marshall Plan 203
Marshall Society 101
Martin, Ed. 232
Martin, William McChesney, chmn., Fed. Reserve Board 7, 41, 47, 111–12, 131–2, 160, 185, 201–3, 213, 252, 263
Mason, Jim 203
Massey, Vincent, Gov. General of Canada 20–1
Maude, Evan, Treasury 75, 97, 103, 106
Maudling, Reginald, Ec. Sec. to Treasury, etc. 11, 16, 33–4, 91–2, 94–5, 143, 146, 152–3, 157, 216, 219, 223–4, 228, 230, 232, 237, 252, 254–6
May, Stacy 133
Meehan, George, Dept. of Commerce 16, 121
Mehta, G. L., Indian Ambassador to U.S.A. 18
Mendés-France, P., French Prime Minister 15, 18
Menzies, Sir Robert, Australian Prime Minister xxii, 5–7
Mikardo, Ian 215
Miller, Johnny 19
Millikan, Max 139
Milliken, Senator 19
Mills, Lord 58, 94, 174, 178–9, 194, 216, 224, 230, 232, 236
Moffat, A. L. 16, 19
Monckton, Sir W., Minister of Labour 24, 26, 176
Monetary policy 14, 29, 33, 59–61, 65, 97, 116, 123, 138; *see also* Radcliffe Committee
Money, stock of 124–5, 128, 135, 144–5, 191–3, 202, 209
Monnet, Jean 228–9
Morris, Lord Justice 119, 123
Morris, Sir Philip 173, 180, 187, 218, 229
Mynors, Humphrey, Dep. Governor, Bank of England 43, 104, 127, 152, 212, 222, 229–31, 246, 250

Naqvi, Dr 83
Nasser, Gamal Abdel 72, 74, 76, 96, 102, 109
National Bureau of Economic Research (N.B.E.R.) 111
National Coal Board 23, 70, 173
National income, doubling of 23, 25
National income forecasts (N.I.F.) 8, 10, 12, 24, 30, 100, 173, 180, 185, 191, 212, 223, 225, 230, 255, 258
Nationalised industries 67, 70, 96, 104, 106, 117, 119, 122–3, 186; prices 171
National Union of Railwaymen (N.U.R.) 27, 230
Nehru, B. K. 213
Nehru, J., Indian Prime Minister 82–4
Neild, R. R., Economic Section 70, 72, 75
NIESR (National Institute) 103, 148, 194
Nitze, Paul 41, 78, 201, 249, 256
Nixon, Richard 47, 161, 201–2, 248, 253
NJAC 25
NPACI 217

O'Brien, L. K. 66, 68, 99, 104, 116, 123, 127, 212
O.E.E.C. 38, 46, 112, 114, 187, 203, 219, 222, 228–9, 237
O.E.C.D. 263 *see also* Export Group; Working Party No. 2
Oil 49, 74, 84–5, 93, 100, 190, 199, 203; *see also* Suez
Opie, Roger 124, 156
Ottawa Agreements of 1932 44
Overseas Corporation Tax 48
Owen, John, Treasury 11

Paarlberg, Ass. to U.S. President 233
Pace, Frank, V.P. then Pres., General Dynamics Corp. 250
Padmore, Sir Thomas, Treasury 20, 117–21, 125, 128, 135, 164–6, 168, 170–1, 180, 189–92, 206, 216–18, 223, 230, 241
Pakistan 4
Paish, F. W. 140
Pant, Pitambar 83, 176
Parsons, Sir Maurice, Bank of England 177, 187, 197, 226, 251–2, 257
Peel, Sir Robert 35
Petch, Louis, Treasury 5, 11, 20–4, 33, 60, 62, 71, 75
Pflimlin, Pierre, French Minister of Finance, then P.M. 162
Phelps Brown, E. H. 191, 214
Phillips, Commonwealth Bank of Australia 234
Pitblado, David, Treasury 58, 258
Plan G 72–4, 76, 79, 82
Playfair, Sir E., Treasury 20–1, 38–9, 165–6, 218–19
Plowden, Sir E. xiii-xv, 8–9, 19, 21, 26, 33–4, 46, 55–6, 71, 75, 80, 86, 104, 117–18, 153, 165, 167, 173–4, 188, 192, 194–7, 205, 216–19, 222–5, 230, 241, 252–3, 259
Plumptre, A. W., Canadian Ministry of Finance 113
Poole, Oliver, chmn. Conservative Party 134
Powell, J. Enoch, Fin. Sec., Treasury ix, 94, 136, 140, 143–4, 228, 241
Powell, Richard, Perm. Sec., Ministry of Defence, then Board of Trade 218–19, 230–1, 256
Prices, increasing; *see* Inflation; retail 64, 82, 173, 196; plateau 82, 87, 104; stable 169; *see also* Commodity prices
Prochnow, Herbert 48, 133
Proctor, P. D., Treasury 205
Productivity 198–9
Profits 24, 60, 63, 220
Protectionism 12, 41, 113, 202, 204, 219, 225
Public expenditure 8, 57, 59, 63, 65, 91, 93, 95, 143, 157, 177, 192, 235
Public Works Loan Board (P.W.L.B.) 140

Radcliffe Committee 91, 99, 101, 104, 107–8, 111, 139, 145; evidence 116, 118, 121–2, 128, 133, 135, 147, 197; report 174, 176, 208–11, 213, 220–1
Radcliffe, Lord 91, 104, 108
Railways 24, 31, 70, 75
Raisman, Sir J. 176, 216
Randall, Clarence 12; Report 7, 11–12
Raphael, C., Treasury 193
Rasminsky, L., Bank of Canada 113–14
Rate of exchange, floating 3–4, 14, 28–9, 43–4, 74, 85, 123, 153, 172; *see also* Devaluation
Rationing, of petrol 100
Reddaway, W. B. 197
Reflation 154–5, 164, 177
Rent control 44, 137, 169
Repton, U.S. Treasury 203, 227, 232–3
Resale price maintenance 221, 224
Reserves of gold and dollars 82, 84–5, 91, 126, 145, 148, 151, 172, 185, 260
Revaluation of Deutschmark 261
RFC securities 74, 84, 186–7
Richenberg, L., Economic Section 96, 107–8
Rickett, D. H. F., Treasury 13, 20, 38–9, 46, 122, 138–9, 153–4, 164–8, 170, 177, 186–7, 193, 197, 200–3, 222–3, 226, 238, 256–7
Riddleberger, E. C. A. 232
Riefler, W. W., Fed. Reserve Board 7, 16, 41, 47, 110–11, 132–3, 201, 214

Roads 23–4
Robarts, D. J., Barclays Bank 104, 153
Robbins, Lord 119, 123, 126–8, 134, 217
Roberts, F. N., Customs and Excise Dept. 39
Robertson, General Brian, chmn. British Transport Commission 26
Robertson, Sir Dennis 123–4, 129, 136, 165, 187, 189, 191, 217
Robertson, Jack 24
Robinson, Joan 123
Robot xiv-xv
Rockefeller, Nelson 201, 214
Roll, Eric 253
Rooke, J. S., Dep. Consul-General, New York 133
Roosa, R. V., Fed. Reserve Bank of New York 214, 249, 256, 263, 265
Roosevelt, F. D. 41, 265
Rooth, Ivor, Man. Dir., I.M.F. 16, 77
Rosenstein Rodan, Paul 138–40
Ross, C. R., Economic Section xvi, 37
Rostow, W. W. 139, 249
Rothschild, Sir E. 210
Rowan, Sir T. L., Second Sec., Treasury 4–13, 17, 20, 29–30, 33, 36–9, 42–52, 58–62, 71–3, 77, 81–5, 95–100, 107–14, 121–3, 147, 151–3, 159–62, 165–71, 174, 180, 193, 197, 223
Rubber 4, 11

Sachs, Alexander 243–4
Saithenyn, Prince 27
Salisbury, Lord, Lord President 20, 32, 76, 87, 92, 94, 104, 106, 224
Samuelson, Paul 249, 253, 256, 265
Sanderson, Basil 250
Saulnier, R. J., chmn., Council of Economic Advisers 41, 109, 111, 129–31, 159–62, 233
Saunders, C. T., Central Statistical Office xviii, 37
Sayers, R. S. 99, 108, 116, 118, 128, 134, 145–6, 174, 220
Scammell, W. S., Economic Section 75, 103, 156, 173
Schlesinger, Arthur 78, 265
Schmidt, Erik Ib, Danish Ministry of Finance 66, 82
Schools 24
Schwartz, George 120
Sellon, Perry 78
Selwyn Lloyd, John, Foreign Secretary, then Chancellor x, 92, 95, 236–7, 241 ff
Sharp, Evelyn 216
Simon, J. E. S. 216
Sixes and Sevens 225–7, 246, 249, 264
Slump, fear of 177–8, 225–7, 246, 249, 264
Smithies, Professor Arthur 133
Snoy, Baron 113
Social Services 9, 91, 144, 259
South Africa 14
Southard, Frank, U.S. Treasury 151, 204, 264
South-east Asia 15, 40
Special deposits 230, 234–6, 266
Sproul, Allan, Fed. Reserve Bank of New York 47
Stafford, Jack, Board of Trade 189
Stamp duty 186
Stassen, H. E. 11, 15, 19
Statistics, alterations in 260; guide to 244; improvements in 70
Steel industry 25
Sterling area working party 102; balances 50, 74, 86, 102, 139, 155, 176, 261; credits 5; confidence in 92, 100; transferable 28–9, 42, 122, 153; *see also* Convertibility
Stevens, John M., Bank of England 193
Stevenson, Adlai 47, 78, 139, 201, 249
Stevenson, Matthew, Treasury 5, 11, 70, 79–80, 96, 108, 128, 158
Stewart, Michael, Economic Section 246
St. Laurent, Canadian Prime Minister 114
Stocks and stockbuilding 37, 139, 148, 152, 253
Strachan, Andrew 17
Strath, William, Treasury 20, 24–6, 38, 46, 167, 174, 195, 216, 224
Strikes 24, 26, 36, 41, 75, 93, 103, 105, 155–8, 164, 199, 230
Subsidies 119; agricultural 9; fishing 197; food 9, 44, 57, 59–64, 100, 120, 133, 190
Suez Canal 72, 74, 120, 133, 190; blocked 82, 86; group 92; withdrawal from 87, 92–4, 96, 100–1; re-opening of 102, 105–6; 'an economic Suez' 125
Summits 200, 224, 226
Survival, principle of 115
Swaps of currencies 206, 243–4, 263–4
Symons, R. S., Treasury 177

Taft, R. 18
Tariffs 14, 21, 28, 31–2, 73, 76, 225, 248–9
Tax increases 231; reductions 188, 192, 196; capital gains 58, 60–1, 242; entertainments 101; expenditure 256; income 28, 65, 71, 87, 100, 186, 194, 234; indirect 100; profits 154, 156, 190, 234, 258; purchase 31, 34, 44–6, 59, 63, 102, 125, 186, 234; regulators 261; sales 46; sur- 26, 258, 260, 267
Terms of trade 148, 185, 199
Tewson, V., T.U.C. 67, 108
Texas Railway Commission 95

Thompson-McCausland, Lucius, Bank of England 47, 187, 197
Thorneycroft, Peter, President, Board of Trade, then Chancellor ix, 21, 30, 33, 39, 76, 91–2, 94–145, 146, 153, 158, 164–6, 179, 185, 191–3, 215, 220, 241
Thorold, Guy, Treasury 109, 129, 132, 177, 223
Thorp, Willard 132
Tied loans 213
Tinbergen, Ian 82, 226
Toner 15–16
Trade rules 8, 12, 18, 28
Trade unions 64, 119, 124, 129, 138, 158, 164, 199, 215; unable to hold wages steady under full employment 67
Transport and General Workers Union (T.G.W.U.) 119, 164
Travel allowance 21–2
Treasury bills 59, 101, 104, 127, 146, 194, 251, 254; deposit receipts 127–8; organisation 71, 170–1; staff 51
Treaty of Rome 72, 113, 265
Trend, Burke St John, Treasury 20, 26, 33, 51, 58, 61, 75, 164, 267
Triffin, Robert, Yale University 261–5
Trinidad G.1 Co. 74
Troup, A. W., Economic Section 75, 103, 107
Truman, Harry, President of U.S.A. 41
Tube Investments 188, 230, 259
T.U.C. 46, 67–9, 74, 81, 168, 223
Tuke, A. W., chmn, Barclays Bank 33
Turhill, U.S. official 227
Tyerman, Donald, Editor, *The Economist* 144

Underdeveloped countries 47, 130, 163, 252; *see also* Aid
Unemployment 22, 43, 57, 100, 102, 127, 163, 168, 172, 175, 177, 179, 185, 188–9, 192, 195–6, 198, 205, 212, 219, 235, 253–4, 257–8
Uniscan 187
United Nations 74
United States, committee on aid 202–3; on price stability 202; balance of payments deficit 201, 205–6, 215, 233, 246, 248, 251; economic outlook 3–4, 16, 40, 47–8, 129–50, 153, 159–60, 169, 202; fear of recession 49; proposal for informal U.S.-U.K. committee 129–30, 149, 213; *see also* Sir Robert Hall (visits to United States)
U.S.S.R. 19, 137, 174–5

Van Lennep, Emil 228
Venezuela 203
Verdon Smith, W. R., British Aeroplane Co. 108
Vickers 174
Vinter, Peter, Treasury 195

Wages 43, 46, 59, 63, 68–70, 72, 80, 91–2, 106, 110, 116–17, 126–7, 144, 164, 179, 199, 220, 235, 256; policy 23–5, 45–6, 66, 93, 127, 145–6, 157–8, 202, 217; *see also* Guiding light, Wages Policy Committee
Waiver clause (in American loan) 47–8, 102
Wall, John 216
Wallich, Henry, Fed. Rserve Board 201–2, 214
Wallis, Allen 202, 214
Watkinson, Harold 174, 216, 242
Watts, Nita, Economic Section 37, 266
Watts, Philip, Economic Section 156, 266
Waugh, Sam, President, Exim Bank 11, 40, 48–9, 109, 232
Way, Richard, Dep. Sec., Ministry of Supply 216, 219
Weeks, Sinclair, Sec. of Commerce 12
Welfare state 106, 186
Whidden, Jay 249
Whitby, Miss 3
Whitehall Dining Club 193
Whitehead, Commander 133
Williams, Professor 47
Williams, U.S. Dept. of Commerce 48
Willis, George, U.S. Treasury 132, 203
Wilson, Geoffrey 75, 85, 202, 214, 232
Wilson, J. Harold, Shadow Chancellor 61, 86, 98–9, 107, 137, 140, 146, 148, 218, 220, 236, 251
Wilson, Sir Horace, former Perm. Sec., Treasury 71
Wilson, Sir Roland 4
Wilson-Smith, Sir Henry 11
Winnifrith, A. J. D., Treasury 164–5, 167–8, 171, 205
Women in the Civil Service 115
Wood, T. 202
Woodcock, George, T.U.C. 67, 99, 108, 168
Woods, Sir J. J. 108, 230
Working Party No. 2, O.E.C.D. 163
Worswick, G. D. N. xvii-xix